Living and Working in

Germany

● A Survival Handbook ●

Edited by David Hampshire

Survival Books ● Bath ● England

First edition 2000
Second edition 2003
Third dition 2008
Fourth edition 2011
Fifth edition 2017

Copyright © Survival Books 2000, 2003, 2008, 2011, 2017
Cover photograph: Ramsau, Bavaria © Minyun Zhou (www.dreamstime.com)
Illustrations, cartoons and maps © Jim Watson

Survival Books Limited, Office 169, 3 Edgar Buildings, George St,
Bath, BA1 2FJ, United Kingdom
+44 (0)1305-246283, info@survivalbooks.net
www.survivalbooks.net and www.londons-secrets.com

British Library Cataloguing in Publication Data
A CIP record for this book is available
from the British Library.
ISBN: 978-1-909282-90-2

Printed in China by D'Print Pte Ltd.

Acknowledgements

The editor wishes to express his sincere thanks to all those who contributed to the successful publication of this fifth edition of Living and Working in Germany and previous editions of this book. They include Pamela Wilson (former editor), Chris Norville, Sunny Randlkofer, Gabriele Bohmler, Manja and Romy Welzel, Lilac Johnston, Di Bruce-Kidman, Robbi Forrester Atilgan, Peter Read, David Woodworth and John Marshall. Also many thanks to Jim Watson for the illustrations and maps.

Finally, a special thank you to the many photographers – the unsung heroes – whose beautiful images add colour and bring Germany to life.

The Editor

David Hampshire's career has taken him around the world and he has lived and worked in many countries, including Australia, France, Germany, Malaysia, the Netherlands, Panama, Singapore, Spain and Switzerland.

David is an authority on living and working abroad, and is the author or co-author of over 30 titles, including *Living and Working in Australia, Living and Working in Britain and Living and Working in Spain.* He is also the author of many books about London including *London for Foodies, Gourmets & Gluttons, London's Secrets: Museums & Galleries* and *London's Peaceful Places.*

David now lives in Dorchester, England with his partner Alexandra.

About Survival Books

From the outset Survival Books' philosophy has been to provide the most accurate, comprehensive and up-to-date information available – our titles routinely contain up to twice as much information as some similar books and are updated more frequently. They are written by experts in the field assisted by local researchers and contain invaluable insights, tips, warnings and advice that cannot easily be obtained from official publications or websites.

A Survival Books' guide is more than a reliable reference book; it is a helping hand, a trusty companion, a friend you can turn to when in need of reassurance, encouragement or simply a different perspective on the problems and challenges you face. Don't just survive, but make your dreams come true – with Survival Books.

What Readers and Reviewers Have Said About Survival Books:

"If I were to move to France, I would like David Hampshire to be with me, holding my hand every step of the way. This being impractical, I would have to settle for second best and take his books with me instead!"

Living France

"We would like to congratulate you on this work: it is really super! We hand it out to our expatriates and they read it with great interest and pleasure."

ICI (Switzerland) AG

"I found this a wonderful book crammed with facts and figures, with a straightforward approach to the problems and pitfalls you are likely to encounter. The whole laced with humour and a thorough understanding of what's involved. Gets my vote!"

Reader (Amazon)

"Get hold of David Hampshire's book for its sheer knowledge, straightforwardness and insights to the Spanish character and do yourself a favour!"

Living Spain

"Rarely has a 'survival guide' contained such useful advice – This book dispels doubts for first time travellers, yet is also useful for seasoned globetrotters – In a word, if you're planning to move to the US or go there for a long term stay, then buy this book both for general reading and as a ready reference."

American Citizens Abroad

Important Note

A diverse country with many faces, Germany has a variety of ethnic groups, religions and customs, as well as continuously changing rules, regulations, exchange rates and prices. A change of government in Germany can have a far-reaching influence on many important aspects of life, although it isn't as dramatic as in many other countries (the Germans are far too sensible to disrupt life and commerce simply for ideological reasons). We cannot recommend too strongly that you check with an official and reliable source (not always the same) before making any major decisions or taking an irreversible course of action. However, don't believe everything you're told or read – even, dare we say it, herein!

Useful websites and references to other sources of information have been included in all chapters and in **Appendix A** to help you obtain further information and verify details with official sources. Important points have been emphasised, in bold print or boxes, some of which it would be expensive, or even dangerous, to disregard. Ignore them at your peril or cost!

Note

Unless specifically stated, the reference to any company, organisation or product in this book doesn't constitute an endorsement or recommendation. None of the businesses, organisations, products or individuals have paid to be mentioned.

Contents

8. TELEVISION & RADIO

9. EDUCATION

10. PUBLIC TRANSPORT

11. MOTORING

Author's Notes

♦ Frequent references are made in this book to the European Union (EU), which comprises Austria, Belgium, Bulgaria, Cyprus, the Czech Republic, Denmark, Estonia, Finland, France, Germany, Greece, Hungary, Ireland, Italy, Latvia, Lithuania, Luxembourg, Malta, the Netherlands, Poland, Portugal, Romania, Slovakia, Slovenia, Spain, Sweden and the UK (at the time of writing!). The European Economic Area (EEA) comprises the EU countries plus the European Free Trade Association (EFTA) countries of Iceland, Liechtenstein and Norway, plus Switzerland (which is an EFTA member but not a member of the EEA).

♦ All times are shown using the 12-hour clock; times before noon are indicated by the suffix 'am' and times after noon by 'pm'.

♦ Prices should be taken as a guide only, although they were mostly correct at the time of publication. Unless otherwise stated, all prices quoted usually include value added tax (*Mehrwertsteuer/MwSt or Umsatzsteuer/Ust*) at 19 per cent. To convert from other currencies to euros or vice versa, see www. xe.com.

♦ His/he/him also means her/she/her (please forgive me ladies). This is done to make life easier for both the reader and the author, and isn't intended to be sexist.

♦ British English and spelling is used throughout this book.

♦ Warnings and important points are printed in **bold** type.

♦ A list of Useful Websites is contained in **Appendix A,** Weights & Measures in **Appendix B** and Useful Words & Phrases in **Appendix C.**

♦ A physical map of Germany is included inside the front cover and a political map showing the states (*Länder*) is inside the rear cover.

Schloss Belvedere, Weimar

Introduction

Whether you're already living or working in Germany or just thinking about it – this is **THE** book for you. Forget about all those glossy guidebooks, excellent though they are for tourists; this amazing book was written particularly with you in mind and is worth its weight in *Wurst*. Now in its 5th edition, *Living and Working in Germany* has been fully revised and updated and is intended to meet the needs of anyone wishing to know the essentials of German life. However long your intended stay in Germany, you'll find the information contained in this book invaluable.

General information isn't difficult to find in Germany (provided you speak German) and a multitude of books is published on every conceivable subject. However, reliable and up-to-date information in English specifically intended for foreigners living and working in Germany isn't so easy to find, least of all in one volume. This book was written to fill this void and provide the comprehensive practical information necessary for a trouble-free life. You may have visited Germany as a tourist but living and working there is a different matter altogether. Adjusting to a different environment and culture and making a home in any foreign country can be a traumatic and stressful experience – and Germany is no exception.

Living and Working in Germany is a comprehensive handbook on a wide range of everyday subjects, and represents the most up to date source of general information available to foreigners in Germany. It isn't simply a monologue of dry facts and figures, but a practical and entertaining look at German life.

Adapting to life in a new country is a continuous process; this book is designed to help reduce your 'rookie' phase and minimise the frustrations, although it doesn't contain all the answers. What it **will** do, however, is help you make informed decisions and calculated judgements, instead of uneducated guesses. Most importantly, it will help save you time, trouble and money, and repay your investment many times over.

Although you may find some of the information in this book a bit daunting, don't be discouraged. Most problems occur only once, and fade into insignificance after a short time (as you face the next half a dozen!). The majority of foreigners in Germany would agree that, all things considered, they love living there. A period spent in Germany is a wonderful way to enrich your life and hopefully please your bank manager. We trust that this book will help you avoid the pitfalls of life in Germany and smooth your way to a happy and rewarding future in your new home.

Viel Glück! **(good luck!)**

David Hampshire

July 2017

1.
FINDING A JOB

*F*rom the outside the German labour market may look completely self-sufficient, but in 2015 it was estimated that the country needed to add some 400,000 skilled migrants to its workforce annually – to compensate for an ageing population and low birthrate – in order to maintain its economic strength. Today, Germany has one of the OECD's lowest barriers to immigration for skilled workers, although long-term labour migration is low in comparison with many other countries and many employers seldom recruit workers from outside Germany. Without significant immigration, the working-age population is likely to fall from around 50 million in 2015 to somewhere between 34 and 38 million in 2060, according to government estimates. The influx of refugees in recent years – who lack vocational training or a degree (or German language proficiency) – aren't expected to plug the labour gap, at least in the short term.

If you're a national of a European Union (see below) country, you'll be on an equal footing with the locals in the job hunt, although you may need to speak German. Americans and others without the automatic right to work in Germany must meet visa and work permit requirements (see **Chapter 3**) in order for a prospective employer to justify hiring them in preference to an EU national. In practice, however, if you have skills that are in demand you'll have little problem finding work in Germany, even if you don't speak fluent German.

The Germans take great pride in their role as leaders of the European economy and champions of industrial productivity and engineering excellence. The title of engineer (*Ingenieur*) carries considerable prestige, and degrees and other qualifications are proudly displayed on business cards and letterheads. Education is highly prized in Germany, and many engineers in industry have doctorates. (It's common for engineers to become company bosses.) German national apprenticeship and on-the-job training programmes are the envy of the world – and, for good reason – German workers are renowned for their high levels of skill, efficiency and productivity.

In the '60s and '70s, the Federal Republic recruited large numbers of foreign workers, euphemistically called 'guest workers' (*Gastarbeiters*), mostly from Mediterranean countries, in response to labour shortages. Many guest workers stayed on as long-term residents and by 2015 there were over 3 million foreigners employed in Germany, the largest national groups being from Turkey, the states of the former Yugoslavia, Greece and Italy. At the same time, over 16 million people with an immigrant background were living in Germany, around half of whom had German citizenship. These numbers have been swelled in the last few years by over a million refugees and illegal immigrants.

BREXIT

The most important consideration for British citizens planning to live or work in Germany is

Britain's historic decision to leave the European Union (EU) – termed Brexit (British Exit) – in a referendum held on 23rd June 2016. The actual mechanism to leave the EU began with the invoking of Article 50, which took place on 29th March 2017, leading to a two-year 'negotiation' period after which the UK will no longer be a member of the EU (unless a transitional period is agreed).

Leaving the EU won't just affect the UK's relationship and trade with the EU and the 27 other member countries, but it will also influence the relationship between England and the other countries that make up the United Kingdom (not least Scotland, which voted to remain in the EU, and Northern Ireland, which has a land border with the Republic of Ireland, an EU member). It will also have far-reaching consequences for Britain's future European and world trade relations, exchange rates, cost of living, laws, and – not least – the ability of Britons to live, work and study in Germany and other EU countries (and German citizens to live and work in Britain).

The ramifications of the UK leaving the EU will no doubt take some years to become apparent, but a certain amount of turmoil is expected in the short to medium term. However, the immediate Armageddon forecast by the remain campaign didn't materialise (although the pound predictably fell sharply in value against the Euro and the $US), but the uncertainly regarding future trading arrangements with the EU has caused anxiety among many businesses. However, many experts and analysts believe that the UK could eventually be better off economically as an independent nation able to make its own trade deals.

GERMANY & THE EUROPEAN UNION

Germany was one of the six founder members of the European Community (now the European Union or EU) in 1957, along with Belgium, France, Italy, Luxembourg and the Netherlands. The German government has been a driving force behind the extension of EU membership to poorer countries in eastern and southern Europe, including its neighbours the Czech Republic and Poland, who joined in 2004 along with Cyprus, Estonia, Hungary, Latvia, Lithuania, Malta, the Slovak Republic and Slovenia. The latest additions to the EU were Romania and Bulgaria in 2007 and Croatia in 2013.

In 2017, the EU members comprised Austria, Belgium, Bulgaria, Croatia, Cyprus, the Czech Republic, Denmark, Estonia, Finland, France, Germany, Greece, Hungary, Ireland, Italy, Latvia, Lithuania, Luxembourg, Malta, the Netherlands, Poland, Portugal, Romania, Slovakia, Slovenia, Spain, Sweden and the UK. The European Economic Area (EEA) comprises the EU countries plus the European Free Trade Association (EFTA) countries of Iceland, Liechtenstein and Norway, plus Switzerland (which is an EFTA member but not a member of the EEA).

Nationals of all EU states (except for Croatia, who must wait until 2020) have the right to work in Germany or any other member state without a work permit, provided they have a valid passport or national identity card and comply with the member state's laws and regulations on employment.

All EU nationals are entitled to the same treatment as German citizens in matters of pay, working conditions, access to housing, vocational training, social security and trade union rights, and their families and dependants are entitled to join them in Germany and enjoy the same rights.

There are, however, still barriers to full freedom of movement and the right to work within the EU. For example, certain jobs in various member countries require job applicants to have specific skills or vocational qualifications. The EU has developed a general system for the recognition of professional and trade qualifications and guidelines for mutual recognition of qualifications (see below). Nevertheless, there are restrictions on employment in the civil service, where the right to work may be limited in individual cases on grounds of public policy, national security or public health. Differences persist among the various German states regarding the civil service status of some occupations, particularly teachers and health professionals.

ECONOMY

Germany is one of the world's wealthiest countries and emerged from the economic crisis as Europe's shining star, with one of the highest per capita gross domestic product (GDP) levels in the EU at around US$45,000. It's also the world's second-largest exporter (previously the world's largest exporter), and its inflation rate, although rising, is among the lowest in industrialised countries.

Thanks in part to its generous social security system, along with the distaste of Germany's wealthy classes for conspicuous consumption and their tendency to understatement, extremes of wealth and poverty aren't as apparent as in many other European countries. Cynics may claim that it's difficult to become rich in Germany because of the high tax rates, particularly on income from 'speculative'

activity; and it's true that those who've made fortunes have almost invariably built them through hard work over a long period, and that people rarely become millionaires 'overnight'. There's also somewhat less stigma attached to receiving social security benefits than in many other countries, and the state benefits system provides a reasonable, if not exactly luxurious, standard of living for those who fall on hard times (although more people fall through its safety net than casual observers notice).

The Germans are justifiably proud of their successes in what they refer to as a 'social market economy'. Less *dirigiste* than their French counterparts, German governments have fostered competition in the marketplace and encouraged enterprise among individuals and businesses. However, the government exercises considerable control over business, both by direct regulation and through high taxes on income and capital; its purpose is to protect economic equilibrium by promoting price stability, high employment, balanced imports and exports, and continuous growth.

Germany's success over the last 60 years has been largely due to the rise of small and medium-size companies (SMEs) – the *Mittelstand* – family-owned and operated industries often established after the Second

World War. Many medium-size companies employ Germany's legendary engineering skills to produce high quality industrial products famous throughout the world.

Today, Germany is the largest national economy in Europe and world's fourth-largest by nominal GDP. In 2016, it recorded the highest trade surplus in the world of $310 billion, making it the biggest capital exporter globally and the world's third-largest exporter with 1.21 trillion euros. The service sector contributes around 70 per cent of total GDP, industry around 29 per cent and agriculture less than 1 per cent. The country's top exports include vehicles (Germany is the third-largest producer of cars in the world, including Audi, BMW, Mercedes, Opel, Porsche and Volkswagen), machinery, chemicals, electronics and electrical equipment, pharmaceuticals, transport equipment, iron and steel, food and drink, and rubber and plastics.

EMPLOYMENT PROSPECTS

Although English is the *lingua franca* of international commerce and may help you to secure a job in Germany, the most important qualification for anyone seeking employment is the ability to speak fluent German. Most Germans study English at school and although only a small proportion are fluent, they're sufficiently competent to make a native command of English less of an advantage in the job market without complementary skills or experience. To find employment in Germany usually requires special qualifications or experience in a field or profession that's in demand.

The public education system is geared toward producing highly skilled workers through on-the-job training and apprenticeship programmes, as well as a large academic elite. By the time a German has earned his qualifications he has considerable experience of the profession or trade he's entering. However, there are many fields and occupations where training programmes haven't kept up with demand and if you have experience in one of these you'll have good job prospects, even without initially speaking German.

Germany has a huge shortfall of engineers and other skilled workers, which is estimated to be holding back the country's growth by around 1 per cent. Mechanical engineering and civil engineering (including architecture) are the principal areas of demand, with tens of thousands of vacancies, while qualified professionals are also highly sought in fields such as IT, natural science (biologists, chemists and physicists) and education. Other areas where there's a shortage of qualified staff include the automobile, chemical, health and machine tool industries.

UNEMPLOYMENT

Unlike much of the rest of the EU, where the average unemployment rate was 8.5 per cent, in early 2017, Germany's unemployment rate was just 3.8 per cent (the lowest since 1980). The number of unemployed was stable at 1.7 million while the number of employed was almost 42 million. The youth unemployment rate was 6.6 per cent, its lowest level since July 1992. Compared with the rest of Europe, Germany has enjoyed very low unemployment rates in the last almost 70 years, averaging just 5.63 per cent from 1949 until 2017; unemployment reached an all time high of 11.50 per cent in April 1950 and a record low of 0.4 per cent in March 1966.

However, the figures mask a sharp disparity between the regions of the former Federal Republic ('West Germany') and those of the erstwhile German Democratic Republic (*Deutsche Demokratische Republik/DDR*) or 'East Germany', now called the *Neue Länder*, where the unemployment rate is nearly double that of the former West Germany.

INDUSTRIAL RELATIONS

In the last 60 years, relations between the unions and employers' organisations have tended to be cordial and constructive, with both sides willing to compromise in the interest of saving or creating jobs. However, the more stressful economic climate of recent years has eroded this consensual approach, which has been exacerbated as pay gaps have widened and working conditions deteriorated. With fewer income raises in Germany, strikes are becoming more frequent than previously, and in recent years have mainly involved public and service sector workers, including train drivers, teachers, post office workers and airline staff.

Like many other aspects of German society, the right to strike is strictly controlled by law and civil servants (*Beamte*) aren't forbidden to strike. Germany has a number of large, powerful national unions, which negotiate regional contracts with employers' groups representing specific industries. A regional contract is binding on all companies within that industry and region, irrespective of whether they're part of the employers' group or not.

All businesses with more than a few employees may establish an elected works council (*Betriebsrat*), comprised of worker representatives, who've an advisory role in management affairs. The works council must be consulted on all significant management decisions, including the hiring and firing of key executives, lay-offs and plant closures, and must be regularly informed about the state of a business. Individuals serving on a works council enjoy privileges and guaranteed job protection under labour laws, while in larger companies representatives of the works council are guaranteed a certain number of seats on the board of directors. They may work closely with local unions but aren't required to be members themselves. Under certain circumstances works council decisions can override those of regionally organised trade unions.

German managers and executives rarely take work home and they almost never work at weekends, which are sacrosanct.

WORK ATTITUDES

Traditional German companies – particularly small and medium-size enterprises (SMEs), whose owner-managers comprise a recognised social class called the *Mittelstand* – often have a strict hierarchical structure with formalised relations between management and workers. Jobs and job titles are often strictly defined by regional industry contracts, with legal distinctions between workers and management. Neither group is keen to take on responsibilities outside their defined duties. Experience, maturity and loyalty are highly valued, and the frequent changing of jobs as a way of increasing your salary or promotion prospects is rare. However, this is beginning to change, particularly in high-tech industries and multi-national companies.

It's expensive to hire and fire employees in Germany, and the works council (*Betriebsrat*) often has the right to review candidates and offer suggestions regarding personnel decisions, even where upper management positions are involved.

The process of hiring new employees (particularly managers and executives) and making business decisions is slower in Germany than in many other developed countries. This is due more to the various levels of review and approval required than to indecision. On the other hand, snap decision-making is considered suspect, and German managers generally prefer to rely on careful planning and a rational, considered approach to solving problems. As a result, many foreigners, particularly Americans, find that they must adjust to a slower pace of working life in Germany.

Many businesses close for two or three weeks during the summer, and employees are generally expected to take the bulk of their annual leave during this period.

Many union contracts stipulate the closing dates each year to coincide with the region's school holiday calendar.

Time spent in the office or on the job is generally highly productive, with little or no time wasted on socialising or idle chatter, except during official (and short) break periods. Socialising with colleagues is usually done primarily in formal settings such as the annual company outing, holiday gatherings and other events.

WORKING WOMEN

The number of women in employment in Germany – over 70 per cent of all women aged between 20 and 64 – is higher than in most other EU nations (only the Netherlands and Scandinavian countries have a higher rate), although most jobs are in the low-wage and temporary work sectors. Overall women earn some 25 per cent less than men and the percentage of working-age women pursuing full-time jobs (around two-thirds) has been stagnating well below the EU average.

Women in Germany comprise around 45 per cent of the workforce and generally enjoy legal protection from discrimination in the hiring process. However, around a third of the female workforce is part-time, compared with just a few per cent of men. There are a number of laws designed to protect women (Frauenarbeitsschutz) from dangerous jobs, excessive overtime or late working. Maternity leave is generous, and time off for family duties (including caring for sick children) is a basic legal right. This can work against women, as many employers are reluctant to hire women of child-bearing age for jobs involving lifting, for example, which would have to be modified during pregnancy (the law requires a female employee to notify her employer as soon as she knows she's pregnant). Employers may also fear losing a key supervisor or manager to extended maternity leave at a crucial point in the business cycle.

Women make up the majority of university graduates in Germany but don't have professional and salary equality with men. There are few top-level women managers and executives and they continue to hold the majority of part-time and lower paid jobs (as in other EU countries). On the other hand, women are well represented in the political sphere in Germany (i.e. Angela Merkel!) and there's an active women's movement. Around 55 per cent of entrants to German universities are women, but far fewer women complete the rigorous business and engineering programmes required for managerial and executive positions. Women in management fields usually have difficulty establishing their credibility with older, more 'traditional' bosses or colleagues.

QUALIFICATIONS

A remarkable number of jobs in Germany are regulated, at least to the extent of requiring formal qualifications. Most qualifications involve a training programme lasting at least two years, with or without supervised on-the-job experience or a formal apprenticeship. Germany has a world-renowned apprenticeship system and offers its young people a dizzying array of training programmes when they finish their school careers. (The system of job-related qualifications is so pervasive that you may hear Germans making jokes about how even jobs such as toilet attendant or road sweeper

Information about qualifications can also be obtained from the European Commission website (http://europa.eu/youreurope/citizens/work/professional-qualifications/index_en.htm) and from www.make-it-in-germany.com/en/for-qualified-professionals/working/guide/recognition.

require a two-year training programme these days.) Qualifications can be highly specific, making it difficult to change jobs unless you've taken a supplementary training programme that meets the requirements of the new job. Employers are required by law to provide continuing training for employees, and a company's annual educational plan must be approved by its works council.

Germany abides by the EU's general system for recognition of diplomas and qualifications, which means that if your field of work is regulated in Germany you must have your qualification formally recognised before you're allowed to work in that field. This obviously applies to professionals such as doctors, nurses and teachers, but recognised qualifications are required to work in many other fields as well, for example as an electrician or computer technician or in the building trades.

Generally speaking, in order to have your home country qualifications formally recognised in Germany you must contact the competent authority (usually a guild, trade association or professional society) for your trade or profession. They will provide you with their requirements, which usually involve the submission of your diploma, certificate or other documentation confirming your training or work experience. You must be able to show that the qualification from your home country is equivalent to the German one, in terms of both duration and subject matter. If there are significant differences in the practice of your profession between the two countries, you may be asked for evidence of mastery of specific areas considered significantly different. This can take the form of job experience, an aptitude test or additional training. Under German law, the competent authority has four months to respond positively to your application; no response after this period is legally equivalent to a refusal, but you're entitled to know the reasons for any negative decision.

All EU member states issue occupational information sheets containing a common job description with a table of qualifications. These cover a large number of professions and trades and are intended to help someone with the relevant qualifications seek employment in another EU country. You can obtain a direct comparison between any EU qualification and those recognised in Germany from the *Zentralstelle für Ausländisches Bildungswesen* (www.kmk.org) and from www.anerkennung-in-deutschland.de.

In the UK, information can be obtained from the National Recognition Information Centre for the UK (www.naric.org.uk), the National Agency responsible for providing information, advice and expert opinion on vocational, academic and professional skills and qualifications from over 180 countries worldwide.

GOVERNMENT EMPLOYMENT SERVICE

The German Federal Labour Office (Bundesagentur für Arbeit, www.arbeitsagentur. de) – also known as the BA, Arbeitsagentur or, colloquially, the *Arbeitsamt* – provides a wide range of employment-related services through some 180 agencies and around 600 offices nationwide. The Arbeitsagentur publishes lists of jobs available throughout Germany and abroad, and provides vocational training,

assessment and re-integration services for disabled people, and vocational guidance for students and others. It also administers various benefit programmes related to employment, compiles labour statistics and conducts market and labour research.

The Arbeitsagentur provides its services free to both job seekers and employers. If you're already in Germany, you can pick up a copy of its weekly magazine, *Markt und Chance*, at any of its offices. This publication contains job vacancies and a 'jobs wanted' section, where job seekers can place adverts, and you can find similar information on the Arbeitsagentur website. The Arbeitsagentur has a department for foreign applicants seeking work in Germany, called the Zentralstelle für Arbeitsvermittlung (ZAV), which also handles placements for Germans abroad.

There's also a European Employment Service (EURES) network, members of which include all EU countries plus Norway and Iceland. Members exchange information regularly on job vacancies, and local EURES

offices have access to extensive information on how to apply for a job, and living and working conditions in each country. The international department of your home country's employment service can put you in touch with a Euroadviser, who can provide advice on finding work in Germany. Euroadvisers can also arrange to have your personal details forwarded to the Arbeitsagentur. The European Commission website (https://ec.europa.eu/eures/public/homepage) contains information about EURES and EURES-related agencies in European countries.

Bear in mind, however, that EURES isn't the fastest or the most efficient way of finding a job in Germany, especially from abroad. As can be expected, national employment services give priority to their own nationals, and jobs aren't generally referred to EURES or other national agencies until after all prospective local candidates have been considered.

RECRUITMENT AGENCIES

In addition to the Arbeitsagentur, many intermediaries post vacancies in German newspapers as 'employment consultants', mostly for management level jobs. In the larger cities there are branches of many of the major international executive recruitment companies or 'head-hunters' (*Kopfjäger*); Michael Page, Korn/Ferry and Heidrick & Struggles all maintain offices in Germany, although they don't normally accept CVs except in response to a specific vacancy.

There's a variety of small to medium-size recruitment agencies in the UK and US that specialise in international placements. Agents advertise in daily and weekly newspapers and trade magazines but don't mention the client's name, not least to prevent applicants from approaching the company directly, therefore depriving the agency of its fat fee!

Websites that regularly list vacancies in Germany include:

- www.careerbuilder.de
- www.craigslist.com
- http://de.theconstructionjob.com
- http://de.theengineeringjob.com
- www.expatengineer.net
- http://germany.xpatjobs.com
- www.jobnet.de
- www.job-office.de
- www.jobpilot.de
- www.jobs.de
- www.jobscout24.de
- www.jobworld.de
- www.monster.de
- www.overseasjobs.com
- www.stepstone.de
- www.thelocal.de/jobs
- www.toytowngermany.com/jobs
- www.xpatjobs.de

In a few instances, agencies advertise directly in international publications to assemble a shortlist of potential job candidates. International companies may list management positions in Germany with recruitment agencies in the UK, particularly if they're seeking multi-lingual, highly experienced or mobile executives.

Most legitimate recruitment services charge the employer a fee based on the annual salary negotiated for the candidate. Fees can run to as much as 40 or 50 per cent of a year's salary, which the head-hunter may have to refund if employees don't survive the initial probationary period (anywhere from one to six months).

Temporary Agencies

In addition to recruitment agencies for permanent positions, there are temporary employment agencies in Germany, such as

Manpower and Adecco, handling either all types of jobs or jobs in specific industries or fields only. To be employed by a temporary agency (*Zeitarbeitsfirma*), you must be eligible to work in Germany and have a social security number. You must usually register, which entails completing a form and providing a CV and references; you can register with any number of agencies. Always ensure that you know exactly how much, when and how you'll be paid. Deductions for income tax and social security are made from your gross salary.

Temporary jobs are also advertised in employment agent (*Arbeitsagentur*) offices, on notice boards in expatriate clubs, churches and organisations, in expatriate newsletters, newspapers and websites.

Because of the long annual holidays in Germany and generous maternity leave, companies often require temporary staff, and a temporary job can frequently be used as a stepping stone to a permanent position. On the other hand, companies may also use temporary agencies as a way of avoiding unlimited contracts, which are difficult and expensive to terminate due to strict German labour laws (see **Employment Contracts** on page 35). To find a temporary agency, look in the Yellow Pages under *Zeitarbeit*, *Personalvermittlung* or *Personalberatung*.

Online Agencies

Nowadays there are many online recruitment agencies and 'job search' sites (simply Google 'jobs in Germany'). Some sites charge a subscription fee to access their vacancy lists, but many permit job seekers to view and respond to vacancies free of charge. It's also possible to post your CV online (again, usually free), but it's wise to consider the security implications of this move; by posting your home address or phone number in public view, you could be laying yourself open to nuisance phone calls or worse.

Note that German sites (those ending .de) don't usually include an English-language version unless a major organisation is involved. However, if your German skills are still rudimentary, you can obtain a rough-and-ready translation using the 'Translate this page' feature on Google.co.uk or Google.com. You'll then be presented with an instant translation of the web page in question – although you shouldn't expect it to be idiomatic or even very accurate!

A useful website for anyone planning to work in Germany is 'Make it in Germany' (www.make-it-in-germany.com/en), which also contains job listings.

CASUAL WORK

Temporary or casual work (*befristete Arbeit*) is usually for a fixed period, ranging from a few days to a few months (or work may be intermittent). Casual workers are often employed on a daily, first-come, first-served basis. Anyone looking for casual unskilled work in Germany must usually compete with newly arrived Turks and eastern Europeans, who are often prepared to work for less money than anyone else (not forgetting one million refugees!). Many employers illegally pay temporary staff in cash without making deductions for social security, insurances and taxes (see **Working Illegally** on page 31), although casual work earnings are subject to the same taxes and other deductions as full-time employment.

Mini-jobs

Labour law reforms in 2003 introduced the concept of the 'mini-job' or minor employment (*geringfügige Beschäftigung*), which allows someone to earn up to €450 per month tax-free, although since January 2013 employers have been 'required' to pay retirement contributions (although they're voluntary). The employer pays a lump sum of 20 per cent (including health insurance, pension fund and wage tax), or 18 per cent in the case of domestic help (pension fund and health insurance).

Mini-job workers – estimated to number over 7.5 million – are mostly women and the elderly. These jobs were intended to legalise informal work in the fields of catering, retail, and domestic work, although they're also popular as second jobs. Mini-jobs are also offered by agencies, start-ups and larger corporations, seeking part-time professional help.

All German industries are allowed to offer mini job contracts, but the most common types of mini jobs are poorly paid (less than €7 per hour) and exist in a deregulated sphere largely outside the traditional job framework and without trade union recognition. They were originally intended for people in transition or who were waiting to get a 'proper' job, but some claim that they were principally designed to reduce the unemployment numbers to save politicians' blushes.

Mini-jobs alone aren't sufficient to cover your living expenses in Germany and don't qualify as valid job contracts for the visa application process.

SEASONAL JOBS

Seasonal jobs are available throughout the year in Germany, the vast majority in the tourist industry. Many seasonal jobs last for the duration of the summer or winter tourist seasons – May to September and December to April respectively – although some are simply casual or temporary jobs for a number of weeks. Some fluency in German is necessary for all but the most menial (and worst paid)

jobs. Additional languages can be a huge advantage, particularly in the tourist industry, as Germany hosts visitors from around the world.

Seasonal jobs include most trades in hotels and restaurants, couriers and representatives, a variety of jobs in theme parks and holiday camps, tour guides, sports instructors, service staff in bars and clubs, fruit and grape picking, and other agricultural jobs.

If you aren't an EU national you must ensure that you're eligible to work in Germany by checking with a German embassy or consulate in your home country before you start looking for a seasonal job. The Arbeitsagentur has reduced the number of seasonal work permits it issues to non-EU nationals to encourage the hiring of Germans and other EU nationals, and non-EU nationals may find it difficult or impossible to secure seasonal work. There are, however, a number of international summer and holiday work programmes that offer work permits and placement assistance, particularly for students (see **Training & Work Experience** below).

Foreign students in Germany can usually obtain a temporary permit for part-time work during the summer holiday period and between school terms.

Fruit & Vegetable Picking

As in many wine-producing countries, grape-picking is a popular late summer job in Germany, despite being boring, badly paid and back-breaking. The major vineyards are on the banks of the Rhine and Moselle rivers, where the harvest usually starts in mid- to late September, depending on the weather. Other fruits that need to be picked by hand include apples and pears, mostly in the south, e.g. Baden-Württemberg and Bavaria. White asparagus (*Spargel*) is popular in Germany and around 90,000 tonnes are harvested annually. The asparagus season (*Spargelzeit*) starts in around mid-April and finishes on June 24th (mid-summer) Germany-wide.

Traditionally, farmers hired fruit pickers from southern and eastern Europe on a 'cash in hand' basis, but the government is cracking down on the use of illegal foreign labour, so in theory it ought to be easier to obtain a bona fide fruit-picking job.

Holiday Camps & Theme Parks

For those who like working with children, German holiday camps offer a number of summer job opportunities, ranging from camp counsellors and sports instructors to administrative and catering posts. The school summer holidays aren't as long in Germany as in some other European countries, therefore the season is correspondingly shorter. There are a number of internet sites devoted to holiday camps and theme park jobs, such as www.transitionsabroad.com/index.shtml, which lists job openings for the coming season.

Germany boasts a dozen or so theme parks (*Freizeitpark*), which all rely to a large extent on seasonal staff. The larger parks may provide on-site accommodation for employees (the cost is deducted from your wages). Positions range from maintenance and catering to performing in shows and pageants that form part of the entertainment. Check local newspapers from January or February for job advertisements for the coming summer season. April is a popular month for parks to hold auditions for performing roles. Theme parks also list employment information on their websites. The better-known parks are listed below.

◆ Europa Park Rust, Europa-Park-Str. 2, 77977 Rust/Baden (07822-77-0, www.europapark.de);

◆ Hansapark, 23730 Siersdorf (04563-474-0, www.hansapark.de);

◆ Legoland, Legoland Allee, 89312 Günzburg (08221-700 700, www.legoland.de);

◆ Moviepark, Warner Allee 1, 46244 Bottrop-Kichhellen (02045-899-0, www.movieparkgermany.de).

◆ Phantasialand, Bergeiststr. 31-41, 50321 Brühl b. Köln (02232-36200, www.phantasialand.de);

◆ Tripsdrill, 74389 Cleebronn/Tripsdrill (7135-9999, www.tripsdrill.de).

Ski Resorts

While Germany isn't as well known for ski resorts and winter sports as its neighbours France, Switzerland, Austria and Italy, it boasts many winter resorts. Cross-country skiing (*Langlauf*) is particularly popular in the Black Forest and parts of Bavaria, and there are many small inns and tourist centres catering to winter sports enthusiasts.

One of the best ways to find jobs in ski resorts is via the internet, e.g. www. adventurejobs.co.uk, www.coolworks.com, www.jobs-in-the-alps.com, www.natives.co.uk, www.skijobs.net and www.snowworkers.com.

TRAINING & WORK EXPERIENCE

A number of organisations run trainee and work exchange programmes for students and recent graduates. For most programmes you must be aged under 30. Some arrange job placements, while others offer work permits for up to 18 months to applicants who find their own placement and meet qualification criteria. Principal programmes include the following:

◆ Technical and commercial students wishing to gain experience by working in Germany during their holidays can apply to the International Association for the Exchange of Students for Technical Experience (IAESTE) in over 60 countries (www.iaeste. org). Applicants must possess a working knowledge of German and be enrolled at an educational institution as a full-time student of engineering, science, agriculture, architecture or a related field of study, or be undergraduates in their penultimate year of study aged between 19 and 30. In the UK, applicants should apply to IAESTE UK, c/o Education Section, British Council (www. iaeste.org.uk).

◆ The Association for International Practical Training (AIPT) provides a career development programme for university graduates and a student exchange programme for US nationals. Both programmes require applicants to find their own internships or job placements but provide them with work permits for up to 18 months. For further information, contact the Association for International Practical Training (www.aipt.org).

◆ For students and those within a term of graduation, the Council on International Educational Exchange (CIEE) provides short-term work permits and job search support for over 30 countries, including Germany. CIEE programmes also include study and volunteer programmes. Contact the CIEE (www.ciee.org) for information.

◆ AIESEC is a student-run, non-profit organisation that provides paid internships in business and technical fields in over 87 countries and territories, including Germany. You can contact the AIESEC chapter at your university for details of qualifications and application procedures. In the UK, contact AIESEC (www.aiesec.co.uk), which also contains contact information for other countries.

◆ For those with an interest in politics, the Bundestag provides an internship programme, which combines work and study in Berlin. Students and teachers interested in exchange opportunities should contact the Deutscher Akademischer Austauschdienst (DAAD, www.daad.de).

◆ *Transitions Abroad* magazine, targeted at Americans, is a good source of information about a wide range of educational and exchange programmes. Its website (www. transitionsabroad.com) contains country-by-country listings of programmes for studying, working, internships and volunteering, all in searchable form.

◆ The EU and EURES have a number of programmes for young people interested in training and work experience outside their home country. Contact your country's national employment services agency or the national trade association for the industry in which you wish to train, who may be able to put you in contact with a suitable German employer. Information about

EURES is available from http://europa.eu/index_en.htm.

SALARY

It can be difficult to determine the salary you should receive in Germany, as salaries aren't usually quoted in job advertisements and are kept strictly confidential. However, Germans are among the best paid workers in Europe, receiving both a '13th month' year-end bonus and a holiday bonus (generally an additional half month's salary or more) during the summer (see **Salary & Bonuses** on page 36). If you're quoted an annual salary, you should therefore divide it by 13.5 (not 12) to determine what your monthly pay will be. On the other hand, the cost of living is high in Germany, as are taxes and deductions for various social insurances (see **Cost of Living** on page 197, **Social Security** on page 183 and **Income Tax** on page 204).

There are a number of international salary comparison websites, including www.payscale.com, www.wageindicator.org and www.worldsalaries.org.

Usually, only starting salaries are negotiable and it's up to you to ensure that you receive the level of salary and benefits commensurate with your qualifications and experience. Minimum salaries exist in many industries for factory or entry-level workers, and the industry agreement for the region may govern pay rises and allowances paid for certain experience or qualifications, unsociable hours, overtime, weekend work or home work, and dangerous or unpleasant working conditions. You don't need to be a union member to be subject to the local industry agreement.

For many employees, particularly executives and senior managers, remuneration

includes much more than monthly pay. Some companies provide benefits such as a company car, interest-free home or other loans, and membership of local clubs or sporting organisations. These benefits are usually taxable, however, and you should take this into account when calculating your take-home pay or comparing job offers.

An overview of salary levels is provided by the current digest (Arbeitnehmerverdienste) of the Federal Office for Statistics (Statistisches Bundesamt), although the figures quoted should be taken only as a guide. The complete digest is available online from the Statistisches Bundesamt website (www.destatis.de/en/homepage.html > Facts & Figures > Earnings & labour costs)

A statutory minimum wage has been applicable in Germany since 1st January 2015, which was initially set at €8.50 (and was increased to €8.84 on 1st January 2017). In addition, there are minimum wages for individual branches and occupations. In April 2015, four months after the introduction of the statutory minimum wage, there were 1.9 million jobs for which workers were paid the statutory gross minimum wage.

SELF-EMPLOYMENT

If you want to be self-employed (*Selbstständiger*) or start a freelance business in Germany, you must meet certain legal requirements, including establishing residence, applying for a work permit (see **Work Permits** on page 54), tax number and trade licence (*Gewerbeschein*); and registering with the appropriate organisation, which is usually a trade or craft guild (*Handwerkskammer*). If you're a non-EU national starting a business (as a foreigner), you must prove that you can afford the investment and will create at least ten jobs. Of course, you must have the appropriate qualification, recognised by the proper authority in Germany, to legally establish yourself as self-employed (see **Qualifications** on page 23).

However, those with a record of practical experience supported by a recognised certificate in another country are able to set up in self-employment in certain fields, e.g. crafts, retailing (from a shop or mobile unit), catering and hotel-keeping, food and drink production, insurance broking, transport services, wholesale and hairdressing. Britons should contact the Department for Business Innovation and Skills through their partner, Business Link (www.businesslink.gov.uk) for information about setting up a business abroad.

In the building trades, the government has cracked down on unqualified and inexperienced foreign labourers, who are seen to take jobs away from Germans. The law requires self-employed construction workers to hold a qualification at least equivalent to that of a German master craftsman (*Meister*) and to have a contract for a specifically defined segment of a building project – down to defining exactly which wall or room they've been commissioned to construct. Many people who've been lured by the prospect of high wages for short-term construction jobs in Germany have encountered hostility on the job.

WORKING ILLEGALLY

Working illegally isn't nearly as easy or as lucrative an option in Germany as it is in some other European countries, and is more dangerous than in most. Germans tend to be law-abiding people, who are knowledgeable about regulations that apply to the workforce. Until some years ago, even the holding of a second job was considered a form of working in the 'black economy' (*Schwartzarbeit*) and was officially illegal. Industrial workers are also well aware of the threat of cheap foreign labour in a country with a high standard of living and low unemployment.

Unscrupulous employers use illegal labour in order to pay low wages and avoid deductions for mandatory social insurances, particularly for foreigners who are unable to obtain residence visas. Foreigners found working illegally are subject to deportation and fines. The employer can also be fined and may be required to reimburse the state for any costs incurred in deporting illegal employees. Even if you aren't caught, if you work illegally you have no entitlement to social security benefits, such as healthcare, unemployment pay or pension contributions. Without the proper paperwork, you'll also be unable to open a bank account, seek medical treatment or rent an apartment.

LANGUAGE

Although English is Germany's unofficial second language (it's taught in state schools from an early age, so most Germans have a reasonable knowledge of English) and many jobs require good English skills, for most positions you must have at least a grasp of basic conversational German. In fact, outside the major cities and tourist areas it may be difficult to find information or help unless you speak some German, particularly in the eastern states.

German belongs to the Indo-European language group and is the mother tongue of over 100 million people worldwide. The standard form of German, which is the form generally taught abroad, is referred to as High German (*Hochdeutsch*), and is widely spoken in northern Germany. It's also the language spoken between Germans from different regions, many of whom have strong accents or dialects. There are several regional dialects, including *Bayerisch* (spoken in Bavaria), *Hessisch* (Hesse), *Schwäbisch* (the southwest, in and around the Black Forest) and *Sächsisch* (parts of Saxony), and the inhabitants of Berlin and Cologne also have distinctive accents. These can be difficult to understand at first if you've learned *Hochdeutsch*. There are

also officially recognised minority languages (as distinct from dialects), e.g. that of the *Sorb* community in eastern Germany, and *Plattdeutsch* and *Frisian* in northern Germany, which those living in these parts will need to be able to cope with.

The good news is that Germans are generally fairly easy-going about their language. If your pronunciation is less than perfect or you use the wrong gender (which is likely, as there are three) or adjective or noun ending (there are five of the former and eight of the latter!), it's very unlikely that you'll be corrected – at least, not in public. Germans recognise that their language can be difficult for foreigners to learn on account of its grammatical complexity.

Particular confusion is caused by the 'alternative' spelling *ss* or *ß*. An attempt

For information about learning German, see page 130.

was made in the mid-'90s to simplify and 'modernise' some spellings – for example, eliminating the *scharfes S* (ß) character. These changes were phased in gradually, rather than being imposed instantly, and you can still expect to see both old and new forms in use as a number of (mainly older) Germans reject such changes as 'dumbing down' of the language. Note that in German, all nouns are capitalised and all pronouns are lowercase except for 'Sie'.

The German language has adopted many English words and terms, particularly from the worlds of business, computer technology and marketing; for example, 'manager', 'marketing', 'computer', 'online' and many other familiar English words are in common use, both in conversation and in print. Needless to say, they're pronounced like German and not like English.

Munich panorama

2.
EMPLOYMENT CONDITIONS

*E*mployment conditions in Germany are governed by German labour law (*Arbeitsgesetze*), collective agreements (*Tarifverträge*), and the terms of an employee's employment contract (see below). Collective agreements are negotiated between unions and employers' associations in many industries, and generally apply to employers and all employees, irrespective of whether they're union members. Agreements specify minimum wage levels for each position in the main employment categories for the industry, as well as controlling the permissible working hours and often even holiday periods. Different rules apply to different categories of employee, e.g. directors, managers and shop-floor workers. Foreigners are employed under the same conditions as German citizens, and part-time employees generally receive the same rights and benefits as full-time employees on a pro rata basis.

German employees enjoy excellent employment conditions and social security benefits, and extensive rights under labour laws, collective agreements and local customs. Labour laws (and there are many) detail the minimum conditions of employment, including working hours, overtime payments, holidays, trial and notice periods, dismissal conditions, health and safety regulation, and trade union rights. The exception is what's termed 'mini-jobs' or minor employment (*geringfügige Beschäftigung*), essentially part-time jobs paying no more than €450 per month, which are outside the traditional job framework and without trade union recognition (see page 27).

An employer's general rules and regulations or terms (*Arbeitsbedingungen*), regarding working conditions and benefits that apply to all employees, are usually contained in a booklet given to employees.

As in many other European countries, all business establishments with more than a handful of workers must have a works council (*Betriebsrat*) – see **Unions & Works Councils** on page 44.

EMPLOYMENT CONTRACTS

Under German law, a contract exists as soon as you undertake a job for which you expect to be paid, although employees have the right to demand a written contract (*Arbeitsvertrag*) formalising the work relationship (*Arbeitsverhältnis*). This relationship is regulated by various labour laws (*Arbeitsgesetze*), which contain specific requirements for virtually every aspect of employment.

The standard employment contract is referred to as an 'unlimited' contract (*unbefristete Vertrag*), meaning that it's for an indefinite period. It usually includes a probationary period of one to six months, depending on the job or industry, before the contract becomes legal and binding on both parties.

A 'limited' employment contract (*befristete Vertrag*) is a contract for a fixed term, usually 6 to 18 months. Normally, the job ends on the expiration date, which must be stated in the contract, but under certain conditions the contract can be extended to up to two years. If an employee continues to work after the end of a limited contract, he automatically falls under the rules for an unlimited contract and is considered a permanent employee of the company, whether or not a written contract exists. Limited contracts are officially used when a company needs a temporary substitute, e.g. when a key employee is on maternity leave, or to complete a specific project, and unofficially when a company wishes to circumvent the strict labour laws by hiring staff for what amounts to an extended probationary period.

All employment contracts are subject to German labour law and references may be made to other regulations such as collective agreements. Anything in contracts contrary to statutory provisions and unfavourable to an employee can be challenged in a labour court (*Arbeitsgericht*), but in principle you're allowed to strike an agreement with an employer that waives some or all of your rights under the law or the collective agreement.

☑ SURVIVAL TIP

As with all contracts, you should know exactly what an employment contract contains before signing it. If your German isn't fluent, you should obtain an English translation or at least have it translated verbally so that you don't receive any surprises later.

Employment contracts usually contain a paragraph stating the date from which they take effect and to whom they apply. Other terms and conditions which may be covered by a contract or by an employer's general rules and regulations are outlined below.

SALARY & BONUSES

Your salary (*Lohn/Gehalt*) is stated in your employment contract, and details of salary reviews, planned increases and cost of living rises may also be included (or these may come under general terms). Contracts normally state the (monthly) gross income (*Bruttoeinkommen*), i.e. before all deductions and withholdings for benefits, taxes and social security. Salaries are generally paid monthly, although they may be quoted in contracts as an hourly, monthly or annual amount, depending on the type of job you're being offered. If a bonus is paid, such as a 13th month's salary or the so-called 'holiday bonus' in the summer, it's stated in your employment contract (see below). If you're quoted an annual salary in your contract, you should divide this by either 13, 13.5 or 14, as appropriate, to arrive at your monthly gross pay.

General points, such as the payment of your salary into a bank account and the date of such payments, are usually included in general terms. You'll receive a pay 'slip' (usually an A4 document) that itemises your salary, bonuses and any commission or special pay rates, and shows tax and other deductions (both your share and your employer's).

Salaries in Germany are generally reviewed once a year, in around November/December, with pay rises taking effect from 1st January of the following year. Annual increases are determined to a large extent by the regional or industry collective agreements that apply to your employer. Small 'merit' increases above the general negotiated pay rise may be granted to individual employees, but the total amounts available for such increases are subject to scrutiny by works councils.

13th Month's Salary & Bonuses

Most employers pay their employees' annual salary in 13 (or sometimes 14) instalments, and not 12. If your employment contract mentions a 'holiday' bonus, this usually means that a '13th month' is paid – half in the summer (usually July) and half at the year end. In some companies, a full extra month's salary is paid both in July and at the end of the year, either in December or early in January, amounting to 14 months' salary. In both cases, the annual salary quoted in your contract is the total you'll receive in a year. Divide this by either 13 or 14 to determine what your 'regular' monthly salary will be. In your first and last year of employment, your 13th month's salary or holiday bonus is paid pro rata if you don't work a full calendar year.

Some employers offer an additional annual bonus (*Gratifikation*) scheme, based on an employee's individual performance or the company's profits. If you're employed for a fixed period, you may also be paid an end-of-contract bonus, depending on the terms of your contract.

Expenses

Expenses (*Spesen*) paid by an employer are usually listed in your employment conditions. These may include travel costs from your home to your place of work, usually consisting of a second class rail season ticket or the equivalent cost, paid monthly with your salary. Companies without an employee restaurant or canteen may pay a lunch allowance or provide luncheon vouchers. Expenses paid for travel on company business or for training and education may be detailed in your contract or general terms, or be listed in a separate document. See also **Relocation Expenses** below.

WORKING HOURS & OVERTIME

Working hours (*Arbeitsstunden*) in Germany vary according to your employer, your position, the industry in which you're employed and the regional or industry collective agreement. The average is around 41 hours per week; in most companies it's 38.5. Some companies are formally on a 35-hour or even four-day working week in order to try to preserve as many jobs as possible.

In manufacturing industries and factories, work may start as early as 7 or 7.30am and finish at 3.30 or 4pm, depending on the length of the official lunch break. Most business premises are open from around 6.30 or 7am until 6 or 7pm. Companies with a 35- or 37-hour working week may close completely on Friday afternoons.

Coffee or tea breaks (*Pausezeit*) are strictly scheduled in Germany, where the right to break time (like everything else, it seems) is enshrined in both law and most union contracts. Breaks usually last 15 or 20 minutes and are strictly monitored. Lunch breaks may be only 30 minutes, although 45 minutes to an hour for lunch is usual in most offices. Eating at your desk is generally frowned upon unless you have urgent work to complete. And don't forget to wish your co-workers 'Mahlzeit' as they leave for their lunch break! (The word literally means 'mealtime'.)

If you work more than the standard number of hours in a week, you must usually be paid overtime at a premium of at least 25 per cent (i.e. 125 per cent of your regular hourly rate). The overtime premium often depends on the time of day when overtime is worked, with overtime after 9 or 10pm subject to higher premiums than overtime worked during 'regular' working hours. Work on Saturdays, Sundays or public holidays is usually paid at premium rates, from 150 per cent ('time and a half') to 200 per cent ('double time'). Employers can offer time off to compensate for weekend or holiday work and this must be at the appropriate premium rate, e.g. double time off for a Sunday worked, time and a half for a Saturday.

Salaried employees, particularly executives and managers, aren't generally paid overtime, although this depends on their employment contracts and their legal classification within the company. Salaried employees may, however, receive compensating time off if they're required to work outside their normal hours.

Flexi-time

Many German companies operate flexi-time (*Gleitzeit*) working hours. A flexi-time system requires all employees to be present between certain hours, known as the core time (*Kernzeit*), e.g. from 8.30 to 11.30am and from 1.30 to 4pm. Core time can start at 7.30 or 8am, which isn't early by German standards. Employees may make up their required working hours by starting earlier than the required time, reducing their lunch break or working later. Smaller companies may allow employees to work as late as they wish, provided they don't exceed the maximum permitted daily working hours. Because flexi-time rules are often quite complicated, they may be contained in a separate set of regulations.

RELOCATION EXPENSES

Relocation expenses in Germany depend on your agreement with your employer and are usually included in your employment contract or general terms. If you're hired from outside Germany, your air ticket and other travel costs are often booked and paid for by your employer or his representative. You can usually also claim any incidental travel costs, e.g. for transport to and from airports. If you travel

by car to Germany, you can usually claim a mileage rate (actually a kilometre rate) or the cost of an equivalent flight.

An employer may pay a fixed relocation allowance based on your salary, position and family size, or he may pay the total cost of removal. Most German employers pay your relocation costs up to a specified amount, although you may be required to sign a contract which stipulates that if you resign before a certain period elapses (e.g. five years), you must repay a percentage of your removal costs, depending on your length of service. An allowance should be sufficient to move the contents of an average house and you must normally pay any excess costs yourself. If you don't want to ship your furniture to Germany or have only a few belongings to ship, it may be possible to purchase furniture locally up to the limit of your allowance. For international relocations, it's common to receive an extra month's salary to cover incidentals, such as electrical equipment you must replace. When the company is liable for the total cost, you may be asked to obtain two or three removal estimates.

Generally you're required to organise and pay for the removal in advance. Your employer usually reimburses the equivalent amount in euros after you've paid the bill, although it may be possible to have them pay the bill directly or make a cash advance. If you change jobs within Germany, your new employer may pay your relocation expenses when it's necessary for you to move house. Don't forget to ask, as they may not offer to pay.

INSURANCE & PENSIONS

Social Security

All German employees, foreign employees working for German companies and the self-employed must enrol in the German social security (*Sozialversicherung*) system. Social security includes disability, health, long-term care and unemployment benefits, work accident insurance and pensions. Contributions are usually calculated as a percentage of your gross income and are deducted at source by your employer. The cost of social security contributions is split 50-50 between you and your employer. Social security contributions are high (to cover the comprehensive and generous benefits available) and can easily total 40 per cent or more of your gross pay, i.e. your share will be around 20 per cent. For more information, see **Social Security** on page 183.

Health Insurance

Health insurance is mandatory for all workers in Germany and is considered part of the social security system. Employees can choose from a number of state-run health insurance providers for cover for themselves and their families. Above certain salary levels, employees can choose to have private health insurance. For further information see page 191.

Unemployment Insurance

Unemployment insurance is compulsory for all employees of German companies and is covered by social security contributions. For details see **Unemployment Insurance** on page 186.

Salary Insurance

Salary insurance for sickness and accidents is included under social security, usually as part of your health or work accident cover. For information, see **Chapter 13**.

Company Pension Fund

Due to the comprehensive German state retirement scheme (see page 189), private or company pensions weren't previously considered necessary and many companies didn't offer a private pension scheme. However, this has now changed, particularly as the state has been forced to scale back its benefits, and the decreasing birth-rate in Germany means there are fewer taxpayers to support the ageing population. Employees now have a right to have part of their earnings paid into a company pension plan under a deferred compensation arrangement.

If you work for a large international company, you may have the option to continue contributing to a company pension plan in another country while you're working in Germany.

For further information about private pension plans in Germany (usually through banks or life insurance companies), see **Supplementary Pensions** on page 191.

HOLIDAYS & LEAVE

Annual Holidays

Your annual holiday entitlement (*Urlaubsanspruch*) depends on your employer, and the collective agreement (*Tarifvertrag*) under which he operates. Under German labour law, all employees working a five-day week must receive a minimum holiday allowance of 20 working days (i.e. four weeks) per year. In fact, in most industries, 25 days (or five weeks) is standard and the average is almost 30 days. Part-time employees receive a pro rata holiday allowance based on the number of days they work per week. For example, if you normally work three days a week, your annual holiday allowance will be 15 days (five weeks at three days a week). Employers cannot count official German public holidays (see opposite) as annual holiday.

Some collective agreements provide for longer annual holidays or grant extra days to employees based on their age or long service. In some industries, the collective agreement may call for a summer shut-down, when all employees are required to take the same two or three weeks' holiday while a factory or business is closed. An individual employer may also declare a holiday shut-down, but this must be announced in advance and be approved by the works council. Many businesses close between Christmas and New Year, sometimes requiring employees to use part of their holiday allowance.

Be sure to ask about the process for requesting holiday dates, particularly if the bulk of your holiday time is already committed to business closure periods. There's usually a formal process for submitting holiday requests, often surprisingly early in the year. Senior employees are given priority over more junior workers under contract rules or other regulations, but only if they make their preferences known according to the rules. Employees with children have priority regarding holidays taken during local school breaks, and married people are often allowed to schedule their holidays at the same time as those of their spouse, whether they work for the same company or not.

Under German law, new employees are entitled to take holiday only after six months' work (the usual probationary period), but some employers permit you to take holiday before you've completed your

Public Holidays

Date	Holiday
1st January	*New Year's Day (Neujahr)
6th January	Epiphany (Heilige Drei Könige) – Baden-Württemberg, Bavaria and Saxony-Anhalt
March or April	*Good Friday (Karfreitag), Easter Sunday (Ostern)
	*Easter Monday (Ostermontag)
1st May	*May Day or Labour Day (Maifeiertag or Tag der Arbeit)
May or June	*Ascension Day (Christi Himmelfahrt)
	*Pentecost or Whitsun (Pfingsten/Pfingstmontag)
	Corpus Christi (Fronleichnam) – Baden-Württemberg, Bavaria, Hesse, North Rhine-Westphalia, Rhineland-Palatinate and Saarland
August	Assumption Day (Mariä Himmelfahrt) – Bavaria and Saarland
3rd October	*Day of German Unity (Tag der Deutschen Einheit)
31st October	Reformation Day (Reformationstag) – Protestant areas
1st November	All Saints Day (Allerheiligen) – Catholic areas
November	Day of Repentance (Buss und Bettag) – Saxony
24th December	Christmas Eve (Heilige Abend)
25th December	*Christmas Day (Weihnachten)
26th December	*Boxing Day (2. Weihnachtstag or St. Stephen's Day)
31st December	New Year's Eve (Sylvester)

* Obligatory holidays

probationary period. Before starting a new job, check that your new employer will approve any planned holidays, particularly if they fall within your probationary period.

Public Holidays

Public holidays (Feiertage) vary from state to state (Land) and sometimes from community to community within a given state, depending on whether the predominant local religion is Catholic or Protestant. The most important public holidays are shown in the box (the nine days prefixed by an asterisk are compulsory); Christmas Eve and New Year's Eve are normally also observed but are often only half-day holidays. Some holidays apply to certain states only, as noted.

In predominantly Catholic areas, there may be semi-official holidays for Mardi Gras (Karneval) in February, such as Weiberfastnacht in Cologne and Düsseldorf, Fasching in Bavaria and Baden-Württemberg, or Rosenmontag in Bonn, Cologne and Düsseldorf. Baden-Württemberg and Bavaria are the states with the most public holidays each year, usually 12 or 13.

If a public holiday falls on a weekend, there's no substitute weekday holiday. If a holiday falls on a Tuesday or a Thursday, many workers (particularly civil servants) are also allowed to take the preceding Monday or following Friday off, known as a 'window day' (*Fenstertag*). Many German companies close over the Christmas and New Year period, e.g. from midday on 24th December until 2nd January, all employees being required to take part of their annual holiday allowance on the days that aren't public holidays.

Sick Leave

Employees are entitled to six weeks' paid sick leave on full salary for the same illness (except in the case of pregnancy – see **Parental Leave** below). However, the period is generally unlimited, provided your doctor gives you a sick note (*Arbeitsunfähigkeitsbescheinigung* or, more commonly, *Krankmeldung*) stating that you're unable to work, in which case your health insurance pays 70 per cent of your salary. Should you become ill again with a different illness, you'll be paid full salary (for up to six weeks).

Special Leave

Most German companies provide additional days off for moving house, your own and a family marriage, the birth of a child, the death of a close relative, and other major life events. Grounds for compassionate leave (*Sonderurlaub*) are usually outlined in collective agreements.

Parental Leave

Under German law, mothers and mothers-to-be are entitled to a wide range of physical and financial protection in the workplace. The low birth rate has caused the government to frequently review the Mother Protection Law (*Mutterschutzgesetz*, abbreviated to *MuSchG*) in order to make parenthood more financially attractive, in addition to protecting the mother from discrimination and physical harm in the workplace.

A woman must notify her employer as soon as she's sure that she's pregnant, by submitting a notification form from her doctor to the personnel or human resources department. This notification activates the provisions of the Mother Protection Law, which include not only her right to time off when the baby is born, but also restrictions on the type of work she may do during her pregnancy (see below), additional rest periods and other benefits. While pregnant or on maternity leave, an employee cannot be fired for any reason, provided the employer has been properly informed of the pregnancy. Maternity protection is the same for all women, irrespective of their length of employment or marital status.

Maternity leave normally starts six weeks before the projected birth date and continues for eight weeks after a baby is born, although this can be extended on doctor's orders. This is regarded as normal sick leave (see above), during which the employee receives her regular salary, although part or all of it may actually be paid by her health insurance provider.

Either parent has the right to (unpaid) child-rearing leave (*Elternzeit*) of up to three

years, two of which must be taken before a child reaches its third birthday. During this leave, either parent is eligible for state parent benefit (*Elterngeld*) for a period. *Elterngeld* is paid at 67 per cent of your average net salary for the last 12 months, subject to a minimum of €300 and a maximum of €1,800, and is available to a parent going on leave or working up to 30 hours per week. If the mother stays at home, she's entitled to 12 months' *Elterngeld*; if the father stays at home for all or part of the 12 months, an additional bonus of two months is added – a rule designed to counter discrimination in the workplace against young women and to encourage fathers to take leave.

The mother and father can take the 14 months in any combination: for example, seven months with the mother at home and seven months with the father, or even both parents simultaneously so that they can spend the first months together with their child. The agency which officially provides advice about *Elterngeld* varies from state to state. There are websites available with a calculator (*Elterngeldrechner*) to help you calculate the amount of money you can earn during your leave.

A new scheme, called *ElterngeldPlus*, was introduced in 2015 and is intended to provide more flexibility in using the benefit. If the parent reduces the weekly working time to 15 hours or less, the benefit is reduced by half (ranging from €150 to €900), but can be drawn for double the length of time. An individual parent can choose between the use of up to 12 months of *Elterngeld*, up to 24 months of *ElterngeldPlus*, or a combination of the two. Under *ElterngeldPlus*, an additional bonus of four instead of two months are subsidised if the father reduces his weekly working time to 15 hours or less. Single mothers can claim two extra months of *Elterngeld* or *ElterngeldPlus* and four extra months of *ElterngeldPlus* if they

work in four sequential months between 25 and 30 hours per week.

To encourage both parents to equally engage in childcare, the new concept of a 'partner bonus' provides for four extra months of benefit for each parent if both parents work not less than 25 or more than 30 hours a week. Whereas the *Elterngeld* and *ElterngeldPlus* concept implies that one parent takes a period of leave while the other works normal hours, the bonus concept encourages both parents to take parental leave. It's designed to encourage leave-taking mothers to work more hours per week and fathers to take leave and reduce their weekly working hours.

Employees cannot be dismissed once they have made a request for parental leave and during child-rearing leave you continue to earn credits in the state pension plan as if you were working. Provided you comply with the notification procedures and don't extend your leave beyond the permitted period, your employer must allow you to return to the same job at the same or a higher salary, taking into account general increases in wages.

EDUCATION & TRAINING

Employee training is taken seriously in Germany, whether it's conducted in your own office or another location. Training may include management seminars, technical courses, language lessons or any other form of continuing education. If you need to learn or improve your language proficiency in order to perform your job, the cost of study may be paid by your employer.

Most employers in Germany are required by law to allocate a set proportion of their gross payroll for employee education and training, and must develop a formal training plan covering all employees. The works council (*Betriebsrat*) must review and approve the training plan, and ensure that the amounts spent are appropriately distributed to benefit workers at all levels in a company. A portion of the training budget is usually available to members of the works council to attend courses covering labour law, management, finance and other areas related to their responsibilities.

It's in your interest to investigate courses of study, seminars and lectures that you feel will be of benefit to you and your employer. Most employers give reasonable consideration to a request to attend a course during working hours, provided you don't make it a full-time occupation. If you decide to pursue a formal degree or certification programme requiring several months or years to complete, some companies may agree to pay for the programme (including books, examinations and other costs), but only if you sign an agreement to reimburse them should you leave the company within a certain number of years (generally no more than five) after you complete the course.

UNIONS & WORKS COUNCILS

Trade unions in Germany are highly organised and play an important role in the 'social market economy'. By far the largest and most powerful union organisation is the Deutsche Gewerkschaftsbund (DGB), which is an umbrella group for the eight industrial unions that operate throughout Germany. The DGB unions represent all workers in specific industries, irrespective of their job titles or professions, and have around 6.2 million members. For example, the well known and powerful IG (Industriegewerkschaft) Metall negotiates for all workers in the metalworking and information technology industries, including factory workers, janitorial crews, office workers and management, irrespective of whether they're members.

Normally, unions negotiate directly with the industry employer organisations, and agreements are concluded which establish the terms and working conditions for an entire industry, rather than individual companies or categories of employee. In addition to the DGB unions, there's a union for German civil servants (i.e. government employees), the Deutsche Beamtenbund (DBB), which is the main employee organisation for civil servants, with over 1 million members.

In large companies with multiple locations, there's usually a works council in each location, and there may also be an all-company works council, whose representatives are guaranteed a certain number of seats on the company's board of directors.

Under German law, unions are allowed to organise strikes on company premises but 'closed shops' are banned. Civil servants aren't permitted to strike in Germany, although they may belong to a union. Most private employees have the right to strike, but due to the system of strict co-operation between works councils and management, strikes are rare and usually of short duration (an hour or so – just long enough to hold a march and make a point). Employees in the private sector (including management employees) cannot be dismissed for striking, although there are rules and regulations governing exactly how and when strikes must be announced and conducted.

to use work time for council business, attend meetings and undergo training relating to their position. The industry-wide unions work closely with works councils and with management, often providing training programmes and general legal advice on key issues.

OTHER TERMS

Probationary & Notice Periods

For most jobs there's a probationary period (*Probezeit*), ranging from one to six months, depending on the type of work, the position and the employer. The duration of the probationary period is limited by law, according to the pay level and legal classification of the employee, and normally isn't renewable or extendable. The period is usually stated as part of the employment contract or collective agreement. During the probationary period, either party may terminate the employment contract without stating a reason, unless otherwise stated in the contract. If you work, even for a few hours, after the end of the official probationary period, you're deemed to have been hired permanently, irrespective of whether an employment contract exists.

Your notice period depends on your employer, profession and length of service, and is usually stated in your employment contract and general employment conditions. If it isn't stated, the legal notice period applies, both to the employee and the employer. The legal notice period varies from one month (which must end on either the 15th or the last day of a calendar month) to seven months, for employees with over 20 years' service.

It isn't unusual for managers or executives to have contracts requiring them to work to the

Works Councils

All businesses with more than five employees must elect a works council (*Betriebsrat*). The delegates to this council or committee are elected from among the employees and serve as an advisory board to management, with their duties and responsibilities spelt out in German labour law. The works council must have regular access to all important financial information and be kept informed of a company's major operating and marketing strategies. It must be consulted before any significant decisions are made that affect the workforce, including redundancies, relocations, or changes in working conditions or schedules.

The works council is consulted on the need for overtime or reduced hours and many day-to-day administrative matters, including the hiring and firing of employees, including executive managers. If the survival of the company is threatened, the council can make an agreement with the employer to suspend benefits granted in a collective agreement for a certain period. The works council also handles individual grievances and brings issues affecting the workforce to management's attention.

All council delegates enjoy special protection from dismissal. They're allowed end of the calendar quarter (i.e. March 30th, June 30th, September 30th or December 31st) following the three months' notice period. This means that, if you submit your notice on 3rd April, for example, you may be expected to work until the end of September. The notice period may rise to six months or even a year, after a few years in the job, which, if applicable, will be noted in your employment contract.

It's possible to waive part or all of the notice period if both sides agree, although this normally requires that the departing employee gives up his right to a redundancy payment, which may amount to several months' salary and is partly tax-free. If an employer goes bankrupt and cannot pay you, you can terminate your employment without notice. Other valid reasons for not giving notice are assault or abuse of you or a colleague by your employer, or other gross violations of the terms of your employment contract.

Part-time Job Restrictions

Restrictions on part-time employment (*Nebenarbeit*) are usually detailed in your employment conditions. Most German companies don't allow full-time employees to work part-time (i.e. moonlight) for another employer, particularly one in the same line of business. You may, however, be permitted to take an additional part-time teaching job or similar part-time employment (or you can write a book!).

Changing Jobs & Confidentiality

Companies in a high-tech or highly confidential business may have restrictions on employees moving to a competitor in Germany or within Europe. You should be aware of these restrictions, as they're enforceable under German law, although it's a complex subject and disputes must often be resolved by a

court of law. German laws regarding industrial secrets and general employer confidentiality are strict but, like most German labour laws, include considerable protection for employees. If you breach this confidentiality, you'll be dismissed and may be unable to find further employment in Germany.

Retirement

The official German retirement age (*Ruhestand*) is currently 65 but will be progressively increased to 67 by 2030, depending on your date of birth and sometimes your profession. To avoid raising contributions too far or allowing pensions to fall, the government may increase the retirement age further, e.g. to 69 by 2060. However, under new retirement reforms introduced in 2014, a person who has worked for at least 45 years from the age of 18 – that is those born before 1st January 1953 and receiving their pension for the first time on or after 1st July 2014 – is allowed to retire at age 63 with a full state pension.

If you wish to continue working after you've reached the official retirement age, you may be required to negotiate a new employment contract.

Dismissal

The rules governing dismissal and redundancy (severance) pay are complicated, and generally depend on an employee's length of service, the reason for the dismissal (e.g. misconduct or redundancy) and whether the employee has a protected status, such as that enjoyed by works council (*Betriebsrat*) members, who can be dismissed only for 'serious misconduct'.

After your probationary period, you can be dismissed only for a valid (and stated) reason, and the proposed dismissal must be reviewed and approved by the works council before notice is given. The works council can oppose the dismissal of an employee if they feel that the grounds are unfair or lacking in substance. In the event of an 'economic' lay-off involving a number of employees, an employer is obliged to submit a written plan to the works council, detailing the reasons for the action, the method for selecting the employees to be made redundant and the redundancy package being offered. The council must then be given time to review the plan and all the supporting documentation, comment, and offer suggestions or alternatives for minimising the number of redundancies.

Irrespective of the reason for the dismissal, a strict procedure must be followed. This involves the formal notification of the employee (or each employee in the case of mass redundancies) by letter to his or her home address. The letter must include the official reason for the termination, make reference to any previous disciplinary actions or warnings (if applicable), and indicate the effective employment termination date in accordance with the legal or contractual notice terms. You're usually expected to work up to your termination date, even though that date may be three months or more away. If you're being fired for a serious offence (e.g. stealing from the company or assaulting a co-worker), you may be barred from returning to work; however, the employer must usually pay your salary for the full notice period.

A dismissed employee is entitled to accrued holiday pay, and may receive a redundancy payment that's determined according to his normal pay rate, years of service, family situation and any extenuating or unusual circumstances. There's no legally prescribed minimum, but each region and industry has guidelines for what's 'fair' under various circumstances, usually calculated as a number of months' salary.

If any of the procedural details of the dismissal have been overlooked or poorly carried out (particularly involving the notice period), or if the stated reasons are deemed deficient, you can apply to a labour law court (*Arbeitsgericht*) and demand to be reinstated in your old job (at which point, the employer may restart the dismissal process, being particularly careful not to miss any of the details this time). A labour law judge can also require an employer to increase the redundancy payment to comply with local standards or to compensate for other injustices committed during the dismissal process. In the case of mass dismissal, the works council may insist on negotiating a redundancy package (*Sozialplan*).

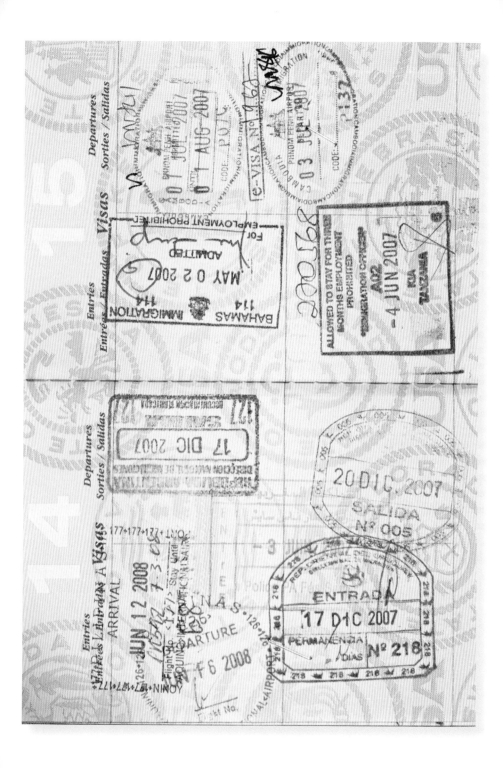

3.
PERMITS & VISAS

*B*efore making any plans to visit Germany you must ensure that you've the necessary identity card or passport (with a visa if necessary) and, if you're planning to work or stay long term, the appropriate documentation to obtain a residence and/or work permit. There are different requirements for different nationalities and circumstances. Nationals of EU and EEA countries (Iceland, Liechtenstein and Norway) plus Switzerland can legally live and work in Germany, and may enter the country with a valid passport or photo identity card. No visa or work permit is required, with the exception of Croatia, whose nationals generally require a work permit until 2020.

Although it isn't widely known, Germany is one of the world's most popular immigration destinations, where around 11 million people were born elsewhere, i.e. over one in every eight inhabitants is an immigrant, rising to one in seven among the working population. Overall, one in five people in Germany has a migrant background.

The migrant population was swelled by some 1.1 million refugees in 2015 (the highest in history), putting enormous strain on the country's ability to process asylum claims and testing confidence in Angela Merkel's right-left coalition government. Immigration slowed in 2016, but the country still welcomed another 280,000 asylum-seekers.

Permit and visa infringements are taken seriously by the authorities, and there are penalties for breaches of regulations, including fines and even deportation for flagrant abuses.

BREXIT

The decision of the UK to leave the European Union (termed 'Brexit' – see page 17), due to take effect no later than the end of March 30th 2019 (assuming the process takes two years to complete), could end the automatic right of Britons to live and work in Germany (and for German citizens to live and work in the UK). This doesn't mean that there will no longer be immigration between the countries, but prospective workers or residents will probably need to qualify and obtain a permit before doing so.

One of the main reasons many Britons voted to leave the EU was the high and uncontrolled immigration from EU countries, which has resulted in net EU migration (people arriving minus those leaving) of around 1.5 million in the last decade; in total some 3.2 million EU citizens live in the UK, compared with around 1.2 million UK nationals in EU countries.

VISAS

The requirement to obtain a visa before entering Germany changes periodically according to the German Foreign Office's assessment of the risk of illegal immigration (according to the outbreak of wars, civil unrest, economic collapse and other global disruptions). It's a rough rule of thumb that the poorer the country you're coming from the higher the probability that you'll need a visa for even a short visit, although in most cases visas are required only for stays of more than three months.

EU, EEA and Swiss nationals don't require a visa to visit Germany for any purpose. After three months in the country, however, they must register their residence at the *Einwohnermeldeamt* (see **Registration** on page 61).

Nationals of American Samoa, Andorra, Antigua and Barbuda, Argentina, Australia, Bahamas, Barbados, Bermuda, Brazil, Brunei Darussalam, Canada, Channel Islands, Chile, Costa Rica, Croatia, El Salvador, Guam, Guatemala, Honduras, Hong Kong (HK-SAR), Iceland, Isle of Man, Israel, Japan, Liechtenstein, Macao (SAR), Macedonia (biometric passports only), Malaysia, Mauritius, Mexico, Monaco, Montenegro (biometric passports only), New Zealand, Nicaragua, Panama, Paraguay, Puerto Rico, St Christopher and Nevis, San Marino, Serbia (biometric passports only), Seychelles, Singapore, South Korea, Uruguay, the USA, Vatican City, Virgin Islands, Venezuela and the US Virgin Islands don't require a visa for stays of up to three months, provided they don't intend to do any paid or self-employed work.

Nationals of all the above countries except Australia, Canada, Iceland, Israel, Japan, New Zealand, South Korea, and the US may not enter Germany as a tourist and change their status to that of an employee, student or resident, but must return to their country of residence and apply for a visa.

Nationals of former Soviet Union countries, most African and Asian countries and some South American countries require a visa to enter Germany for any purpose.

Holders of diplomatic passports from certain countries may be exempt from visa requirements.

A visa is usually stamped in your passport, which must be valid for at least four months at the time of entry into Germany. Visas may be valid for a single entry only or for multiple entries within a limited period.

For up to date information about visas for any country, see www.doyouneedvisa.com.

Short-stay or Schengen Visas

A short-stay visa, also referred to as a 'Schengen Visa', is valid for 90 days and is usually valid for multiple entries as well as free circulation within the countries that are signatories to the Schengen agreement: Austria, Belgium, the Czech Republic, Denmark, Estonia, Finland, France, Germany, Greece, Hungary, Iceland, Italy, Latvia, Liechtenstein, Lithuania, Luxembourg, Malta, the Netherlands, Norway, Poland, Portugal, Slovakia, Slovenia, Spain, Sweden and Switzerland.

The Schengen Agreement (named after a Luxembourg village on the Moselle River where the agreement was signed in 1995) introduced an open-border policy between the member countries. The United Kingdom and Ireland aren't members but are signatories to the Schengen police and judicial cooperation treaty. Bulgaria, Croatia, Cyprus and Romania aren't yet part of the Schengen Area, but have a visa policy that's based on the Schengen scheme.

A Schengen visa is generally issued for tourism, business travel or family visits. It also allows holders to come to Germany for short training courses, internships or to exercise a salaried occupation, subject to obtaining a temporary work permit, e.g. for artists on tour, sportspeople playing in championships, employees seconded to provide services, etc. You may also need a Schengen visa to transit through Germany.

A Schengen visa usually costs €60 (there's a reduced fee of €35 for nationals of some countries) and allows you to travel freely between all Schengen member countries. Under the Schengen agreement, immigration checks and passport controls take place when you first arrive in a member country from outside the Schengen area, after which you can travel freely between member countries for a maximum of up to 90 days in a six month period.

Certain applicants for a Schengen visa must submit their visa application in person, together with all the necessary documents, at the Germany consulate responsible for their place of residence. For information about applying for Schengen visa in the UK, see www.ambafrance-uk.org/how-and-where-to-apply-for-a-visa.

Schengen visa holders aren't permitted to live permanently or work in Europe. Foreigners who plan to take up employment or a self-employed activity in Germany (or any Schengen country) may require a long-stay visa, even if their home country (nationality) is listed on the Schengen visa-free list.

Non-EU nationals who are resident in Germany (or another Schengen country) are issued with a Schengen ID card that allows them to travel freely to all Schengen member countries without a visa.

Business Visas

Business visas are valid for up to 90 days in a six-month period. Although it's possible to act as managing director, teacher, university scientist, sportsperson, actor, model or journalist on the basis of a business visa, business persons may only attend contract negotiations and buy or sell goods for an employer abroad. All other economic activity is considered work and cannot be performed with a business visa.

Transit Visas

Nationals of certain countries changing aircraft in Germany require a transit visa. These include nationals of Afghanistan, Bangladesh, the Democratic Rep. of Congo, Eritrea, Ethiopia, Ghana, India, Iran, Iraq, Jordan, Lebanon, Nigeria, Pakistan, Somalia, Sri Lanka, Sudan, Syria, and Turkey. Exceptions include:

◆ those who hold a visa for Australia, Israel or New Zealand and have a valid boarding pass to one of these countries;

◆ those who have 'leave to remain in the UK for an indefinite period' or a 'certificate of entitlement to the right of abode in the UK';

◆ those who have a valid visa or residence permit for any EEA country or Canada, Switzerland or the US;

◆ some diplomatic passport holders.

If a stopover requires accommodation in Germany, full visa regulations apply (see above).

RESIDENCE PERMITS

All foreigners are permitted to stay in Germany for up to three months without a residence permit (*Aufenthaltserlaubnis*), although some require a visa (see above). After this time, all non-EU nationals must have a residence permit. EU nationals need only to register at their local council.

Non-EU nationals and nationals of Australia, Canada, Israel, Japan, New Zealand, South Korea and the US can apply for a permit during their first three months in Germany – if you know from the outset that your stay in Germany will be longer than three months, it's wise to start the process immediately after your arrival – or you can apply in advance at a German consulate in your home country if this is likely to be more convenient or you require a work permit (see page 54). All other nationals must apply in their country of domicile for a residence permit, which cannot be sent to you in Germany.

Before applying for a residence permit you must first register at the local registration office (*Einwohnermeldeamt* – see page 61), where you'll receive a confirmation form (*Anmeldebestätigung*) as proof of your registration and a tax card (*Lohnsteuerkarte*). The application forms for a residence permit are available from the local foreigners' office (*Auslandsbehörde*), which is often in the same building as the registration office. Once you've completed the forms, you must compile the necessary supporting documentation, which includes some or all of the following:

◆ two completed forms;

◆ two passport photographs, showing a full and unobstructed frontal view of your face, which must measure between 32 and 36mm from the bottom of the chin to the hairline, and be printed at 600dpi on high-quality paper;

◆ a valid passport and one copy of the relevant pages;

◆ proof of health insurance;

◆ proof that you have a place to live, e.g. a signed statement or lease (*Mietvertrag*) from your landlord;

◆ proof of means of support (usually a letter from your employer). If you're married to a German citizen, this isn't usually necessary.

◆ a 'certificate of health for a residence permit' (*Gesundheitszeugnis für Aufenthaltserlaubnis*), which can be obtained from any registered German doctor or local health office (*Gesundheitsamt*) and costs between €100 and €150 from a doctor, or around half as much from a health office. In some states, your blood must be tested for HIV.

◆ a 'certificate of good conduct', which can be obtained from your home country's

embassy or your local police station or consulate in Germany.

Exact requirements depend on the German state (*Land*) where you'll be resident and your marital status – for example, the last two items (listed above) aren't required everywhere – check with your local Aliens Department, which can be found in the Yellow Pages under *Ausländerbehörde* or *Kreisverwaltungsreferat*. Being married to a German citizen makes the process simpler and also means that you're exempt from the fee, which is normally around €50.

You must then take the completed application forms and documents to your local *Ausländerbehörde* (check the business hours as most are closed in the afternoons and many are open for just a few days a week). There's usually a long queue for non-EU nationals and you should plan to arrive at least an hour before closing time. In larger towns and cities, there's usually a ticket system such as you find at a post office. If you aren't sure or don't understand the instructions posted in German, ask the receptionist.

When you're called for an interview they will go through a checklist to confirm that you have all the necessary documents, and, assuming your paperwork is in order, you'll be asked about your job and planned stay. Obviously the preferred language is German, but many officials can speak enough English to manage the interview, although you may want to arrange for someone to come with you to translate.

At the end of this process, and having paid your fee (if applicable), you receive a residence permit for a period of between six months and five years – the duration depending largely on your country of origin. For example, EU nationals are entitled to a five-year residence permit, although you must specifically apply for one and you must have either a job in Germany or evidence of means of support in order to qualify. Non-EU nationals are normally issued with a one-year permit, renewable annually at the *Ausländerbehörde* for a fee of €20; you must apply for a new permit before your existing permit expires.

After five years, EU citizens are entitled to an open-ended residence permit (*Niederlassungserlaubnis*), provided they still meet the necessary criteria for residence. Non-EU nationals can apply for a *Niederlassungserlaubnis* after five years (three years if they have a German spouse), provided they've worked and paid into the system for that amount of time. To obtain an open-ended permit, you're required to be able to speak at least basic German as well as to have proof of employment or means of support. If you're unable to speak German, you must take an integration course (*Integrationskurs*).

Your residence permit must be attached to a current passport in order to be valid. This means that if your passport expires while you're in Germany, you must go through the process of applying for a residence permit again when you receive a new passport. Therefore, if your passport is due to expire in the near future it will pay you to renew it early.

Students

In order to remain in Germany for longer than three months, all students from non-EU countries must have a residence permit. The application procedure is the same as for other non-EU nationals.

A certificate of matriculation (*Immatrikulationsbescheinigung*) is necessary to obtain health insurance and student discounts, e.g. for public transport.

However, the documentation required for students is different and includes:

♦ two passport photographs;

♦ a valid identification card or passport;

♦ proof of health insurance;

♦ a rental contract;

♦ proof of adequate financial resources – the minimum amount required varies with the area, but is generally around €700 per month;

♦ certificates of school or university examination results;

♦ certificates proving your ability to speak German, or confirmation of enrolment in a German course (*Deutschkurs*);

The requirement regarding proof of financial resources is strict. It isn't sufficient to say that you plan to work, even if you've obtained a work permit. If you cannot provide the required proof, a possible solution is to obtain a formal statement from a third party that he'll assume responsibility for your living expenses, accompanied by evidence that he has sufficient financial resources. Alternatively, you can deposit funds in a bank account sufficient to finance your studies and living costs for one year.

Students from Andorra, Australia, Brazil, Canada, El Salvador, Honduras, Iceland, Israel, Japan, Liechtenstein, Monaco, New Zealand, Norway, San Marino, South Korea, Switzerland and the US can wait until after their arrival in Germany before starting the visa application process. However, it's advisable to start it immediately upon arrival, as it can take up to ten weeks. Other nationals must begin the application process at a German consulate or embassy in their home country, and obtain a permit before travelling to Germany.

WORK PERMITS

There are stiff fines for employers who hire people without residence and work permits, therefore most will demand that you have both (if applicable) before starting work.

EU Nationals

Citizens of countries that joined the EU before 2004 don't require permits to work in Germany. Citizens of countries that became EU members in 2004 and 2007 (and probably future members) must apply for a work permit (*Arbeitserlaubnis*) at the relevant Labour Office (*Arbeitsagentur*), which can be found in the Yellow Pages or on the internet under *Arbeitsagentur*.

Nationals of new EU countries must register with the local council and take their registration certificate (*Anmeldung*) to the local employment office (*Arbeitsagentur*) and apply for a work permit. This can take eight weeks to obtain, so you can apply for a work permit before arriving in Germany. After working for a year, you're eligible for an unlimited work permit (*Arbeitsberechtigung*).

There's usually a qualifying period for new EU countries, e.g. most citizens of Croatia will need work permits until 2020. Exceptions include graduates working in jobs corresponding to their qualifications (and their family members), trainees on in-company training programmes and Croatians who've already lived in Germany for three years. Otherwise you must have a permit from the Federal Employment Agency and a definite job offer.

Non-EU Nationals

Non-EU nationals (including those from the US and Canada), must obtain a work permit, but the application is combined with that for a residence permit, and the work permit is likewise stamped in your passport. German law prohibits employers from hiring non-EU nationals unless they're unable to find an EU national who's qualified and available to fill a position. As a non-EU national applying for a work permit, you therefore require evidence from a prospective employer that he wishes (and is permitted) to hire you. This is typically a copy of an employment contract (*Arbeitsvertrag*), but it can be a letter or written statement offering you a job. You must also provide a detailed job description provided by your prospective employer along with a statement explaining why you, a non-EU national, are uniquely qualified for the position. You may also be asked to provide copies of your educational, professional and trade qualifications.

After the work permit application forms and supporting documents have been filed and approved at the *Ausländerbehörde,* you pay the fee and your permit is stamped in your passport on the spot.

If you're a non-EU national married to a German citizen, the procedure is simplified and it isn't necessary to find a job before applying and your permit will be valid for any job, including self-employment.

Blue Card Scheme

In April 2012, European Blue Card legislation was implemented in Germany, allowing highly

skilled non-EU citizens easier access to work in Germany, subject to certain requirements. The Blue Card is an approved EU-wide work permit allowing high-skilled non-EU citizens to work and live in any country within the EU, excluding Denmark, Ireland and the UK. The Blue Card provides a fast-track procedure for non-EU citizens to apply for a work permit, which is valid for up to three years and can be renewed thereafter. Those granted a blue card are given a series of rights, such as favourable family reunification rules.

Applicants must have a university or college degree and an employment contract with a German company for a position with a minimum salary of €49,600 per year (2016) or €38,688 for certain occupations with a severe shortage of skilled labour, e.g. engineers, academics and doctors.

A useful website for qualified professionals wishing to work in Germany is 'Make it in Germany' (www.make-it-in-germany.com/en), which also contains job listings.

Self-employed & Freelance Workers

Non-EU nationals may work freelance, which (in Germany) means that you have three or more employers but no fixed contract (with social security, benefits, etc.), but you must have received a letter from the prospective employers to receive a freelance work permit. To receive a permit to start a business, you must usually make an investment of at least €250,000 and create a minimum of five jobs. However, the requirements can be relaxed with the support of the local chambers of commerce or similar organisations, which confirm the business plan's socioeconomic value for the region. Investors are eligible for grants, tax reductions and loans to help build their business.

The above conditions also apply to the non-EU spouses of German nationals, usually for the first three years of residence. Any limitations will be stated on your residence permit, and the official issuing the permit will tell you exactly what's permitted and what isn't. Restrictions are lifted when an open-ended residence permit (*Niederlassungserlaubnis*) is issued (see **Residence Permits** on page 52).

☑ SURVIVAL TIP

If you plan to work freelance, make sure that you inform the official before he issues your residence permit/work permit.

If you own your own business, you must apply for a trade licence (*Gewerbeschein*) at the local tax office (*Finanzamt*). The same form will also provide you with a tax number (*Steuernummer*), which isn't the same as a tax card (*Lohnsteuerkarte*) – see page 205. If you're freelance, you need only a *Steuernummer*, but to get one you complete the same form as for a trade licence. The two most important things on the form are your projected earnings – which you should underestimate in order to avoid paying a hefty pre-tax payment – and whether you charge VAT (*Mehrwertsteuer*) on your services. If you invoice your customers, you'll have to include VAT at 19 per cent, which you must later pay

to the *Finanzamt*. Freelancers must also pay social security (see page 183).

Students

All students except those from EU countries must be authorised by the *Ausländerbehörde* to work in Germany. Generally students may work for either 90 full days or 180 half-days per year. Exceptions may be made if there's a close connection between your studies and a desired job (typically a job on the university campus or one organised by the university), in which case you may work during terms without a permit. If you wish to work before commencing or after completing your studies in Germany, you must obtain a work permit. Otherwise, holding a wage-earning job while a student is illegal and can be grounds for expulsion from the country, even if you have time remaining after completing your studies.

There are, however, programmes that allow for the reciprocal exchange of students seeking short-term paid employment in Germany. The largest and best known of these programmes is administered by the Council on International Educational Exchange (www.ciee.org). You must apply for and receive a work permit before leaving your home country. There's a fixed fee, and opportunities exist for three or, in some cases, six months' employment. At the conclusion of your studies, you may be permitted to remain in Germany with a student visa for up to 18 months to seek employment.

Working Holiday Programme

Germany has working holiday agreements with Australia, Brazil, Canada, Chile, Hong Kong, Israel, Japan, South Korea, New Zealand and Taiwan. Under the working holiday programme, visa holders can remain in Germany for up to 12 months and take holiday jobs to help finance their stay.

Applicants must be aged 18 to 30 (35 for Canada), be single (unaccompanied by a spouse or children), have proof of sufficient funds, possess a return air ticket or equivalent funds, and have health insurance for the duration of their stay.

Brandenburg Gate, Berlin

10 EU

50

EURO

BCE ECB EZB EKT EKP 2002

Passenger Ticket and Baggage Check

CONTINENTS

EUROPEAN UNION

UNITED KINGDOM OF
GREAT BRITAIN
AND NORTHERN IRELAND

4.
ARRIVAL

O n arrival in Germany, your first task will be to negotiate immigration and customs. Fortunately, this presents few problems for most people, particularly citizens of EU and EEA countries and Switzerland . However, non-EU nationals coming to Germany for any purpose other than as visitors usually require a visa (see page 49).

In addition to information about immigration and customs, this chapter outlines a number of tasks that must be completed before (or soon after) your arrival, and includes suggestions for finding local help and information.

IMMIGRATION

When you arrive in Germany from another Schengen country (see page 50), there are usually no immigration checks or passport controls. If you're a non-EU national and arrive in Germany by air or sea from outside the EU, you must go through immigration for non-EU citizens. Unless you require a visa to enter Germany, however, the official will usually do little more than look at your passport to see that you vaguely resemble the photograph, although at major border posts they may feed your details into a computer to check whether you're wanted for a crime in Germany. Residence and work permits are handled by the local authorities at your final destination, rather than on entry to the country.

☑ SURVIVAL TIP

Note that you should always carry your identity card, passport or residence permit in Germany.

All non-EU foreigners residing in Germany for longer than 90 days must obtain a residence permit (see page 52). Failure to apply for a residence permit before three months have expired is an offence and may result in a fine or even expulsion from Germany. Most EU nationals who visit Germany with the intention of finding employment (or starting a business) have no restrictions and need only register their presence (see **Registration** below).

CUSTOMS

The Single European Act created a single trading market and changed the rules regarding customs (*Zoll*) for EU nationals. The shipment of personal (household) effects to Germany from another EU country is no longer subject to customs formalities, although it might be useful to have an inventory of the items you're bringing with you. For more information, see the German Customs website (www.zoll.de/en/home/home_node.html).

Visitors

Imported belongings aren't subject to duty or valued added tax (VAT) if you're visiting Germany for less than 90 days, provided their nature and quantity doesn't imply a commercial aim. This applies to private cars, camping vehicles (including trailers or caravans), motorcycles, aircraft, boats and personal effects, but all means of transport and personal effects imported duty free mustn't be sold or given away in Germany and must be exported before the end of the 90-day period.

If you cross into Germany by road, you may drive through the border without stopping. However, any goods (and pets) that you're carrying must fall within the exempted categories, and mustn't be the subject of a prohibition or restriction. Customs officials can stop anyone anywhere in Germany for a spot check, e.g. to search for drugs or illegal immigrants.

Non-EU Residents

If you're a non-EU resident planning to take up permanent or temporary residence in Germany, you're permitted to import your furniture and personal effects free of duty. These include vehicles, mobile homes, pleasure boats and aircraft. However, to qualify for duty-free import, articles must have been owned and used for at least six months. VAT must be paid on all items owned for less than six months that were purchased outside the EU, as well as on those purchased in the EU if a VAT receipt cannot be produced.

To import personal effects as a non-EU national, you must contact the local customs office (*Zollamt*) in the area where you'll be resident and provide documentation showing that:

♦ you've been living outside Germany for at least 12 consecutive months prior to your entry. (This requirement may be waived if there are unusual circumstances, such as when you're transferred abroad and back to Germany by the same employer.)

♦ you've given up your residence outside Germany, i.e. documents showing the termination of your lease or employment, the sale of your home or a statement from your employer stating that you've been transferred to Germany;

♦ you're establishing residence in Germany; i.e. a lease agreement, a statement from your German employer or your registration receipt (*Anmeldung*) from the local authorities in the area where you'll be living.

To import a vehicle into Germany duty-free, it must have been registered in your name for at least six months prior to its importation. You may be required to have it inspected to check that it meets German standards and, if you're coming from another EU country, that VAT was paid at the time of purchase. Imported vehicles may be used tax-free for six months only. For more information, see page 148.

All items must usually be imported within a year of the date of your change of residence, either in one or in a number of consignments. If you cannot bring in all your goods within your first year, you can apply for an exception. In this case, your remaining goods must be imported as soon as possible after the initial consignment and no later than three years after your move.

If you use a removal company to transport your belongings to Germany, they'll usually provide all the necessary forms and take care of the paperwork. On the arrival of your shipment, the removal company will ask you to send copies of the clearance documents (see above) so that it can attend to the formalities with the local customs office before delivering your goods. Always keep a copy of all forms and communications with customs officials, both in Germany and in your previous or permanent country of residence. You should have an official record of the export of valuables (e.g. jewellery, works of art and antiques) from any country, in case you wish to (re-)import them later.

The EU requires that currency, jewels or precious metals worth €10,000 or more must be declared at customs at the first border crossing into the EU and at any subsequent EU border crossing. There are detailed and strict regulations regarding the importation of guns, rifles or ammunition into the country, and certain types of pets and plants require prior approval and health certificates.

REGISTRATION

Everyone in Germany, including German citizens, must register with the local residents' registration office (*Einwohnermeldeamt* or *Bürgeramt*), and there are fines for those who fail to comply. Registration (*Anmeldung*), which simply involves reporting your address, must be done within one or two weeks of taking up residence in a private dwelling in Germany (including accommodation with friends), or within two months of taking up residence continuously in the same hotel.

To find out where the local registration office is located, you can consult the phone book under *Stadtverwaltung* – which shouldn't be confused with the *Rathaus*, both of which are often translated as 'town hall' – or you can check online by visiting www.meldeaemter.de.

There are set times for registering, usually before midday, and you should phone to check or look on the notice detailing *Sprechstunden* (business hours), which is usually located at the main entrance area of the *Stadtverwaltung*. On arrival, take a number slip from the inevitable machine and wait until your number is called. You need the following documents when registering:

◆ a valid passport or national identity card;

◆ a copy of your lease or rental agreement (*Mietvertrag*) as proof of accommodation or a signature from the landlord on the registration form;

◆ a completed registration form (*Anmeldeformular*).

After you have registered you receive a certificate of registration (*Meldebestätigung*).

If you move to a different state within Germany, you must de-register before you leave, although when you register in some states, the town where you were previously registered is notified. De-registration is also required when you leave the country. Fortunately this process is straightforward and the forms can be returned by post.

CHURCH TAX

One item on the registration form to pay careful attention to is the question asking you to state your religion. If you list a Christian religion or Judaism, you'll automatically be registered to pay church tax (*Kirchensteuer*).

This is calculated as 8 (Bavaria and Baden-Württemberg) or 9 per cent (rest of the country) of your income tax (*Einkommensteuer*). No one cares whether you actually practise the religion or attend services, so if you wish to avoid this tax you should answer the question with the word *'keine'* (none) – no justification for your answer is required. Muslims, Hindus, Sikhs and members of other religions can, at present, register their beliefs without being taxed, although there's some discussion about implementing a tax in the future.

If, due to ignorance of the tax implications, you previously indicated a (taxable) faith, your decision can be rescinded, but not without some effort and inconvenience on your part – and, of course, there's a fee.

A decision to extend church tax to capital gains income (or the profit earned from selling an asset) in recent years has sparked a sharp decline in church membership.

INCOME TAX CARD

When you register as a resident, you should ask for an income tax card (*Lohnsteuerkarte*), even if you haven't started work. This will be required for your income tax payments. When registering your tax class (*Steuerklasse*), you must show evidence of your marital, family and employment status. The tax card must be given to your employer when you start work and will be returned to you at the end of the year with a summary of your annual income; it must be included when you file your income tax return (*Einkommensteuererklärung*). Provided you haven't moved to another district during the

Tax Number

A tax number (*Steuernummer*) is required if you wish to work freelance or be self-employed. You apply for it at the tax office (*Finanzamt*). For more information, see page 205.

year, a new *Lohnsteuerkarte* will be sent to you the following January. For more information, see page 205.

EMBASSY REGISTRATION

Nationals of some countries are required to register with their local embassy or consulate as soon as possible after arrival in Germany, and most embassies like to keep a record of their country's nationals resident in Germany. Embassies and consulates are usually an excellent source of information, and if you have a problem with German bureaucracy they can be contacted for help and advice.

FINDING HELP

One of the main difficulties facing new arrivals in Germany is how and where to obtain help with day-to-day problems, e.g. finding a home, enrolling your children in school and obtaining insurance. This book was written in response to this need. However, in addition to the comprehensive information contained in this book, you'll require detailed local information. How successful you are at finding it depends on your employer, the town or area where you live (Frankfurt's residents are better served than, for example, Baden-Baden's), your nationality and your language proficiency.

As you'd expect, there's a wealth of general local information available in German – although it isn't designed for foreigners and their particular needs – but little in English, and other foreign languages. You may find that your friends and colleagues can help, as they're often able to proffer advice based on their own experiences and mistakes, although this may be inappropriate or irrelevant to your situation.

Your local council is usually an excellent source of reliable information, but you must speak German to benefit from it. Similarly, public libraries often have lots of free government publications (in German) about many different subjects, usually located near the entrance. Some companies may have a department or staff whose job is to help new arrivals settle in, or they may contract this task out to a relocation company. Unfortunately most German employers seem totally unaware of (or uninterested in) the problems and difficulties faced by their foreign employees.

A good source of information and help can be found in the American Women's Clubs (AWC) located in Berlin, Cologne, Düsseldorf, Hamburg and the Taunus region around Frankfurt. AWC clubs provide comprehensive information in English about both local matters and topics of more general interest, and many provide data sheets, booklets and orientation programmes for newcomers to the area. Membership is generally limited to Americans or those with active links to the US, e.g. through study, work or a spouse who works for a US company or the US government, but most publications and orientation programmes are available to others for a small fee.

AWC clubs are part of the Federation of American Women's Clubs Overseas (FAWCO), which can be contacted through its website (www.fawco.org). In Munich, the English-speaking International Women's Club (IWC), which fulfils much the same functions as the AWC, is

open to women of all nationalities (www. internationalwomensclub.org). A useful list of clubs is published by Expatica (www.expatica. com/de/out-and-about/groups-and-clubs-in-germany_101761.html).

In addition to the above, there are many social clubs and other organisations for expats in Germany, including Anglo-German 'friendship' clubs and other English-speaking organisations, whose members can help you find your way around. They may be difficult to locate, as small clubs run by volunteers often operate out of the president's house and they rarely bother to advertise or take out a phone listing. Many embassies and consulates provide information regarding clubs for their nationals, and many businesses (particularly large multinational companies) produce booklets and leaflets containing useful information about clubs or activities in the area.

Bookshops may have some interesting publications about the local region, and tourist and information offices are also good sources. Finally, don't forget to check the internet, where you can find the websites of expatriate groups as well as local newspapers, government offices, clubs and organisations.

Tübingen, Baden-Württemberg

5.
ACCOMMODATION

*F*inding affordable accommodation can be difficult in Germany due to an enduring housing shortage, particularly in the major cities where increasing demand, lack of supply and strong economic growth have increased property prices and rents. Government programmes intended to remedy the situation resulted in a building boom during the '90s, but since then fewer and fewer homes have been built. Many developers have taken advantage of state aid to build luxury accommodation with rents to match, so that the government still finds it necessary to provide housing subsidies for many citizens.

Expect to pay around a third of your net income for housing and energy costs in most areas of Germany, or up to 50 per cent in the major cities. Around 55 per cent of the population rent their homes, although it's much higher in the major cities, e.g. 86 per cent in Berlin, 79 per cent in Munich and 76 per cent in Hamburg, where property is most expensive.

Home ownership is far lower in Germany – around 45 per cent – than in most of the rest of Europe and the lowest in the EU. The German housing market was one of the few worldwide that avoided a slump in the wake of the 2008-2009 global financial crisis and property prices have historically remained fairly stable. However, in the last five years prices have ben rising inexorably – by as much as 25 per cent in some areas (in Munich, Germany's most expensive city, property prices have risen by over 80 per cent in the last decade) – with buyers encouraged to invest in property due to low interest rates and bond yields.

TEMPORARY ACCOMMODATION

On arrival in Germany, you may find it necessary to stay in temporary accommodation for a few weeks or months, perhaps while waiting for your furniture to arrive or while looking for a property to rent or buy. Some employers provide rooms, self-contained apartments or holiday houses (*Ferienwohnungen*) for transferred employees and their families as part of their moving and relocation costs, but usually for a limited period only.

Many hotels and bed-and-breakfast establishments cater for long-term guests and offer reduced weekly or monthly rates. Serviced apartments (or apartment hotels) are available in most large cities, comprising furnished apartments with their own bathrooms and kitchens, which are cheaper than a hotel and more convenient for families. In more rural areas, particularly in the south of Germany, you can rent self-catering holiday accommodation by the week or month, although this can be prohibitively expensive and may be impossible to arrange at short notice during the main summer holiday season.

GERMAN HOMES

Most Germans live in various forms of multi-family housing – apartments, duplexes, 'triplexes' and semi-detached properties – particularly if they live in or near a major city. Detached, single-family houses (*Einfamiliehäuser*) are normally available only in rural areas, although 'housing estates' are beginning to spring up on the edges of cities and towns. Most of the available housing has been built since 1950; a property described as *Altbau* (literally 'old building') may date from before 1914, as there was little building in Germany between the wars. Old properties generally command a high price (whether for sale or rent), despite their age and possible lack of modern conveniences, due largely to the Germans' romantic attachment to older styles. Timber and mortar buildings (*Fachwerk*) are particularly popular and can command top prices, even when in poor condition. Note, however, that the term *Altbau* may simply refer to an existing house or building, as opposed to a brand new one.

Exacting building standards and the German liking for modern conveniences ensures that new buildings (*Neubau*) are solidly built to high standards. Nearly all building nowadays is in stone or reinforced concrete, and wooden or wood-frame buildings are rare. Germany is also a world leader in luxury prefabricated houses (see www.hanse-haus.co.uk, www.huf-haus.com/en.html and www.weberhaus.co.uk). All modern homes have central heating, usually oil or gas. Air-conditioning is rarely provided, nor is it often required, given Germany's generally moderate summer climate.

Size

When it comes to housing in Germany, size really does matter! The cost of a home, whether to buy or to rent, is determined by its floor space, measured in square metres (*Quadratmeter*, abbreviated as *qm* or m^2, where $1m^2 = 10.76ft^2$). Furthermore, as with many things in Germany, there's a strictly regulated method – stipulated by the German Standards Institute (Deutsches Institut für Normung/DIN) – for determining the official size of a dwelling.

The following areas are included in the calculation of habitable living space:

- living rooms and bedrooms;
- kitchen, bathroom and toilet;
- entrance halls, hallways and cloakrooms;
- cupboards and stairways inside the dwelling;
- enclosed porch or balcony areas that can be heated for winter use.

The following areas aren't included in the calculation of habitable living space:

- storage areas outside the main living area, for example in a cellar or garage;
- lofts;
- utility or machine rooms;
- any space where the ceiling height is less than 1m.

The following areas are calculated at 50 per cent of actual floor space:

- any space where the ceiling height is greater than 1m but less than 2m;
- open balconies, porches and roof gardens and uncovered decks or terraces;
- enclosed porch or balcony areas that cannot be adequately heated during winter.

When comparing the price of properties, it's important to bear in mind the above points. For example, a 60m² apartment may have only 55m² of indoor living space because there's a 10m² balcony, while a rooftop unit (*Dachwohnung*) with the same official size of 60m² could yield only 45 or 50m² of usable living area if it has a large roof garden.

The average home in the west German states is around 90m² and the average in the east 75m². In university towns such as Freiburg or Leipzig, you can sometimes find 'apartments' with just 12m² of living space, and even then it doesn't guarantee a low rent. Generally, a 70-80m² property is considered the average size for a small family, a couple or a well off single person. Larger apartments, particularly those over 100m², are considered up-market, if not luxury dwellings. Larger properties are generally more difficult to find and are more likely to be listed with estate agents than standard-size properties.

Number of Rooms

The number of rooms is also important in determining whether a given house or apartment fits your needs. An advertisement or information sheet will include not only the size of a property but also the number of rooms. The way rooms are counted is, oddly enough, not subject to any standards, although certain conventions apply. Normally only the bedrooms, living room and dining room are included. A half-room indicates that there's a dining area off the main living room that isn't separated by a door that can be closed (doors are very important in German homes) or a bedroom under 10m². Kitchens, bathrooms and toilets aren't included in the room count.

Thus, an apartment advertised as 3.5 rooms probably has two bedrooms with a living room and dining area. A four-room dwelling usually has three bedrooms and a living room but could have two bedrooms, a separate dining room and a living room. Separate dining rooms are rare in modern properties, although you could of course use a spare bedroom as a dining room. Bathrooms, showers and toilets are usually listed separately in advertisements.

Kitchens

One of the biggest shocks for many newcomers to Germany is that you aren't just expected to supply your own light fittings, but must literally provide the kitchen sink (plus cupboards and other fittings) as well. If you view an apartment or house before the previous tenants have vacated it, you could offer to buy the fittings from them (*Ablöse*) – if you like what you see and the outgoing tenants agree to sell them. If you don't include fixtures and fittings in the purchase contract, however, the chances are that they'll be gone when you move in.

The advantage of this arrangement is that you don't have to limit your house-hunting to apartments with dishwashers or a certain kind of cooker, if that's what you want. However, you must allow extra in your budget to cover the cost of fitting out a kitchen. Sometimes landlords will provide a kitchen and charge you a separate rent for its use, otherwise you must provide your own kitchen cupboards and appliances, even in rented accommodation.

Kitchen fittings in Germany come in standard-size units, so mixing and matching appliances with cupboards isn't difficult. For those tiny student apartments, there are even compact, all-in-one units consisting of a sink, a small refrigerator and a cooker in a single, stainless-steel box. The Germans like modern conveniences and sturdy, well-engineered products, and you'll have no problem finding state-of-the-art appliances when shopping for new ones. Ceramic induction hobs are popular, as are ovens equipped to handle a variety of cooking methods: forced hot air, baking, grilling or microwaving, all at the flick of a switch or knob.

> ## ☑ SURVIVAL TIP
>
> Bear in mind that most shops must order in a kitchen, unless you're buying a display model or other special unit, delivery usually taking 3 to 12 weeks.

Many Germans still prefer rather small refrigerators – generally the type that fit under kitchen worktops – but larger upright fridge-freezer combinations are becoming more popular, and you can also buy side-by-side American-style fridge-freezers complete with water and ice dispensers. While these may be tempting (particularly to Americans), you should ensure that you can fit such a large item into your kitchen along with all the other appliances, worktops and cupboards you may want. Connecting the water supply may involve running pipes along the walls in full view unless you can place your refrigerator next to the sink, although you can buy American-style fridge-freezers that don't require plumbing.

As you may imagine, there's an active market in used kitchen fittings. Most furniture stores and do-it-yourself (DIY) shops sell new cupboards and appliances and can arrange for installation. Keep an eye out for offers – often a display unit will be sold for an attractive price, particularly when new models are introduced. However, sale prices only apply to a kitchen of the exact size and construction shown in the advertisement. Any changes in size, colour, knobs, handles or appliances will increase the cost.

By law, you must have the plumbing and electrical connections for a cooker connected by a qualified tradesman. If you hire someone to install your kitchen or have the store where you purchased it do the installation, they'll usually organise a plumber and electrician for you, while some independent kitchen installers are certified in all the necessary trades and can do the entire job.

GARAGE OR PARKING SPACE

Public transport in most cities and towns in Germany is frequent and convenient. As a result, it's possible to live and work in many areas without owning a car. If you own a car, you'll probably have to rent a garage or parking space for it, as on-street parking is difficult to find in most residential areas. Most modern apartment blocks have parking spaces or garage space available for an additional monthly fee. You may have the option of buying or renting a garage or parking space in the building itself or within its grounds, which may belong to someone other than the owner of your apartment. If you're lucky enough to find an apartment with a garage or parking space, the cost will be itemised separately on the lease or in the purchase contract.

If there are no available parking spaces in or around your building, you may be able to rent a space in a nearby covered car park or garage or even in another apartment building. Parking spaces for rent are advertised in local newspapers and in apartment building entrance halls.

The cost of a parking space varies according to its size, type (e.g. covered garage or outside parking space), location and other factors, such as security. Generally, you should be able to find adequate parking for around €100 per month.

MOVING HOUSE

Once you've found a home in Germany, it usually takes only a few weeks to have your belongings shipped from within continental Europe. From anywhere else it varies considerably, e.g. four weeks from the east coast of America, six weeks from the west coast of America and the Far East, and around eight weeks or longer from Australasia. Customs clearance is no longer necessary when shipping your household effects from one EU country to another. When shipping your effects from a non-EU country to Germany, you should enquire about customs formalities in advance, or you may encounter numerous problems and delays. Removal companies usually take care of the administration and ensure that the right documents are provided and correctly completed.

For international removals, you should use a company that's a member of the International Federation of Furniture Removers (FIDI, www.fidi.org) or the Overseas Moving Network International (OMNI, www.omnimoving.com),

with experience in Germany. Members of FIDI and OMNI usually subscribe to an advance payment scheme providing a guarantee; if a member company fails to fulfil its commitments to a customer, the removal is completed at the agreed cost by another company or your money is refunded.

Some removal companies have subsidiaries or affiliates in Germany, which may be more convenient if you encounter problems or need to make an insurance claim. Obtain at least three written quotations before choosing a company, and, if you're moving from overseas, give careful thought to how you plan on shipping your belongings. Most employer-sponsored overseas moves allow for a limited airfreight shipment of around 250kg (550lbs), which should arrive at your new home within a week or two. Make sure you include the items that you'll need most.

Bear in mind that moving house rarely goes smoothly and it's a chaotic and stressful time for all involved. You're entitled to a day off from work to move house under German law and you should plan on taking it, if only to enjoy a moment of peace and quiet once the removal van has left!

Freudenberg, North Rhine-Westphalia

ESTATE AGENTS

The quickest and easiest way to find a property, either to rent or buy, is to contact an estate agent (*Immobilienmakler, Wohnungsmakler* or, more often, just *Makler*). If your employer is paying your relocation costs the agent's fees (for a rental property at least) will usually be covered, particularly if your employer is keen to have you settle in and start work quickly. If not, however, you should be aware that it will be expensive.

> On average, an agent's fee for a purchase is around 3 per cent and it's the buyer who pays, therefore on a purchase price of €400,000 you should reckon on paying around €12,000 plus VAT at 19 per cent.

If you rent an apartment or house through an agent, you must pay a finder's fee (*Provision*), which generally runs to two to three months' rent plus VAT at 19 per cent. Therefore, if you find an apartment for €1,000 per month through an agent, it will cost you a minimum of €2,000 plus VAT before you pay the first month's rent or the rental deposit (usually three months rent)! The agent involved in the purchase of a home may charge you anywhere from 2 to 7 per cent of the purchase price (plus VAT).

What agents do to earn these hefty fees varies considerably. Somewhat surprisingly, the profession isn't stringently regulated in Germany and almost anyone can set himself up as an estate agent after doing a three-day training course (mostly dealing with business registration and taxes) and paying a local licensing fee. All an agent is obliged to provide is a referral (*Nachweis*) or some form of mediation (*Vermittlung*) in the transaction. In some cases, the agent may do nothing more than provide a list of properties meeting your requirements, along with (possibly) the name and phone number of the current tenant, so that you can arrange a viewing of the property. Others will arrange an appointment for you, but may not accompany you when you view a property.

However, most reputable agents, particularly those used to dealing with foreigners, will handle all aspects of a transaction, including scheduling visits, accompanying you to properties, and assisting in negotiations with the landlord or vendor. Officially, an agent is a mediator between the parties and isn't a representative of one side or the other. His fee, however, is determined by the selling price or monthly rent, so he obviously wants to get the highest price or rent possible.

It's possible to find your own accommodation in Germany without using an agent, but it takes time and organisation. Many Germans spend weeks, months or even years conducting house-hunting searches, whether to rent or buy. An agent can help you to make the most efficient use of a short house-hunting trip and may reduce the time (and therefore money) you spend in temporary accommodation on your arrival. Most agents have English-speaking staff.

To find a reputable agent, the best approach is to ask around. Your employer and co-workers will be able to advise you on those they've used and can recommend – or those to be avoided! Most banks have a property (*Immobilien*) department handling both rental and purchase properties. Doing business with a bank's estate agent can be an advantage, in that the bank has an interest in protecting its reputation by exercising control over its real estate agents. When dealing with a bank's property department, you'll be encouraged to arrange financing or insurance through the bank, but this can work in your favour if you let it be known that you also require banking services.

You can contact as many agents as you wish, but be careful to keep track of which one referred you to which property. If a second agent shows you a listing sheet for a property you've already seen, you must notify the second agent of the duplication in writing and return any listing sheets or other information you received about the property. If you don't, you may find yourself liable for two agents' fees, although this is more likely when you're buying than renting.

RENTED ACCOMMODATION

Renting is common in Germany, where some 55 per cent of the population rent rather than own their homes. One reason is that the property market is usually stagnant (although this has changed in recent years) and most Germans don't consider owning their own home to be a good investment, but rather a form of insurance for retirement. Tax benefits only go to property owners who let a property and tenants have considerable security of tenure in Germany, where rental costs and regulations are strictly controlled by law.

Most rental properties in Germany are let unfurnished. Furnished properties (*möbeliert*, abbreviated to *möbl.* in advertisements) are difficult to find, other than for short-term lets or student accommodation. Unfurnished properties consist of floors, ceilings, windows, doors and walls, and not much more. The bathroom and toilet will have permanently installed fixtures – sinks, baths, showers and toilets – but you must provide everything else. Expect to provide your own lighting fixtures, curtain rods and even kitchen fittings, unless you can do a deal with the previous tenants to buy theirs (see **Kitchens** on page 67).

Check whether a garage or parking space is included in the rent, particularly if you don't have (or intend to buy) a car!

Finding a Rental Property

The easiest way to start your search is on the internet. Many *Immobilien* websites exist that allow you to set the parameters of your search, e.g. size, location, price, balcony, etc. Usually, you can see webcam views of the rooms and maps of the location. You can generally contact landlords directly through the website. However, useful as the internet may be, you shouldn't neglect local newspapers and bulletin boards, as many older landlords prefer this approach for finding tenants. Most German newspapers (see www.onlinenewspapers.com/germany.htm) contain rental advertisements, usually concentrated towards the end of the week in Thursday, Friday and Saturday editions.

> Advertisements may be placed by property owners seeking to let properties or by vacating tenants looking for someone to take over their lease (*Nachmieter gesucht*) before the notice period expires.

If you don't want to pay a hefty *Makler*'s fee (see **Estate Agents** opposite), avoid responding to advertisements placed by letting agents. It's also fairly common in Germany for

Rental Advertisement Abbreviations

Abbreviation	Full Term	Meaning
2MMK	2 Monate Miet Kaution	2 months' rent for security deposit
EBK	Einbauküche	Built-in kitchen
KM or WM	Kaltmiete/Warmmiete	Heating excluded/included
Nfl.	Nutzfläche	Usable space
Stpl.	Stellplatz	Parking space
TG	Tiefgarage	Underground garage
Wfl.	Wohnfläche	Living space
Zi	Zimmer	Rooms

apartment seekers to place advertisements in local papers or on websites such as www.wg-gesucht.de ('accommodation sought' in English). This isn't as desperate a ploy as you may think. A 'for rent' advert can easily attract 50 to 100 phone calls in the day or two after it appears, particularly in areas where housing is in short supply. Therefore landlords usually check the advertisements of would-be tenants before subjecting themselves to this onslaught.

Placing an advertisement to find a property to rent may be particularly fruitful if you have special requirements – such as seeking a large apartment (over 100m^2), one that accepts large pets, or when you require a ground floor (Erdgeschoss) apartment or wish to be near a particular school or other facility. German landlords appreciate stability, therefore if you're a professional being transferred by a large company or are in some other 'prestige' occupation (professors, doctors, lawyers, etc.), mention this in your advert.

Be sure to ask around among your colleagues, friends and acquaintances, as rented accommodation can often be found by this method. Many businesses maintain a bulletin board (schwarzes Brett) for the use of employees, which is usually a good way of finding rentals as well as furnishings (e.g. kitchen units) for sale. If your German is up to it, you can also find accommodation via the internet, e.g. on www.immowelt.de, www.immobilienscout24.de, www.immonet.de, www.wohnungsboerse.net and www.wohnung-jetzt.de. There are also websites that specialise in flat sharing, e.g. www.easywg.de, www.studenten-wg.de and www.wohngemeinschaft.de.

Rental Costs

Rental costs vary considerably across Germany but are generally related to the size of a property, measured in square metres (m^2), rather than the number of rooms or bedrooms (see **Size** on page 66). Your local council office (Stadtverwaltung) can tell you the typical rent per square metre for a particular town or district (known as the Mietspiegel). Some towns impose upper limits on rental charges, although enforcement may be lax. Many communities include energy efficiency factors in the calculation of their local Mietspiegel, in which case it's called Öko-Mietspiegel.

The national average monthly rent for a 2-bed 80m^2 apartment (excluding heating costs) in a good area of a major city is €600 to €1,000 and €1,000 to €1,500 for a 2-bed house. In small town and rural areas, rents are usually less than half those in the major cities. However, in Munich, Germany's most expensive city, you can easily pay over €1,000 per month for a tiny (40m²) studio apartment.

Rents are normally quoted 'cold' (*kalt* or *Kaltmiete*), which means without heating or other costs. Additional costs (*Nebenkosten* – see below) are added to the base rent each month for such things as heating, water, taxes, rubbish disposal and other extras, and maintenance costs for the building and grounds. If the rent is quoted as *warm* or *Warmmiete*, heating costs are included.

You're also expected to pay a security and cleaning deposit (*Kaution*), which is usually equal to two or three months' base rent. The deposit must be paid into a separate bank account in your name and the passbook given to your landlord for safe keeping during the term of your lease. The landlord is required to provide proof that the account still holds your deposit in the form of annual statements from the bank (including interest payments). It's sometimes possible to negotiate the payment of the security deposit in two or three instalments at the beginning of your lease.

It's possible to take out insurance rather than pay a lump sum security deposit (*Kaution*), which involves paying a monthly fee (see www. wohnungsboerse.net/kautionsfrei).

Rental Contracts

A rental contract (Mietvertrag) is usually a standard document and can be quite long – most rental contracts run to seven or more pages of small print. Like many contracts in Germany, housing rental contracts are often open ended, although some landlords specify a minimum term of a year, particularly for a new tenant. Even a contract with a defined term, however, will automatically be renewed unless you follow the prescribed notice procedure (Kündigung). You should read a contract carefully before signing it; if you have any doubts or questions about the terms have them translated or explained to you. Many standard contracts include marginal marks, such as exclamation marks or asterisks, flagging paragraphs and provisions considered particularly important or most likely to cause problems (for the landlord, that is!).

The contract will first identify the property that you're renting: not only the address and number or location of the property, but also its official size (in square metres) and what other

☑ SURVIVAL TIP

If you encounter any problems with your landlord, you should go to the Tenants' Protection Association (*Mieterschutzverein*, www. mieterbund.de), an organisation that provides legal advice for a nominal fee.

areas, facilities or privileges are included in the rent. You should ensure that a garage space or parking space is listed (if applicable), as well as cellar storage areas, balconies, garden space, and the right to access laundry or drying rooms in a building. If your landlord is providing a built-in kitchen, this must also be listed. The contract should include or refer to a list of the keys for the property and its common areas.

The contract must list the base rent, the monthly allocation for additional costs (see **Additional Costs** opposite) and any other costs, such as a parking space or garage, to arrive at your total monthly payment (*Gesamtmiete*). You'll be given a detailed list of items covered by the incidental charges, such as a caretaker (*Hausmeister* or *Hausdienst*) and grounds and building maintenance (e.g. lift, hallway lighting and TV aerials). Planned rent increases should be noted in the contract, particularly if you're renting a new property, or (at the very least) the method used to calculate and notify you of increases.

Most landlords expect you to pay your rent by automatic bank transfer or standing order (*Lastschrifteneinzugsverfahren*) and this is usually stipulated in the contract, along with the day of the month on which the rent is due and the penalty for late payment. Make sure that your wages are paid into your account in time to cover your rent payment, as fines for late payment are steep and it can take a long time to recover your good standing in the eyes of a landlord once he suspects that you're unreliable.

If you have a pet or intend to get one, you must ensure that permission is written into the contract. While it generally isn't too difficult to find landlords sympathetic to pet ownership, most standard contracts require specific permission (and occasionally a small additional deposit) for a pet to be kept legally.

In general, tenants are expected to maintain everything inside their home, which means that it's up to you to deal with plumbers, carpenters or electricians should anything go wrong in your apartment. Normally, you're free to decorate your home as you wish, e.g. paint the walls, hang wallpaper, put up shelves or hang pictures. However, when you move out you must return it to the same condition as it was in when you moved in (unless otherwise agreed with your landlord). Most contracts also specify that the tenant must replace the carpeting, repaint walls and complete other renovation at specific intervals during the lease term, e.g. every three years or so. If you move out before major renovation is due, you may still be liable for a pro rata share of the estimated cost, which will be withheld from your deposit unless

you make other arrangements. These terms must all be detailed in the rental contract.

Some landlords require evidence that you have adequate insurance to cover them and adjoining properties in the event of damage to the property. Policies covering personal effects (*Hausratversicherung*) and personal liability (*Haftpflichtversicherung*) are widely available from around €150 to €200 per year (see **Chapter 13**). Sometimes policies include legal cover (*Rechtsschutz*), which can also be useful in certain circumstances.

ADDITIONAL COSTS

Whether you're renting or have bought a home, you must usually pay monthly incidental charges (*Nebenkosten*). A monthly allocation for incidental charges will be calculated when you move in, based on how many people will be living in the property, and your estimated use of common resources (based on the usage of the previous tenants).

At the end of each year (or, more usually, in January or February of the following year), your actual usage of heating, water and other utilities is calculated. You'll receive a letter informing you of the date and approximate time of the official meter reading to determine your actual usage of communal services (usually water and heating costs). It's important that you're available to let the meter reader in on the appointed date, or leave a key with a neighbour or give the caretaker authorisation to enter your home with the meter reader. The official meter reading is usually done by an independent company (the cost is added to your incidental charges), and if they need to make a separate trip to read your meters on another day, you must pay an extra charge.

Shared costs that cannot be metered or measured are apportioned to your property according to the size of your living space in relation to the building or complex. For example, if a building contains four apartments of equal size, each tenant/owner pays 25 per cent of the total costs for the whole building. If you've been paying too much towards your share of common costs, you'll receive a refund at the end of the year, and your monthly contribution for the next year may be reduced. On the other hand, if you haven't paid enough over the year, you'll receive a bill, and your monthly communal charges will be increased the following year. In any event, you'll receive a statement of your actual communal charges for the year, along with the calculations used to determine your share of each item.

For tenants, incidental charges are paid to the landlord each month with your rent. If you own a home that's part of a managed sub-division or housing estate, you make monthly payments directly to the builder or management company (*Hausverwaltung*).

BUYING PROPERTY

Buying a house or apartment in Germany is considered a 'major life decision' and it's something a newcomer should consider very carefully before doing. If you're staying for a relatively short period (say, less than five years), you're probably better off renting. Due to the chronic shortage of housing, the German government has tended to offer financial incentives to builders rather than to homebuyers. You may find that home ownership in Germany carries few of the tax benefits that you're used to in your home country; e.g. the interest paid on a mortgage or other property-backed loan isn't tax deductible unless you're letting the property. However, buying a home is some 40 per cent cheaper than renting in the long term.

An important factor to consider with regard to buying property in Germany is that it doesn't free you from most of the communal aspects of German life. If you buy

an apartment, you must still deal with the building maintenance company and the onsite caretaker, and are still subject to house rules (see page 78). It's highly likely that some or most of your neighbours will be renting their apartments and, in any case, house rules apply to everyone living in a building; some homebuyers are unpleasantly surprised to find that they cannot keep pets or must put up a certain colour of curtains, even in their own homes! Moreover, in addition to your mortgage or other loan repayments, you must pay the various incidental charges – for example, heating, hot water, building maintenance

> In 2016, the average price of a home in Germany was €242,000 (average area 126m²), although in Munich (the most expensive city) this would only buy you an apartment of 44m². In an affluent Munich suburb, prices can be as high as €10,000 per m².

and the caretaker's salary. Even some single-family (detached) houses are part of a 'community' and you may have a surprising amount of charges to pay at the end of each year.

The mix of tenants and owners in most buildings can complicate the house-hunting process. For example, you may find a property you want to buy, but the owner is letting it to long-term tenants, so it could be as much as a year after buying before you can move in. Of course, you'll be receiving rent from the tenants during this period, but you'll need to find temporary accommodation in the meantime.

Germans don't generally consider buying a home to be a good investment. Most properties in larger cities increase in value by only 2 or 3 per cent per year in real terms (after taking inflation into account), while those in undesirable locations may stagnate or even lose value. The government's efforts to encourage the building of new housing may cause the price of existing housing to dip, which could lose you money in the short term. Add to this the fact that you're liable for capital gains tax if you sell a property within ten years of purchase (see page 212). However, in recent years property prices have risen much faster than inflation and in 2017 property was looking like a good investment.

Property Prices

Property prices are often quoted exclusive of land, as the cost of land varies greatly from place to place, and are calculated on the same basis as rental costs, i.e. per square metre (m²). While most land costs between €400 and €800 per m², in prime locations it can be well over as €2,000 per m², whereas in less desirable towns in east Germany it can cost as little as €100 per m².

Fees

You should expect to pay a deposit (*Eigenkapital*) of 10 to 25 per cent of the price, plus the following fees and taxes:

♦ if you use a *Makler* to help you find a home, his fee is usually negotiable and may be anywhere between 2 and 7 per cent (plus VAT) of the purchase price (see **Estate Agents** on page 70), with the average around 3 per cent;

♦ a notary fee of 1.2 to 1.5 per cent (see **Conveyancing** below);

♦ A property transfer tax (*Grunderwerbsteuer*) of 3.5 to 6.5 per cent (3.5% in Bavaria to 6.5% in Brandenburg, Saarland, Schleswig-Holstein and North Rhine-Westphalia);

♦ a land registry registration fee of 0.8 to 1.2 per cent;

♦ a 1 per cent mortgage fee if you have a mortgage.

Conveyancing

Conveyancing (or, more correctly, conveyance) is the legal term for processing the paperwork involved in buying and selling a property and transferring the deeds of ownership. In Germany, all transactions involving property ownership (*Grundbesitz*) must be registered in the official land register (*Grundbuch*) of the local authority (*Gemeinde*) for the area where the property is located.

Contracts for buying and selling property recorded in the *Grundbuch* must be overseen by a public notary (*Notar*), who ensures that all applicable laws are observed and that the appropriate fees and taxes are paid and recorded. The notary is an agent of the state and acts as a neutral third party, representing neither the buyer nor the seller in the transaction, but ensuring that the terms and conditions of the contract of sale (*Kaufvertrag*) have been met. It isn't unheard of for a notary

to refuse to validate a contract because specific terms of the agreement haven't been settled between the buyer and seller.

The issues you must decide before your appointment with a notary include:

♦ the exact price of the property;

♦ the payment schedule;

♦ who's paying the notary's fee or how it's to be divided;

♦ the exact date of transfer of the property;

♦ any payment of rent between the parties if the transfer date doesn't coincide with the buyer's or seller's moving dates;

♦ a list of repairs or other work to be completed by the vendor prior to the hand-over;

♦ any special features or conditions of the sale, e.g. if the seller is including the kitchen or appliances in the price.

At your meeting with the notary you must provide personal identification (usually your passport and residence permit if you're a foreigner) and confirmation of your financing. Normally, there aren't any restrictions or prohibitions on foreigners buying or selling property in Germany, although financing a property purchase is a complicated business (see **Mortgages** on page 204).

With all these documents and confirmations to hand, the notary draws up the sale's contract and ensures that it's registered with the appropriate offices and bureaux of the local government. Notaries' fees are regulated by law and you should receive an itemised list of precisely what's included. Usually this consists of a fee for the preparation of the contract, which varies according to the selling price, plus four or five fixed fees for registering the sale with each of the various government offices and tax authorities. Notary fees are fixed by law and are usually between 1.2 and 1.5 per cent of the property price (see **Fees** above).

HEATING & HOT WATER

In most apartment buildings, heat is supplied by a central heating furnace, usually oil or gas, which is the responsibility of the caretaker. By law, heating is switched on on the 1st October and off on the 30th April. Most modern buildings allow for the regulation of heat within each apartment, usually on a room-by-room basis. In buildings with radiators, there should be a thermostat and control on each one. Some new buildings have under-floor heating, but there's usually a means of controlling the heat in each room and it isn't uncommon to find under-floor heating combined with radiators in some rooms, particularly bedrooms. German homes are solidly built, so insulation isn't usually a problem, particularly in new buildings.

Each apartment connected to a shared water tank is metered separately, although it isn't uncommon to find that hot water costs are apportioned (by apartment size) in relation to a building's overall water usage.

If you can control the level of heat, there will be a meter (often several) somewhere in your apartment – usually in a cupboard or some other out-of-the-way place. In some apartments there's a meter on each radiator. In some cases, you're permitted to read the meter yourself and register the readings online on your provider's website, or provide them by post or telephone. Note also that rental contracts hold the tenant responsible for maintaining an adequate temperature in the home to ensure that no damage occurs. If there's a cold snap while you're away on holiday, for example, you could be liable for burst pipes – not only for the damage to your own apartment but also for any damage caused to neighbouring apartments.

In newer buildings there are sometimes individual hot water tanks in each apartment, in which case you pay directly for the heating of your water through your electricity bills.

In older houses and apartments, you may find a small water-heating unit for each sink or basin where hot water is needed, and a larger water heater for the bath, which you may have to remember to 'fire up' before use. With this arrangement, you'll need to buy a water heater for your kitchen sink if there isn't one installed when you move in. Kitchen water heaters often allow you to rapidly heat a small amount of water to boiling point, which can be handy for making a quick pot of tea or coffee, instant soups or other convenience foods.

It may come as a surprise to some foreigners that household appliances in Germany, such as washing machines and dishwashers, are connected only to the cold water outlet. Appliances that require hot water have a built-in water heater and heat up just the right amount of water for a single cycle. (Incidentally, this means that even the most expensive dishwashers and washing machines require nearly an hour to complete a full cycle, due to the need to heat the water.) If you plan to import a washing machine or dishwasher, you should therefore check whether it will work with a cold-water intake.

HOUSE RULES

All apartment blocks have house rules (*Hausordnung*), some of which may be set by the local council and are enforceable by law (particularly those regarding noise and siesta periods). You should receive a copy on moving into an apartment or when you sign your rental or sales contract. They apply to everyone living in a building, whether a tenant or owner, therefore it pays to check the rules before making an offer on an apartment that you're interested in buying. If you don't understand them, you should have them translated. Some of the more common house rules are:

♦ a noise curfew between 10pm and 6am;

♦ a siesta, e.g. from noon to 2pm, during which you mustn't make any loud noise, play music or sing, or (most important of all) use any power tools. This is to allow young children and pensioners an undisturbed afternoon nap.

> Your neighbours will be familiar with the house rules and will be only too happy to point out any transgressions. If in doubt, you should ask the caretaker for clarification.

♦ no bathing or showering between 10pm and 6am. Sometimes there's even a restriction on flushing the toilet during these hours, lest you disturb your neighbours' slumber. If you work nights, however, you're exempt from this rule.

♦ no loud noise on Sundays and public holidays. In some areas (mostly the south), hanging out washing to dry and mowing the lawn are also forbidden on Sundays, even in detached houses. In some areas, hanging laundry to dry on balconies is prohibited if it can be seen from the street.

♦ restrictions regarding where children may play or ride their bicycles;

♦ restrictions on the storage of bicycles, carts, children's toys or other personal objects in hallways or ground floor entrances or on balconies;

♦ restrictions on the use of laundry or drying room facilities, including cleaning after use. Laundry hanging is often done in rotation, so it may be necessary to find out what day is allotted to you. You aren't usually permitted to hang laundry to dry in an apartment due to the risk of mould.

♦ responsibilities for cleaning common areas, gardening, snow removal and other maintenance chores;

♦ the requirement to keep the front door to the building locked between 8pm and 6 or 7am. Usually, the occupants of the ground floor apartments are responsible for locking the front door at the appropriate hour in the evening.

♦ the requirement to separate and prepare rubbish for collection according to the local council regulations, with 'recyclables' separated into a number of categories (see **Rubbish & Recycling** on page 83);

♦ the requirement to air (*luften*) your flat for at least one hour a day to prevent mould;

♦ the requirement to use the correct cleaning agent (listed in the lease) for your flat's parquet floors.

INVENTORY

One of the most important tasks on moving into a new home is to complete an inventory (*Inventur*) and condition report (*Bestandliste*). This includes the state of fixtures and fittings, the cleanliness and condition of the decoration, and anything missing or in need of repair. The form should be provided by your landlord (or by the builder if you're buying or renting a new property), and any problems must be listed on this form, which you sign and return by the deadline stated. If the problems or damage noted aren't put right or repaired within a reasonable time, you may be entitled to a

reduction of your rent for the period they're left unresolved. If you're buying a home, the condition report should be used to document any work or repairs that the seller has agreed to undertake. If possible, this list, along with the deadlines for completing the work, should be submitted prior to your meeting with the notary, so that it can be officially registered with the contract and sale.

If you're renting, a property should be spotless when you move in, as this is what your landlord will expect when you move out. Any damage that isn't noted on the condition report when you move in will be charged to you when you move out, so you should check a property thoroughly and return the report promptly to your landlord.

ELECTRICITY

Germany is one of the world's largest consumers of energy, and not surprisingly, Germans pay some of the highest electricity rates in Europe. The electricity companies were privatised in 1998, and what has developed is a network of electricity brokers (*Strombrokers*), who purchase power from the large generating companies and sell it to individual consumers under a variety of tariffs and plans. Within two years of privatisation, there were over 1,000 electricity companies, mostly brokers, in Germany. To find a list of local electricity suppliers, look in the Yellow Pages under *Elektrizitätsgesellschaften* or *Energie-versorgung* (energy supply). A full list of electricity brokers can be found at www.stromseite.de/stromanbieter.

Electricity is generated using a variety of fuels – primarily lignite, hard coal and enriched uranium. The heavy use of lignite was a major source of pollution in the former East Germany, while hard coal produced from German mines is expensive and uneconomical for privatised power companies. Although

nuclear power stations supply around 20 per cent of Germany's electricity, the government is committed to closing all nuclear plants. They've extended the deadline to 2021, however, to allow time for further development of alternative and renewable energy resources, which would reduce air and water pollution levels. The government is also in a heated debate over whether they should levy a nuclear power tax on energy providers. Some brokers market themselves as purveyors of 'green' power generated primarily by wind or solar energy. Despite privatisation, it seems likely that electricity prices in Germany will continue to remain fairly high in comparison with other European countries (particularly France, which has no plans to scrap its nuclear plants).

☑ SURVIVAL TIP

A number of websites allow you to compare electricity (and gas) costs, including www.billig-strom.de, www.stromauskunft.de, www.stromtarif.de, www.stromtarife.de, www.stromtip.de and https://1-stromvergleich.com/compare-energy-prices (in English). However, you need to take recommendations with a pinch of salt as comparison sites may be paid to promote certain deals/companies.

Power Supply

The electricity supply is delivered to homes at 220 to 250 volts with a frequency of 50 Hertz (cycles). If you're coming from a country that operates on the same voltage, most of your appliances will require only a change of plug to fit German sockets (*Steckdosen*), which are recessed into the wall (particularly in modern buildings) and have two small earth contacts. German plugs (*Stecker*) have two round pins, usually with two earth (or ground) contacts on the side, if an appliance requires an earth.

Televisions and video recorders are the most notable exceptions, but this relates to the transmission systems in use rather than the power supply. North American or other 110V appliances aren't usable in Germany unless they can be switched or converted to the higher voltage.

German plugs aren't fitted with fuses. Instead, the electrical circuits are protected by either a fuse box or a circuit breaker panel. Most modern buildings have a circuit breaker panel containing several switches, usually labelled to indicate the circuits or apparatus they control. When there's a short circuit or the system has been overloaded, the relevant breaker is tripped and the power supply is cut. To reset the circuit breaker, you must flip the switch to the 'off' position (when the circuit 'blows', the switch moves only to the half-way position) and then back to the 'on' position to restore power. However, before reconnecting the power, switch off any high-wattage appliances such as a washing machine or dishwasher.

Make sure that you know where the fuse or circuit breaker box is located, and keep a torch handy so that you can find it in the dark. In most apartment buildings, there's a circuit breaker panel in the entrance hall, or one in each main hall connecting apartments. When you move into a new home, there'll probably be no lighting fixtures but just bare wires hanging from the ceiling or walls which are colour-coded.

Suppliers & Tariffs

Following the privatisation of the electricity market, hundreds of electricity brokers (*Strombrokers*) have sprung up, each offering a variety of rates. The effect of so much competition has been to lower prices, or at least those displayed in advertising, although electricity rates are still among the highest in Europe. The differences in pricing structures, however, make comparison between brokers' rates and those of traditional utility companies almost impossible. Unlike brokers, most local utilities offer lower tariffs at night (*Nachttarif*), and many appliances are equipped with timers or start-delay systems so that thrifty Germans can take full advantage of these.

You can compare rates via the Verivox energy comparison website (Verivox (www.verivox.de).

There are, however, other factors to take into consideration besides the price per unit at various times of the day, including the minimum length of the contract you're obliged to sign, whether you must pay a deposit, whether you must pay for the entire year in advance and the notice period (*Kündigungsfrist*) required. German consumer magazines and other publications publish frequent comparisons of companies offering the lowest rates. Companies producing electricity in environmentally friendly ways, i.e. green energy, usually have the most expensive tariffs (some companies offer new customers gifts as an inducement).

Sometimes the kWh rate depends on using a minimum amount each month or quarter, and some brokers reduce the kWh rate if you agree to a higher monthly fixed fee. These plans may be more economical for heavy electricity users, but it's difficult to evaluate competing claims if you don't know your usage. Brokers may require you to report your meter readings at regular intervals (with penalties for late reporting). Bear in mind the following when evaluating offers:

♦ It's unwise to sign a contract committing you to any power company for more than a year.

♦ The notice period for cancelling a contract or changing suppliers should be no longer than four to six weeks.

♦ Ensure that there are no conditions attached to the cancellation of your contract, such as a penalty payment or the need to produce a copy of a signed competitor's contract before you can cancel.

♦ Make sure that you read and understand all the small print regarding matters such as minimum consumption and your obligations to confirm or report meter readings.

♦ Changing your electricity supplier consists only of giving notice (usually by phone) and reporting the meter readings at the changeover date.

In your first year, a monthly or quarterly rate is estimated based on your family size and the size of the property you're occupying, and you're asked to pay this amount each month or quarter via your bank to the local electricity utility. At the end of the year, there's an official meter reading and you settle with the electricity company, which then sets a new monthly or quarterly rate for the coming year, based on your actual usage.

GAS

Gas isn't widely available in homes in Germany, although local utility companies are starting to promote its use as a 'clean' fuel for heating. It's supplied by local companies, usually part of a town or regional utility, which are listed in the Yellow Pages under *Gasversorgung* (or you can do an internet search). Some make introductory offers to homeowners and builders who wish to install gas central heating in new or renovated properties. In remote rural areas, homes may have a bottled gas cooker or heater. Most apartment buildings are designed to accommodate only electrical appliances in kitchens, and it generally isn't possible to change to gas.

WATER

Water in Germany is generally hard, which means that you must have plenty of decalcification liquid on hand to keep your kettle, iron and other equipment and utensils clean. Tap and shower fixtures must be decalcified regularly. Distilled water, or water melted from the frost build-up in your refrigerator or freezer, should be used in some electric steam irons, although you should check the manufacturer's instructions; some brands of steam iron are made to be used with unfiltered tap water, and these have a decalcification system of their own which should be periodically cleaned. It also pays to decalcify dishwashers and washing machines from time to time. (Some detergents include decalcifying agents.)

There are a number of filter systems that can improve the quality of small quantities of water used in cooking, and reduce or eliminate the lime (*Kalk*) build-up on heating elements

and in pots and pans. These normally require you to pour water through a filter into a pitcher or other storage container (such as Brita water filters) before using it. Other systems consist of a small filter fitted to a kitchen tap. Filters for both systems are available in supermarkets and other shops, and generally need to be replaced every month or two. It's possible to install elaborate household decalcification equipment, although systems are generally expensive and aren't practical for installing in rented premises. Water isn't fluoridated in Germany.

Water costs are included in the incidental charges for all apartments and for most houses in Germany. Costs are based on your actual usage and there may be multiple meters, particularly if laundry or other washing facilities are located in a common area.

RUBBISH & RECYCLING

The Germans have been sorting their rubbish for years and recycling is a way of life. Most cities and towns require the sorting of household rubbish into several categories, including – at the very least – paper, cardboard, glass, plastic and metal. Many towns also collect organic waste (*Biomüll*) for composting, and old clothes, bed linen and curtains for the poor (*Altkleidersammlung*). You should check with your local *Stadverwaltung* for the exact requirements for each category and how 'recyclables' should be prepared for collection, as this may vary from town to town. For example, some councils require that white paper be separated from coloured paper, while others insist only that brown cardboard be kept separate from paper. A few smaller councils require only that recyclable material be separated into 'round' (bottles, cans, jars, etc.) and 'flat' (paper, cardboard, plastic, etc.).

Most towns provide each building with standard-size coloured bins for each type of rubbish and recyclable waste. The collection of rubbish and recyclables is usually 'metered' for billing to building owners or maintenance companies, the cost being distributed to building occupants as part of their incidental charges. Often bins have a bar-coded label which indicates the 'owner' of the bin, whether the homeowner or the management company of the apartment block. Each time a bin is emptied the bar code is 'swiped' and the owner is charged according to the size of the container. A large container costs more to empty each time, so many building owners try to make do with the smallest possible bins, even if they fill up long before the next collection day!

 Caution

Certain hazardous materials (paint, paint thinner, cleaning solvents, motor oil, etc.) should be taken to the local recycling and disposal centre. Information published by your local council will include the location of the nearest recycling centre, its hours of business, and disposal requirements.

Leaving rubbish in plastic sacks alongside official rubbish bins is a violation of house rules (if not local laws) and you can be fined if you're identified as the culprit.

Bottles

Glass deposit (*Pfand*) bottles are standard throughout Germany for most juices and fizzy drinks, including beer (wine bottles are the main exception). The price of these drinks includes a deposit to ensure the return of the bottle and the plastic crate (if you buy in bulk). When you return the empty bottles and crates to the shop where you made your purchase you're refunded the deposit in cash or as a credit on your purchase (on the same visit).

So-called one-way plastic bottles (*Einwegflaschen*) carry a €0.25 cent deposit, and can be returned to almost any supermarket and deposited in a machine, which dispenses a voucher to claim a refund from the cashier. When a machine isn't available, you can return your bottles to a drinks counter or to the cashier. Hard plastic bottles that you buy at kiosks (e.g. at railway stations) have a €0.15 *Pfand*, but must be returned to the kiosk you bought them from (write it on the bottle!). Bottles made of polyethylene terephthalate (labelled *PET*) don't have a *Pfand*.

Non-deposit glass bottles (including wine bottles) should be disposed of in the appropriate glass recycling bin, e.g. for clear, brown or green glass. Many towns provide 'bottle banks' in car parks.

Packaging

German shops are required by law to retain (or take back) packaging materials, e.g. cardboard boxes, plastic bags and Styrofoam, for all products sold. Many supermarkets and other large shops provide a bin in the car park or near the main entrance to collect this material. If you have furniture or large appliances delivered to your home, the delivery service must take the packaging material away for you. In fact, if you have your household goods moved by a professional mover, they must offer either to take the packing boxes away with them after they've unpacked your belongings, or to pick up the empty boxes once you've unpacked them yourself.

Empty packing boxes (particularly heavy-duty ones used for international moves) can be sold for a couple of euros each to people who are moving or who need storage boxes.

Other Recycling

Large objects, such as unwanted household furniture, broken appliances or building debris, may be collected once or twice a year on dates announced by your local council (*Stadtverwaltung*). In many areas, during the evening before the pick-up, you'll see people inspecting the items that their neighbours have put out for disposal. By the time the trucks show up the next morning, many of the still-serviceable articles will have vanished, leaving only the real rubbish to be picked up. This form of 'direct' recycling is technically illegal, but is tolerated by most local governments and residents.

You can usually request a collection of large items (for a fee) by contacting your council offices. In some communities, this is the only way of disposing of large or bulky items, so you may wish to arrange a pick-up with one or more neighbours in order to share the cost.

Used batteries mustn't be deposited with regular household rubbish for collection, but should be returned to shops, where they're collected for proper disposal (there's usually a box near the checkout). Shops are required to provide this facility if they sell batteries or battery-powered devices.

old town hall, Bamberg

6.
POSTAL SERVICES

*T*here's at least one post office (*Postamt*) in every German city or town, a total of some 13,000 nationwide, although they're disappearing in small villages. As in many other countries, privatisation has put an end to the traditional role of the post office. The German Post Office (Deutsche Post) no longer operates the telephone system or offers banking services, and is now responsible solely for delivering post. (When the Post Office was privatised in 1994, its banking and telephone operations became the Deutsche Postbank AG and the Deutsche Telekom AG respectively). However, it's still possible to open a savings or cheque account at a post office, deposit and withdraw cash, pay bills and perform a number of other banking transactions. Many post offices still have one or more telephone booths, although as they're no longer operated by the same company (there's a surcharge for using them).

Now that it has lost its responsibility for telecommunications and banking and can concentrate almost entirely on delivering post, Deutsche Post provides one of Europe's best postal services. Packages and express post are delivered by DHL, a subsidiary of Deutsche Post and the world's leading delivery network, although customers aren't aware of using a different service.

Deutsche Post has a useful and informative website (www.deutschepost.de/en/home.html), and produces a number of free publications describing its products and services, the most comprehensive of which is entitled *Serviceinformationen* (available free from post offices).

BUSINESS HOURS

It's difficult to generalise about post office business hours, although offices usually open from around 8 or 8.30am until 6pm on weekdays and until noon on Saturdays.

Generally, the larger the city, the longer the main post office (*Hauptpostamt*) remains open. Main post offices are usually located next to main railway stations (*Hauptbahnhof*), and are often open for a short time on Sundays. Post offices at major airports (e.g. Frankfurt) may be open 24 hours a day, while smaller post offices may close for lunch (usually between 1 and 2.30pm). Post offices located in shops may open earlier or close later than ordinary post offices, depending on the business hours of the shops in which they're located.

Post office opening hours are displayed at the entrance. However, if you need to locate or check the opening hours of a post office in a rural area, you can do so by phoning 228 4333111 between 7am and 8pm on weekdays and from 8am to 2pm on Saturdays. Alternatively you can use the search option (*Filialsuche*) on the 'Online Services' page of the Deutsche Post website (www.deutschepost. de).

LETTER POST

Ordinary letters posted at main post offices before 9am are usually delivered the next working day anywhere in Germany. Delivery times to other countries are more difficult to estimate as a result of varying service standards in the country of destination, but average 2.2 days for Belgium and the Netherlands, 2.3 days for the UK and 4.3 days for Italy – which says a lot more about the (in)efficiency of Italy's postal service than Germany's!

Most post offices sell a variety of envelopes in various sizes, including 'bubble-pack' envelopes for sending fragile, but relatively flat items.

Rates

Postal rates for letters are based on a combination of size, weight, quantity (e.g. bulk deliveries), type of delivery, and even the content and purpose. In 2011, the post office revised its international rates and now has a single rate for all international mail, whether it's destination is France or New Zealand. A complete list of rates would be encyclopaedic and beyond the scope of this book, but the most common categories are listed below:

- ◆ **Postcard** (*Postkarte*): €0.45 within Germany and €0.90 international;

- ◆ **Standard letter** (*Standardbrief*): A 'standard letter' is 25-90mm wide and 140-235mm long. It must be no more than 5mm thick and weigh no more than 20g. Postage is €0.70 within Germany and €0.90 to the rest of the world. American readers should note that the standard US 'business size' envelope (9.5in/241mm) is too long for this category of post, therefore it's advisable to use standard German envelopes.

- ◆ **Compact letter** (*Kompaktbrief*): Despite its name, this has the same maximum width and length as a standard letter, but can be slightly thicker and heavier: up to 10mm and 50g respectively. The cost is €0.85 within Germany and €1.50 to the rest of the world.

- ◆ **Large letter** (*Grossbrief*): A domestic large letter may be 70-250mm wide and 100-353mm long, a maximum of 20mm thick and with a maximum weight of 500g. The postage is €1.45 within Germany.

- ◆ **International large letter** (*Grossbrief International*): International *Grossbriefe* may be a minimum of 90mm wide and 140mm long, with a maximum combined length + height + width of 900mm and a maximum weight of 500g. The cost is €3.70.

- ◆ **Maximum letter** (*Maxibrief*): This is the largest size letter that can be sent to domestic destinations. The length is 100-353mm, width 70-250mm, thickness a maximum of 50mm and the weight up to 1kg. The postage is €2.60 within Germany.

- ◆ **International maximum letter** (*Maxibrief International*): International *Maxibriefe* may be a minimum of 90mm wide and 140mm long, with a maximum combined length + height + width of 900mm with a maximum weight of 1kg. The fee is €7 worldwide.

- ◆ **International maximum letter 2** (*Maxibrief International*): This is the largest letter that can be sent abroad, which can have the same measurements as the 'International maximum letter' (above) but with a maximum weight of 2kg. The postage is €17 worldwide.

Note that when buying stamps from a machine, you receive your 'change' in stamps!

A *Plusbrief* is an envelope with pre-printed postage. They're available at post offices and online and sold in packs of between three and ten. They're stamped for various uses and sizes, for example standard post (within Germany), standard (rest of the world), compact and large letter post, and are available with or without windows. For an extra charge, it's possible to personalise *Plusbriefe* with your address, company logo and photo.

Certain materials addressed to blind recipients, including Braille texts, audio tapes and similar materials, and weighing up to 7kg, can be sent free of charge. Particular rules apply – enquire at a post office for details.

Stamps can be purchased at any post office or from stamp machines outside post offices. Alternatively, you can print postage vouchers via your PC (see www.deutschepost.de and click on 'Shop').

Addresses

The correct format for addressing envelopes in Germany is as follows:

Herrn Hans Handel
Goethestr. 12
D-65193 Wiesbaden
Germany

Note that the street number follows the street name and the postcode (*Postleitzahl*) precedes the name of the city. You may occasionally see envelopes with the postcode and city name on the second line and the street address on the third. This is an old format and its use is discouraged due to the increasing mechanisation of mail sorting.

Mechanisation also requires that addresses begin no more than 14cm (around 5.5 inches) from the right edge of the envelope. This has the effect of moving the address considerably further to the right than is customary in many countries. Although senders of individual letters can safely disregard this rule, businesses sending mass mailings must be aware of it. Booklets containing formats and rules such as this are available free from post offices.

A list of postcodes is available for inspection at any post office and they can also be found via the Deutsche Post website (www.postdirekt. de/plzserver).

Registration & Insurance

There are various kinds of registered (*per Einschreibung*) letters. A letter which is recorded only by the postman (*Einwurfeinschreiben*) costs €2.15 plus postage. If you want a letter signed for by the recipient (*Übergabeeinschreiben*), who may not be the addressee, the cost is €2.50 plus postage. For greater security, materials sent as *Übergabeeinschreiben* may also be denominated *eigenhändig* for an additional €4.65. This ensures that delivery is to the addressee or his legal representative only, who must sign for the item. If you want a return receipt (*Rückschein*), which costs an additional €4.65, it must be signed by the recipient and is returned to the sender.

There are many categories of insurance (*Versicherung*) for various kinds of post. Ask for details at a post office.

PARCELS

The most convenient way to send parcels is by using the standard boxes available in the *Packset*, an assortment of pre-cut and pre-folded boxes available from post offices. The designations, sizes and prices are as follows:

Parcel Rates		
Designation	**Dimensions (cm)**	**Cost**
XS	22.5 x 14.5 x 3.5	€1.49
S	25 x 17.5 x 10	€1.79
M	37.5 x 30 x 13.5	€1.99
L	45 x 35 x 20	€2.49
F	37.5 x 12 x 12	€2.49

The F box is designed to take a standard bottle, e.g. of wine. *Packset* boxes include address labels and (all but the XS size) sealing tape.

The variety of parcel-post categories and rates is even greater than that for letter post. Generally speaking, parcels weighing up to 1kg (30 x 30 x 15cm) cost €3.89 and parcels up to 2kg (60 x 30 x 15cm) costs €4.39 within Germany. A domestic parcel weighing 10kg (120 x 60 x 60cm) cost €8.49 and €16.49 for 31.5kg. The cost of international parcels varies depending on the destination, e.g. parcels to

the UK costs from €8.89 up to 2kg (L+B+H = 90cm) and up to €44.99 for a parcel weighing 31.5kg (120 x 60 x 60cm).

EXPRESS POST

It's possible to send letters and parcels by express post, which should arrive on the next day. Express letters (*Express Briefe*) cost from €11.90 to €14.90 depending on the weight (the maximum is 2kg). Express packages (*Express Pakete*) via DHL cost between €10.90 (500g) and €44.90 (20-31.5kg) for domestic addresses; for an extra charge you can arrange to have your package arrive by 9am, 10am or 12pm the next day.

Postage for international express parcels is determined by the weight and delivery zone: zones 1-5 include countries in Europe, Zone 6 is Eastern Europe, Russia, Turkey and North America, Zone 7 is Asian countries, Zone 8 includes some South American countries, Australia and parts of the Middle East, and Zone 9 is the rest of the world. There are no published tariffs (they're no doubt too complicated for a normal person to calculate), therefore you must take your package to a post office to find out the cost. DHL services, delivery times and costs are contained in a downloadable file (www.dhl.de/content/dam/images/Express/downloads/dhl-express-preise-und-laufzeiten-012017.pdf).

COLLECTION & DELIVERY

Post boxes are yellow with a black stylised post-horn symbol and are usually mounted on building walls. Collections from boxes outside main post offices are usually made every few hours, while in residential neighbourhoods, boxes may be emptied only once a day (collection times are displayed on the front of boxes). There's one postal delivery per day in most of Germany, from Mondays to Saturdays, usually in the morning.

If the postman requires a signature or payment of import duty, VAT or excess postage when you aren't at home, he'll leave a form showing where you can pick up the item (not always the nearest post office). Pay particular attention to the collection time '*heute jedoch nicht vor…*' followed by a time, as you cannot collect mail before the time and day (*heute* = today) stated.

Most post offices provide a *Postlagerservice* service, whereby post is held for up to three months while you're away (e.g. on holiday) and upon your return you collect it from the post office at the pre-arranged time. You may also authorise others to collect it (authorisation must be given in writing). The service must be arranged a minimum of five working days in advance and costs €9.90 for one month and €11.90 for three months.

You can obtain a post office box (*Postfach*) at your local post office for a one-off registration fee of €19.90. There are no further charges. Post office box addresses should be in the following format:

[your name]
Postfach [box number]
[post code] [city]
Germany

The box number should be written with the digits grouped in pairs, e.g. Postfach 23 45 67. Note that the post code of your box is usually different from that of the post office where the box is located!

POST OFFICE BANKING

Although the post office sold its banking operation when it was privatised, the resulting banking company, Deutsche Postbank AG, transacts most of its business at post offices and has branches at many post offices in Germany, as well as 3,000 cash machines (ATMs) throughout the country. Postbank customers can also use ATMs belonging to Dresdner Bank, Commerzbank, Deutsche Bank and Hypovereinsbank free of charge.

Postbank services include the following:

◆ bill payment (in person, by post or electronically), cash deposits and withdrawals;

◆ Postbank debit card free with account;

◆ Postbank MasterCard or Visa card;

◆ postage-paid envelopes for sending *Zahlungsverkehrsvordrucke* (see **Paying Bills** below) or other transactions;

◆ deposit insurance;

◆ option to open a current account (*Postgirokonto*) or a savings account (*Postsparkonto*).

A *Postgirokonto* is among the cheapest bank accounts and, provided you deposit at least €1,000 per month you're eligible for a *Giro Plus* account, for which there's no maintenance fee. If you don't fulfil this condition there's a monthly fee for a standard account.

PAYING BILLS

A red-and-white payment form (*Zahlungsverkehrsvordruck*) is usually included with all bills you receive by post in Germany, but you aren't obliged to use the form to make payment if you wish to pay via online banking. If you use the form you can pay the bill via a bank account or at a post office. There's no charge for the transaction provided you have an account at the bank where you're making the payment.

Most payment forms are partially completed with the payee's name, account number (*Kontonummer*), branch code (*Bankleitzahl*) and the amount due, so you usually need only enter your own account number and branch code. You can also use blank payment forms provided by your bank for payments, in which case you have to enter all the information yourself. Make sure that you sign the form, however, or payment will be rejected.

When paying bills either online or with payment forms, you must enter the payee's name and bank data and the amount. The payee's bank data (*Bankverbindung*) is shown at the bottom of the payee's letter or statement in the following format:

Dresdner Bank Stuttgart,
BLZ 600 800 00,
Ktonr. 987 654 321

BLZ is the abbreviation for *Bankleitzahl* (branch code) while *Ktonr.* is the abbreviation for *Kontonummer* (account number). If more than one bank is listed, you can make the payment to any of them. It isn't strictly necessary to enter the name of the payee's bank on the form, but if you omit it, you must make sure that you've entered the branch code correctly.

When writing figures in Germany (or anywhere in continental Europe), you should cross the down stroke of the number 7 in order to avoid confusion with the number 1, which is often written with a leading upstroke and resembles a seven to many non-Europeans. Germans (and other Europeans) write the date with the day first, followed by the month and year, not as Americans do, with the month

first. For example, 1.11.2017 is 1st November 2017 and not 11th January 2017. To confuse matters further, the International Organisation for Standardisation (ISO) has introduced a new date format with first the year, the month and then the date, which is slowly being accepted in Germany.

☑ SURVIVAL TIP

The conventional US way of writing the date, with the month first and slashes between the digits (e.g. 1/11/2017 for 11th January 2017), is unknown and must never be used in Germany.

Meersburg am Bodensee (Baden Wuerttemburg)

7.
COMMUNICATIONS

*B*efore the German telephone network operated by state-run monopoly Deutsche Telekom (DT – now also called T-Home, but referred to as DT here) was privatised, telephone rates in Germany were among the highest in Western Europe. In accordance with EU legislation, the German government privatised DT and offered 500 million shares (representing around 25 per cent of the company) to the German public. Despite the reputation of Germans as cautious investors, the privatisation proved wildly successful and provided DT with much-needed capital to modernise and widen its range of services and prepare for competition. Despite these changes, DT's customer service still has a 'public service' quality, perhaps because over 95 per cent of fixed lines are still owned and managed by DT.

There are now so many companies competing for your business that calculating who's offering the best deal is a challenge. To add to the complexity of choosing a provider, nowadays many companies offer internet, mobile and TV services, in addition to fixed-line telephone services.

EMERGENCY NUMBERS

There are two nationwide emergency numbers (*Notrufnummern*) in Germany: 110 for the police (*Polizei*) and 112 for fire (*Feuerwehr*) and ambulance services (*Rettungsdienst/ Rettungswagen*). In some remote areas there are local numbers for ambulance services, although the fire department will connect you. You should be able to call either of these numbers free from any public phone, including card phones, although with some old payphones you may need to insert coins first, which are returned after the call.

In many phone booths there's an emergency services 'lever' in a case near the phone. Pulling it to the green side automatically connects you to the police, the red side to the fire department; needless to say, misuse of this facility is punishable by a heavy fine.

See box overleaf for a list of numbers.

INSTALLATION & REGISTRATION

The easiest way to get a standard telephone line installed in your home is to register by telephone, online or visit a Telekom (0800-330 1000, www.telekom.de/en) shop, which can be found in most cities (to find your nearest shop, see www.telekom.de/start/telekom-shops?wt_ mc=alias_9998_telekom-shops/telekom-shop-finden). To set up a new account you'll need proof of identification, proof of address (*polizeiliche Anmeldung*), and your bank details to set up a direct debit payment facility.

DT (and other service providers) offer package deals which include line installation. If your property already has a line you must usually wait just a day or two for connection rather than the couple of weeks it takes to install a new line. The fee for installing a line is around €60.

DT has a range of tariff packages to suit different needs. There are options for free

Emergency Numbers/Helplines

Number	Service
Police	110
Ambulance	112
Fire	112
First aid emergency (Ärztlichen Notdienst)	19 222
Non-emergency medical (doctor on call)	116 117
Air rescue	(0711) 70 10 70
Nurse advice line	0800 47 59 23 30
Toxic substance emergency (BfR)	19240
Suicide hotline	0800-111 01 11
Kids and youth hotline	0800-111 03 33
Parental hotline	0800-111 05 50
Alcoholics Anonymous	19295
AIDS hotline	0180 331 94 11

weekend and evening calls or for fixed rates on local calls for up to one hour. However, you can choose from a wide range of service providers, many of whom offer cheaper deals than DT.

USING THE TELEPHONE

Using the telephone in Germany is much the same as in any other country, with a few German eccentricities thrown in for good measure. When dialling a number in your local area, dial the number only. When dialling anywhere else you must add the area code before the subscriber's number. There's no standard method of writing German phone numbers. Some advertisements and company letterheads insert spaces between every two digits, while others prefer to separate the area code (Vorwahl) from the rest of the

Useful Numbers

Number	Service
030-40 50 40 50	credit card and mobile cancellation (all credit & debit cards and mobiles)
*116 116	credit card and mobile cancellation (the same as above)
0900-11 22 499	ADAC (German motoring club) traffic report
*22 499	ADAC traffic report
0800-11 10 111	spiritual guidance (Catholic)
0800-11 10 222	spiritual guidance (Protestant)

* from mobile phones only

Useful Telephone Phrases

English	German
I'd like to speak to ___ .	*Ich möchte mit ___ sprechen.*
Could you connect me with ___ ?	*Könnten Sie mich mit ___ verbinden?*
___ is not in.	*___ ist nicht hier/im Hause.*
I will try again later.	*Ich versuche es später noch einmal.*
I would like to leave a message for __.	*Ich möchte ___ eine Nachricht hinterlassen.*
You've reached the wrong number.	*Sie sind falsch verbunden.*
Could you ask ___ to call me back?	*Könnten Sie ___ bitten zurückzurufen?*

number with a dash or full stop or put it in brackets. In this book, dashes are used to separate the code, and spaces are inserted every three or four digits in the subscriber's number.

Answering the Phone

Germans generally answer the phone by stating their last names; so don't expect a cheery 'Good morning' when you ring somebody. When making a call, Germans identify themselves first, before asking for the person they're calling, therefore if you don't want to be thought pushy or rude it's best to do likewise. Similarly, it may be considered impolite to ring a private home after 9pm.

SERVICE PROVIDERS

Since privatisation, a plethora of companies has offered telephone services, which has resulted in the lowest telephone costs in German history. Internet, fixed-line, mobile and cable providers compete with DT in offering telephone/internet packages, normally for a fixed monthly rate (called *Flatrate* in Germany) of around €9.95 for unlimited use. The major telephone and internet (see page 101) service providers include:

As in most EU countries, nowadays most people in Germany use their mobile phones for calls, text and internet on the go, but a landline is still necessary if you want a fast internet service.

1und1: www.1und1.de
Deutsche Telekom: www.telekom.com
O2: www.o2online.de
Tele2: www.tele2.de
Vodaphone: www.vodaphone.de

To compare the prices and packages offered by each company (which change frequently), you can use a comparison website such as www.billiger-telefonieren.de or www.teletarif.de.

CHARGES

How much you're being charged for a particular call is often almost impossible to calculate, as most telephone service providers offer only package deals, which may include the rent of a telephone, a certain number of 'free' calls or minutes, a discount on calls from fixed lines to mobile phones (*Festnetz zu Mobil*) or to selected countries (a benefit that may be called '*CountrySelect*' or '*CountryFlat*'), and in some cases also internet access, cable TV services and/or a mobile phone contract. To further complicate the matter, there may be a variety of tariff periods, depending on whether a call is local or national. Note also that all charges are based on one-minute intervals (*1-Minuten-Takt*) or part thereof.

Some companies (including DT) have simplified their services so that there's a flat rate for all calls from one fixed line to another fixed line in Germany (whether local or not),

which may be included in your flat rate plan. Rates for international calls vary according to the country you call. Companies offer various packages which may include free calls to a fixed number of countries (chosen by you) or a geographical group of companies.

Calls from a fixed line to mobile phones are much more expensive than calls to fixed lines, which again vary depending on your service provider and your call plan.

BILLS

Telephone bills (*Rechnung*) are issued monthly, whether by DT or another provider. Bills show the charges for the previous month, based on units. For an additional fee you can request an itemised phone bill showing all calls made. A standard phone bill includes the information shown in the box below (in alphabetical order).

You can choose to receive your bills by mail or by email. Your telephone bill must be paid within 14 days of its date. If you're late paying

---

Deciphering Your Phone Bill

German	English
Andere Dienstleistungen	Additional services provided by Telekom
Anschlüsse an . . .	Services to . . . (i.e. other providers' services)
Bei Rückfragen Telefon	Telephone number for billing queries
Cityverbindungen	Local calls
Deutschlandsverbindungen	National calls (i.e. outside the local area)
Inlandsauskunft, Auslandsauskunft	Calls to information services
Kundennummer	Customer reference number
Mobilfunknetz	Connections made to mobile phone services
Monatliche Beträge	Monthly basic fee (including any rented equipment)
Rechnungsbetrag	Total amount due (including 19 per cent VAT)
Rechnungsdatum	Date of billing
Rechnungsnummer	Billing number
Regionalverbindungen	Regional calls
Rufnummer	Customer's telephone number
Weltverbindungen	International calls

there's a penalty, and if you fail to pay after being sent two reminders your service may be disconnected, in which case, there's a fee to be reconnected and your telephone number may change! Automatic payment from a bank account can be arranged by simply authorising a standing order (*Lastschriftverfahren*).

PUBLIC TELEPHONES

Public phone boxes in Germany used to be easy to spot by their bright yellow colour, but only a few of these remain; new booths are pink and are far fewer in number. Although DT claims to have thousands, finding a public phone can sometimes be a challenge, although there's usually at least one at post offices; in hotel foyers, hospitals, restaurants and pedestrian areas of cities; outside the gates of military bases; at *Autobahn* service areas, airports, railway and bus stations; and near sports stadia.

As elsewhere in Europe, most public phones in Germany no longer accept cash but require a phone card (*Telefonkarte*). These

are available in denominations of €5 and €10 from DT offices, post offices and newspaper kiosks. The cost of each call is subtracted automatically from the balance on the card. An increasing number of phone booths accept international credit cards (*Kreditkarte*), particularly those at airports, railway stations and hotels, although there's a €1 fee per call when you pay by credit card. The other payment option is a 'money card' (*Geldkarte*), which costs €0.10 per call.

Only a few payphones – mainly at airports and railway stations – accept coins. Some phones have an illuminated counter indicating the credit remaining; when '*Bitte Zahlen*' (please pay) flashes, it's time to insert more money. Some phone booths, indicated by a bell logo can receive calls, which is useful if you run out of money as you can ask the person you're calling to ring you back.

In addition to payphones, there are public internet terminals (mostly in railway stations and at airport terminals) in Germany, where you can check your emails, surf the internet and send text messages. You can pay by credit card or telephone card.

Telephone Directories

All DT subscribers are entitled to a free copy of their local telephone directory and Yellow Pages, but directories aren't delivered to your door. You must collect copies, normally from your local post office – subscribers receive a postcard explaining the procedure each year. Some post offices accept old directories for recycling.

Information about the phone system is provided in seven languages, including English, at the front of phone books. You can look up numbers in directories (other than your local directory) at a post office, although the quality of directories varies, as Germans have the inconsiderate habit of tearing out the pages they want.

Directory Enquiries

The phone numbers for domestic directory enquiries (*Auskunft*) are 11833 or 11867 and for international enquiries 11831; there's also an English-language service on 11837. A call to these information numbers will cost you at least €1.99 per minute from a landline and possibly more from a cell phone. This service is available free online including www. dastelefonbuch.de, www.dasoertliche.de, www. gelbeseiten.de and www.suchen.de or www. teleauskunft.de.

MOBILE PHONES

The mobile phone market in Germany is dominated by three main operators: Telekom (a subsidiary of Deutsche Telekom (www.telekom. com, branded as T-Mobile between 2002 and 2010), O2 (www.o2online.de, which recently merged with Eplus) and Vodafone (www. vodafone.de).

Germany conforms to the GSM digital standard used by most countries (the main exceptions being Japan and most of the US), which means that those moving to Germany from another European country, Africa, Australia

New EU regulations came into force in June 2017 that abolished 'roaming' charges – the extra fees charged by mobile phone companies when a phone is used abroad – in all European Union countries. All calls and texts when using a foreign registered mobile phone in Germany – or a German-registered phone in another EU country – are now charged at the user's domestic rate.

or most of Asia can use their existing GSM phone and must purchase only a new SIM card or have their phone 'unlocked'. This can be done by your service provider, sometimes free, or you can do it yourself by finding the code on the internet – search for 'unlock mobile phone' – and giving the brand and model number of your phone and its International Mobile Equipment Identity (IMEI) number, which is normally found under the battery.

The cost of mobile phones (*ein Handy*) ranges from around €200 to €500 without a contract, but if you take out a contract (usually for two years) the phone is provided 'free' or for a nominal fee. A typical mobile phone contract requires you to pay at least €15 a month, which usually includes free calls (a number of 'free' minutes) and a number of free texts per month.

You can buy mobile phones from specialist dealers and department and chain stores. Retailers have arrangements with service providers/networks to sell contracts along with phones, so you shouldn't bank on receiving impartial advice from retail staff. Ask your friends and colleagues for their recommendations and shop around, comparing not only phone prices but also the features and additional services provided. Above all, compare the monthly fees and the charges for calls to different mobile networks and international calls. Retailers worth checking out include Base (www.base.de), Blau (www.blau. de), Congstar (www.congstar.de), Dein Handy (www.deinhandy.de), Fonic (www.fonic.de) and Preis24 (https://preis24.de).

If you're an infrequent user or mainly want a mobile phone to receive calls, you can get an inexpensive pay-as-you-go (pre-paid) phone from phone shops (no contract) from around €30.

There's an active market in second-hand mobile phones in Germany, from companies such as https://asgoodasnew.com, www.gebrauchteshandy.de, www.handy-gebraucht.de, www.handy-market.com and www.rebuy.de.

INTERNET

T-Online (www.t-online.de), a former subsidiary and now a business unit of Deutsche Telecom, is the largest internet service provider in Germany, offering a variety of tariffs depending on the kind of internet connection you choose. ADSL/DSL (asymmetric – digital subscriber line) connection costs from around €19.95 per month for unlimited access at speeds of up to 200mB/s (with a fibre optic line) for the first 12 months, after which the cost increases. T-Online offers inducements to change providers (as do other ISPs), including free periods (no monthly fee) and a start bonus. The best deals usually involve a combination of telephone and internet connection (dubbed 'call and surf'), and cost between €35 and €45 per month (unlimited), depending on the speed you choose.

Hundreds of smaller ISPs advertise on the internet and in newspapers and magazines and on television and radio. Prices and services vary, but you should be wary of signing up with a 'new' service, however attractive the offer, as many fail in their first few months leaving users high and dry. The main ISPs (in addition to T-Online) include – in A-Z order – 1und1 (www.1und1.de), rated the number 1 ISP in most consumer magazines in 2016, Congstar (www.congstar.de/DSL-Festnetz--

> Generally all internet service providers in Germany offer DSL with speeds of at least 6Mb/s up to 200Mb/s in areas with fibre optic lines.

709d.html), O2 (www.o2online.de/dsl-festnetz), Tele2 (www.tele2.de), Unity Media (www.unitymedia.de), Versatel (www.versatel.de) and Vodaphone (https://zuhauseplus.vodafone.de/internet-telefon). You can compare deals from the main ISPs online via websites such as DSL Germany (http://dsl-germany.com/en/biglist.php) and All ISPs (www.allisps.com/en/offers/germany).

You can sign up with a free email service, such as Google Mail (www.google.com/gmail), Hotmail (www.hotmail.com) or Yahoo Mail (www.yahoo.com) and access your email from any computer with internet access, e.g. at a library or an internet café. Most ISPs also provide a secure webmail service, which allows you to check your email via a web browser (e.g. Internet Explorer or Mozilla Firefox) on any computer with an internet connection.

Satellite Broadband

As with many other parts of Europe, Germany's broadband performance varies from region to region, depending on how remote your home or business is, and whether a fast ADSL (e.g. fibre) service is available. Satellite broadband provides a fast and reliable service irrespective of your location (although it can be affected by

inclement weather), allowing you to work from home, stream films and TV programmes, and keep in touch with friends and family via email from anywhere in Germany. (Many providers use the KA-SAT high throughput Ka-band satellite, the first European satellite designed exclusively for Internet access.)

In recent years the quality and range of satellite internet offers has improved considerably, both in the speeds available and low fees, and there's now a wide range of options available. The main suppliers include Sky DSL (www.skydsl.eu), Europa Sat (UK 01869-397292, www.europasat.com) and Tooway (www.tooway.de).

Most providers offer a basic service starting at around €20 to €30 per month, to which you need to add a fixed monthly sum for telephone calls starting at around €7 per month, (more if you wish to include mobile calls). However, if you choose the telephone option you don't need to take out a fixed telephone line subscription (*abonnement*) with DT or another provider.

With most offers the satellite and equipment (satellite dish, etc.) costs around €350, but it may be possible to pay for it through a higher monthly charge. Most suppliers require you to take out a contract for a minimum of 12 months or longer.

Internet Telephony

If you've a high-speed ADSL (e.g. fibre) broadband connection – or a mobile with internet connection –- you can make long-distance and international phone 'calls' free (or almost free) to anyone with a broadband connection using VOIP (voice over internet protocol), which has revolutionised the international telecommunications market in recent years.

A leading company in this field is Skype (www.skype.com), now owned by Microsoft (and included in Office 365), with over 75 million users worldwide, while others include Ring Central (www.ringcentral.co.uk) and Vonage (www.vonage.co.uk). There are numerous other companies in the market (a web search for 'VOIP' will throw up dozens), some of which also allow you to call landline phone numbers.

All you need is access to a high-speed broadband service – which can be via a PC, smartphone, tablet, laptop or even a TV – and you're in business. Calls to other computers anywhere in the world are free, while calls to landlines are charged at a few cents per minute.

For information about Skype, see https://support.skype.com/en/faq/FA10613/how-do-i-make-a-call-on-skype.

Schloss Glücksburg, Schleswig-Holstein

8.
TELEVISION & RADIO

*T*elevision and radio services in Germany are operated by both public and private broadcasting companies. The two 'national' public TV channels, ARD and ZDF, are run by a network of *Länder*-based broadcasters and funded by advertising and TV and radio licence fees, which are collected and distributed by an agency of the federal government. The regional authorities also produce and broadcast programmes targeted at their local audience using the so-called 'Third Channel' of public TV. There are nine Third Channels, whose regions don't correspond to Germany's 16 states.

The public broadcasters are bound by European regulations requiring at least 51 per cent of programming be European in origin; an increasing amount of programming is produced in Germany – everything from soap operas to drama series. The ever-popular quiz shows can be useful for those learning German, as many are based on word play or other language skills. The Germans also produce a wide range of chat shows, some of which are indistinguishable from their American counterparts, often right down to the sets used (but with different guests!).

German audiences are keen on news programmes and documentaries, particularly 'investigative reporting' or consumer-oriented *exposés* of overpriced tourist packages, food scares, shoddy builders and crooked estate agents. Late-night programming is often on the exotic (and erotic) side, with some documentary-type shows dedicated to exploring sexual themes. At weekends, don't be surprised to find soft porn films starting around midnight (often dubbed into German).

As in many countries, around half of German viewers say they find little or nothing worth watching on TV!

TELEVISION STANDARDS

Germany has over 20 million households with TV, of which around 16 million receive their TV via cable and the rest via satellite and terrestrial. Terrestrial reception had lost most of its users by the '90s due to extensive cable and satellite coverage. Germany switched from analogue to digital terrestrial TV broadcasts in 2008-9 (analogue broadcasting was switched off in 2011). However, despite the switchover to digital TV, sales of HDTV televisions haven't taken off in Germany in the way that they have in some other countries, e.g. the UK.

The standard for TV reception in Germany isn't the same as in many other countries. Together with much of the rest of continental Europe, Australia and New Zealand, Germany uses a standard called PAL B/G that differs from the PAL-I standard used in the UK. This means that TVs imported from the UK (and France and the USA, which have different systems) are unusable unless they're multi-standard. For those planning to leave Europe after their stay in Germany, a multi-standard set-up is the best buy.

The German mains supply is 220-240 volts at 50 Hertz (cycles), presenting an additional problem for those wishing to use equipment manufactured for the US market, which operates at 110 volts, 60 Hertz. When bringing camcorders or other playback devices from foreign countries, check that your German TV can support playback of the foreign standard.

If you're buying a DVD player locally, make sure that it will playback your DVDs (take one with you and check) if you aren't from Europe (see **DVDs** on page 110).

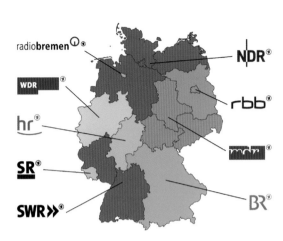

TELEVISION CHANNELS

Without cable or satellite TV (see below), you'll normally be able to receive only the three public broadcasters (ARD, ZDF and the local regional channel – although in many states it's possible to receive more than one regional channel). If you're in an area that receives more than one regional station, don't be surprised to find that both (or all) regional channels are showing the same programmes at the same time. Public stations are permitted to show advertisements (commercials) only during scheduled breaks between programmes and at certain times of the day.

There are nine regional channels in Germany, listed below, which co-operate to produce programmes for the TV network known as Das Erste (The First).

The smaller regions, such as Bremen and the Saarland, contribute to the nationwide TV programme *Das Erste*, but broadcast few regional programmes.

Regional TV Stations (see map above)

Station	States
Bayerischer Rundfunk/BR	Bavaria
Hessicher Rundfunk/HR	Hesse
Mitteldeutscher Rundfunk/MDR	Saxony, Saxony-Anhalt and Thuringia
Norddeutscher Rundfunk/NDR	Hamburg, Lower Saxony, Schleswig-Holstein and Mecklenburg-Vorpommern
Radio Bremen/RB	Bremen (also a television broadcaster)
Rundfunk Berlin-Brandenburg/RBB	Berlin and Brandenburg
Saarländischer Rundfunk/SR	Saarland
Südwestrundfunk/SWR	Baden-Württemberg and Rhineland-Palatinate
Westdeutscher Rundfunk/WDR	North-Rhine Westphalia

Most private broadcasters' programmes are available only via cable or satellite. There are channels dedicated to children's programmes (such as Ki.ka), to music (Viva Plus), shopping (Home Shopping Europe) and news (N-TV), as well as more general stations such as Kabeleins, Pro7, RTL, Sat1, Sonnenklar TV and Vox. Private stations are financed by advertising revenue, and the limitations on the frequency and duration of advertising are much less restrictive than those for public broadcasters. Commercial breaks can extend to ten or even 15 minutes.

Private station broadcasts are dominated by American series and films, German talk shows and 'reality' and 'magazine' shows; science and nature programmes are also popular. Nearly all imported shows are dubbed into German. The German public is also fond of classic British comedy. Not only will you find reruns of *Monty Python's Flying Circus*, *Mr. Bean* and *Fawlty Towers*, but you can watch them in English, as they're subtitled rather than dubbed.

The American Forces Network (AFN TV) is available in areas where there are US military installations, but you need an NTSC standard TV or VCR to receive it. You may also be able to receive British Forces Broadcasting Service TV (www.bfbs.com/tv/country_guides/germany) in the Lüneburg-Osnabrück area.

CABLE TELEVISION

In most cities and many rural areas, the majority of buildings are wired for cable TV, which enables households to receive over 30 TV stations and at least as many radio stations. In theory, you can request a cable connection to anywhere in Germany, but the cost in a remote rural area will be prohibitive if cable TV isn't already installed locally (in which case you can opt for satellite TV). To have an existing cable connected is as easy as informing the building superintendent that you want it. In

most apartment blocks the entire building is wired for cable and all you need to do is connect your TV to the cable outlet.

The downside of cable TV is that you have no choice of provider but must use whichever has the local contract, although in some large apartment buildings a number of local and national companies operate an in-house cable network which is fed by its own satellite antenna on the roof, not the local cable operator.

There are two major cable operators in Germany: Unity Media in Hesse and North-Rhine Westphalia and Baden-Württemberg, and Kabel Deutschland in the other 13 states. All companies offer around 200 digital (DVB-C) channels, which includes some 70 basic channels plus a number of pay-per-view channels and subscription-based packages. In addition to the pay-TV broadcasters, Premiere and, in some networks, Arena, are also available.

The cost of the connection is billed to you either as part of your incidental charges

(*Nebenkosten* – see **Additional Costs** on page 75) or directly by the cable provider. Cable fees range from around €20 to €30 per month, depending on the options you choose. You can save money by paying the fees annually or six months in advance, rather than quarterly or monthly.

The selection of channels varies with the provider according to local needs and tastes, but the most popular stations, such as Kabel 1, Pro7, Sat 1, VOX, ARD, ZDF, RTL, MTV, VIVA, Eurosport and CNN International, are usually available. In border areas, you're likely to be offered public TV channels from neighbouring countries, as well as Arte (formerly a French-German co-operative channel but now becoming a pan-European enterprise).

Some stations are scrambled and require a decoder. An additional monthly fee is payable directly to the relevant broadcaster for this service (occasionally on a pay-per-view basis). For an extra fee you can receive additional English channels: National Geographic, AXN, Extreme Sports, ESPN Classic, Playhouse Disney, Toon Disney, Boomerang, Sailing Channel, MTV Hits and Dance, VH-1 Classic, NASN, BBC Prime, and TCM (Turner Classic Movies). Details of how to subscribe to pay TV channels are available via TV adverts, in TV stores and via the website of your local cable provider.

SATELLITE TELEVISION

A large number of the satellite channels serving Germany are unencrypted, which means you need only a satellite dish to receive them. The two main European satellite providers are Astra (www.ses-astra.com) and Eutelsat (www.eutelsat.de). The signal from some stations is scrambled (the decoder is usually built into the receiver), and viewers need a Digibox and must pay a monthly subscription fee to receive programmes.

German Satellite Television

Digital satellite television has been available in Germany since 1996, and all of the 30+ TV stations now broadcast their satellite signal in digital (DVB-S) format. To watch digital TV you require a decoder, called a D-box (Digibox), which you can buy either separately for around €100 or as part of a programme package deal.

A list of digital German satellite service providers can be found on www.digitalfernsehen.de.

The main satellite broadcaster in Germany is Sky Deutschland (www.sky.de) – not to be confused with Sky Television in the UK (although owned by the same company) – which offers individual programme packages from €16.99 per month. The interactive receiver allows you to receive digital and HD TV and radio programmes, and provides access to an on-screen programme guide, search function and automatic software updates.

Customers must usually sign up for 12 months. It's recommended you have a phone line available (which is connected to the D-box) if you wish to use interactive services.

UK Sky Television

It's possible to receive Sky TV (www.sky.com) throughout Germany, which provides access to up to 350 channels, including all the BBC and ITV channels. Sky offers a number of packages, including films and exclusive live sports events. To receive Sky television you need a Sky digital receiver (digibox) and Sky viewing card, plus a satellite dish. In recent years Sky reduced the footprint (the area of coverage) and the further you are from the UK the larger the dish you'll require; in the west of the country an 80-100cm dish is sufficient but in the east and south you'll require a 1.2-1.8m dish. However, if you're unable to install a satellite dish, there are various internet-based products available.

It's possible to subscribe in the UK or Ireland (personally, if you've an address there, or via a friend) and then take your Sky receiver and card to Germany. Alternatively, you can buy a digibox and obtain a Sky card in Germany with a European Sky TV subscription. A number of companies offer this service including Insat International (www.insatinternational.com), Sky Europe (www.skyeurope.tv/sky-subscription-germany) and Skycards.eu (www.skycards.eu/watch-sky-tv-in-germany).

You can also watch British TV via a computer and web browser, although most UK TV services are blocked outside the country. Catch-up services use your IP (internet protocol) address, making it impossible or difficult to watch catch-up TV, although it's possible to get around this using a virtual private network (VPN) or proxy server, which channels your network traffic so that it appears to be coming from a different country (e.g. the UK). This is illegal, although it's estimated that some 65 million people worldwide regularly access, for example, the BBC catch-up TV service this way.

TV PROGRAMME GUIDES

There's a bewildering choice of TV guides in Germany, some of which are published weekly and some fortnightly; they come and go with alarming frequency. Guides are available from supermarkets as well as newsagents and are published early, therefore it's sometimes difficult to buy the current issue. Some magazines include satellite and cable programmes, while others also include radio programmes. Certain publications concentrate on films while others are dedicated solely to series, soaps or police series. The most popular guides include *HörZu* (www.hoerzu.de), *TV Movie* (www.tvmovie.de) and *TV Today* (www.tvtoday.de).

There are a number of internet sites where you can design your own programme guides according to your tastes and the cable or satellite programmes you can receive. One particularly comprehensive website is www.eurotv.com, which has the advantage of being in English, although it carries programme listings for most European countries. Most TV stations in Germany (and elsewhere) have a website and some German websites offer some programme information in English.

Satellite Programme Guides

Most satellite stations provide comprehensive programme information. Satellite TV programmes are also listed in some expatriate newspapers and magazines in Germany, and programmes are also available online.

TELEVISION & RADIO LICENCE

Since 2013 a television (and radio) licence fee of €17.50 per month (€210 per year) has been mandatory for all German households, irrespective of whether you own a TV or radio (or how many you own). The fee is payable to ARD ZDF Deutschlandradio (*Beitragsservice*) and helps maintain the broadcast services of the ARD, ZDF and the regional channels. Those on the minimum wage or unemployed are exempt from paying the licence fee and people with certain disabilities pay a reduced fee.

Registration forms (*Anmeldung*) are available from banks and post offices, or you can register via the internet (www.rundfunkbeitrag.de). You can pay by standing order (*Lastschrift*) from a bank account, monthly or annually. On leaving the country don't forget to file a licence cancellation form (*Abmeldung*) to stop your payment standing order (which can be done via the above website)

When buying a new television in Germany an address is normally requested, and the retailer is obliged to inform the *Beitragsservice* of the sale.

DVDS

Although most people get their films (and music) online nowadays via streaming and pay-to-view services such as Amazon Prime, Netflix and NowTV, DVDs are still available to rent or buy in Germany. To rent a DVD, you must usually join a rental club and pay an annual fee, after which you can rent videos for as little as €1 (e.g. 'classic' films) up to around €12 for the latest Hollywood blockbusters. A popular way to rent DVDs and videos is via the internet, e.g. Amazon (www.amazon.de) or Video Buster (www.videobuster.de), which

---

DVD Zones

DVDs may be encoded with a region code, restricting the area of the world in which they can be played. The code for Western Europe is 2 (North America is zone 1), while discs without any region coding are called all-region or region 0 discs. However, you can buy all-region DVD players and DVD players can be modified to be region-free, allowing the playback of all discs (see www.regionfreedvd.net and www.moneysavingexpert.com/shopping/dvd-unlock).

---

offers rental DVDs from as little as €2.50 for seven days including delivery.

Many shops and petrol station sells DVDs at prices ranging from €6 to €25. You can buy English-language videos via the internet and through mail-order book and video catalogues. Check with local expatriate clubs for English-language videos available for sale or swap.

RADIO

The good news for radio enthusiasts is that radios have the same standards the world over, meaning there are generally few problems with equipment compatibility. The only significant difficulties are likely to be experienced by Americans, who may find that their VHF radios with digital tuning don't work properly in Europe. The reason for this is that the American broadcasting standard calls for a broader tuning bandwidth than in Europe (10kHz rather than 9kHz).

FM (VHF) stereo stations flourish in Germany, to the extent that it's almost impossible to obtain a broadcasting licence due to the lack of available frequencies. A short-wave (SW) radio is useful for receiving international stations such as the BBC World Service, Voice of America, Radio Canada and Radio Sweden. Most stations are also available via cable and satellite. Digital radio (DAB) broadcasts are also widespread in Germany, although you need a digital radio to receive them. However, before taking a DAB radio to Germany, check that it's compatible with the German system.

German Radio

There's a wide choice of German radio stations, both public and private, although most are regionally orientated. All musical tastes are covered, from classical to youth and oldies' stations, with most stations broadcasting a variety of music. A list of all radio stations in

and programmes can be found on the BBC website. The BBC World Service (plus BBC Radio 1, 2, 3, 4 and 5) is also available via the Astra and Eutelsat satellites.

Many other foreign stations offer worldwide broadcasts for expatriates keen for news from home, including Radio Australia, Radio Canada and the Voice of America. Check broadcasters' websites for programme schedules.

Internet Radio

If you have an internet connection you can listen to hundreds of radio stations via websites such as www.internetradiouk.com (for UK radio stations) – including all the main BBC stations – www.live-radio.net/us.shtml (US radio stations plus stations worldwide) and www.internet-radio.com, which has links to hundreds of music stations from around the world which you can choose by genre.

You can also access a comprehensive list of internet radio stations via Wikipedia (https://en.wikipedia.org/wiki/list_of_internet_radio_stations) or you can search for a station online simply by typing its name into a search engine such as Google.

Germany is available on Wikipedia: https://en.wikipedia.org/wiki/List_of_radio_stations_in_germany.

Deutsche Welle (www.dw.com/en/radio/s-32771) – the equivalent of the BBC World Service (see below) – broadcasts in German and English (as well as in many other languages) across the globe.

A list of German radio stations streaming live on the internet can be found at www.listenlive.eu/germany.html and www.surfmusic.de/country/germany.html.

English-language Radio

If you live near a US or British military base, you'll be able to pick up English-language stations, e.g. the British Forces Broadcasting Service (BFBS) of the Rhine Army (www.bfbs.com/radio) in the Lüneburg-Osnabrück area, while those living in central and southern Germany can receive AFN Radio (www.afneurope.net), which caters to the American forces in Europe and is popular for its country-and-western music among German listeners, as well as homesick Americans.

The BBC World Service (www.bbc.co.uk/worldserviceradio) broadcasts on various wavelengths and frequencies and you should be able to receive a good signal on one of them in Germany. A list of frequencies

First day at school

9.
EDUCATION

O ne of the first countries to introduce compulsory schooling, Germany has no national education system as education is a responsibility of the individual states (*Länder*). Consequently, there are as many school systems as there are states (i.e. 16), all with different structures and methodologies. The introduction of a unified school system for the whole of Germany has been a perennial topic of discussion among the chattering classes, but up to now little has come of it.

In the 2015 OECD (www.oecd.org/pisa/pisa-2015-germany.pdf) Program for International Student Assessment (PISA) study of the achievements of 15-year-olds in 34 OECD countries (plus a number of G20 and partner countries), Germany performed above average in the three subjects assessed: mathematics, science and reading.

Education is compulsory in Germany for at least nine years (ten in some states), children beginning full-time education at between five-and-a-half and seven, depending on the time of year they were born. Education in state schools is free, from primary school through to – and including – university. Free education is also provided within the state system for the children of foreign residents in Germany, although non-resident, non-EU students require a student visa (see page 53).

Unlike some other Europeans, Germans have always viewed their education as almost entirely egalitarian. For example, kindergarten teachers aren't allowed to teach the alphabet or reading, so that all children start off on an even footing. The disadvantage of this system is that learning disabilities, such as dyslexia, often remain unnoticed or are ignored; those with such difficulties are simply considered 'dumb' and put at the back of the class. There are special schools for those with perceived or genuine mental and physical disabilities, but every attempt to create special schools for exceptionally intelligent or gifted children has been met with fierce opposition, from both the general public and politicians.

Nevertheless, the education system is highly competitive and selective, and separates the brighter students from the less academically gifted on entry into secondary schools. Formal tests are conducted each year from primary school onwards, and the results carry considerable weight in determining the type of education (and hence the likely future career) a child can expect. And although there are no close equivalents of France's elite *Grandes Ecoles* or the US's Ivy League universities, there are nonetheless good and bad universities – and the differences between them can be considerable.

Critics of the German education system complain that, unlike British and US schools, which emphasise developing the whole person, the German system (like the French) is focused entirely on academic achievement and consequent career advancement. Most German state schools offer little in the way of extra-curricular activities.

The German teaching style is generally more formal than in many other countries, including the UK and the US, with little contact between pupils and teachers outside classrooms. In some city schools, discipline has become a problem in recent years, owing partly to tensions arising from the high proportion of children from ethnic minorities, who constitute 50 per cent or more of pupils in some districts in large cities.

On the plus side, academic standards are generally high, with well qualified teachers and commendable results (at least by German standards); some 95 per cent of pupils gain a school-leaving certificate and around 30 per cent the general university entrance qualification. German schools have also been quick to embrace the potential of new technology, most having fast internet connections, and each child, whatever his level of natural ability, is given the opportunity to study for a trade, diploma or degree.

A strong emphasis is placed on workplace training, and few school-leavers go into a job without it. Everyone up to the age of 18 must attend some form of educational institution (full- or part-time) and it's normal practice for those leaving school at 16 to attend a technical college or train as an apprentice. In today's highly competitive labour market, both parents and students are acutely aware that qualifications and training are of paramount importance in obtaining a good job, although these don't have to be academically orientated.

Local school information (possibly available in English) can be obtained from the municipal administration centre (*Stadverwaltung*) or the education office (Amt für Schule or Behörde für Schule, Jugend und Berufsbildung), which is usually located at the Stadverwaltung but may be in a separate building.

In fact, a graduate of a *Fachhochschule*, where studies have a strong technical bent, is more likely to get a job than a university graduate.

Further information about German schools, both state and private, can be obtained from German embassies and consulates abroad, and from foreign embassies, educational organisations and government departments in Germany.

ADAPTING TO THE SYSTEM

Generally, the younger your child is when he enters the German school system, the easier he'll be able to cope. Conversely, the older he is the more problems he'll have adjusting, particularly as the school curriculum is more demanding at a higher level. Teenagers often have considerable problems learning German and adjusting to German school life, particularly children from the UK or USA who haven't learnt a second language. In some schools, foreign children who cannot understand the language may be neglected and just expected to get on with it. In your early days in Germany, it's important to check exactly what your children are doing at school and whether they're making progress (not just with the language, but also with their other lessons).

As a parent, you should be prepared to support your children through this difficult period. If you aren't fluent in German, you'll already be aware how frustrating it is being unable to express yourself adequately, which can easily lead to feelings of inferiority or inadequacy – in children as well as in adults. It's also important to ensure that your children maintain their native language, as it can easily be neglected (studies show that the children of English residents in non-English-speaking countries tend to lose their ability to read and write English).

For many children, the challenge of living in a foreign country is stimulating and provides

(when children begin to learn languages more slowly), many of whom encounter great difficulties during their first year.

Until recently, the German state school system generally made little or no concession to non-German speakers, e.g. by providing intensive German lessons. However, this has changed (largely due to the immigrant PISA results mentioned above) and now most German states are required to provide extra German language training to children of immigrant backgrounds who are beginning primary school. These classes may take place in the child's pre-school, in his designated primary school or in both, and can help to ease the burden for non-German-speaking children. The possibility of immigrant children taking part in these classes after the start of the school year can vary from region to region. It may be worthwhile enquiring about the availability of extra German classes before deciding where to live. Bear in mind that while attending extra language classes, children may fall behind in other subjects.

Foreign children are tested (like German children) and put into a class suited to their level of German, even if this means being taught with younger children or slow learners. In some states (e.g. Bavaria) they're tested before starting primary school (*Grundschule*), and held back a year if their German isn't considered good enough.

If your local state school doesn't provide extra German classes – and outside large cities this is likely to be the case – your only

invaluable cultural, as well as educational experiences. Your child will become a 'world' citizen, less likely to be prejudiced against foreigners and foreign ideas. This is particularly true if he attends an international school with pupils from many different countries, although many state schools, particularly in the larger cities, also have pupils from a variety of countries and backgrounds. Before making major decisions about your child's education, it's important to consider his ability, character and long-term requirements.

LANGUAGE

There are many considerations to take into account when choosing an appropriate school in Germany, not least the language of study. The only schools in Germany using English as the teaching language are a few foreign and international schools (see page 124). For most children, however, studying in German isn't such a handicap as it may at first appear, particularly for those aged under ten. Many young children adapt quickly and some may become fluent within six months (if only it were so easy for adults!). However, children don't all adapt equally well to a change of language and culture, particularly children aged over ten choice will be to pay for private lessons or send your child to another (possibly private) school, where extra tuition is available. Some parents send a child to an English-speaking school for a year followed by a state school, while other parents find it easier to throw their children in at the deep end than to introduce them gradually. It all depends on the character, ability and wishes of the child.

Whatever you decide, it will help if your child has some intensive German lessons before arriving in Germany (see **Learning German** on page 130). It may be possible to organise an educational or cultural exchange with a German school or family, before coming to live in Germany, which will be a considerable help in integrating a child into the German language and culture.

STATE SCHOOLS

The German state education system has traditionally been highly regarded, and is for the most part well organised and adequately funded (not that teachers would ever agree!). However, each state (*Land*) sets its own standards and objectives and develops its own education programme. The education ministers of German states meet periodically to debate current issues and establish minimum standards, although all attempts to institute a unified state education system have been vigorously opposed.

Co-education (mixed classes of girls and boys) is normal in German state schools and is even required by law in some states. There are very few all-male or all-female schools.

A general criticism of German state schools often made by foreigners is the lack of extra-curricular activities such as sport, music, drama, and arts and crafts. There's the occasional track-and-field contest, but state schools have few if any sports clubs or teams and if your child wants to do team sports he must join a local club. This means that you'll have to ferry children back and forth for games and social events (Americans will be used to this!). A list of organised activities for children and young people can usually be obtained from the town hall, and the local church may organise some activities.

Having made the decision to send your child to a state school, you should stick to it for at least a year to give it a fair trial. It will take a child at least this long to begin to adapt to a new language, the change of environment and the different curriculum.

Enrolment

Enrolling your child in a German school is usually straightforward. In fact, provided you're officially registered as a resident, your local school will write to you some time before the start of the school year inviting you to register your child for classes (this applies if you move to Germany from abroad or within Germany). You'll be informed about any medical certificates that you must provide and any items you must buy (see below), and you're then required to visit the school during normal office hours to complete the necessary forms. Even if you've decided to send your child to another (e.g. private) school, you must notify your local state school and tell them what alternative arrangements you've made.

School Hours

Most state schools operate only in the morning and early afternoon, Mondays to Fridays. The standard school day is from 8am until 1pm, with a maximum of half an hour's variation either side of these times. The original rationale for this arrangement was that the afternoon and early evening would be devoted to a demanding homework regime, although, as the social climate has become more relaxed, children increasingly tend to look upon this as 'free time' for sport and leisure. Nevertheless, children are required to do at least two hours' homework per day, and parents are expected to help them – which places an additional burden on parents, who must also provide lunch for their offspring and supervise them during the afternoons.

All-day schools (*Ganztagsschulen*) were introduced in the last few decades and now number some 17,000 nationwide. All-day schools include more extra-curricular activities and tutoring with homework, with lessons continuing until 4 or 5pm, sometimes with evening activities. Another solution for working parents is the *Hort* or *Mittagsbetreuung*, which provide the same services as an all-day school (e.g. afterschool activities, tutoring), but may be in another location. The important difference between the two is that a *Hort* also provides this service during school holidays, whereas the *Mittagsbetreuung* doesn't. If the *Hort* is in another location, a pick-up service may be provided. Like a Kindergarten space, a *Hort* place is difficult to come by and you should apply to as many schools as possible (as early as possible).

The situation is further complicated by the fact that school hours can vary from day to day. In most schools, children don't go to school in the early morning if they have no classes scheduled, and if their last class finishes before the end of the school day, they're free to go home. Similarly, if a teacher is off sick and the school cannot arrange a replacement (a fairly common occurrence), children may be sent home without warning. Parents with two or more children face a scheduling nightmare, as each child may have a quite different school schedule.

Holidays

Summer holidays normally last six weeks, but the start and finish dates vary from state to state. Before the introduction of this system, most Germans tried to have their holidays at the same time, causing monumental traffic jams on motorways and congestion on public transport. Each year a school holiday schedule for the whole of Germany is issued (see www.schoolholidayseurope. eu/choose-a-country/germany.html#autumn-holiday or www.feiertagskalender.ch/ferien. php?geo=3059&jahr=2017&hl=en).

> There are additional short holidays of two to four days, which vary from state to state. Schools are also closed on church, state and national holidays that don't fall within a holiday period (see **Public Holidays** on page 41).

In general, the northern and central states start their summer holidays in mid-June to early July, the eastern states in mid-July and the southern states as late as the end of July or early August. It's common for German families to go on holiday the day after the school holidays commence and return the day before school starts again.

In addition to the summer holidays, there are the following school holidays:

♦ Two weeks in autumn, which used to be termed 'harvest holidays' and were originally intended to give children in rural areas time off school to help their parents with the farm work (nowadays the nearest most German children get to a harvest is the fruit and vegetable section of the local supermarket);

♦ Two to three weeks at Christmas;

♦ Rose Monday (the day before Shrove Tuesday, i.e. two days before the beginning of Lent) and Hag Thursday (the Thursday of the week preceding Rose Monday). In regions where *Fasching* (Carnival) plays a major role, holidays can extend from Hag Thursday to Rose Monday or even Ash Wednesday.

♦ A one- to two-week break at Easter, which usually starts on the Monday before Easter;

♦ 10 to 14 days around Pentecost (in May or June).

Some states allow you to withdraw your children from school for 'compassionate' reasons and/or to observe religious holidays that aren't provided for by the state. All absences from school (including those due to illness) must be justified in writing. It's advisable to co-ordinate any planned absences with your child's teacher so that he doesn't miss any important activities or annual tests. Removing your child from school for a period of more than a couple of days without prior agreement with school officials can lead to a substantial fine, and for persistent offenders, imprisonment for parents and the placement of a child in foster care!

Summer camps, so much a feature of a child's upbringing in North America, aren't part of the state educational system in Germany. There are, however, some summer camps organised by Boy and Girl Scout organisations, certain church groups, political parties and commercial organisations.

Health & Accidents

As a rule, there's no school nurse in German state schools and health problems are generally referred to a family doctor or the nearest hospital. Vaccination programmes exist in each state, but only a few are mandatory. In some states a school doctor makes regular examinations and provides vaccinations at a school, while in others healthcare is left to the discretion of parents. There are optional bi-annual dental checks at schools, which are free of charge.

Schools are insured for accidents that occur on their premises during school hours and on the way to and from school, provided children take the shortest route between their home and school, and don't interrupt the journey for any non-school-related reason. Other accidents should be covered by a family's health insurance, which is mandatory for all employees and some self-employed people. Busy roads near schools are usually manned by volunteer traffic patrols (usually retirees), who help children cross the street safely by stopping the traffic.

Equipment

The equipment (books, uniform, materials, etc.) necessary to start school in Germany vary from state to state, although all pupils require the following:

♦ School bag (a rucksack is most commonly used);

♦ Pencil case, pencils, erasers, sharpeners, watercolours, brushes, coloured pencils or crayons and a fountain pen (most German schools and teachers are opposed to the use of ballpoint pens during primary education, and some schools insist on the use of fountain pens throughout a child's education);

♦ An assortment of lined writing pads or notebooks (colour-coded), binders, graph paper for maths and plain (unlined) paper for drawing;

♦ Gym shoes (plimsolls), a T-shirt and a towel for sports and exercise periods. Some states also require a tracksuit. A sports bag is required if the gym kit doesn't fit into the normal school bag.

There are mandatory schoolbooks for all ages, which are provided free by schools in some states, while in others parents must pay for them. In some cases, books are provided free of charge only if a child's parents earn less than a certain amount. If you have several children it's therefore advisable to tell them to look after their books, so that they can be used by their younger siblings (the required book for a particular level seldom changes). Parents must also be prepared to cover the cost of materials for cookery and handicraft lessons.

Children may need a sleeping bag for the annual school excursion, which may be a day trip to a nearby site or a few days of camping or staying at youth hostels. Excursions, which aren't free, tend to be longer the older a child is, and a week's holiday abroad (e.g. in Majorca) just before graduating from secondary school isn't uncommon.

School uniforms are rare, although students usually devise their own 'uniform', and in some areas the theft of designer clothes by gangs is widespread and has resulted in children being told to dress down and not wear expensive clothes to school.

Parents are required to provide their children with food for mid-morning breaks, although snacks may be available from vendors who visit schools during breaks or from local shops. School caféterias are rare, as most children are home by lunchtime (unless it's an all-day school). Some schools offer a 'milk-for-breakfast' programme, through which parents

can arrange for their children to be given warm milk or a chocolate drink during break periods.

Nursery School

Attendance at nursery school (*Kindergarten*, meaning literally 'children's garden') from the age of three is voluntary in Germany and parents are required to pay a fee, although subsidies are available to those on average and low incomes from the Youth Authority (*Jugendamt*). While there are sufficient nursery school places to meet demand in the eastern states, in some western areas there aren't nearly enough. Indeed, some parents enrol their children at birth to ensure a place. Nursery school generally lasts from two to three hours in the morning, although children can be supervised for up to nine hours or at other times (e.g. for shift-working parents) if required; the fee is higher for longer hours.

Children normally attend nursery school from Mondays to Fridays, although some nursery schools are also equipped to look after the children of weekend workers. Nursery school is generally a good way to integrate your pre-school children into German life. Note, however, that in many nursery schools all children from the ages of three to six play together, with no attempt to segregate them into groups or activities. This means that children must be prepared to face a degree of rough-and-tumble; as one expatriate parent in Germany commented: "Kindergarten is wonderful for the children – they really learn how to defend themselves!"

In some towns there are *Kinderkrippen*, a kind of crèche for children under three, providing the same service.

Primary School

Children start primary school (*Grundschule*) between the ages of five-and-a-half and seven depending on the month they were born. A child may be held back one school year due to health, insufficient German knowledge or other factors.

The first day of primary school is considered a very important event in a child's life in Germany and a degree of ceremony accompanies it, including photos taken by professional photographers. It's customary to provide children starting school with a bag of sweets (*Schultüte*) resembling a colourful dunce's hat upside-down, with an inscription such as 'my first day at school'. These bags can be purchased at stationery shops and supermarkets in a variety of colours and sizes, but are sold empty and must be filled with treats purchased separately.

Despite a recent ruling by Germany's Supreme Court that crucifixes on the walls of classrooms infringe on religious freedom and should be removed, there's hardly a classroom in southern Bavaria without one.

and arithmetic. In addition children receive a basic introduction in other subjects they'll be studying at secondary school, including history (*Geschichte*), geography (*Erdkunde*), social studies (*Sozialkunde*), biology (*Biologie*), physics (*Physik*), chemistry (*Chemie*), music (*Musik*), art (*Kunsterziehung*) and sport (*Sport*). Religious education (*Religionslehre*) classes, which focus on Christianity, are mandatory everywhere with the exception of some eastern states, where a non-religious equivalent (called 'ethics') is substituted.

Nowadays, with a growing immigrant population, many of whom are Muslims, ethics is an option at most schools; however, this can cause an unhealthy segregation between Christian and non-Christian students. There's a strong Catholic tradition in southern Bavaria and, if your child attends a state school in this region (except in Munich, which is more cosmopolitan), you'll probably have to accept this as part and parcel of his education.

Primary school normally lasts for four years (six in Berlin and Brandenburg). In Bavaria, however, *Grundschulen* and *Hauptschulen* (see **Secondary School** below) are amalgamated into *Volksschulen*. After this (in most states), parents receive a recommendation from the child's teachers concerning the type of school most appropriate for the child's continuing

State School Grades

Grade	Assessment	Meaning
1	*Sehr gut*	very good
2	*Gut*	good
3	*Befriedigend/ zufriedenstellend*	reasonable/satisfactory
4	*Ausreichend*	sufficient
5	*Mangelhaft*	deficient/unsatisfactory
6	*Ungenügend*	poor/insufficient

The total number of weekly lessons at primary school varies from 20 to 30 depending on the class, i.e. the age of the child. The main subjects are reading, writing

Secondary School

After primary education, children normally go to one of three types of secondary school: *Hauptschule*, *Realschule* or *Gymnasium*. In some states, however, there are also *Gesamtschulen*. These four types of secondary school are described below.

Hauptschule

This type of school is designed for those who are less academically gifted and expected to enter a manual trade on leaving school. The main subjects studied are German, arithmetic, history, work studies (*Arbeitslehre*) and crafts. In some states the *Hauptschule* curriculum includes a foreign language (normally English, French or Russian). The number of weekly lessons (each of which lasts 45 minutes) is between 30 and 33.

After five or six years, a *Hauptschule* graduate generally enters an apprenticeship (*Lehre*) in a manual trade, although those with good grades may apply for an apprenticeship in a commercial or medical profession. Once a *Hauptschule* student has obtained his school certificate (*Hauptschulabschluss*) he can go on to study part-time for vocational qualifications at a *Berufschule*.

Realschule

Realschulen are designed for those who will be entering an apprenticeship in a commercial trade or medical profession such as nursing. Here the emphasis is more on mathematics and language skills than on crafts. In most states, at least two foreign languages (usually English and French) are taught, the number of weekly lessons being between 30 and 34. *Realschulen* include specialised schools such as trade schools (*Handelsschule*). The leaving certificate, awarded after a final examination, is called the *Mittlere Reife*.

education. This is based on the teachers' assessment of the child's performance, abilities and interests, and teachers can veto the admittance of a child to a *Gymnasium* or *Realschule* if, in their view, the child hasn't achieved the necessary standard. In some states, failing to pass a year (grade) precludes a child from attending a *Gymnasium*, and failing the same year twice or any grade three times means that a child is automatically enrolled in a special school for slow learners.

Reports & Tests

Children at German schools are regularly tested in a range of subjects, and each year receive two reports (one at the end of each term). Performance levels are traditionally indicated by a grade from 1 to 6, as follows:

Most 'private' schools are found in Bavaria and North Rhine-Westphalia, where a periodic debate breaks out about reducing government funding to such schools.

Gymnasium

Equivalent to a British grammar school, this is the type of school for students with the most academic promise and is designed to prepare them for university or a 'high-end'

apprenticeship. This is the most demanding level of secondary education, with lots of homework and pressure to perform, and between 32 and 40 lessons per week.

Classes at a *Gymnasium* consist of a group of mandatory subjects, including English, French, German, mathematics, chemistry, physics, history and religion/ethics, and a group of optional subjects (electives), such as advanced chemistry, advanced physics, advanced mathematics, Greek and Latin. The optional subjects selected depend on the career intentions of the student (a classical language, for example, may be compulsory for those hoping to pursue a career in medicine).

Gymnasium concludes with the *Abitur* examination, the number of subjects examined varying with the state. Upon passing the *Abitur*, a student is awarded the *Zeugnis der Allgemeine Hochschulreife*, which entitles him to study the subject of his choice at a university or equivalent institution (provided a place is available).

Because German university education is free, all but the best are 'filtered out' in *Gymnasien*, and it's possible that after one or two years, your child's teachers may recommend that he transfers to a *Hauptschule* or *Realschule*. It may be wise to accept this suggestion, because in Germany it's much better to have a low-level qualification than no qualification at all. In most states, failing two years at any point in your school career automatically sets you back to a lower level education, and in all states a child is allowed just two attempts to pass the final examination.

The *Abitur* is generally reckoned to be more demanding than the UK's A Levels but less so than the French *baccalauréat*. It's widely (but not universally) recognised as an international university entrance qualification, although a student may also need to prove his capabilities in the relevant teaching language (if not German).

Gesamtschule

These are found in some parts of Germany (particularly the east) and are equivalent to a comprehensive school in the UK, where education for children of all abilities is provided under one roof, with some common classes. The traditional three-track system (*Hauptschule, Realschule, Gymnasium*) still applies, leading to three levels of graduation, although there's more opportunity for a late-developing child to move to a higher level of schooling within a *Gesamtschule*.

PRIVATE SCHOOLS

There are various alternatives to the state school system in Germany, although most aren't strictly private, and some claiming to be so are, in reality, dependent upon government funding and may operate under the same rules as state schools. Private schools normally have a higher standard of instruction but longer hours. Many new private schools are bi-lingual (English-German), which is a great advantage. At a semi-private school, the fees are determined on a sliding scale according to your income, and the school cannot be elitist about entrance requirements as they must meet a foreigner/class quota.

The largest network of private schools in Germany is *Waldorfschulen* (www. waldorfschule.de), which are 'alternative' schools based on the philosophy of Rudolf Steiner (1861-1925), known as anthroposophy. Similar in many respects to Montessori schools, which generally extend from kindergarten through to the early years of secondary education, Waldorf schools emphasise the importance of developing creativity in a child, and the curriculum places considerable emphasis on the arts. Waldorf schools have spread across the world since the first was founded in Stuttgart in 1919, but they're most heavily concentrated in Germany (although Steiner was Austrian), where there are over 230. A Waldorf school education is radically different from standard German (and most other European) schooling, and if your child must later change schools he may have trouble adapting. Students from Waldorf schools may also face prejudice from traditional Germany university admission boards.

Religious schools can also be found throughout Germany, although most depend on state funding for their survival. They operate to a large extent like German state schools, although with a greater emphasis on religious and moral instruction. Catholic schools constitute the largest group in this category, although the Lutheran Church has a nationwide network, and there are also Jewish and Moslem schools. Religious schools are heavily oversubscribed, as they're perceived to be better than state or other private schools. There's no need for a family to be practising members of a particular faith for their children to attend a religious school, but children must show due respect for its beliefs and traditions and will, of course, be required to abide by its customs, e.g. concerning diet and dress.

A limited number of pupils can attend Department of Defense Educational Activity (DODEA) schools – known as K-12 schools – run by the US Department of Defense, which are located on American military bases throughout Germany. Normally, these schools are for the children of US (and some other NATO) military personnel and other government workers. All others must apply for permission, and relatively few are approved (the admission criteria are – intentionally? – nebulous). Fees at K-12 schools are high, but they provide extensive sports facilities and instruction (basketball, American football, wrestling, track and field, and sometimes hockey and baseball) for both boys and girls. The comprehensive DODEA website (www. dodea.edu) has sections of interest to parents and potential pupils (and to those seeking teaching positions), and is frequently updated with news.

Other private school options include international schools in Germany (see below), private day schools in neighbouring countries, e.g. France or Switzerland, and boarding schools abroad. There are only around 50 boarding schools (*Internate*) in Germany.

International Schools

Germany's international schools are mostly situated in cities or regions with a high concentration of diplomats or multinational companies. Most use English as their main teaching language and are based on the American educational system. Schools range from kindergarten level to secondary schools offering the American high school diploma or International Baccalaureate. Tuition fees are generally around €10,000 or €12,500 per year, while other fees such as transport, registration and extra-curricular activities add a further around €3,000. Among the most popular international schools are:

◆ Bonn International School (www.bonn-is.de).

◆ Frankfurt International School (www.fis.edu), which has a second campus in nearby Wiesbaden (see below). The brochure claims an average class size of 20 students.

◆ International School Berlin/Potsdam (www.berlin-international-school.de). This school has become very popular as the German government and foreign embassies are located in Berlin, and many pupils are from the families of diplomats.

◆ International School of Stuttgart (www.international-school-stuttgart.de). Many of the parents of pupils enrolled at this school, which opened in 1998, work at the Daimler Benz and IBM plants.

◆ International School Wiesbaden (www.fis.edu) – a branch of the Frankfurt International School.

◆ Munich International School (www.mis-munich.de).

Enquire at your country's embassy or consulate about international schools near where you'll be living.

APPRENTICESHIPS

The vast majority of German school-leavers go into an apprenticeship (*Lehre*) rather than straight into a job. There are around 330 state-recognised occupations in Germany, ranging from publisher to ladies' tailor, carpenter to dental surgery assistant, photographer to car mechanic. All require a two- to four-year apprenticeship, the exact length of which depends on the demands of the job. Participants who've passed the *Abitur* examination may have their apprenticeship shortened by six months or even a year if they perform exceptionally well.

An apprentice receives a low salary, which is increased annually. Roughly half the working week is spent on the job and the other half at a vocational school (*Berufsschule*), where the apprentice learns the theoretical and practical skills officially required for his occupation (although not necessarily used in the workplace!). The syllabus is set out with detailed national training regulations for each occupation, drawn up by the relevant federal ministries in consultation with employers' organisations, business associations and trade unions, with the aim of ensuring a uniform qualification for each occupation in Germany.

For those who've successfully completed an apprenticeship and want to obtain a higher qualification in their chosen field, there's the *Fachabitur* (an advanced vocational certificate of education), which enables a student to attend a polytechnic (see page 127). A *Fachabitur* can be obtained by attending a vocational school, either full- or part-time.

An apprenticeship concludes with an examination marked by a board of examiners comprising employer and employee representatives and vocational school teachers. Successful candidates are awarded a certificate of fellowship (*Gesellenbrief*) in manual trades, a business assistant's certificate (*Kaufmans Gehilfen Prüfung*) in commercial occupations or a medical assistant's diploma (*Abschlussprüfung zur Arzthelfer/Apothekergehilfe*) in the case of medical assistants and chemists' assistants.

The German labour office (*Arbeitsagentur*) offers cross-training programmes (*Umschulung*) for those trained in occupations that are gradually becoming obsolete, to enable them to move into another field with better employment prospects.

For more information about apprenticeships, see www.planet-beruf.de and the Bundesagentur für Arbeit website (www.arbeitsagentur.de/content/1478794651750).

Master Programmes

After working for three years as a qualified tradesman (*Gesele*), you can attend classes to become a master tradesman (*Meister*). There are two kinds of *Meister* programme, one designed for someone wishing to run his own skilled trade business and the other for someone wanting to manage a company's apprentice programme. In most trades it's mandatory to have a *Meister* or engineer managing the business and an 'industry master' (*Industriemeister*) in charge of apprentices. There's no master tradesman qualification in medical or commercial professions. For the latter, a licence (*Lehrberechtigung*) is required to train apprentices. Any doctor, dentist or chemist is authorised to train assistants. For those wishing to attend these classes full-time but lacking the

funds, there's a Federal Tuition Assistance Programme from BAföG.

HIGHER EDUCATION

Germany has over 400 higher education institutions, including state universities (traditional and technological), private universities and colleges of education, as well as a large number of specialised establishments, such as colleges of theology, colleges of art, polytechnics and colleges of public administration (the last admitting only graduates). Anyone who passes the *Abitur* is guaranteed entry to one of these institutions, which are attended by some 30 per cent of secondary students (around 2 million).

The duration of higher education courses depends largely on students themselves. The period prescribed is usually four to six years, but most students take longer over their courses, which are completed at an average age of almost 29 (in comparison with age 23 in the UK and 24 in the US).

An excellent English-language website for prospective university students is www.educations.com/study-guides/europe/study-in-germany.

State Universities

German state universities include those at Augsburg, Bayreuth, Berlin, Bielefeld, Bonn, Bremen, Cologne, Dortmund, Dresden, Dusseldorf, Erlangen, Essen, Frankfurt, Frankfurt-an-der-Oder, Göttingen, Hamburg, Hanover, Heidelberg, Kaiserslautern, Karlsruhe, Leipzig, Mainz, Mannheim, Marburg, Munich, Münster, Osnabrück, Passau, Potsdam, Rostock, Saarbrücken, Stuttgart, Tübingen, Ulm, Weimar and Würzburg. Germany's oldest higher education institutions are the universities of Heidelberg (founded in 1386), Leipzig (1409) and Rostock (1419).

Since 1960 many new universities have been established in Germany, although many universities suffer overcrowding, with lecture halls packed to the rafters and many courses heavily over-subscribed. Nevertheless, in international comparisons, most German universities rate highly in terms of results.

Only students with the highest *Abitur* grades may choose the university they wish to attend; all others are allocated places by the Central Office for the Allocation of Study Places (Zentralstelle für die Vergabe von Studienplätzen/ZVS) in Dortmund. The allocation depends on two factors: your *Abitur* grades, and the length of time you spend waiting for a place. The *Abitur* is graded from 1 to 6, where 1 is the highest pass and 6 is a fail; the better your grades, the better the university you'll be sent to. However, many fields of study have access restrictions. For example, if you wish to study medicine, you must usually have at least a grade of 1.5.

If your grade is too low for direct admission, you can sometimes obtain access to a university education by learning a related profession first. For example, doing a three-year apprenticeship as a medical technical assistant greatly improves your chances of getting into medical school if you have low *Abitur* grades. If you fail to gain admission at your first attempt, you can improve your chances by reapplying a term or a year or two later; presumably, the fact that you're prepared to wait for admission means that you're unusually keen to obtain a place – and the longer you wait, the more likely you are to be accepted.

Great Hall, Heidelberg University

German students usually have at least one part-time job, which is one reason why they take much longer than their European counterparts to complete their studies.

Foreign students' numbers in Germany are around 150,000 or some 8 per cent of the intake to higher education establishments, over a third of whom obtained their university entrance qualification in Germany (so-called resident foreign students). Nevertheless, the government, anxious that the country could suffer academic isolation, is keen to attract more foreign students, and knowledge of German is no longer necessary. Many courses leading to internationally recognised bachelors and masters degrees are now available in English. Even for foreign students, tuition is free, and graduates are encouraged to remain in Germany to help bridge the country's skills gap.

If you wish to study at a German university but have non-German educational qualifications, your prospects will depend largely on whether your qualifications were awarded inside or outside Europe. All European qualifications (including British A Levels and the International Baccalaureate) are recognised as equivalent to the *Abitur* for the purposes of university admission. Non-European qualifications, however, including those from the US and Canada, require additional certification in order to be recognised. Each state's ministry of education has a different policy for evaluating such qualifications, with costs likely to include an administration fee plus the cost of official translations of school reports and qualifications.

Private Universities

Germany also has a number of private universities, which fall into three categories.

◆ **Private universities:** These are similar to state universities but usually affiliated to a religious organisation and focus on subjects such as theology. You must pay the tuition costs yourself.

◆ **Elite, industry-sponsored institutions:** These are designed to train the second-level management of large corporations. Gaining access to these is even more difficult than to state universities but, once you're in, a glittering career in senior management is all but guaranteed.

◆ **International universities:** Mostly of US origin, these include the well known Schiller International University in Heidelberg (www. siu-heidelberg.de). International universities mostly offer US-style diplomas, which aren't automatically recognised in Germany or in the rest of the EU, but are designed largely to allow American students a period abroad. Tuition fees are high.

Polytechnics

Polytechnics (*Fachhochschulen*) were originally intended to improve the skills of blue-collar workers but are now fully-fledged, university-level institutions. However, one tradition remains, which is that only technical subjects are taught there. Some states insist that the diploma contains the letters *FH* to show that it was obtained at a *Fachhochschule*. Some graduates from traditional universities refer rather disparagingly to polytechnic graduates as 'narrow gauge scholars'. However, an *FH* designation usually isn't a disadvantage for a graduate but quite the opposite. Many employers seek those with *FH* degrees because of the practical skills and experience they have, and such individuals are more likely to find employment shortly before or after graduation than those from regular universities.

There are specialised schools for many fields of the medical profession; these are often private, meaning that students must pay for their board and tuition. Many companies and institutions (e.g. Deutsche Telekom) operate their own polytechnics to train their engineers.

Accommodation

After gaining a university place, your first challenge will be to find somewhere to live. Although university and polytechnic courses are free, accommodation can be expensive and difficult to find. Many universities have halls of residence (*Studentenwohnheim*), but few have anywhere near enough places to meet demand, and getting a room in a hall is almost equivalent to winning the national lottery! (Not many years ago, one university had to provide homeless students with 'containers' to live in, which were originally designed for earthquake victims.) If the cost of accommodation is likely to be a problem for you, as it is for many German students, you should apply for a place at a university in a smaller town rather than in a large city, as rents are usually lower.

Degrees & Titles

There are essentially three types of degree: a *Magister*, which is a purely academic qualification, usually in an arts subject; a

Diplom, which is similar but in a science subject; and a *Staatsexamen*, which is taken by future teachers and tests their knowledge of the relevant school curriculum. Teacher-trainees must also take a second (*zweites*) *Staatsexamen* after practical experience in the field. After six terms (semesters), you take an intermediate exam (*Zwischenprüfung*), which is often regarded as the equivalent of a British BA degree, although it confers no qualification. In order to become more competitive (and comprehensible!) internationally, German universities are gradually replacing the *Diplom* and *Magister* degrees with Bachelor's and Master's degrees.

The highest qualification is a doctorate, which is highly prized – most Germans who've earned a doctorate wish to be addressed as '*Herr/Frau Doktor*'. Those with doctorates from other EU countries have the right to use the title also, but those with an American PhD can call themselves 'Doctor' in Germany only if their qualification has been recognised by a state's Ministry of Education. The procedure for this can be complicated, depending on the state. In some states (Berlin, for example), it's as simple as sending a copy of your diploma to the registrar's office, while in others you may feel as if you're doing your thesis all over again (and you must have all relevant documents translated by officially recognised translators at considerable cost).

Grants

Most German students were given grants until the early '80s, when funds were first limited to those who couldn't afford to study, then geared to the level of their financial needs, and finally converted into a loan which must be repaid (after finding a job). The situation that applies today is some way from the original intention, which was to allow anyone who qualified the opportunity to study at a university.

Student subsidies are administered by the Bundesausbildungsförderungsgesetz (BAföG), which roughly translates as Federal Promotion of Education Authority, but is the name for the assistance it provides as well as the body that dispenses it.

To qualify for a subsidy you must be an EU citizen, have a parent who has worked in Germany for at least three years or possess a permanent resident permit *(Niederlassungerlaubnis)*. To apply for a subsidy, you must provide statements showing not only your own financial resources but also those of anybody who may reasonably be expected to support you. Those under the age of 27 must provide earnings statements from their parents, and a divorced person may even be required to supply an earnings statement for his ex-spouse.

If your means (or those of your parents) are below the qualifying limit, the state pays 50 per cent of your subsidy in the form of a grant and 50 per cent as an interest-free loan, which you have up to 20 years to repay (exemptions and reductions apply to certain categories of student). There's no interest for the first five years after completion of your studies, after which you must pay a minimum monthly sum. Applications are processed locally in the town or city where you wish to study, and full information is provided (in English) on the BAföG website (www.bmbf.de/en/the-german-federal-training-assistance-act-bafog-provides-educational-opportunities-2010.html.)

DISTANCE LEARNING

Although magazines in Germany are filled with advertisements for correspondence schools, there's only one German state institution whose certificates are recognised by all European countries – the Fernuniversität (distance university) Hagen (www.fernuni-hagen.de/english). This is roughly equivalent to the UK's Open University and broadcasts some lectures via television and the internet. The Fernuniversität is designed for those who cannot afford to take time off work to study, and conditions are a little more relaxed than at normal universities. The disadvantages are that it usually takes longer to earn a diploma than through a 'normal' university, and the subjects available are somewhat limited.

Graduates of other distance learning universities, particularly those situated overseas, may have trouble getting their qualifications recognised in Germany.

EVENING CLASSES

An inexpensive way to learn German or another language in Germany is at the people's high school (*Volkshochschule*), which originated in the early 20th century as a popular education institution for the 'masses'. Schools were sponsored by left-wing political parties, including the Social Democrats, in a similar way to Workers' Educational Association (WEA) courses in the UK, although today they're government-run.

Volkshochschulen (*VHS*) offer courses in almost every imaginable subject, from basic basket weaving to ocean sailing. They also run one-day seminars on topics such as tenants' rights and weekend courses on how to repair your bicycle. The most popular courses are foreign languages, but psychology, computers, health and 'new age' subjects are also widely available, some of which may have waiting lists. Course fees seldom exceed €250 per term, plus the cost of books and other course materials.

Each *VHS* publishes a course catalogue, many running to hundreds of pages, which are usually distributed free (but sometimes for a nominal fee) via bookshops and municipal buildings. There are three ways to enrol: in person at a *VHS*, by post or online at www.

vhs.de. Enrolment periods and availability vary greatly. Places are limited, therefore you should book early. Some *VHS* courses offer an official certificate (e.g. in German proficiency) or a high school diploma, whole others are just for fun.

Private schools are less popular, probably because most Germans don't think that the quality of instruction justifies the generally high fees. Those that exist mostly survive thanks to government contracts and company clients such as international banks.

LEARNING GERMAN

If you want to make the most of the German way of life and your time in Germany, it's essential to learn German as soon as possible. For those living in Germany permanently, learning German isn't an option but a necessity. Although it isn't a particularly easy language to learn, even the least linguistically talented person can acquire a working knowledge of German. All that's required is some hard work, help and, particularly if you have only English-speaking colleagues and friends, perseverance.

Most people can help themselves a great deal through the use of books, tapes, DVDs, CDs and CD-ROMs and web-based courses. Many 'virtual classroom' courses allow you to speak to and interact with an online teacher, but for most people, attending a 'real' course (combined with one or more of the other methods listed above) is likely to be the best solution.

There's certainly no shortage of possibilities. German classes are offered by language schools (including branches of large corporations such as Berlitz), German and foreign colleges and universities, private and international schools, foreign and international organisations, local associations and clubs, and private teachers. Tuition ranges from language courses for beginners through

☑ **SURVIVAL TIP**

Your business and social enjoyment and success in Germany will be directly related to the degree to which you master German.

specialised business-related or cultural courses, to university-level courses leading to recognised diplomas. If you already speak German but need conversation practice, you may prefer to enrol in an art or craft course at the local *Volkshochschule* (see **Evening Classes** above).

There are language schools (*Sprachschulen*) in all German cities and large towns. Most run various classes, from which you can choose according to your language ability, how many hours you wish to study a week, how much money you have to spend and how quickly you want (or need) to learn. There are 'extensive' courses, comprising four to ten hours' teaching per week, 'intensive' courses (10-20 hours) and, for those for whom money is no object (hopefully your employer!), 'total immersion' courses, where you study for up to nine hours a day for five days at a cost of between €1,500 and €2,500, depending on the school. Note, however, that not everyone benefits from such intensive study, and it's generally better to spread your lessons over a longer period.

One of the most famous German-language teaching organisations is the Goethe Institut (www.goethe.de), a government-funded non-profit organisation with around 150 branches in over 90 countries across the world and 13 centres in Germany. The Goethe Institut runs general, specialist and intensive courses. The recommended method (not always possible in practice) is to start with a course in your home country at level one (*Grundstufe 1*), followed by courses at levels 2 and 3 in Germany. Courses cover speech, pronunciation, reading, writing and grammar.

All Goethe Institut instructors are university graduates with additional training in teaching German as a foreign language. Many have studied abroad or worked at an overseas branch and the high quality of the teaching is widely acknowledged. Unfortunately, the costs are high (e.g. a two-week part-time course costs around €500) and so is the number of participants (up to 16). The Goethe Institut publishes a free annual leaflet (in many languages), *Learn German in Germany*, which contains up-to-date information about the courses available at its centres in Germany, with an overview of course content, dates and prices. Goethe has a free online facility to help you practise your German skills (see www. goethe.de/prj/dfd/en/home.cfm).

You may prefer to have private lessons, which are a quicker, although generally more expensive, method of learning a language. The main advantage of private lessons is that you learn at your own pace and aren't held back by slow learners or left floundering in the wake of the class genius. You can advertise for a teacher in your local newspapers, on shopping centre/supermarket and university notice boards, and through your or your spouse's employer. Don't forget to ask friends, neighbours and colleagues if they can recommend a private teacher. Private lessons by the hour cost from around €50 at a school or €30 to €40 with a self-employed tutor.

Another possibility is to find someone who wants to learn (or improve) his English and work out some kind of reciprocal arrangement with them. This can be a very economical (or even free) way of learning German, although it depends on your having the time (and inclination) to give 'lessons' as well as to receive them.

UK citizens wishing to visit Germany to study the language and culture may be interested in programmes offered by the British Council. The Council also organises a range of international education and training exchange programmes, including the English Language Assistants' Programme, which enables modern language graduates and undergraduates to spend a year working as a language assistant in a foreign school. The British Council website contains practical information on a wide range of opportunities to work and study abroad. For information, contact the Education Section of The British Council (www.britishcouncil.org) or its office in Germany (www.britishcouncil.de/en).

ICE, high-speed train

10.
PUBLIC TRANSPORT

*P*ublic transport (*öffentlicher Verkehr/öV*) in Germany is efficient, clean, safe, comfortable and comprehensive. Integration between different modes of transport is good, although not quite up to the gold standard of Switzerland. The main modes of public transport within Germany are air, train, tram, bus and metro (subway). There are also river and lake ferries and cable cars, although these tend to be localised and cater mostly for tourists. Until 2013, inter-city services were provided largely by air and rail, although the country is now served by a comprehensive network of inexpensive inter-city bus services, alongside international bus services provided by companies such as Eurolines. Frankfurt is the hub of both rail and air services in Germany.

In major cities – and to an increasing extent also in rural areas – public transport is organised by a public transport authority (*Verkehrsverbund*), which contracts services to different companies and is responsible for integrating fares within the region, so that one ticket is accepted on all modes of transport within a city or region. Rural transport, by contrast, can be patchy, with infrequent services outside school hours. Weekend services, particularly outside tourist areas, can be sparse.

Fares may be considered high by some foreigners (although not the British). Rail fares aren't based simply on distance but also take into account the quality and speed of trains, which means that money can be saved by choosing slower trains when speed isn't important. If you're commuting regularly, it's worth buying a weekly, monthly or even an annual ticket. Many transport systems grant extra privileges to season ticket (*Abo*) holders, such as allowing other family members to accompany them free of charge during the evenings and at weekends. You can use season tickets to travel at any time on all modes of transport within the designated zone(s), with the exception of long-distance trains.

TRAINS

Newcomers are sometimes confused by the terminology used in Germany for rail systems, which include main-line railways (*Eisenbahn*), trams or light rail (*Strassenbahn*), underground (*U-Bahn*) and suburban trains (*Stadtschnellbahn* or more commonly *S-Bahn*). This section is primarily concerned with man-line railways; for other forms of rail transport, see **City Trains, Trams & Metros** on page 139.

The railway network in Germany is extensive and has seen huge investment in recent decades, with high-speed lines being built and others upgraded to cater for high-speed trains. Most main lines are electrified, as are suburban lines around the main conurbations. After unification, the railway systems of the former East and West Germany were merged to form Deutsche Bahn AG (DB AG). However, following directives from the European Union (EU), the operating arm of DB

AG was split into several companies, the most important of which are DB Reise & Turistik AG (long-distance passenger services) and DB Regio AG (local passenger traffic).

Huge investments have been made in high-speed lines in recent years and Intercity-Express (ICE) high-speed trains now connect many major cities across Germany, including Frankfurt, Hamburg, Stuttgart, Mannheim, Munich, Cologne, Berlin and Dresden. If you plan to explore neighbouring countries, international ICE trains connect Germany with Austria (Wien, Innsbruck), Belgium (Brussels, Liège), Denmark (Copenhagen, Arhus), France (Paris), the Netherlands (Arnhem, Utrecht, Amsterdam) and Switzerland (Basel, Zürich, Interlaken). In Brussels or Paris, you can connect with the Eurostar service to London, providing high-speed rail connections between Germany and the UK.

> There are currently five different types of the ICE in operation: the ICE 1, ICE 2, ICE 3, ICE T and ICE Sprinter. From December 2017 over 100 new ICE 4 trains will be added to the fleet by 2023.

Investment isn't restricted to high-speed services. In many conurbations, a new generation of rolling stock for *S-Bahn* and regional trains has been introduced, providing new standards of comfort and security. Several rural lines have benefited from tilting trains, enabling higher speeds on routes where new infrastructure cannot be justified.

In addition to DB, there are a number of private railway companies in Germany, operating branch lines or small self-contained networks. Many are fully or partly owned by the states and in several recent cases have been successful in obtaining operating contracts for regional passenger services from the *Verkehrsverbünde*, and are now fully integrated into the local transport network.

First-class rail travel is popular in Germany, and not just among expense-account businessmen. One reason is that discount fares (see **Fares** on page 137) also apply to first-class tickets, and many passengers consider the extra comfort and space well worth the extra cost.

General railway information is available from the DB website (www.bahn.de/en), which has links to many other information pages, plus timetables.

Types of Train

Passenger trains are classified according to their speed, the distance they cover, and the type of service they offer, as shown below:

♦ *InterCity Express* (*ICE*): Deutsche Bahn's flagship trains travel at up to 320kph (200mph) on selected routes, usually with regular-interval timetables. Seating, entirely of the reclining variety, is arranged in either compartments or open-plan carriages (coaches), with panoramic windows and air-conditioning. You can plug a headset into the audio system in your armrest to access six music channels, while individual video screens and a copy of the *Financial Times Deutschland Kompakt* are available free in first class. First-class seats also have sockets for laptops and an amplified mobile phone signal for business travellers. First class passengers receive breakfast and a taxi service at their destination. The *ICE T* is a tilting train that takes bends at up to 220kph (138mph). Needless to say, *ICE* trains are the most expensive to use.

♦ The *ICE Sprinter* is DB's fastest direct trains between cities, taking less than four hours between Frankfurt/Berlin, Hanover/Hamburg and Munich. Complimentary snacks, soft drinks and daily newspapers are provided for first class passengers, who can choose from three 'comfort categories'; other features include an electricity socket and a service call button at each seat, not to mention card telephones. There's also a cocktail and espresso bar, and hire car bookings can be made from trains (and be waiting at the station on your arrival).

◆ **InterCity (IC)**: express trains operating on major internal routes at a speed of up to 200kph (125mph), with first- and second-class carriages, usually including a restaurant or bistro car.

◆ **EuroCity (EC)**: *IC* trains serving destinations outside Germany;

◆ **InterRegioExpress (IRE)**: limited-stop trains connecting regional centres, with a minimum two-hour frequency and an average speed of at least 90kph (55mph);

◆ **Schnellzug (D)**: other limited-stop fast trains, including international services, e.g. to Rome, Warsaw and Budapest;

◆ **StädteExpress (SE)**: limited-stop local trains linking with the major conurbations;

◆ **RegionalExpress (RE)**: local trains operating a limited-stop service;

◆ **RegionalBahn (RB)**: local trains stopping at all stations on their route;

◆ **S-Bahn** (originally *Stadtschnellbahn*): suburban services inside the *Verkehrsverbünde* (see **City Trains, Trams & Metros** on page 139).

Each train has a unique number (like the flight number for aircraft) which is prefixed by one of the above abbreviations, so there should be no confusion about the type of train or the fares applicable. Most trains have a sign on each coach indicating its destination and route details. *ICE* trains usually have on-board electronic displays, as well as an information screen at the entrance area to carriages, providing details of connections and other information. When not otherwise in use the screen shows the train's speed.

Restaurant or bistro and trolley facilities are available on *IC*, *ICE* and *EC* trains. *IRE* trains also usually have a bistro car as well as a trolley service. A small number of *RE* and *SE* trains offer a limited refreshment service from a trolley. As in France, double-decker trains are becoming increasingly common on *RE* and *SE* services (these have been in use much longer in eastern Germany and are often found there in rural areas).

Accommodation

Accommodation on trains varies with the train type. *ICE* trains have carriages that are mostly 'open', with two or three compartments at the end of each coach. *EC* and *D* trains have carriages with either compartments or open accommodation, whereas *IRE* trains have a mixture of compartments and semi-open 'bays'. On *ICE* trains, you can book a particular seat, whereas on other trains you can choose only between a compartment or an open carriage, a window or a corridor seat and (if you book two seats) facing or adjacent seats. All trains are non-smoking.

Note that you cannot choose a forward-facing or backward-facing seat, as many trains change direction during the course of their journey, although in older *IC* trains seats in first-class 'open' carriages are reversible. Virtually all trains, including some *S-Bahn* trains, have both first- and second-class carriages.

On *Sprinter* trains (see above), accommodation is divided into four zones, which you choose when booking your ticket and seat:

◆ **Office Zone:** clear mobile telephone reception, fax service and business magazines for sale;

◆ **Silence Zone:** quiet atmosphere (mobile telephone- and computer-free), seats in rows, a choice of music programmes with headphones, and blankets and pillows available;

◆ **Club Zone:** individual choice of films (DVD players), clear mobile telephone reception, area for families with children, and a coach equipped for disabled passengers;

◆ **Traveller Zone:** the second-class area with none of the above creature comforts.

The majority of coaches in *EC* and *IC* trains are air-conditioned, as are all *ICE* trains and the latest generation of *S-Bahn* trains. Many trains have toilets with wheelchair access. *ICE* trains have two toilets per carriage (male and female) in second class.

Tickets

You must buy a ticket before travelling by train. If you don't, you'll end up paying a higher fare or even a penalty. Bear in mind that ticket checks are routine, as each train usually has a team of staff rather than a single conductor. Tickets for rail travel can be purchased from a variety of sources, including the following (the last two being the cheapest):

◆ travel centres or booking offices at stations;

◆ authorised travel agents (note that you may be charged an additional handling fee by the agency);

◆ ticket machines at stations. These are usually 'touch screen' and tickets may be purchased with cash (notes and coins), money card (*Geldkarte*), debit card (*EC Karte*) or by credit card.

◆ via the internet (www.bahn.com/en/view/index.shtml) using a credit or debit card; tickets can be posted to you, collected at a nominated station, or printed via a machine by entering a personal identification number (PIN). You can also print them on a computer at home if you're a *BahnCard* holder (see below) or have a credit card.

◆ Tickets can be purchased on board some long-distance trains but a surcharge is payable. Tickets cannot be purchased on local trains operated by a *Verkehrsverbund* and anyone discovered travelling without a ticket is regarded as a 'black traveller' (*Schwarzfahrer*) or 'fare dodger' and liable to an on-the-spot fine. Fines vary depending on the *Verkehrsverbund* but average around €40.

◆ *RE*, *SE* and *S-Bahn* trains operating within major conurbations can be used with the same ticket.

Fares

DB's fare structure is intended to be simple but not everyone has found this to be the case, and a pocket calculator is a useful accessory for travellers. A huge range of fares is offered with many discounts, some of which can be combined. Prices are based on the speed and comfort provided as well as the distance covered. Premium trains attract premium fares and there's no set 'per kilometre' tariff; the longer the journey, the lower the fare per kilometre. The most common fares are summarised below, some of which are subject to availability:

♦ **Standard (basic) fare:** These vary with the length of the journey, longer journeys costing less per kilometre. There are no discounts on these fares, except for those with *Gruppe & Spar* tickets (see below). You may either exchange your ticket for another or obtain a full refund if you decide not to travel, provided you do this before the day of validity (there's no charge).

♦ **Kostenloser Kindermitnahme:** Children up to 14 can travel free when accompanied by their parents or grandparents. If they're on their own, they receive a 50 per cent discount. They can receive a further 25 per cent discount if they have a *Bahncard* (see below).

♦ **Mitfahrer-Rabatt:** One person pays the full fare and up to four others travel for half price. For groups of six or more, Gruppe & Spar tariffs apply (see below).

♦ **Europa-Spezial:** Starting from around €40 one-way you can travel to many popular European destinations. Tickets are booked online and travel must be completed within one month.

♦ **London-Spezial:** Starting from €59 one-way for travel to London, tickets must be booked online and travel completed within one month.

♦ **Sparpreis 25 & 50:** These discounted tickets are subject to availability and,

although you may cancel, a fee of between €15 and €30 is incurred, depending on how late this is done. Two under-14s count as one adult. You receive a discount of between 25 and 50 per cent when you book three days or more in advance and a 50 per cent discount at weekends. This deal is also applicable with the *Mitfahrer-Rabatt* (see above).

♦ **BahnCard:** A discount card offering a 25, 50 or 100 per cent discount on all fares, including Mitfahrer-Rabatt, Kostenloser Kindermitnahme and Sparpreis fares. The *BahnCard* 25 and *BahnCard* 50 offer holders a 25 or 50 per cent discount respectively on standard long distance rail fares, while a Mobility *BahnCard* 100 allows unlimited free travel on most of the German railway network.

♦ **Gruppe & Spar**: 50 to 70 per cent discounted fares apply to six or more people travelling together (two under-14s counting as one adult) and are subject to availability. These tickets can be booked between six months and one year in advance.

Other tickets: Rail & Fly tickets are airline tickets that include free or reduced-price travel on German railways. Other tickets offer reduced fares for journeys to specific destinations at specific times, such as for the annual carnival in Berlin. They're explained in detail at www. bahn.de.

♦ **Schönes-Wochenende-Ticket:** a 'beautiful weekend ticket' valid nationwide (and in some areas of Poland) on Saturdays and Sundays from midnight to 3am the following day, e.g. from midnight Friday/Saturday to 3am on Sunday, for unlimited travel on local trains (*RE*, *RB*, *SE*, *S-Bahn*) in second class. The cost is €40 for up to five people travelling together, or for parents or grandparents with an unlimited number of their own children or grandchildren up to 14 years of age. The *Schönes-Wochenende-Ticket* is also valid on many local *U-Bahn* trains, trams and buses (you can take a bicycle with you for an additional payment). Remember to write your name (or the name of someone accompanying you) on the ticket before travel begins.

◆ **Länder-Ticket:** This is a 'rover' ticket that allows unlimited travel in one of Germany's 16 federal states for a little as €3 per person. It's valid from 9am any weekday until 3am the following day on local trains (*IRE, RE, RB* and *S-Bahn*) in second class, along with other forms of local public transport. Up to five people, or parents/grandparents with an unlimited number of their own children or grandchildren up to the age of 14, can use it. Conditions vary slightly from state to state. Remember to write your name (or the name of someone accompanying you) on the ticket before travel commences.

◆ **Local transport system all-inclusive tickets:** Usually up to 72 hours' unlimited travel in a particular city and surrounding area, using the entire local transport network. Ticket prices vary but they're usually a bargain and are listed on the DB website, where you select the state and local area to view the details.

Bookings

Bookings can be made for all *ICE, IC, EC, IRE* and *D* trains up to three months in advance to a few minutes before departure. The latest *ICE* trains have automatic booking systems, allowing seats to be reserved even after a train has left its starting station. Bookings (fee €2) are highly recommended on inter-city routes, particularly on Fridays and Sundays, when trains can become very crowded, even in first class. If you want to reserve a seat for a disabled person (and companions) contact the Mobilitäts Service Zentrale (01805-512512).

Bicycles

Bicycles can normally be taken on local trains (*RE, SE, S-Bahn, RB*) and on the *U-Bahn*, and stored in luggage and entrance areas, provided space is available, although in some cases their transportation is restricted to certain carriages (indicated by a bicycle logo). Bikes can also be taken on some long-distance trains, indicated by a similar logo. Booking is recommended during peak holiday times between the beginning of March and the end of November. Reserving a place for your bike is obligatory on some long-distance trains, but is free. DB provides advice and assistance on its cyclist's hotline (01805-599 6633).

If you don't want the hassle of taking your own bike with you, you can hire one on arrival through DB's 'Call-A-Bike' service, available in over 50 cities. For information, see www.callabike-interaktiv.de. More traditional bike hire companies usually operate close to stations, but these aren't associated with DB and rates vary.

Information

Large electronic displays show train departure and arrival details and platform information. Note, however, that only a limited number of stops for any given route are shown on these. At the entrance to each platform is a display board indicating the next arriving or departing train, again with the main (but not all) destinations. On the platform itself there's usually a *Wagenstandanzeiger*, a diagram showing each carriage for every train stopping at the platform with its number (and destination, if different from the rest of the train), alongside a series of letters from A to E. These letters relate to sections (*Abschnitte*) marked on the platform surface, so that it's easy to see precisely where your carriage will stop. This is important on long platforms where trains may stop for only a few minutes and you won't have time to rush from one end to the other looking for your carriage. This information also appears in simplified form on the platform display screen.

DB has an easy-to-use website in English (www.bahn.com/en/view/offers/other/seat-reservation.shtml) that provides extensive details of train times, categories of trains and offers, e.g. saver fares. If you don't want the expense of an *ICE*, for example, you can exclude this type of train, or any other, from your search.

DB's online information isn't restricted to Germany and information about all European railways can be accessed via the website, together with a range of bus and other local transport information.

CITY TRAINS, TRAMS & METROS

Some 13 cities and regions are served by urban rail networks (S-Bahn), while many cities (around 50) have tram (Strassenbahn) networks and a few also have metro (*U-Bahn* – underground, subway) networks.

City Trains (*S-Bahn*): There is no easy definition of an *S-Bahn* (an abbreviation of *Stadtschnellbahn*) system, which is the most local type of railway stopping at all stations in and around a city. They're much slower than mainline railways but usually serve as fast crosstown services within a city. Most *S-Bahn* systems are built on older local railways or in some cases parallel to an existing dual track railway. Most use existing local mainline railway tracks, but a few branches run on purpose built lines. Trains typically use overhead electricity lines or a third rail for traction power.

Lines may run alongside a metro network (or be superimposed on it) and often operate underground in the city centre and can be distinguished by a sign showing a green circle with a white 'S' in the centre (*S-Bahn* line numbers have an 'S' prefix). Peak hour or less-frequent services on branch lines have a different number, usually an extra digit; for example, the S11 may be a peak hour variation of the S1. At a main station, the *S-Bahn* often runs from underground platforms (*Gleis*) separated from the main part of the station. The prefix for night lines is 'N', which applies to both trams and buses.

Most *S-Bahnen* are operated by DB under contract to the local *Verkehrsverbund*. Stopping points are normally further apart than on the *U-Bahn* and trains are generally less frequent – every 15-20 minutes is typical – with routes extending into the surrounding towns and countryside. Nevertheless, both *U*- and *S-Bahnen* are fully integrated into city transport systems and can be used with normal city transport tickets. Some *S-Bahn* trains have first-class carriages. If you want to take advantage of the exclusivity (it's rarely any more comfortable than standard class) you must buy a *Zuschlag* ticket from a machine.

Trams (*Strassenbahn*): Some 50 German cities operate tram (*Strassenbahn*) or light rail (*Stadtbahn*) services, an increasing number of which run underground in city centres. In the Ruhr, high-speed tramlines are also referred to as the *U-Bahn* (metro) but confusingly often have the word *Stadtbahn* superimposed on the U. The

Stadtbahn scheme is not to be confused with the *S-Bahn* (see above), which commonly is a *suburban* railway operating under the Railways Act, while the *Stadtbahn* typically is an *urban* railway operating under the Tramways Act. In the last 30 years there has been a renaissance in tram and light rail systems, during which older systems have been modernised and expanded and many new networks built.

Metro (*U-bahn*): The term U-Bahn was created at the beginning of the 20th century in Berlin, where Germany's first metro system opened in 1902. Only Berlin, Hamburg, Munich and Nuremberg have genuine metro (*U-bahn* or *Untergrundbahn*) networks, with all other cities having upgraded tramways. Sometimes, as in Stuttgart, Frankfurt (where only line U4 is a true metro line) and Cologne, these have developed into an independent metro railway (*U-Bahn*), and stations are distinguished by large signs showing a white 'U' on a blue background.

U- and *S-Bahn* services are both numbered, in contrast with similar services in other countries, where a line may have a name and/ or a colour allocated to it. *U-Bahn* routes, not surprisingly, are numbered with a U prefix.

BUSES

The are two main types of buses in Italy, city or local buses and long-distance and rural buses.

City Buses

In all major cities, and in many smaller towns, bus services are provided by a division of the local authority (*Verkehrsbetriebe* or *Stadtwerke*). The scale of these operations varies enormously, from the extensive route networks of Berlin, Hamburg and Munich to just two or three routes in small towns. Services are mainly operated with standard buses, although there are trolleybuses in some towns, e.g. Eberswalde (northeast of Berlin), Esslingen (south of Stuttgart) and Solingen (in the Ruhr). In Wuppertal there's the *Schwebebahn*, a suspended monorail operating along the River Wupper, which isn't merely for tourists but is an integral part of the local transport system.

In the major conurbations, bus services are co-ordinated by the regional *Verkehrsverbund*, where common fare systems and timetables cover all public transport within the area. The largest example is the Verkehrsverbund Rhein-Ruhr, covering an area of over 5,000km^2 (1,930mi^2) in the industrial Ruhr area, incorporating almost 900 routes providing services to over 20 major towns and cities in the region. Such services are integrated with local trains (*S-Bahn*) operated by Deutsche Bahn (DB).

In some towns, local bus services are also provided by a DB subsidiary company. Some can be identified by a variation on the old DB bus livery of strawberry pink and grey, although many companies are now introducing their own liveries.

If you have a *BahnCard* (see page 137), you should check whether the service is run by DB or a subsidiary, as you're entitled to a discount on DB services.

Regional bus companies are mainly owned by DB and tend to offer inter-urban (although not inter-city) services, as well as services linking major towns to outlying villages. In most cases, these operate in conjunction with regional train services and generally the bus terminus is adjacent to the railway station. However, services are severely limited on some rural routes, the frequency of buses being calculated per week rather than per day. Many services cater mainly for schoolchildren (although anyone can use them) and therefore operate only from Mondays to Fridays (sometimes also Saturdays) at the start and end of the school day, and not at all during school holidays.

Bus (and tram/trolleybus) services don't generally operate between around 1am and 5am, but most larger cities have an hourly night bus service – indicated by an 'N' prefix – covering the most popular destinations.

Long-distance Buses

While most European countries have had a system of long distance buses for decades, intercity bus travel was virtually non-existent in Germany until 2013. Under a 1930s law, the German railways were protected from competition from intercity buses on journeys over 50km. However, in 2013 this protection was removed, leading to a significant shift from rail to bus for long journeys. Intercity buses now offer budget friendly transport alternatives to a wide range of domestic, and a handful of international, destinations. Buses may be slower and less comfortable than trains but in many cases are much cheaper.

Flixbux (www.flixbus.com) controls around 90 per cent of the long distance bus market in Germany, offering 100,000 daily connections to over 1,000 destinations in 20 European countries. The company expanded organically (green buses!), buying several competitors, and offers very competitive fares. You can buy tickets online via their bus app, in a FlixBus store or directly from the bus driver. Snacks and drinks are available from drivers, and buses have free wifi and plug sockets for laptops (etc.). There are a number of smaller competitors, including Deinbus (www.deinbus. de/en).

Deutsche Bahn's IC (InterCity) bus service provides a comfortable and inexpensive way to travel from abroad to many German cities and vice versa. Passengers benefit from scores of connections to other modes of long-distance and regional transport. You can travel for as little as €10 single from, e.g. Eindhoven to Dusseldorf or from Berlin to Rostock, with an IC Bus saver fare. You can choose your personal entertainment programme in the IC Bus entertainment portal on most routes. For more information see www.bahn.com/en/view/offers/bus/index.shtml.

Eurolines (www.eurolines.de/en) predates the opening of the bus market in Germany and offers both domestic and international services, particularly to eastern European countries. It also offers a business class service on selected routes.

A useful website for international bus travellers is Bus Radar (www.busradar.com), an intercity bus search engine for inexpensive bus tickets.

> ## ☑ SURVIVAL TIP
>
> Several public transport authorities offer the facility to book a taxi to meet a bus or tram at a nominated stopping point, particularly during the evening or at night. There's usually no extra charge for this service.

FERRIES

There's a variety of ferry (*Fährboot*) and shipping services in Germany. Major rivers, such as the Rhine and Main, have a number of ferry crossings for cars and foot passengers, and some major cities include ferry services in their range of public transport services, which are usually covered by a standard ticket. Examples are the river services in Hamburg and the lake services in Berlin, each of which forms an integral part of the local public transport system. Ferry services on Lake Constance (*Bodensee*) are provided by the Stadtwerke Konstanz Company; the *Bodensee Pass* offers a 50 per cent reduction on transport in this area, including ferries.

A number of companies operate international ferry services between Germany and the Baltic states and Scandinavia. There are also good connections from the German mainland to the outlying Frisian Islands, usually run in conjunction with trains or express buses.

CABLE CARS & FUNICULARS

Cable cars (*Seilbahnen*) and rack railways (*Zahnradbahnen*) can be found in the more mountainous areas of Germany, particularly the northern Alps in Bavaria. Here you'll find the famous *Zugspitzbahn*, an electrified rack railway running some 18.6km (12mi) from Garmisch-Partenkirchen at an altitude of around 700m (2,300ft) to the top station at 2,650m (8,694ft).

Funiculars (*Drahtseilbahnen*) are found in several of the hillier towns in Germany, and include the *Nerobergbahn* in Wiesbaden, operated by a water-balance system, the two-stage line in Heidelberg and an ancient line in Stuttgart. Stuttgart also has the only rack railway (actually a tramway) to be integrated into a city transport network (at Degerloch on Route 10). Dresden has a hill-climbing *Schwebebahn* (suspension railway) and a more conventional funicular.

TAXIS

Taxis are easy to identify in Germany, where they're painted in a standard cream livery and have an illuminated '*Taxi*' sign on the roof. Many are Mercedes or other quality makes. Fares are fixed by local authorities and shown on a meter inside the vehicle, and usually consist of a minimum fare plus a variable kilometre or elapsed time rate. Rates for evenings and weekends are usually higher. Taxis can be hailed in the street or hired from official taxi ranks (stand) at railway stations, airports, and bus and tram termini. Taxis can be summoned to your home by telephone for around €1. If you need to stow luggage in the boot there's a fee of around €1 per bag.

Uber

Uber (www.uber.com/info/uber-in-berlin) operates an inexpensive taxi service in Berlin and other German cities using private drivers operating private cars, which can be booked via a mobile phone using a special app. To start using Uber as a passenger, you must signup and create an account, after which you download and install an app on

your mobile phone. Bookings are made via the app and payment is via a debit or credit card, so you don't need to pay (or tip!) the driver. You must be aged 18 to use Uber (or 21 to be a driver).

Needless to say regular taxi services (and private 'minicabs') have been hard hit by Uber – which is allegedly already worth some $60 billion worldwide! – and licensed taxi drivers have staged protests in a number of cities. A number of court rulings – for example regarding using unlicensed drivers – in Germany and France have gone against the company and it can expect more legal challenges.

AIRLINE SERVICES

Germany is well served by airlines, both domestic and international, and boasts the fourth-busiest airport in Europe (Frankfurt), as well as numerous smaller airports. The national carrier is Lufthansa (see below), which is supported by a number of large charter holiday airlines.

Lufthansa

The national airline, Lufthansa, is one of the world's largest passenger and freight carriers, flying to around 200 cities in some 85 countries and operating over 700 aircraft. It was a founding member of the 'Star Alliance' with 28 other major airlines, including Air Canada, Air New Zealand, British Midland, Continental, Singapore Airlines, SAS Scandinavian, Thai, United Airlines and US Airways. One of its most successful innovations has been the 'Miles and More' frequent flyer reward programme, which recognises air miles flown with other Star Alliance members (see www.miles-and-more. com for more information).

Lufthansa's hub is Frankfurt Airport, with a secondary base at Munich International Airport. Flights within Europe offer business and economy classes, while intercontinental flights include first class. Lufthansa aircraft are equipped throughout with leather seats, which can be widened in business class to provide additional room. All flights are non-smoking. Passengers can make bookings via the Lufthansa website (www.lufthansa. com), which also provides flight information, timetables, offers and other information. Economy seat assignments can be reserved only on intercontinental flights (on European flights seats are allocated at check-in). Flights are often full during school holiday periods (see page 117), which are listed in most diaries and calendars, therefore you should book early.

In addition to check-in facilities at airports, Lufthansa provides a check-in service at certain railway stations, including Cologne, Frankfurt and Stuttgart, where you can check in your luggage and receive boarding cards. On the return trip you can check your bags at the airport and pick them up at the station. You can collect your ticket from a quick check-in machine, the check-in counter or online (choosing your seat and printing out your own boarding pass). You can fly to any airport in Germany and continue your journey by rail from just €29 to almost anywhere in Germany (see www.lufthansa.com/uk/en/rail-and-fly-in-germany).

Over 60 airports around the world provide dedicated lounges for holders of Lufthansa first, business and frequent traveller cards, and at a further 80 airports you can use the executive lounges of its partner airlines.

Other Airlines

Other German airlines include Air Berlin (www. airberlim.com), Germany's second-largest airline and Europe's seventh-largest in terms of passenger numbers. It maintains hubs at Berlin's Tegel and Düsseldorf airports and operates a domestic network to around a dozen cities, plus some European and intercontinental services (mainly to the Caribbean and the Americas)

CityLine (www.lufthansacityline.com), a Lufthansa subsidiary, offers some 350 flights per day to 60 destinations in continental Europe. It has hubs at Frankfurt and Munich airports, flying Embraer E-190/195 and Bombardier CRJ-900 aircraft.

Condor (www.condor.com) is a German holiday airline based in Frankfurt whose flights are mostly sold as part of a holiday package. It's a subsidiary of the British Thomas Cook Group, but partners with its former parent Lufthansa. It's the largest such airline in Germany, and provides around 500 flights a week during the peak season to over 70 international destinations. Its modern fleet consists of Boeing 757, 767, and Airbus A320 aircraft.

Airports

The main international airports in Germany are Berlin (Tegel and Schönefeld), Cologne-Bonn, Dusseldorf, Frankfurt (see below), Hamburg and Munich. There are many smaller airports that provide limited international services, including Dresden, Hanover and Leipzig-Halle, some of which handle only charter flights.

Long- and short-term parking is available at all major airports, including reserved parking for the disabled, and all major airports have wheelchairs and ambulance staff on hand to help disabled travellers, although it's wise to make arrangements in advance. Lufthansa also provides flight attendant services (for a fee) for children aged over five travelling alone. International airports have shopping centres that are usually open 24 hours a day, seven days a week. The table below shows the contact details (flight information, etc.) for Germany's major airports and bus or rail services to the city centre.

Frankfurt

Frankfurt International is Germany's most important airport and the fourth-busiest in Europe (after London-Heathrow, Paris-Charles de Gaulle and Amsterdam Schipol), handling over 60 million passengers a year. The airport is huge with two terminals (a third is being constructed), five 'halls' (A-C in Terminal 1, D and E in Terminal 2) and six floors (four

Airport Contacts & Public Transport

Airport	Website	Telephone	Transport to City Centre
Berlin Tegel	www.berlin-airport.de	0180-5000 186	Express bus X9 or bus109 (20 to 25 mins)
Berlin Schönefeld	www.berlin.airport.de	0180-5000 186	S-Bahn to Hauptbahnhof (30 mins)
Cologne-Bonn	www.airport-cgn.de	02203-4040	Shuttle bus 170 (20 mins)
Dusseldorf	www.flughafen -duesseldorf.de	0211-4210	S-Bahn S7 (13 mins)
Frankfurt	www.frankfurt-airport.de	0180-5372 4636	S-Bahn S8 or S9 (12 mins)
Hamburg	www.ham.airport.de	040-50750	Airport Exp. bus (25 mins)
Hanover	www.hanover.airport.de	0511-9770	S-Bahn S5 (12 mins)
Munich	www.munich-airport.de	089-97500	S-Bahn S1 or S8 (40 mins)
Stuttgart	www.flughafen-stuttgart.de	01805-948 4444	S-Bahn S2 or S3 (25 mins)

☑ **SURVIVAL TIP**

After checking in, you'll find the gate number for your flight (if known) on your boarding card. Gate numbers consist of a Hall letter (A to E) and a number. It's wise to locate your gate well in advance of the departure time as it may entail a long walk.

For passengers requiring overnight accommodation, there's a Sheraton Hotel in the terminal complex and at least 15 other hotels nearby, many accessible by courtesy shuttle buses and taxis. There's a hotel information and booking desk in each terminal. Several hotels offer a 'park & fly' service, with a room rate combined with short or medium-term secure parking.

in Terminal 1 and two in Terminal 2); finding your way around can be difficult, and you may have to walk long distances. It may be worthwhile perusing the airport website (www. frankfurt-airport.de) and printing a map. The two terminals are linked by the free 'Sky Line Shuttle', a driverless electric train running every two minutes (journey time is also two minutes). The Sky Line 'station' in Terminal 1 is above Departure Hall B, and in Terminal 2 it's on Level 4. You must take the shuttle to get from Hall C to Hall D.

11.
MOTORING

With the fourth highest level of car ownership in Europe after Luxembourg, Cyprus and Italy, Germany has some 50 million registered cars or around 600 vehicles per 1,000 inhabitants. Although the country has an excellent road system, which includes some 226,500km (140,312mi) of main roads, it's notorious for traffic jams (*Staue*) which can be encountered at any time. In addition to the expected congestion during rush hours, roads are usually clogged during school and public holidays, when millions of Germans take to their cars.

Germany's motorway (*Autobahn*) network covers some 13,000km (8,000mi) and provides direct connections between most German cities. There's no official speed limit on around half of Gernam motorways, where speeds in excess of 160kph (100mph) are common and high-performance cars can be seen – if you don't blink – zooming by at well over 200kph (125mph). However, Germany is a relatively safe country in which to drive, with a road death rate of around 4 people per 100,000 population, which is lower than France (around 5 per 100,000) but higher than the UK (3 per 100,000).

The German authorities are strict regarding traffic laws and police the roads assiduously and effectively, using not only patrol cars but also cameras, which are more common than in most other European countries. Cameras are stationed at strategic points (such as traffic lights) throughout the country, and photographs show not only your number plate and the date, time and location, but also your face (or the face of the person who has stolen your car!). You may not be aware that you've been caught on camera until a traffic ticket arrives in the post a few days later.

In order to reduce air pollution, most German cities have established 'Environmental Green Zones' (Umweltzonen) in recent years, indicated by a sign. To drive in such a zone a vehicle must meet certain exhaust emission standards, according to a vehicles environmental badge (a coloured windscreen sticker): green (class 4), yellow (class 3) and red (class 2). However, since 2017, if a vehicle doesn't qualify for a level-4 (green) environmental sticker it's likely to be barred from all green zones; vehicles without a valid badge can be fined €80. Green zones also apply to foreign-registered vehicles, which can obtain an environmental badge prior to visiting Germany (see www.environmental-badge.co.uk).

> To check whether alpine passes are open, visit www.alpineroads.com, where you can even see live webcam footage.

Traffic information is readily available thanks to regular radio and TV announcements, where the audience is encourage to call to warn others about accidents and jams. Recorded traffic information is also provided by the German motoring organisation ADAC (224 99) and signs on motorways show the radio frequency on which road and traffic bulletins are broadcast.

IMPORTING A VEHICLE

If you plan to bring a motor vehicle to Germany, either temporarily or permanently, you should be aware of any restrictions or requirements that may apply. All vehicles manufactured outside the EU must meet German specifications (see **General Operating Licence** on page 150) and may therefore need to be modified. The question of finding parts and service facilities for foreign-made vehicles should also be considered before deciding to import a car rather than buying one in Germany. Add to this the cost of import duty and VAT (see below) and you may think twice before bringing a car with you.

> You're permitted to drive an imported vehicle with foreign number plates for up to 12 months, provided the vehicle's registration remains valid (a registration document with a German translation is required), but duty and tax (where applicable – see below) must normally be paid after six months.

Duty & VAT

Vehicles registered in a non-EU country are normally subject to import duty (*Zoll*) and value added tax (*Mehrwertsteuer*), either when entering Germany or at a later date. Normally, vehicles imported for private use for a maximum of six months (which don't need to be consecutive) in any 12-month period are exempt from duty and tax. It's strictly forbidden to lend, hire, give or sell a temporarily imported vehicle to a citizen of an EU member country. If this exception applies, VAT must be paid at the time of importation and is refunded by the customs office upon departure.

If you're moving from a non-EU country and establishing residence, your vehicle may be considered part of your household goods and therefore exempt from taxation provided the following criteria are met:

- you can prove that you've been resident outside the EU for the last 12 months;

- the vehicle has been in your possession and was registered abroad by you at least six months before your arrival in Germany;

- you register your residence in Germany;

- the vehicle is for personal use only;

- the vehicle is immediately registered with the local motor vehicle office (see **Registration** below);

- the vehicle isn't given away, sold, lent or hired in the year after its importation.

If no duty or tax is payable, a customs exemption certificate (*Unbedenklichkeitsbe scheinigung*) is issued. This document is required when registering the vehicle in Germany (see below). In the case of non-EU vehicles that don't qualify for exemption, the following charges are levied, irrespective of the type of vehicle being imported:

- import duty of 10 per cent, based on the purchase price plus freight costs and insurance to the place of destination in Germany;

◆ value added tax at 19 per cent, based on the purchase price plus freight costs and import duty.

You're required to present a dealer's invoice as evidence of the purchase price of the vehicle. If, however, customs officials don't consider this a fair and accurate representation of the vehicle's market value, they may calculate their own figure by reference to a dealer's car buying guide (the standard one is the *Schwacke Liste*) or obtain a certified appraisal (*Wertgutachten*). Appraisals can be arranged in Germany with local branches of the Dekra (www.dekra.de) organisation (listed in telephone books and on the internet), but the authorities recommend that private importers without a recent invoice for their vehicle or who ship an uncommon type of car should have their vehicle appraised before declaring its value.

Once payment has been made, a customs receipt or clearance certificate (*Zollquittung*) is issued, which is required when registering a vehicle in Germany (see below). Some shipping agencies will complete the clearance and customs formalities on your behalf.

TECHNICAL INSPECTION & EMISSIONS TEST

A regular technical inspection (*Fahrzeughauptuntersuchung* or *HU*) made by a certified expert is required by law for all vehicles registered in Germany. An inspection must be made when a car is imported or is three years old and thereafter every two years. The Technischer Überwachungsverein (TÜV) and the private Dekra organisation (www.dekra. de) maintain test centres in most towns and cities, listed on the internet.

The inspection costs between €50 and €60, depending on where you live, and a re-inspection after a failure €10 to €30, which must be carried out within one month of the original inspection. The car's mechanical condition is checked for compliance with the relevant safety standards, which cover brakes, lights, chassis, shock absorbers, tyres, etc. The vehicle is also tested for general roadworthiness. You don't always need an appointment and can just turn up at an inspection centre and have it done on the spot, although it's advisable to make a booking.

If your vehicle fails the inspection you're told what repairs or alterations are necessary before it can be re-tested. When your vehicle is approved a small circular sticker (*TÜVplakette*) is affixed to the rear number plate by the test centre and a certificate issued; these state the expiry date (the number in the inner circle indicates the year when the next inspection is due and the outer circle the month). If you're discovered driving a vehicle with an expired inspection sticker you can expect to be fined and given a short period in which to have the car tested; if it isn't tested within this period, you won't be permitted to drive it until it passes the inspection. You must also pay a fine for an overdue inspection, which depends on how long overdue it is. After any major alterations or accident repairs, a vehicle must be tested to determine whether the modifications or repairs influence its handling or operating characteristics, in which case its certificate can be revoked.

An exhaust emissions test (*Abgassonderuntersuchung* or *AU*) is also required and is carried out at the same time as the *BU* and thereafter every two years for modern vehicles. Older vehicles (generally those manufactured before 1980) must be tested annually. The test costs between €20 and €40, which includes any necessary minor repairs. You receive one sticker for both the *BU* and *AU* tests. German-registered vehicles must also display an environmental sticker (*Umweltplakette*), which is required to enter a green zone (*Umweltzone*) in most German cities. Note that if a vehicle doesn't qualify for a (level-4) green environmental sticker it's likely to be barred from all green zones.

Certificates for both the technical inspection and emissions test are required when registering a motor vehicle (see below), and must be carried in the vehicle or by the driver at all times.

REGISTRATION

You must register your vehicle if one or more of the following apply:

◆ the vehicle was purchased in Germany;

◆ you've imported a vehicle and plan to stay longer than 12 months;

◆ you've imported a vehicle whose foreign registration has expired.

Only residents and resident companies can register a vehicle, either directly or via an authorised representative with power of attorney.

GENERAL OPERATING LICENCE

Vehicles can usually be registered only if a general operating licence (*allgemeine Betriebserlaubnis*) for the model has been issued by the Federal Motor Vehicle Authority (Kraftfahrtbundesamt/KBA), which certifies that the model conforms to German technical, safety and pollution-control standards. The general inspection is instigated by the manufacturer or importer when a new model is launched, and the KBA issues a specification (*Kraftfahrzeugbrief* or *Kfz-Brief*) for each model listing its principal technical features (a copy is automatically issued to car buyers by the manufacturer or a dealer). If you don't have

it, one can be obtained from the local motor vehicle licensing office (*Kfz-Zulassungsstelle*).

☑ **SURVIVAL TIP**

Even when an imported non-EU model has been granted a general operating licence, modifications may be necessary to meet German safety and environmental standards.

You're strongly advised not to make any substantial modifications to a licensed vehicle without obtaining expert advice or you could invalidate the general operating licence. If you feel compelled to turn your hatchback into a roadster, you can engage a KBA-certified expert (*Kfz-Sachverständiger*) to issue the necessary title after performing a technical inspection, but be warned: such 'private' general vehicle inspections don't come cheap.

Privately imported vehicles (particularly those manufactured in America and Japan, relatively few of which are sold in Germany) may not have the required operating licence. If a licence hasn't been issued, it's your responsibility to supply the necessary technical data. To avoid the time-consuming and expensive procedure of establishing the technical specifications of a car via a general inspection, you should contact the manufacturer of your vehicle before shipping for information about the VIN (vehicle identification number), year of manufacture, vehicle type and other technical data, including:

◆ engine capacity;

◆ power (in horsepower or kilowatts);

◆ maximum speed;

◆ emissions data;

◆ admissible wheel and tyre sizes;

◆ admissible gross front/rear axle weight.

You must also provide the date of the vehicle's first registration, which determines the standards that apply to it. If the vehicle doesn't have valid number plates, you need to request temporary 'red plates' (*rote Kennzeichen*) from the local motor vehicle licensing office in order to drive it to the inspection station.

Procedure

To register a vehicle in Germany, you must apply at the local motor vehicle licensing office (*Kfz-Zulassungsstelle*) in the town where you live, with the following documents:

♦ proof of identity and residence, e.g. passport and registration card;

♦ a customs clearance certificate stating payment of, or exemption from, the relevant duty and tax (see **Duty & VAT** on page 148);

♦ proof of ownership, e.g. a bill of sale or commercial invoice;

♦ proof of liability insurance cover (*Privathaftpflichtversicherung* – see **Insurance** on page 154), which takes the form of a copy of your policy (*Versicherungsdoppelkarte*), obtainable from your insurer;

♦ an export permit (from your previous country of residence), if applicable;

♦ vehicle documents, including the specification (*Kfz-Brief* – see above);

♦ technical inspection and emissions test certificates (see above).

You must pay a fee of between €15 and €45 in cash (the authorities don't accept payment by credit or debit cards), and are given a receipt and your vehicle registration certificate (*Kfz-Schein*) as well as three stickers to be affixed to the number (licence) plates, which you must then purchase (you're told where to obtain them). Plates cost between €30 and €100, depending on their size (non-standard plates are available for certain makes of car).

The stickers verify the validity of the vehicle registration and that the vehicle has passed the technical and emissions inspections (on the rear plate, alongside the one issued by the technical inspection centre – see **Technical Inspection & Emissions Test** above). Nothing should be affixed to your windscreen. Be prepared to attach your plates before driving away!

Number Plates

The first one to three letters of a German number plate indicate the district (*Kreis*) where the vehicle is registered. Large cities generally have a single registration letter (e.g. F for Frankfurt and S for Stuttgart), while smaller districts have two or three letters. You can therefore tell whether a vehicle is 'foreign' to your district or region. Number plates must be changed if you move to a new district for longer than three months. Standard plates show the letter 'D' for *Deutschland* and the EU logo, therefore no separate country code sticker is required.

VEHICLE (ROAD) TAX

Vehicles registered in Germany are subject to an annual vehicle or road tax

(*Kraftfahrzeugsteuer* or *Kfz-Steuer*), which is payable soon after registration. An 'application' is filed automatically when a vehicle is registered and you receive a bill (*Kfz-Steuerbescheid*), which should be paid at your local tax office (*Finanzamt*). If the tax exceeds €500 it can be paid in equal half-yearly instalments (plus a surcharge of 3 per cent) or quarterly instalments if it exceeds €1,000 (plus a 6 per cent surcharge). Tax is paid a year in advance and any unused portion will be refunded.

The amount payable is determined by the size of a vehicle's engine as well as its carbon dioxide (CO_2) emission levels. The (engine size) tax is €2 per 100cc for gasoline engines and €9 per 100cc for diesel engines. Vehicles emitting less than 95 gms/km are exempt from the CO_2 portion of the tax, while vehicles with emissions above this level pay €2 per g/km. The tax can be calculated online at www.bundesfinanzministerium.de/Web/DE/Service/Apps_Rechner/KfzRechner/KfzRechner.html and www.kfz-steuer.de/kfz-steuer_pkw_neu.php.

In 2017 the German parliament agreed to introduce a road toll for foreign registered cars. Under the plan foreign drivers could have to pay up to €130 per year (depending on a vehicle's emissions) to use German roads; German drivers would also have to pay the toll but would receive a rebate on their road tax.

Electric vehicles are exempy from road tax for ten years.

BUYING A CAR

After you discover what's required to import a vehicle into Germany, you're likely to decide against bringing a car with you (unless you're pathologically attached to your existing car), and will therefore need to buy or hire one (see page 164) in Germany.

New Cars

Germany is the world's third-largest manufacturer of cars and the largest producer of high-quality cars. German-made cars aren't cheap, however, nor necessarily cheaper to buy in Germany than elsewhere, although prices are generally lower than in the UK.

> When you buy a new car, a dealer can assist you with the registration process – all you need do is provide the necessary documents.

Haggling over the price of a new car is possible, although significant discounts aren't easy to negotiate; you may have more chance of success by saying that the price is acceptable only if some options are included.

Note, however, that you should expect to pay not only the list price but also several fees, including 'dealer preparation' and VAT (*Mehrwertsteuer* or *MWSt*). In contrast with most other items sold in Germany, VAT isn't always included in the list price of new cars, therefore you should make sure you know the final (end) price, including all taxes and fees.

There are certain circumstances that allow exemption from VAT: for example, diplomats and military personnel enjoy tax-free status, irrespective of how long they remain in Germany; and non-EU nationals don't have to pay VAT on a vehicle if they leave the country within 12 months of the purchase date. Registration fees and insurance premiums must also be paid before you can drive a new vehicle.

Among German manufacturers, Audi and BMW offer discounts for diplomats and other short-term residents, while BMW, Mercedes-Benz and Porsche offer a 'tourist delivery programme' for US residents through their dealers in the US. You pay for the car in the States, pick it up on arrival in Germany and, when you leave again, drop it off at a handling agent, who ships it to the US for no extra charge.

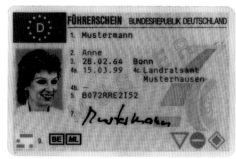

German driving licence (front)

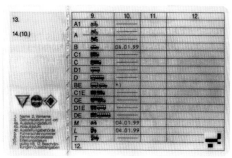

German driving licence (back)

Electric Vehicles

Electric/hybrid vehicles have yet to have much impact in Germany – less than 1 per cent of sales in 2016 were PEVs – although the country has an extensive network of charging stations (see https://ev-charging.com/at/en).

DRIVING LICENCE

Ensuring that you're licensed to drive in Germany can be very simple or infuriatingly complicated, depending mainly on whether your licence originates from an EU country or not. Those in the EU have few problems (see **EU Licences** below). On the other hand, for those coming to Germany from certain non-EU countries and planning to live there for longer than six months, obtaining a German driving licence (*Führerschein*) may be one of the most frustrating experiences of your stay.

EU Licences

EU residents enjoy reciprocal recognition of driving licences for an unlimited period, and you don't need to obtain a German licence even if you become a permanent resident in Germany – unless you have a driving licence of a category other than class B (e.g. allowing you to drive professionally or an HGV) and want to have the same privilege in Germany, in which case you must obtain the appropriate German licence. However, you'd be unwise not to obtain a German licence in any case, as you can have a foreign licence revoked for anything other than a minor infringement of the road rules (see **Licence Penalty Points** below).

EU nationals can obtain a German licence from a driving licence office (*Führerscheinstelle*) without needing to take

a written or road test, a privilege known as *Prüfungsfreiheit*, although there's a small fee.

Non-EU Licences

If you have a valid non-EU driving licence, you can legally drive in Germany for up to six months. Once the six months have elapsed, you must obtain a German licence. Those with licences issued in the following countries or states (irrespective of their nationality) can obtain a German licence without having to take either a written or a road test, a privilege known as *Prüfungsfreiheit*: Andorra, the Channel Islands, Croatia, Isle of Man, Israel, Japan, Monaco, New Caledonia, French Polynesia, San Marino, Singapore, South Africa, South Korea, Switzerland and some US states. Those with licences issued in a non-EU country or a country that isn't listed above, must take a

German road and written test in order to obtain a German licence.

In order to obtain a German licence, irrespective of whether your licence exempts you from taking a German driving test, you must have your licence transcribed (validated) within your first six months in Germany. Therefore, if you have a non-EU licence and plan to stay for longer than six months you should start the process of obtaining a transcription and applying for a German licence as soon as possible after your arrival. If the country or state where your licence was issued enjoys *Prüfungsfreiheit* (see above) but you fail to have your licence transcribed within your first six months in Germany, you must take German theory and practical tests.

Licence Penalty Points

As in many other countries, if you infringe the rules of the road, you receive penalty points on your licence. If you accumulate a certain number you must attend a course designed to correct your bad habits and, if you continue to incur penalties, your licence can be suspended for a period. You should be particularly careful if you're driving with a foreign licence (see above), as penalty points don't apply and you can have your licence withdrawn for even a fairly minor infringement.

INSURANCE

Car insurance in Germany is strictly regulated by law and supervised by the state authorities. The following categories of insurance are available:

◆ **Third party** (*Haftpflichtversicherung*): the most basic insurance, which covers you for the cost of third party damage or injury in accidents for which you're responsible. This cover is compulsory for all motor vehicles.

◆ **Part comprehensive** (*Teilkasko*): known in the UK as third party, fire and theft cover, and similar to comprehensive cover in North America. It includes cover against fire, natural hazards (e.g. rocks falling on your car), theft, a broken windscreen and damage caused by a collision with animals. You can usually choose to pay an excess (*Selbstbeteiligung*), e.g. the first €200 to €1,000 of a claim, in order to reduce your premium.

♦ **Fully comprehensive** (*Vollkasko*): as in the UK, and equivalent to the combination of comprehensive and collision cover in North America. It covers everything included under *Teilkasko* and also damage to your own car for which you're responsible, e.g. by driving into a lamp post. Again, you can pay an excess to lower your premium. Fully comprehensive cover is compulsory when you lease a car or purchase one on credit. Experts recommend this cover for new cars up to three years old, after which you need to consider whether it makes financial sense due to the high premiums and the lower value of the vehicle (unless it's a Bugatti).

To ensure that any passengers injured in your car are well provided for in the event of an accident, extra passenger insurance (*Insassenversicherung*) is recommended, and costs only a little extra.

Although EU regulations allow you to insure your car with any EU insurer (and therefore possibly save money), a vehicle licensed in Germany must be insured with an insurer 'registered' in Germany. If you take out third party insurance with a German insurance company and wish to increase your cover to fully comprehensive later, you aren't required to do this through your third party insurance company but can shop around for the best deal.

Motorists insured in any EU country are automatically covered by third party insurance in all EU countries, as well as in Andorra, Croatia, Iceland, Liechtenstein, Norway and Switzerland.

Green Card

Under recent EU regulations, possession of an international insurance certificate (commonly referred to as a 'green card', although in many countries it isn't green) is no longer compulsory within the EU. However, it's still wise to obtain one from your insurance company, as it can help prevent problems and delays in the event of an accident in another country, and if you're travelling outside the EU it may be obligatory. In most countries, you need only inform your insurance company that you want a green card to prove your cover, and they'll provide one free of charge (some insurance companies provide them automatically).

If you have fully comprehensive insurance, you should obtain a green card, as without one you'll be insured only for third party damage. If you're insured in the UK, however, your insurance company may provide a free green card for a limited period only, e.g. 30 or 90 days. (This is to discourage the British from driving on the continent, where they're a danger to other road users – most of them don't even know which side of the road to drive on!) Note that a green card must be signed to be valid.

Schutzbrief

Even if you're covered by your insurance policy when driving in other EU countries, the additional protection of a *Schutzbrief* (literally 'protection letter') can be well worth the extra cost. A *Schutzbrief* is offered by most insurance companies and motoring organisations (see page 165) and the benefits vary between companies. It usually covers breakdown assistance, repairs, the removal of a damaged vehicle, emergency car hire, the train fare home, the transport of you or your passengers to hospital if necessary, and repatriation by air of the sick and injured, as well as the return of your car to Germany after an accident or mechanical fault outside the country rendering it unfit to drive.

Costs vary quite widely, but you can get good coverage for around €35 per year. Check before buying, however, as the price of most new cars includes protection similar to that afforded by a *Schutzbrief* for the first three years.

Premiums & No-claims Bonus

The cost of car insurance in Germany is high, although premiums vary depending on a number of factors – not least the insurance company. A novice driver usually pays 25 per cent more than the standard rate, while someone with the best possible record – usually 18 or 21 years without a claim – pays just 30 per cent of the standard rate. You must normally have a year of accident-free driving before you qualify for the standard rate. German drivers must complete a two-year probationary period after passing their test, during which they pay the highest rates. The rate for third party cover can be as high as 240 per cent of the standard rate. If you're in this category, it pays to shop around, as there are huge differences in premiums between insurers.

When buying car insurance (or any other kind of insurance), it's wise to shop around a number of insurance companies and compare rates and cover. The same car, driver and circumstances can attract quotes which differ by over 30 per cent. Note that an insurer may offer excellent rates for certain classes of vehicle and/or drivers, but may be uncompetitive for others. Some may offer discounts for such considerations as off-road parking, but others may have a lower rate even without a discount.

If you had a no-claims bonus with a previous insurer, this is usually taken into account by a German insurer, although German insurance companies aren't obliged to do so. To substantiate a no-claims record, you need to obtain a letter from your previous insurer stating how many years you've driven without making a claim. In Germany, no-claims discounts apply only to third party and fully comprehensive cover. You're placed in a 'no-claims class' (*Schadenfreiheitsklasse* or *SF*) according to your number of years without a claim. For each claim-free year, you're automatically moved into a higher *SF* class, which usually leads to a premium reduction. If you're involved in an accident for which you're deemed wholly or partly responsible, you may lose some or all of your no-claims

bonus, and can expect your premiums to rise significantly the following year.

High discounts take longer to accrue in Germany than in some other countries, and you may need 21 years' claim-free driving to qualify for the maximum discount of 65 or 70 per cent (compared with as little as five years in the UK, for example).

If you discover that you can obtain better rates in your particular classification from another insurance company, you're permitted to switch, but only at the end of your insurance year. If you're switching third party cover, you must give written notice a month in advance, while terminating part or fully comprehensive cover requires three months' notice. Notice should be given by registered letter (*Einschreiben*) which requires a signature to confirm receipt by your insurance company. Your new insurance must begin no later than one day after the last day of your old insurance. Be sure to arrange this well in advance of the date you need the new policy to commence, in order to allow time for billing and payment processing. Bills are usually sent out 30 days in advance to ensure that payment is received by the due date.

Breakdown Insurance

Breakdown insurance (*Pannenservice*) in Germany and other European countries is provided by car insurance companies and German motoring organisations (see page 165), as well as by some car manufacturers. If you are or have been a member of a motoring organisation in another country, check with them before you move whether they have a reciprocal agreement with a German motoring club. If you've purchased a new car in Germany you may already have breakdown cover, at least during the initial warranty period provided by manufacturers. Some credit card companies (e.g. American Express and Diners Club) offer

Road Sign Shapes & Colours	
Design	Meaning
red triangle	warning
red circle	restriction
blue circle	requirement
square/rectangle	guidance
diamond	priority
octagon	stop

this type of insurance for their members. If you have a company car breakdown cover is usually provided by your employer.

ROAD SIGNS

Germany generally adheres to the international road sign system. With a few exceptions, most signs conform to the following shapes and colours:

An online guide to traffic signs in Germany is provided by the ADAC (www.adac. de/_mmm/pdf/fi_verkehrszeichen_engl_ infobr_0915_30482.pdf).

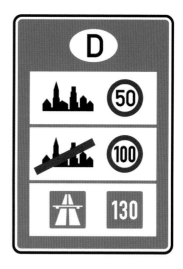

SPEED LIMITS

Around 50 per cent of German motorways have no speed limits, while others have either permanent or temporary (depending on weather conditions or traffic density) speed limits. Maximum speed limits are posted on signs with red circular borders, while a blue circular sign with a number in it is a minimum speed limit. The latter most commonly show 60kph (37mph), the minimum speed on motorways. There are also blue square signs, which show 'recommended' maximum speeds (see below). Note that speed limits aren't always posted and it's up to motorists to know the prevailing speed limit in the absence of signs.

Caution

If you're caught exceeding the speed limit significantly you could be hit by a huge fine and lose your driving licence for a period.

In cities and towns, the maximum speed limit for all vehicles is 50kph (31mph) unless otherwise posted. Many residential and school areas are designated a '*30 Zone*', where the maximum speed limit is 30kph (18mph); the 30kph limit remains in force until you pass a 30kph sign with a diagonal line through it, indicating a return to the usual 50kph limit. Even more restrictive are the traffic calming zones found on some residential streets, which are indicated by blue signs showing an adult playing ball with a child in front of a house. Traffic here is limited to walking speed, i.e. 7kph (4mph). In fog on any type of road, the maximum speed is reduced to 50kph (31mph).

Outside cities and built-up areas (except on motorways), the speed limit for vehicles under 3.5 tonnes, without trailers, on a normal two-lane road is 100kph (62mph). For vehicles weighing between 3.5 and 7.5 tonnes, and those towing, the maximum permissible speed is 80kph (50mph); above 7.5 tonnes, the limit is 60kph (37mph).

Despite their reputation as unregulated race tracks, German motorways are often subject to speed restrictions. Limits of between 90 and 120kph (56 to 75mph) are typical on stretches with constant heavy traffic, near urban areas or with tight bends. Construction zones (*Baustelle*), which seem to be everywhere, can have limits as low as 60kph (37mph). There are also sections with night and wet-weather speed restrictions. Trucks and vehicles towing trailers are limited to between 60 and 110kph (37 to 68mph) on all motorways; a truck or car with a trailer weighing under 7.5 tonnes may travel at up to 80kph (50mph).

Where there are no signs stating otherwise, drivers are advised (although not obliged) not to exceed 130kph (82mph). The absence of a general motorway speed limit isn't without controversy. The Green Party, with its strong environmental platform, has pushed for a national speed limit as low as 100kph (62mph), claiming that air pollution created by high-speed driving has caused widespread destruction of trees and forests. As a compromise, some limits have been set in heavily forested areas, but a general limit remains unlikely. It appears that the government fears the reaction of the millions of citizens who own luxury cars and have a predilection for high-speed driving. No matter how highly petrol is taxed, the cost doesn't seem to persuade many drivers to slow down.

ALCOHOL & DRUGS

The laws regarding drinking and driving are taken just as seriously as beer in Germany. If you want to enjoy a few drinks it's wise to have someone with you who won't be drinking who will drive you home or use public transport. Riding a bicycle isn't an acceptable alternative; if you're caught riding a bike on public roads while over the legal limit for driving, your driving licence can be suspended.

The legal limit in Germany is 50mg per 100ml of blood and 0mg for novice drivers and those aged under 21. The penalties for driving while over the limit are severe. Breath tests can be performed by the police at any time (even if you're driving correctly), and those found in violation of the law can lose their licence as well as being heavily fined.

If you have an accident while under the influence of alcohol it will be expensive. Your insurance company isn't obliged to pay for damage to your car or any other vehicle that you damage. You can also be held personally liable for all medical expenses and property damage resulting from an accident. There will also be a fine, starting at several thousand euros, and if you're unable to pay it you may find yourself facing a jail sentence of up to five years! The courts may decide that alcohol was a factor in an accident even when a driver's blood alcohol content was below the legal limit; anything above 30mg is likely to put you at fault.

Driving under the influence of 'recreational' drugs isn't taken lightly either. If you're found to have been driving with traces of marijuana, hashish or cocaine in your system, your licence will be withdrawn for at least a year. You'll also incur penalty points, be fined and need to undergo a psychological examination before you receive your licence back.

RULES OF THE ROAD

All motorists in Germany must be familiar with the *Strassenverkehrsordnung* (rules of the road), which are available in book form and distributed by the Federal Transport Ministry

(also available from bookshops). There are many online guides to driving in Germany including www.gettingaroundgermany.info/regeln.shtml.

Under German law, you're required to carry your vehicle registration certificate (*Kraftfahrzeugschein* or *Kfzschein* – see **Registration** on page 150) and driving licence at all times when driving a vehicle. It's wise to have copies of these documents (in case the car and/or your documents are stolen) and to keep the originals on your person or at home. If you're stopped by the police and don't have the required papers, you can be fined. When driving outside Germany, it's wise to have a green card from your insurance company (see page 155) and a blank accident report form (*Unfallbericht*), both of which can be obtained from your insurance company.

WINTER DRIVING

Most of Germany doesn't experience such severe winters as many of its neighbouring countries. Except in a few high altitude regions, such as the Bavarian Alps and the Black Forest, driving conditions aren't usually hazardous for prolonged periods during winter. However, most motorists who rely on their cars for regular transport fit snow tyres (*Winterreifen* or *Schneereifen*) at the start of the winter. In some rural areas, roads aren't cleared of snow by the authorities, making snow tyres a necessity. Snow tyres may be used on vehicles of up to 3.5 tonnes from 1st November until 31st March; vehicles are then restricted to 80kph (50mph).

☑ SURVIVAL TIP

If you have an accident on snow in a vehicle that isn't fitted with snow tyres, you may be considered at fault if the other vehicles involved have snow tyres, irrespective of other circumstances.

If there are signs showing a tyre covered by chains, it's compulsory to fit chains (*Schneeketten*) when there's snow. These signs are generally found only at the highest altitudes, but even if you don't see them it's wise to fit chains when there's thick snow. Buy good quality chains and practise putting them on and removing them before you get stuck in the snow; even getting the container undone can be a trial when you have numb fingers, let alone fitting the chains!

In mountainous areas, the edges of many rural roads are marked by two-metre high poles in case of snow.

GERMAN DRIVERS

Ever since Carl Benz invented the first practical motorcar in 1885, Germans have been in love with their cars and care for them like a member of the family (often even better!). Only Americans are more devoted to their cars, and it's said that depriving a German of his car is like amputating one of his limbs. On the other hand, the Germans, being more ecologically minded than many other Europeans, are prepared to forgo their cars for more environmentally friendly means of transport when practicable. The number of Germans who own bicycles and use them surprises most visitors, and it's common to see bikes on the top or back of cars on their way to a weekend or holiday destination.

Germans take it for granted that anyone driving in Germany will stick to the rules of the road (except for speed limits), and the rigorous process of earning a driving licence contributes greatly to the general competence of motorists. Predictability is as important when driving as it is in every other aspect of life in Germany. Thus Germans drive precisely, if not always with any particular degree of courtesy or understanding beyond that specifically called for by the rules of the road.

Despite the high speeds permitted on German motorways, there are relatively few serious accidents on them. Most serious crashes occur on ordinary roads outside built-up areas, and speeding or impatience are frequently a prime cause. Minor accidents happen mostly in cities. Patience isn't common among

German drivers and although sounding your horn is prohibited within city limits (except in an emergency), it's overlooked by many. Impatient and aggressive drivers are identifiable by their fondness for tailgating and reminding you with their horn that a red light may turn green at any second.

When driving on a motorway, you may feel that you've strayed onto a racetrack. Even if the traffic in the 'slow' lane is moving at the recommended maximum speed of 130kph (82mph), some drivers will constantly change lanes, often cutting in with no more than a few metres to spare, in order to gain a few 'places'. The one thing that preserves some kind of order in this potential chaos is the German respect for the 'car hierarchy'. In the outside lane, where tailgating is the norm, there's an unwritten code that a VW will yield to an Audi, which will yield to a Mercedes or BMW, while the kings of the highway drive Porsches (Germans don't give way to foreign-registered vehicles, whatever their make!).

MOTORCYCLES

To drive a motorcycle of up to 50cc (with a maximum speed of 45kph) on German roads, you require a class M licence and must be aged at least 16 years old. Obtaining a licence involves attending a driving school, as you must pass a written rules test and a practical test. If you already have a class A1, A, or B driving licence, however, you can ride any vehicle in class M without obtaining further permission. Most driving schools teach motorcycle as well as car driving, although specialist motorcycle driving schools exist. Once you're authorised to take your bike on the road, you can obtain a number plate from an insurance company at the same time as paying your road tax and obtaining the mandatory third party insurance.

There are two classes of driving licence for motorcycles over 50cc: A1 and A. To apply for the A1 classification, you must be aged at least 16 and your motorcycle must have an engine capacity of no more than 125cc or an engine power not exceeding 11kW. If you're aged under 18, your bike must be capable of a speed no greater than 80kph (50mph). If you wish to drive a larger motorcycle, you must be aged at least 18 and have a class A licence. If you're aged 18 to 25, obtaining this is a two-stage process: first you must take instruction, and pass written and practical tests entitling you to ride motorcycles with an engine power not exceeding 25kW, and a power-to-weight ratio of not more than 0.16kW/kg, for two years after obtaining your licence. After two years' experience without any major accidents, you're permitted to ride any motorcycle. If you're aged

over 25 you needn't undergo the two-year probationary period, but may ride any bike after undertaking the required practical training and passing the corresponding test.

The registration procedure for a motorcycle is the same as for a car (see page 150). Your motorcycle must also pass a technical inspection and emissions test every two years, and you must pay annual vehicle tax (see page 151).

All motorcyclists must use dipped (low beam) headlights and wear a crash helmet at all times when riding, and must have at least third party insurance.

PARKING

Once you've successfully navigated the roads, kept out of the way of other drivers and reached your destination, you may find yourself with a new challenge: finding somewhere to park. In most heavily populated residential areas and business districts, there's an acute lack of parking space. In many larger cities areas are reserved for resident parking, whereby residents must obtain a permit (*Anwohner Parkausweis*) from the local town hall.

Legal street parking is indicated by a blue sign with a white P, although wherever you park there must be at least 3m (10ft) between the middle of the street and your car. This may require that you park partly or completely on the pavement. When this is permitted (for vehicles up to 2.8 tonnes only),

it's indicated by a sign with a P showing a car parked on two levels. There must be sufficient room left for pedestrians on the pavement. Cars may park on both sides of a one-way street, provided there's room for vehicles to pass between them. Parking is normally only permitted facing the direction of the traffic flow.

Vouchers, Discs & Meters

If the time permitted for parking on a street or in a car park is limited, parking will be controlled by one of the following methods:

◆ **Parking voucher** (*Parkschein*): When you see the sign '*Nur mit Parkschein*', you must buy a voucher from a nearby machine (*Parkscheinautomat*) before leaving your vehicle. Modern machines accept debit cards and money cards and also accept payment via a mobile phone (instructions are provided); if a machine accepts cash a notice will tell you what coins or notes are accepted. Vouchers must be placed behind your windscreen where they can clearly be seen, and you must return to your car before the expiry time printed on the voucher.

◆ **Parking disc** (*Parkscheibe*): In shopping areas in particular, you'll often see a blue sign with a picture of a white parking disc and the white letter 'P', which denotes that the use of a parking disc is required. Discs can be obtained free of charge or for a nominal cost from petrol stations, motor accessory shops, news-stands and kiosks, and from the ADAC and other motoring organisations (see page 165). You must turn the dial to indicate the time of your arrival

Parkhaus 200m

(you may round it up to the next half-hour) and put it behind your windscreen. The time by which you must leave is automatically displayed on the disc.

◆ **Parking meter** (*Parkuhr*): These aren't as common as the other two methods and operate in the same way as in other countries. Coins must be inserted for the amount of time you wish to park. If a meter is defective, you're permitted to park with a disc. The maximum parking period is shown on the meter.

If you're caught exceeding your allotted time, you're fined between €5 and €40. It's illegal to return once your time has expired to insert more coins in a meter or to adjust a parking disc, penalties for which are similar to those for over-staying your time.

Car Parks

Blue-and-white 'P' signs not only indicate street parking but are also used to give directions to off-street car parks (*Parkplatz*). An inverted (and flattened) 'V' over the P (like a roof) indicates a covered car park (*Parkhaus*). In many larger urban areas there are electronic signs indicating which car parks and garages have spaces available (*frei*) and which are full (*besetzt*). These signs may also show the number of spaces available.

Most covered car parks are completely automated: you take a time-stamped ticket at the entry barrier, which then rises to allow you to enter. You take your ticket with you when you leave your car, and when you're ready to leave you pay at a machine (*Parkenkasseautomat*), usually located near the entrance. Once you've paid the ticket is validated and returned to you. You then have around 15 minutes in which to return to your car and exit the garage. At the exit gate you insert your ticket into the machine

and the gate will open. Payment at the exit isn't possible, and you'll be extremely unpopular with the motorists behind you in the exit queue if you forget to pre-pay! Using a car park for up to an hour usually costs at least €5, although additional hours are usually cheaper.

There are exceptions to this general principle, as some car parks still have people who collect payments. Even so, they aren't at the exit gate but rather in a booth at a pedestrian entrance, so you still need to pay and have your ticket validated before returning to your car.

FUEL

Unleaded petrol (*Bleifrei*) and diesel (*Diesel*) are available at all garages in Germany (leaded has been phased out.) Although diesel fuel (around €1.22 per litre in early 2017) is cheaper than petrol (€1.35 per litre, unleaded 95 octane), vehicle taxes for diesel cars are higher. There are three grades of unleaded petrol: regular (*Normalbenzin*) 91 octane, super (*Super Bleifrei*) 95 octane and super plus (*Super Plus Bleifrei*) 98 octane.

Depending on where you fill up, the price of petrol varies by up to ten cents per litre. As you'd expect, petrol stations on motorways are the most expensive. The best places to fill up tend to be petrol stations associated with supermarkets, and, of course, those in areas where there's lots of competition.

Electric Vehicle Charging

Germany has an extensive network of charging stations (see https://ev-charging.com/at/en/), although relatively few are fast chargers.

Petrol stations in Germany are usually self-service. Opening hours vary, but they aren't controlled like those of shops. Some are open from 7 or 8am until 10 or 11pm, others 24 hours a day. Many petrol stations are less interested in selling you petrol than goods (at high mark-ups), on which they make the bulk of their profits.

Payment is usually made after petrol has been purchased and to a person rather than a machine. Petrol pumps that accept credit cards are rarer in Germany than in some other European countries. Provided a petrol station is open it's usually manned by at least one person. When you've filled your tank, you go to the cashier and tell him the number of your pump. Unless otherwise stated, garages accept payment in cash or by debit card. Most petrol stations also accept credit cards, although you shouldn't rely on paying by card in rural areas.

You're permitted to carry up to five litres of petrol in a vehicle in an approved can in Germany. However, different rules apply in other countries, so check with a German motoring club before taking a can of petrol over the border. It's illegal to run out of fuel on a motorway, for which you'll be fined if caught.

The main operator of motorway petrol stations in Germany is the Tank & Rast company, which has hundreds of outlets across the country offering (as the name suggests) facilities for relaxation as well as fuel. A free booklet, which includes a map showing the location of all services, is available at motorway service areas and from Autobahn Tank & Rast GmbH & Co KG (https://tank.rast.de).

CAR HIRE

Major international car hire (rental) companies, such as Avis (www.avis.de), Europcar (www.europcar.de), Hertz (www.hertz.de) and Sixt (www.sixt.de) are all represented in most German cities (Note: Budget goes by the name of Sixt in Germany). A website that provides car hire price comparisons is www.billiger-mietwagen.de. Cars can also be hired from local garages and offices in most towns – look under *Autovermietung* in the Yellow Pages or on the internet. Business hours vary with the location of the office; those at airports having the longest opening hours.

Although far from cheap, car hire isn't as expensive as in some other European countries. The basic daily rate with limited free mileage (100-200 km per day) for a small car (e.g. Ford Fiesta or VW Polo) starts from around €20 per day or €100 per week, but is likely to be double this when all the 'extras' and taxes are added. German hire cars usually have manual transmission (stick shift) and if you want an automatic you must order one when booking and pay extra. You must also pay a surcharge for more than one driver. Hire costs not only vary between companies but also depend on where you hire a car. Hiring from an airport is the most expensive option and if you can get to a city by public transport you'll get a better deal, although it may not be worth the inconvenience for a short hire.

Most car hire companies in Germany require drivers to be aged over 21 and some have a minimum age of 25, with an upper limit of around 70. You must, of course, have a valid driving licence. It isn't necessary to hold a German driving licence unless you've been living in Germany for more than six months, in which case your home licence will no longer be valid in Germany (though it will be in your home country – see **Driving Licence** on page 153). By law, non-residents are required to possess an EU driving licence or an International Driving Permit (IDP).

Most major companies allow you to collect a car in one city and drop it off in another for no additional fee, although if you want to do this you must check that it's permitted and whether there's a surcharge. If you plan to travel outside Germany this must also be allowed and noted in the contract – and check that the vehicle is properly documented for international travel, even within the EU. Most companies permit travel to other western European countries but not anywhere east of Germany.

Vehicles should be equipped with the necessary emergency equipment (i.e. warning triangle and first-aid kit) and you may want to check that you have a parking disc (see **Parking** above). In winter, hire cars may be fitted with studded tyres and you can usually request snow chains and ski racks if you're heading for the mountains. Car phones and baby and child seats are available from many companies for a fee, e.g. €10 per day for a child seat, which is required by law in Germany.

ROAD MAPS

Good road maps are readily available in Germany and reasonably priced. Falk publishes an excellent hardcover atlas and DVD-Rom which covers all of Germany and sells for around €25. The most popular street atlases are those published by Shell.

The average hardcover Shell edition sells for around €16, with soft-cover versions available from €7 to €13. The ADAC motoring club (see **Motoring Organisations** below) publishes low-price maps that are widely available in Germany and abroad.

Street maps and atlases can be purchased at bookshops, newsagents' and kiosks everywhere, while there are shops specialising in maps in the major cities. Other sources of maps include the telephone book, where you'll find local street maps with indexes, and tourist information offices. You can also display and download maps from the internet.

Many modern cars are fiited with satellite navigation (satnav), which – if not provided – can usually be upgraded to include Western European maps. You can also purchase Satnavs with Western European maps from companies such as Garmin and TomTom.

MOTORING ORGANISATIONS

There are two main motoring organisations or clubs in Germany – the Allgemeiner Deutscher Automobil Club (ADAC, www. adac.de – also available in English www. adac.de/mitgliedschaft/adac_membership) and the Automobilclub von Deutschland (AvD, www. avd.de) – plus a few smaller organisations, such as Auto Club Europa (ACE, www. ace-online.de).

The ADAC, which was established in 1903, is by far the largest and best known, and provides products and services extending well beyond the usual motoring requirements. It has a large network of shops selling road maps and motoring accessories,

A·D·A·C

WINTERFAHRT
GARMISCH-PARTENKIRCHEN
13. mit 17. FEBRUAR 1925

and also maintains driving practice areas for learners and foreigners who need to take practical driving tests. The ADAC also provides translations of foreign licences and legal advice regarding accidents and other motoring-related problems, with the initial consultation free to members.

You can purchase motoring legal protection (*Rechtschutz*), which covers your legal costs in the event of an accident. Many services aren't included in the standard membership fee, although members are usually entitled to a discount. Services offered by ADAC, AvD and the other smaller clubs include:

♦ emergency roadside assistance;

♦ assistance if you've locked yourself out of your car;

♦ estimation of repair costs and verification of repairs/servicing and bills;

♦ travel bureau and ticket office services;

♦ hotel finding and booking;

♦ road maps, tour guides and tourist information;

♦ advice on buying cars and valuations of used cars;

♦ car insurance;

♦ travel insurance.

There are two levels of ADAC membership (*Mitgliedschaft*): standard membership for Germany (€49 per year for a single person over 23, €69 per year for a couple and €89 for a family of two parents and one child aged 18-23) and ADAC Plus with worldwide cover (€84 for

The highest category of membership of motoring organisations provides more extensive cover and assistance outside Germany through reciprocal agreements with other national breakdown services.

a single person, €109 for a couple and €134 for a family, as above). There's also separate membership for young people age under 23 years.

Basic annual membership of the AvD costs €34.90 (Germany) and €64.90 (worldwide). Entitlements vary with the organisation and if you want anything more than basic emergency breakdown cover it pays to shop around and compare the benefits offered.

If you break down on a motorway, go to the nearest emergency phone (indicated by arrows along motorways and other main roads), lift the receiver and tell the operator you require assistance and which motoring organisation you belong to. Be ready to give your membership number. If there isn't an emergency phone nearby, the number to call from a mobile is 222-222 for the ADAC or 0180-2222 222 from a fixed line phone. The equivalent for the AvD is 0800-990 9909. If you aren't a member of a motoring organisation the nearest available breakdown service will still be sent to help you, but you must pay.

Most European motoring organisations have reciprocal agreements with the ADAC, AvD or ACE.

RULES FOR PEDESTRIANS

Pedestrians (*Fussgänger*) must wait for a green light before crossing the road at a crossing with a pedestrian traffic light, irrespective of whether there's any traffic. You can be fined €5 for failing to do so or for crossing the road dangerously, although it's more likely that you'll simply be run over! Pedestrian crossings that aren't at traffic lights are indicated by thick black stripes on the road known as zebra stripes (*Zebrastreifen*). Although motorists must (and in Germany usually do) stop when you're waiting at a crossing if you show your intention to cross the road you should never assume that a car will stop.

If an accident results from your crossing the street without proper regard to traffic controls, you're liable for any resulting damage or injury, although, not surprisingly, you can take out liability insurance (*Haftpflicht*) against this eventuality.

Zwinger Museum, Dresden (Saxony)

12.

HEALTH

*T*he German healthcare system is widely acknowledged as being among the best in the world. It provides near-universal cover and ensures that almost everyone, irrespective of income or social status, has the same access to healthcare. The infant mortality rate in Germany is 2.8 deaths in the first year for every 1,000 live births – one of the lowest in the world – and average life expectancy at birth in 2015 was 78.7 for men and 83.4 for women.

As in most western countries, the healthcare system is, however, an enormous financial drain on the government and private industry (which foots part of the bill) as well as on individuals, and cost-cutting reforms have been implemented in recent years and more are in the pipeline. Such reforms inevitably meet stiff resistance from a population unaccustomed to paying for their health and medical needs other than through their health insurance. As in most developed countries, however, a declining birth rate has unbalanced the system so that a decreasing number of workers must pay for the extended life spans of an increasing number of retirees. Health insurance (*Krankenkasse*) contributions (see page 185) are 15.5 per cent of gross income, of which employees pay 7.9 per cent.

When you register with the health authorities you're sent a plastic eHealth Card, which you must sign. There's a microchip in the card where your medical data is stored. Children are covered for free until age 18 under their parents' health plan. Medications and even some over-the-counter items are also free, provided they're prescribed by a paediatrician.

One area in which Germans are surprisingly less than health-conscious is smoking, with

some 25 per cent of the 15+ population smokers and around 35 per cent of those aged 18-25, despite punitive taxes, smoking bans, etc. A smoking ban in all 16 federal states covers all public buildings including nightclubs, restaurants, cafés and bars. Exceptions are made for some small bars and premises with separate smoking rooms, outdoor eating areas and parks.

Paradoxically, despite their general salubrity, most Germans regularly worry about their health. They fear most medical problems known to modern man and visit the doctor frequently – comforted by the knowledge that their health insurance will pay for everything. (Germans visit the doctor almost once a month on average.) Employees are generally entitled to unlimited paid sick leave (although after six weeks of sickness, the payment is reduced) provided they receive a doctor' sick note (*Krankmeldung*) stating that they're unable to work (see **Sick Leave** on page 42).

Perhaps the biggest health mystery in Germany is a 'disease' unknown to the rest of the world called *Kreislaufstörung*. This roughly translates as 'circulatory disorder' and covers everything from mild headaches and tiredness to heart problems. In some cases, it can also mean 'I don't feel like going to work today, but don't want to use any of my annual leave'. Since the disease is so vague and all encompassing, some Germans claim a form of it regularly, and it's often difficult to determine how serious the underlying problem is – if indeed there is one.

EMERGENCIES

In a life-threatening emergency, you should ring for an ambulance (dial 112), which will take you to the nearest hospital accident and emergency (A&E) department. Germany has a public ambulance service, which is efficient, and you're normally attended to without delay at A&E. If necessary, ambulance crew will begin treatment en route and, if you're able to, you should give them details of your health insurance (see page 185).

> ### ☑ SURVIVAL TIP
>
> When visiting a hospital or clinic, take proof of your health insurance, although you're unlikely to be refused treatment if it's urgently required.

If you need a doctor outside regular surgery hours, you should first try to contact your family doctor (keep the number by your phone). If the surgery is closed, there should be a recorded message telling you how to reach your doctor or a locum service standing in for the practice. This, of course, will be in German, so it's wise to ask in advance how a practice handles emergencies. If you don't have a family doctor or yours cannot be reached, you can call the Emergency Doctor's Service (*Ärztlicher Notdienst* or *Ärztlicher Bereitschaftsdienst*), a free 24-hour public service. The number for your area will be listed at the front of your local Yellow Pages. The GPs in a district usually take it in turns to act as an emergency doctor (*Notarzt*) at night, and offer advice and, if necessary, visit you or send an ambulance.

If you have a dental emergency or your pet is in dire need of medical attention, the numbers to call are listed in your Yellow Pages under *Zahnärztlichen Notdienst* (dental emergencies) and *Tierärztlicher Notdienst* (veterinary emergencies).

ACCIDENTS

If you have an accident resulting in an injury to yourself or to a third party, inform the following as required:

♦ a doctor if treatment is necessary;

♦ the police;

♦ your accident insurance company;

♦ your employer, if it will affect your ability to work (if you have an accident at work, report it to your manager or boss as soon as possible).

An accident report form must be completed for all accidents where medical treatment is necessary and which result in a claim on your insurance, e.g. car, health or third party liability. Your health insurance policy will normally pay for medical treatment only if you remain in Germany, and journeys abroad while undergoing a course of treatment as the result

of an accident may require the consent of your insurance company.

HOSPITALS & CLINICS

Hospitals are signposted by the international sign of a white 'H' on a blue background. To find a list of hospitals in your area, look in your phone book under the heading *Krankenhäuser* (the singular is *Krankenhaus*) or online. Hospital care is excellent in Germany, but you may notice a number of differences in admission and other procedures from those you're used to in your home country. Your family doctor requests a bed for you, but your care is taken over by a doctor at the hospital. Either your medical records are transferred to the hospital or, if you're undergoing a regular procedure, you're given your records to take with you.

The kind of room you're allocated depends on whether you're covered by state or private insurance (see **Chapter 13**). A privately insured person is usually assigned to a single room, while those with state insurance usually share with up to three others; you can request a single room, but you must pay the extra cost yourself.

As a consequence of the growing concern over the cost of state healthcare in Germany, patients aged over 18 pay a fee of €10 to €15 per day for a maximum of 28 days per year, i.e. up to a maximum of €280 to €420, after which there's no further charge. They're also required to pay €5 to €10 of the cost of transport (by ambulance or taxi, for example) for necessary medical treatment. Those under age 18 and people on low incomes are exempt from these charges.

Some insurance companies are also ending the widespread practice of admitting patients the day before surgery, by refusing to pay the bill for the extra night unless it's shown to be necessary. Nevertheless, Germans stay in hospital longer than people in many other countries.

Because German doctors aren't usually inclined to discuss treatment with their patients, it may pay you to read up on your condition and possible treatment alternatives before entering hospital. If you don't speak fluent German and cannot find any useful books in English, you may wish to check the internet, where there's a wide range of English-language sites, including those of the American Academy of

Family Physicians (www.familydoctor.org) and Patient Information Publications (www.patient. co.uk). German doctors will, of course, answer your questions or address any concerns you may have, but you must know what to ask. If language is a problem, you may also wish to take a German-English dictionary with you. Most doctors can speak at least some English, but nurses and other hospital personnel may not, although there will be someone around to interpret if there's a major problem.

Germans tend to be less concerned about privacy than most English-speakers. Gowns aren't issued during examinations and there are usually no curtains surrounding beds. Therefore, if you don't wish to suffer 'exposure', be sure to bring a nightdress or pyjamas, dressing gown and slippers; you should also take towels and toiletries. Don't, however, bring too many things as you'll have only a small locker in which to store them.

Visiting hours vary with the hospital, the level of care you require and whether you're in a private room. In a hospital ward, visiting hours are usually from 2 to 8pm. Small children aren't welcome as visitors. If a child must go into hospital, a parent can usually spend the night there. Mobile phones aren't usually allowed in hospitals (although people bring them anyway), therefore a telephone on which you can make outgoing calls is normally provided next to the bed, but to activate it you must buy a card from a machine in a public area on your floor. This can cost anything from €10 to €25 and there's a fee for just turning the phone on, after which charges for calls are deducted from the card. If you have unused time, the card machine will refund your money when you leave. The same procedure goes for the television, which is charged on the same card as the telephone.

Meals and meal times in hospitals conform to the usual German practice, breakfast consisting of rolls or bread with jam, meat or cheese. (Expect to be woken at the crack of dawn.) Large hot meals are served at lunchtime and supper is a simple meal based on bread or rolls. There's usually a choice of menus and you may also keep your own food and drinks by your bed, unless you have a special diet.

DOCTORS

You should take the same care when selecting a doctor (*Arzt*) in Germany as you would in your home country. In general, German doctors aren't particularly open to discussion and questions about your treatment, so if this is

important you may need to do some searching before you find someone who meets your needs. If possible, it's preferable to obtain recommendations from colleagues or friends. Doctors are listed by their specialities in the Yellow Pages under *Ärzte* and on the internet. Most doctors in Germany have at least a basic level of English, but this isn't the case with nurses and nursing assistants. If this is a significant factor for you, check before making an appointment.

The healthcare system allows you to visit any doctor you choose, which means you may consult any doctor or specialist who will accept you as a patient. If you're unhappy with the diagnosis or treatment given by a doctor, you're free to consult another to obtain a second opinion. However, it can be difficult or impossible to obtain an appointment with certain specialists without a referral from a general practitioner (*Praktischer Arzt*).

Note that some doctors don't accept payment via the state system. Signs outside the surgery indicate this; if you're relying on the state system, look for '*Kassenarzt*' or '*Alle Kassen*', which indicates that patients from all the public health insurance providers or *Krankenkassen* are accepted. Absence of such a sign indicates either that the doctor is a specialist or that he hasn't been able to obtain the official blessing of the *Krankenkassen* because the maximum number of doctors they'll recognise in that district has been reached. It doesn't necessarily indicate a higher quality of service.

Once you've found a doctor you like, it's preferable to consult only him (whenever possible) in order to establish a relationship, and for the convenience of having your medical records in one place. Most people have a regular or 'house' doctor (*Hausarzt*).

Doctors' surgeries are usually open during normal office hours except for a two-hour lunch break, with perhaps a late afternoon or early evening surgery one day a week. They're generally closed one day per week – usually Wednesday. City doctors usually have longer surgery hours than those in small towns and villages, where hours may be more irregular. When you call a doctor's surgery for an appointment, you're usually given an appointment time (*Termin*) or occasionally told to come any time during surgery hours (*Sprechstunden*). The latter operate on a first-come, first-served basis, but there's usually no difficulty in obtaining an early appointment.

When you register with a doctor you must give your medical card to the receptionist, who will enter your details into a computer. If you're in the state health insurance programme you're charged €10 per quarter for visits to the doctor, irrespective of the number or reason for visits. If you request a test that the doctor doesn't deem necessary you may have to pay extra, depending on what your health insurance policy covers. Similarly, if you consult a specialist without a referral from your *Hausarzt*, you must usually pay €10, but if you need further referrals the specialist can arrange them instead of your *Hausarzt*.

If you're treated by anyone other than a *Kassenarzt*, you'll receive a bill that you must pay yourself; the state health insurance scheme won't reimburse you. If you have private insurance, you must usually pay and then submit the bill to your insurance company for reimbursement.

Complementary Treatment

Complementary medicine has a long tradition in Germany, although it isn't accepted as a viable alternative to normal medical treatment by many doctors. Nevertheless, you may find the surgeries of both a doctor and an alternative practitioner (*Heilpraktiker*) in the same building, and it isn't unknown for someone who has first consulted the former to be referred to the latter (or vice versa). A growing number of GPs offer complementary therapies in addition to conventional medicine. Check your local Yellow Pages or on the internet, where services are listed under the doctor's name.

The most widely available alternative therapy in Germany is homeopathy, which should come as no surprise given that it was founded by a German doctor, Samuel Hahnemann (1755-1843). Homeopathy operates on the controversial principle that a substance that's toxic in large quantities can act as a remedy in smaller measures – rather like a vaccination. Approval for homeopathic treatment in Germany dates back to a law passed in 1939, allowing a homeopath to practise in conjunction with an authorised medical doctor, provided he has passed a qualifying examination. Obtaining a diploma (after a two-year training course) is still necessary to establish a homeopathic practice in Germany.

Standard health insurance – whether state or private – normally doesn't cover the cost of treatment by a homeopath or other alternative practitioners. However, if the treatment is provided by a GP, your insurance may cover the cost, so if you're an advocate of alternative medicine you'll find it pays to register with a doctor who offers such therapies.

MEDICINES & CHEMISTS

Prescription and most non-prescription medicines (drugs) are sold by chemists or pharmacies (*Apotheke*), denoted by a sign showing a large red 'A' with a white symbol of a serpent and a dish on the left-hand side. Apart from throat lozenges, vitamin preparations and some therapeutic lotions, most medicines are (by law) available only from an *Apotheke*. This includes homeopathic products and items that you may be used to buying at your local corner shop or supermarket at home, such as aspirin and cold cures. As such treatments are expensive in Germany, it will pay you to bring an ample supply of non-prescription painkillers, cold remedies and other preparations with you. Even if it doesn't require a prescription (*Rezept*), you must usually ask for a product you want by name. Alternatively, you can describe your symptoms, in which case the chemist (*Apotheker*) will offer a suggestion.

☑ **SURVIVAL TIP**

Before committing yourself to expensive treatment, it's wise to obtain a second opinion, although you should bear in mind that dentists rarely agree exactly what treatment is necessary.

Chemists' opening hours correspond more or less with normal shop opening hours, although if a number are located in one area they usually take turns in opening during the evening. In smaller towns and villages, some chemists are closed on Wednesday afternoons. Chemists display a duty roster on their doors or windows, and at least one will be available at night for emergencies. This information is also published in local newspapers under the heading *Apothekennotdienst*. Another alternative is to check the Yellow Pages for the number that provides a recorded list of chemists open outside normal hours (again under *Apothekennotdienst*).

If you're privately insured, you must pay for all medicines and reclaim the cost from your insurer by sending them the receipt. Some chemists offer a service whereby they keep your records on file and at appropriate intervals prepare a print-out of your purchases for submission to your insurance company (therefore encouraging you to visit them for all your medicines) in conjunction with a small discount on over-the-counter items.

If you're insured under the state scheme, the process is simple. You can take a prescription to any chemist and, provided they have the medicine in stock, they'll provide it. You must usually show your insurance card at the time of purchase and pay a small nominal fee equal to 10 per cent of the cost of prescription drugs and dressings (a minimum of €5 and a maximum of €10). If your gross monthly income is below a certain amount you may be exempt from paying additional charges. Not all medicines are covered, and if your doctor recommends something that isn't covered by state insurance, you must pay the full price at the time of purchase. You must also pay the full cost for certain medications for minor ailments such as cough mixture.

Unlike an American drugstore, a *Drogerie* sells household goods, baby care items, cosmetics and personal hygiene products, but no medicines. You may be able to find some of these items at an *Apotheke*, but prices are generally higher. For health foods and other 'natural' food products, look for a *Reformhaus*; for perfumes and cosmetics, a *Parfümerie*.

DENTISTS

It's wise to be cautious when choosing a dentist (*Zahnarzt*) in Germany, as recent reforms to the state health system have greatly reduced the reimbursements for dental procedures. For example, preventative cleaning is no longer covered by state health insurance. As with visits to a GP, there's a €10 fee for the first appointment per quarter.

Dental treatment is very expensive in Germany and in recent years patients have been cutting back on treatment and even

travelling to other European countries (such as Hungary) for 'dental holidays', where costs are lower. However, if this isn't possible or practicable and you need dental care while in Germany, try to obtain a recommendation from someone (with perfect teeth) who you can trust. Dentists are listed in the Yellow Pages under *Zahnärzte*.

It may be possible to negotiate the price with a dentist to some extent, perhaps by opting for a cheaper procedure. You should ask for a written estimate of all costs for expensive treatment, which is necessary if you want your insurance to cover some of the charges.

OPTICIANS

If you just want your vision checked, you can visit an optician (*Optiker*) or optometrist, which can be found in most towns, selling prescription glasses and contact lenses. An optician will usually adjust your frames free of charge. Ophthalmologists (medical doctors who specialise in examining and treating diseases of the eye) can also do a vision check, but will charge more than an *Optiker*. Ophthalmologists are listed in Yellow Pages and other directories under *Augenärzte* (singular *Augenarzt*), but you need a referral from a GP; if you have state health insurance the cost is covered automatically, but with private insurance you're reimbursed after paying the bill.

On the other hand, state heath insurance doesn't cover the cost of frames and lenses, both of which are expensive in Germany. You could pay twice as much for spectacles in Germany as you would in some other EU countries. However, there are several large optical chains in Germany selling spectacles at lower prices than independent opticians. These include Fielmann (www.fielmann.de) – probably the best-known name due to its widespread advertising – and Apollo (www.apollo.de), a well established chain.

CHILDBIRTH

Although healthcare reforms have reduced benefits in many areas, pregnancy, childbirth and the aftermath attract increasingly generous benefits. Pregnant women and their babies receive excellent care in Germany and every effort is made to ensure the good health of mother and child. Once pregnancy is confirmed, which must be done by a gynaecologist (*Frauenarzt*), you're issued with a 'mother's passport' (*Mutterpass*) that contains all the important details of your pregnancy. It starts with your medical history and, each time you go for a check-up, information such as your blood pressure, weight and ultrasound results is recorded. Your *Mutterpass* must be taken to all pre-natal medical appointments and to the hospital for the birth itself. If you're pregnant you're advised to carry your *Mutterpass* with you at all times in case of emergency.

In your home country, it may be customary to go to an obstetrician for pre-natal care and for him also to deliver the baby. However, this isn't always the case in Germany. A woman normally visits her regular gynaecologist for pre- and post-natal care, while the baby is delivered at a maternity clinic by the medical personnel on duty. It's possible to hire a midwife (*Hebamme*) to assist during the pregnancy, birth preparation and to accompany

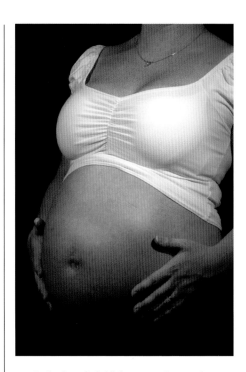

you to the hospital. All these services and prescribed medicines are covered by state health insurance, provided your doctor issues a prescription marked '*Gebührenfrei*'. If you're privately insured, you can arrange to be cared for throughout the pregnancy and birth by the chief obstetrician of the hospital's delivery team.

For the birth of your baby, you can choose between regular hospitals with maternity units, 'birthing centres' and your own home, under the supervision of a midwife. An invaluable magazine entitled *Wo bekomme ich mein Baby?* (Where do I have my baby?) is available from maternity clinics and gynaecologists' offices. It provides a list and description of all the options in your area for having a baby, including information about the type of equipment available in the labour and delivery rooms, the anaesthesia and medication offered, ante-natal classes and post-natal services, and parking and public transport facilities. Women's clubs, such as the American Women's Club (www.fawco.org) may also be able to help. Many website also provide comprehensive information (in English) about having a baby in Germany (e.g. www.howtogermany.com/pages/havingababy.html).

In addition to published information, most hospitals offer at least one 'open house' evening per month, when expectant mothers and partners can obtain details of the services available and inspect the facilities. After you've chosen the hospital or clinic for a birth, you must register with them.

When preparing your things to take to the hospital, you should include the passports of both parents and your marriage certificate. If the latter is in English, you'll need a certified German translation. For a normal delivery, a woman usually spends three to five days in hospital (5-7 days for a caesarean). All German health insurance plans pay for a daily midwife to visit for the first 11 days after a birth, plus a further 16 visits until a baby is two months old. Two house calls and two telephone conferences during weaning are also included. If you're recovering from a particularly difficult delivery or caesarean, you may be eligible for a free housekeeper (Haushaltshilfe) for the weeks following the birth.

The hospital will register the birth for you, but be sure to ask where it has been registered, as it may be necessary to go there in person to collect the birth certificate (Geburtsurkunde). If you're resident in Germany it's also essential to register the child with your home country's local consulate or embassy, for which you'll require the birth certificate. Check the procedure with them or a child may later be denied citizenship of your home country. US passport holders must take their baby to a US consulate, as a Consul General must see it (though how he knows it's yours is anyone's guess!). It's wise to make an appointment as soon as the baby is born, as it can be a month or so before you receive an appointment.

> You must register a baby with the German authorities at the *Einwohnermeldeamt* and apply for a residence permit on its behalf (see **Residence Permits** on page 52).

COUNSELLING & SOCIAL SERVICES

Counselling and general welfare assistance is widely available in Germany. In all major metropolitan areas, you can find help for problems such as alcoholism (Alcoholics Anonymous), drug addiction, compulsive gambling, marriage and relationship problems, and eating disorders. There are also dedicated centres for women or children who are suffering abuse.

For a list of professional counsellors you should check first with your family doctor or, if you have health insurance in Germany, your insurance company. Also check the Yellow Pages under your local social services department. Key words to look for include *Jugendamt* (department for juvenile programs), *Sozialamt* (department of social services), *Sozialhilfe* (social help) and *Sozialdienst* (social work).

HOME NURSING SERVICES

You can insure against the need for home nursing services by taking out a policy called (*Pflegeversicherung*). Policies are provided by the national health service and by private companies. The premiums for state insurance are deducted from your salary; if you have private health insurance you must negotiate a separate home care policy with your insurer.

Since the introduction of long-term care insurance in 1995 there has been a rapid growth in the number of private home care agencies (*Pflegedienste*) in Germany. Your insurance company can assist you in choosing one, and there are various seals of approval that indicate a high quality agency, such as the *Qualitätsgeprüfter Ambulanter Pflegedienst*.

The following services are usually provided by a home nursing service:

- **body care:** for example, bathing, oral hygiene, hair care and shaving;

- **nutrition:** preparing food so that it can be easily eaten and swallowed, and feeding;

- **mobility:** getting in and out of bed, getting dressed and undressed, help with standing, walking and stair climbing, accompanying on excursions outside the home;

- **household needs:** shopping, cooking, cleaning, dishwashing, and changing and washing bed linen.

A basic requirement for the cost of home nursing to be covered by insurance is that the patient requires help for a period of at least six months. The one exception to this rule is when the life expectancy of the patient is less than six months. The level of reimbursement depends on the amount of care required. There are three levels defined by law; your insurance company will determine which applies according to the evaluations of qualified medical personnel.

DEATHS

If a foreign national dies in Germany, one of the first official steps is to contact the appropriate consulate or embassy. They will advise you of the options for burial (locally or in another country), and can also provide the names of funeral directors experienced in preparing the body for transport home, if desired. A consular report may be necessary for probate in your home country, but a consulate cannot issue this document until it receives an official death certificate (*Sterbeurkunde*) issued by the appropriate Registry of Births, Marriages and Deaths (*Standesamt*). You may also wish to request an International Death Certificate from the *Standesamt*, which is issued in several languages.

One important point to note is that a German death certificate (*Sterbeurkunde*) doesn't state the cause of death, without which you may encounter difficulty in settling insurance claims back home. To avoid this problem, you should ask a doctor for a 'cause of death' certificate (*Leichenschauschein*), which is normally issued only when a death occurs in suspicious circumstances. The *Leichenschauschein* and the *Sterbeurkunde* should be issued by the same doctor.

13.
INSURANCE

*I*t's unnecessary to spend half your income insuring yourself against every eventuality from the common cold to being sued for your last cent, but it's important to insure against any event that could precipitate a major financial disaster, such as a serious accident or your house burning down. The German government and German law provide for various obligatory state and employer insurance schemes. These include health, pensions, unemployment, work accident and long-term care insurance – referred to as the five 'pillars' of the social security system, which was the world's first, established in 1883.

Health insurance is mandatory for anyone living and working in Germany. Some 85 per cent of the population receive health treatment under the German social security system, although you can choose to have private health insurance if your salary exceeds a certain level (see **Health Insurance** on page 185). Social security also extends generous protection to students (if they aren't covered by their parents' insurance), the retired and trainees.

There are a few occasions in Germany where private insurance for individuals is compulsory. The most common is third party car insurance. Some landlords require tenants to have third party liability insurance (i.e. to protect the landlord's interests) as a condition of the lease, and if you finance the purchase of a home, you're usually required to have life insurance to protect your lender. If you lease a car or buy one on credit, the lender will insist that you have comprehensive car insurance (*Vollkasko*) until the loan has been paid off. You're responsible for ensuring that you and your family are legally insured in Germany. Voluntary insurance includes supplementary pensions, private health insurance, household insurance, certain third party liability, travel, car breakdown and life insurance. For information about car and car breakdown insurance, see **Chapter 11**.

As with anything connected with finance, it's important to shop around when buying insurance. You can compare rates via the internet, e.g. www.versicherungsvergleich.de and www.tarifchecks.de. Regrettably, however, you cannot insure yourself against being uninsured or sue your insurance broker for giving you bad advice!

If you wish to make a claim against an insurance policy, you may be required to report an incident to your insurer within prescribed time limits or in the exact manner and level of detail outlined in your contract or policy documents. Filing a claim may also require you to provide a list of receipts for any articles damaged or destroyed, police reports or photographs of damage.

You should ensure that your family has full health insurance during the interval between leaving your last country of residence and obtaining health insurance in Germany, particularly if you have a health problem that may not be covered by a new policy. If you're planning to live in Germany without working you're required to have adequate medical insurance (cover must be at least equal to the

☑ SURVIVAL TIP

Obtain legal advice for anything other than a minor insurance claim, whether you're the claimant or someone is claiming against you. Bear in mind that German law is likely to differ from that in your home country or your previous country of residence, so never assume that it's the same.

German state programme) before you'll be granted a residence permit.

INSURANCE COMPANIES & AGENTS

Insurance is one of Germany's major businesses and there are numerous companies to choose from, many providing a broad range of insurance services, while some specialise in certain fields only. The major insurance companies have offices or agencies throughout Germany, including Allianz, AXA and Zürich. In most cities and towns there are many independent insurance agents and brokers (*Versicherungsmakler* or *Mehrfachagent*) who represent a number of insurance organisations and allow you to compare policies from different companies. There are also insurance consultants (*Versicherungsberater*), who will (for a fee) advise you on your insurance requirements and hopefully find you the best policies and rates. Some consultants, however, represent particular insurance companies and accept commission from them so their advice may not be independent.

Many banks have insurance partners (for example, Versicherungskammerbayern is the insurance partner of Stadtssparkasse bank) and include an analysis of your insurance cover as a part of their financial advice and investment service. Department stores and hypermarkets also offer insurance policies, including holiday, travel, car and life insurance.

'Telephone' insurance companies have appeared in recent years and usually offer competitive premiums, although there may be disadvantages to dealing with them; for example, it may be more difficult to obtain information or a decision regarding a claim over the telephone than face to face. In addition, you can find numerous insurance companies via the internet (e.g. www.versicherungsvergleich.de and www.tarifchecks.de), many of which offer do-it-yourself price estimates and the facility to sign up online.

The European insurance market theoretically allows insurers to offer cross-border policies. This means that, if you're coming from another EU country, you may be able to retain many of your insurance policies from that country (particularly life insurance and supplementary pension policies). However, with insurance, as in other matters, there's some discrepancy between theory and practice.

INSURANCE CONTRACTS

Read all insurance contracts before signing them. If you cannot obtain an English translation and you don't understand everything, ask a friend or colleague to translate it or take legal advice. Like insurance companies everywhere, some German companies will do almost anything to avoid honouring claims and will use any available legal loophole. It therefore pays to deal only with reputable companies. Terms and cover can be difficult to compare, as insurers often include a whole range of excesses (deductibles), co-payments, conditions and exclusions, even on 'standard' policies.

Always check the notice period required to cancel (*kündigen*) a policy. In Germany, insurance policies, like most forms of contract, are automatically extended for a further period (usually a year) unless cancelled in writing at least three months before the expiry date. Some types of policy must run for two or more years before they can be legally cancelled. You can cancel an insurance policy before the term has expired only if the premium is increased or if the terms or value of the policy are substantially changed. You won't receive a reminder of cancellation dates and, by the time you're notified that the premium is due, your cancellation date will be long past!

Most forms of insurance are paid via a single annual premium; if you want to make payments on a bi-annual, quarterly or monthly basis (assuming this is possible), you must pay considerably more. Most insurers require a bank transfer authorisation allowing them simply to deduct premiums from your bank account at the appointed times. If you don't pay, you can be sued for the whole premium, plus the credit collection agency's fees and interest.

The good news is that the insurance premiums you pay for the most common forms of insurance can be deducted from your taxable income. This applies to life insurance, private health insurance, long-term care insurance, accident insurance, and forms of liability insurance that insure your person but not your belongings. Social security contributions are automatically deducted from taxable income.

SOCIAL SECURITY

Germany has a comprehensive social security system for all employees, covering healthcare (including sickness and maternity benefits), injuries and illnesses at work, old age (pensions), unemployment, disability and death, long-term care and child allowance (*Kindergeld*). The labour and social services budget comprises the largest item in the federal government's budget.

Social security programmes also include a range of benefits and services available to those on low incomes, such as rent assistance and food and clothing allowances. There's less stigma attached to accepting government 'welfare' than in some other countries – in fact Germans are justifiably proud of their social support network.

Social security cost-cutting measures have been (cautiously) introduced in recent years by politicians such as Angela Merkel, who, while anxious to increase contributions and cut costs, are well aware that they must maintain benefit levels if they wish to remain in power.

The Federal Ministry for Health (Bundesministerium für Gesundheit, www. bundesgesundheitsministerium. de) and the Ministry for Labour and Social Security (Bundesministerium für Arbeit und Soziales, www.bmas.de) provide information on social security and other programmes in a number of languages, including English.

Insurance:
Car
Travel
Home
Health
Life

An excellent booklet in English, called *Social Security at a Glance*, provides a thorough overview of the German social security system (see www.bmas.de/EN/Services/Publications/a998-social-security-at-a-glance.html).

> Employees' social security contributions are automatically deducted from their income by employers, whereas the self-employed must pay their own contributions. Benefits aren't taxed.

Eligibility

All employees and most self-employed people in Germany are automatically enrolled in the state social security system, which also covers their immediate family members, i.e. spouse and children, as well as other dependent family members. Students, trainees and apprentices are covered separately if they don't come under their parents' cover. Those drawing 'wage replacement benefits' (unemployment, disability or old age pensions) are also covered, although they don't make any contributions. You receive a social security card bearing your name and social security number (*Sozialversicherungsnummer*), which verifies that you contribute to the statutory social insurance system.

Social security agreements exist between Germany and over 30 other countries, including all EU nations, Norway, Lichtenstein, Iceland, Switzerland and the US, whereby expatriates may remain under their home country's social security scheme for a limited period. For example, EU nationals transferred to Germany by an employer in their home country, or the self-employed, can continue to pay social security abroad for a year (forms E101 and E111 are required), which can be extended for another year in unforeseen circumstances

(when forms E102 and E106 are needed). Britons can obtain more information from the Department of Work & Pensions website (www.dwp.gov.uk). The names and functions of such forms change frequently, so it's best to check the DWP website before applying. Americans should be aware that the US social security agreement with Germany covers pensions only, and that medical and some survivor benefits under the US social security programme aren't payable to those living outside the USA.

If you or your spouse work in Germany but remain insured under the social security legislation of another EU country, you can claim social security benefits from that country. If you must claim benefits in Germany and have paid contributions in another EU country, those contributions are usually taken into account when calculating your qualification for benefits. There's a mutual agreement between EU countries whereby contributions made in any EU country count as contributions in your home

country when calculating benefits. Contact your country's social security administration for information.

In the UK information is provided by the Department of Work & Pensions (formerly DSS) International Pension Centre (www.gov.uk/international-pension-centre).

Contributions

With the exception of work accident insurance, which is paid entirely by employers, social security contributions are split equally between the employer and employee and are calculated as a percentage of your gross income – in some cases up to a certain salary level. In general, you should expect around 20 per cent of your gross salary to 'disappear' in your social security contributions (treatment for shock is covered!). Normally, the employer's share of the contribution is 'added' to your pay, and then the full amount of the contribution (around 40 per cent) is deducted. Bear in mind that the self-employed must pay the whole 40 per cent themselves – plus tax!

HEALTH INSURANCE

You have three options for health insurance (*Krankenversicherung*) while living in Germany; the government-regulated public health insurance system (*GKV*), private health insurance from a German or international insurance company (*PKV*) or a combination. You can choose a completely private plan if your income is above a certain threshold or if you're self-employed. Around 85 per cent of the population are mandatory or voluntary members of the public health scheme, while the remainder have private health insurance.

Enrolment in the state health insurance scheme (*Gesetzliche Krankenversicherung/GKV*) is mandatory for all employees earning less than a certain monthly salary, which in 2017 was €4,800 (i.e. €57,600 per year). The amount is indexed annually to take account of inflation. If your salary exceeds this level for three years in a row, you must choose between the state system and private health insurance (see page 191). Note that if you choose private insurance, you can have difficulty re-joining the state scheme in future.

Health insurance is provided by a network of non-profit funds who work with the state to administer the national health programme, and you're free to choose from most of them (the exceptions being company or guild funds that don't accept outsiders). Among the most popular are AOK, BEK, BKK, DAK and KKH. It pays to compare the premiums of a number of funds before making a decision because, although benefits are uniform across all insurers, costs vary significantly; the smaller companies are usually among the cheapest. Generally, however, the AOK (Allgemeine Ortskrankenkasse) is among the cheapest and has the largest number of offices nationwide.

> Your employer is obliged to pay you full salary for the first six weeks of an illness, provided you have a doctor's certificate stating that you're unfit for work.

The government health insurance scheme is administered by some 120 *Krankenkassen* and they charge the same basic rate of 14.6 per cent of gross salary plus a possible median supplementary rate of 1.1 per cent (2017) of your eligible gross salary up to a maximum monthly income of €4,350, making a total of 15.7 per cent. The 14.6 per cent is paid equally by employer and employee (7.3 per cent each) but the employee must pay the supplementary rate in full. If you earn more than €4,350 per month you don't pay a higher insurance premium. Rates are determined according to your salary and cover all family members, irrespective of the number of children you have; in other words, a single person pays the same contribution as a married person with several children.

Statutory health insurance benefits are extensive and cover dentistry as well as medical care, and even some spa treatments when recommended by a doctor. However, orthodontics are usually covered only for children up to the age of 18 (when recommended by a dentist), and there's limited cover for spectacles and contact lenses. There's also a provision for the state to pay 70 per cent of your normal salary when you're absent from work due to illness for more than six weeks.

As the government tries to cut the cost of healthcare, co-payments (i.e. the portion of costs patients must pay) have been increasing for such basics as prescriptions, hospital stays, ambulance transport and dental care. However, for most doctors' appointments you simply show your health insurance card, which is sent to you automatically when you register with the national health service, and the doctor bills the insurance company directly. For more information see **Chapter 12**.

LONG-TERM CARE INSURANCE

Long-term (nursing) care insurance (*Pflegeversicherung*) is the most recent addition to Germany's extensive social security benefits. Cover is mandatory and is linked to your health insurance plan. For those in the state healthcare system, the contribution is 2.55 per cent (plus 0.25 per cent if you're aged over 23 and have no children) of your gross salary (up to a threshold of €52,200 in 2017), with half (1.275 per cent) paid by your employer. In Saxony, contributions are higher due to the retention of an extra paid public

holiday each year, Day of Repentance (*Buss und Bettag*).

If you're eligible for private health insurance, you can also shop around for long-term care cover, but you must prove to your health insurance provider that the cover you choose meets the statutory requirements. The cost of private long-term care insurance obviously varies according to the benefits and options you choose. Whether public or private, the cover you select includes everyone in your family without their own insurance.

You're considered to need long-term care if your health insurance company determines that you require frequent or substantial help with day-to-day activities for six months or longer (see **Home Nursing Services** on page 177).

Long-term care benefits include holiday stand-ins for household helpers or caretakers, and extended social security cover for family members who reduce their paid employment in order to care for someone at home. Under the state programme, benefits can be tailored to individual needs, varying from cash reimbursement for private services engaged directly, to contracting services from a social service agency. It's possible to receive nursing care training for family members or others to reduce or eliminate the need for outside services. You may also be eligible for grants for modifications to your home or car, when necessary.

UNEMPLOYMENT INSURANCE

Unemployment insurance (*Arbeitslosenversicherung*) is mandatory for all employees in Germany; the contribution (2017) was 3 per cent of your gross monthly salary (half paid by the employer) up to a maximum salary of €6,350 per month in western states

your employer has given you notice of your impending lay-off or termination, you can register for benefit up to two months in advance so that it takes effect from the first day that you're unemployed. On the other hand, if it's your own fault that you're unemployed, e.g. you quit your job without good reason or were fired for good cause, the *Arbeitsagentur* can impose a holding period (*Sperrzeit*) of up to 12 weeks before paying the benefit. Again, this applies from the date you register as unemployed.

The benefit paid depends on your previous salary and whether or not you have children in your care, as noted on your tax card. Those without children receive around 60 per cent (67 per cent for those with children) of their previous net pay up to a maximum benefit, which varies according to the tax class you were in during the previous year (see **Tax Card** on page 205). Benefit payments are made once a month directly into your bank account. Social security cover for pension, health, long-term care and accident insurance is maintained while you're drawing unemployment benefit.

How long you can continue to draw the unemployment benefit depends on how long you've been working (and paying into the system) and your age. If you've been working only for a year, you're entitled to six months' benefit. For those under 50, the maximum entitlement is 12 months' benefit, and to qualify you must have been employed for at least 24 months in the last three years. For those aged 55 and over with at least 36 months' previous employment, the maximum is 18 months' benefit.

After you've exhausted your unemployment benefit entitlement, you may be eligible for unemployment assistance/welfare (*Arbeitslosengeld II* or commonly referred to as *Hartz IV* – see www.hartziv.org/hartz-iv-rechner. html) if you have no other means of support and no other working household members to

(*Alte Bundesländer*) and €5,700 per month in the eastern states (*Neue Bundesländer*). In order to qualify for unemployment benefit you must have worked (and paid contributions) for at least 12 months in the last three years. The benefit is paid not only when you're unemployed but also when you're on short time work or when an employer is unable to pay your wages, e.g. has gone bankrupt. Part-time employees are also entitled to unemployment benefit when wholly or partly unemployed.

To register for unemployment benefit you must go to the local employment office (*Arbeitsagentur*) with identification, your tax card, social security certificate and any documents previously issued by the *Arbeitsagentur*, such as your work permit or benefit claims. It's wise to register as soon as you become eligible (i.e. the day you become unemployed, provided you've made the required number of contributions), as the benefit is paid only from the date you register; if you put off registering for a couple of weeks, you have no right to backdated benefit. If assist you financially. This form of assistance is a fixed sum of €409 per month for one adult, plus the cost of housing. Additional assistance is provided for unemployed spouses, children aged between 14 and 25 living with their parents and for children under the age of 14. Unemployment assistance is available indefinitely.

If you're drawing unemployment benefit, you must report to the *Arbeitsagentur* at least every three months or whenever they summon you to discuss a possible job opportunity or training to improve your employment prospects. Recent reforms by the government (intent on reducing unemployment levels) mean that officials have become much less relaxed about this. It has become more difficult to turn down work even though you may think it beneath you, unrelated to your area of expertise or inadequately paid. You can also be required to attend classes or training programmes, all of which are provided free of charge.

Technically, you're required to check your letter box for information or requests from the *Arbeitsagentur* or your job counsellor at least once a day while drawing unemployment benefit, although you're entitled to take up to three weeks' holiday while unemployed, provided you notify the office in advance. If you miss an appointment, fail to turn up at classes or training programmes, or fail to follow up on job leads, you can be fined or have your benefit stopped for a number of days or weeks. You may be required to produce proof of your job-hunting efforts and you must notify the office immediately if you find a job, move house or your personal situation changes in any other way, e.g. you get married or divorced or find that you're expecting a baby. There are provisions for paying reduced benefit if you find part-time work while drawing unemployment benefit, but if you don't notify the *Arbeitsagentur* and continue to draw your benefit while being paid for full- or part-time work, you can be charged with fraud.

If you're a citizen of another EU country you may be entitled to receive up to three months' unemployment benefit from Germany if you move to another EU country to seek employment. To qualify, you must notify the *Arbeitsagentur* of your move, and register with the unemployment office in your new country within seven days of your arrival.

WORK ACCIDENT INSURANCE

Industrial accident insurance (*Unfallversicherung*) pays all medical and rehabilitation costs associated with injuries or illness occurring on the job, or while on your way to or from work. In the event of death from a job-related injury or illness, your survivors receive a funeral allowance and pension benefits. This insurance also covers children in school; students attending university or vocational training; those who help at the scene of an accident; civil defence and emergency rescue workers; and blood and organ donors. The contribution is paid entirely by your employer (average around 1.19 per cent of an employee's salary), the amount being based on the employer's health and safety record.

The employer is required to participate in various programmes to evaluate and improve health and safety conditions in the workplace as a condition of the insurance scheme. If you're self-employed and aren't required to have this type of insurance by law or under some other agreement, you can voluntarily obtain cover through the state system.

If you're unable to work (*arbeitsunfähig*) as a result of an injury or illness covered by insurance, 80 per cent of your wages (*Verletzengeld*) will be paid for up to 78 weeks after the statutory six-week period covered by your employer (see **Sick Leave** on page 42). In the event of long-term or permanent disability, you can receive occupational assistance, retraining and any necessary modifications to your car or home.

You must immediately notify your employer if you suffer an injury at work or on the way to or from work, or the educational establishment if the accident involves a child or student. The employer or school is responsible for filing a claim with their insurance provider. Statutory work accident insurance provides benefits irrespective of fault, and exempts your employer from liability claims for work-related accidents or illnesses.

For further information, see the Deutsche Gesetzliche Unfallversicherung (DGUV, www.dguv.de/de/index.jsp) website.

STATE PENSION

Pension 'insurance' (*Rentenversicherung*) is the social security programme that covers old age, invalidity and death benefits for retirees, their families and survivors. All employees must make contributions to the state pension fund, as must trainees, disabled people employed by sheltered workshops, and those doing military or civilian service. Most self-employed people also pay into this plan, although there are some alternatives open to professions with their own social welfare plan (*Sozialkasse*). Artists and those involved in publishing may be exempt from contributions after five years, provided their income doesn't exceed certain limits.

The state pension programme is easily the most expensive of the generous welfare plans in Germany and is the one that employers are most anxious to see reduced (at least, their portion of the cost). The pensions system has come under considerable strain in the years since reunification, due both to high unemployment (particularly in the eastern region) and to an ageing population. A voluntary private supplementary pension scheme has been introduced, which it's hoped will relieve the state of some of its burden (see **Supplementary Pensions** below).

The pension insurance contribution in 2017 was 18.7 per cent of gross salary up to a maximum of €6,350 per month (€76,200 per year) in western states (*Alte Bundesländer*) and €5,700 per month (€68,400 per year) in the eastern states (*Neue Bundesländer*). Employers pay half the sum and employees the other half through payroll deductions, while

the self-employed must pay the full amount themselves.

In order to claim an old-age pension, you must usually have contributed for at least five years (other conditions apply to those with occupational disabilities or work-related illnesses). The normal retirement age (i.e. the age at which you can claim a full pension) for men and women is currently 65, although it's gradually being increased so that anyone born in 1964 or later will have to wait until they're 67 to receive their pension; however, those who've been working and paying into the system for 45 years can retire with full benefits at age 65. Under certain circumstances, women, miners and those on unemployment or disability programmes are eligible for retirement at 62 or 65 with full benefits. A reduced pension for early retirement is available from the age of 63 (depending on your circumstances), and there are provisions for pensioners wishing to go on partial retirement (*Altersteilzeit*) so that they can continue to work part-time.

The pension scheme also provides pensions for surviving family members in the event of the death of an insured person, and partial pensions are available to compensate for reduced earning capacity in cases of long-term illness, injury or other forms of disability.

The formula for determining the level of pension benefit is based on a fairly complicated points system, which takes into account your contributions (and therefore your salary level) and the length of time you've been covered. The total number of points earned is multiplied by a factor corresponding to the type of pension you're claiming (i.e. retirement, disability, survivor, partial, etc.) and your age. The resulting number of points is then multiplied by the current pension 'value', which is based on the monthly pension that an average wage earner would receive after paying contributions for a calendar year. The aim has traditionally been to maintain pensions at around 70 per cent of your previous salary, although it's projected that this will fall to around 67 per cent by 2030.

If you move to Germany after working in another EU country (or move to another EU country after working in Germany), your state pension contributions can be exported to Germany (or from Germany to another country). German state pensions are payable abroad, and most other countries pay state pensions directly to their nationals resident in Germany. Non-EU nationals should check with their respective consulate, embassy or social security agency for details on claiming their national pension while living in Germany. Under the terms of the pension-only social security agreements between Germany and certain countries, including the US and Canada, pension contributions made in Germany may count towards pension qualification or value in your home country.

Your pension cover is continued while you're receiving unemployment or other forms of income-replacement benefit, the relevant agency paying contributions on your behalf. Parents on parental leave are automatically insured during their time off work, without making any contributions.

PRIVATE & SUPPLEMENTARY HEALTH INSURANCE

If your salary exceeds the level where state insurance is mandatory (€4,800 per month or €57,600 per annum in 2017) for three calendar years in a row, you may choose to purchase private health insurance instead of contributing to the statutory scheme (see page 185). You must notify your employer if you choose this option, in which case your monthly premiums will be deducted from your salary and remitted directly to your insurance company by your employer. As with state insurance, your employer contributes half of the cost of your private insurance, i.e. up to a limit of €317.55 for health insurance and €55.46 for long-term care insurance.

☑ SURVIVAL TIP

Many employers limit their contribution to private health insurance to half the maximum statutory rate, so that you must pay all the extra costs if you decide to go private.

Private health insurance provides much more extensive cover than the state scheme, including the option of private or semi-private hospital rooms; 'alternative therapies' such as acupuncture and herbal treatments; eye examinations; glasses and contact lenses; cosmetic surgery; and other treatment that isn't usually available under the state plan. You'll also have a greater choice of medical practitioners with a private scheme, as some doctors restrict their practices to privately-insured patients only (some because it's more profitable, others because the maximum number of GPs allowed to register in a particular administrative area with the Krankenkassen has been reached and they

have no option). However, premiums for private cover can be considerably higher than for state cover, especially if you opt for cover that eliminates most co-payments.

Private insurers can refuse to cover 'pre-existing conditions', so private cover may not be a practical option if you or a family member has existing or recurring health problems.

Another important point to bear in mind when considering private health insurance is that, once you've opted out of the state health insurance system, you cannot go back unless your salary falls below the level where you're entitled to choose. Normally you must make a decision on which health insurance Kasse you want to use within your first three months in a new job; if you aren't sure it's best to sign up with one of the state insurers, as you can always go private later. At the end of each year there's an open enrolment period, when employees who are eligible for private health insurance can choose this option or change insurance companies.

If you wish to (or have to) stay in the state system but want to receive 'private insurance-level care', you can pay extra for supplementary insurance (Zusatzversicherung), either from your state provider or from a private insurance company. You can also choose the type of extra coverage you want, such as dental or homeopathic insurance.

SUPPLEMENTARY PENSIONS

Germans have traditionally placed considerable faith in the national pension scheme and supplementary private pensions were previously considered something of a luxury. However, with legislative moves to limit or reduce state pension benefits, private pension insurance is slowly becoming more popular. Nowadays the government recommends a combination of state, company and private pensions – if you can afford it, of course. If you already have private pension insurance in another country, it may not be necessary (or, in some circumstances, wise) to buy a supplementary pension policy in Germany, particularly if you'll be moving on after a few years. If this is the case, you should obtain expert advice.

Technically, a private pension (*private Rentenversicherung*) in Germany is a form of life insurance investment, where you purchase an insurance contract for a set amount and a set term, usually 25 to 30 years. All policies for private pensions must run for at least 12 years to avoid being taxed as regular investments. At the end of the policy term the accumulated benefits are paid to the insured person, either as a monthly pension or in a lump sum. Where a private pension policy differs from a regular life insurance contract is in the manner in which proceeds are taxed after the death of the policyholder. When the pensioner dies, the remaining sum in the fund (or the face value of the policy if the policy hasn't yet matured) is paid to his heirs. While the pension payments made to the insured are tax-free, however, payments made to heirs after the death of the insured may be subject to tax (either inheritance tax or income tax, depending on the circumstances), whereas the proceeds of a life insurance policy are tax-free in all cases.

Because of the dramatic impact the low birth rate (and low immigration) is having on financing the state pension system, the government has recently introduced the state-assisted private supplementary pension. It's restricted almost entirely to those in the state insurance plan and is designed to soften the blow of future cuts in the state system on those who've been unable to take out a private supplementary pension, and to prevent too wide a chasm emerging between the rich and the less well off. The system involves the government making 'bonus' payments into private pension schemes.

HOUSEHOLD INSURANCE

As few Germans and even fewer foreigners buy their homes, buildings insurance isn't usually a concern in Germany, but contents insurance (*Hausratversicherung*) is essential for most people. Contents insurance normally covers your property in the event of damage by fire, burglary, vandalism, storms and water, and usually replaces damaged items at their current value, including furniture, appliances, clothing and books, as well as jewellery up to certain limits. It also covers you for a limited amount of cash. Contents insurance may also include provision for refunding hotel or rent and transport costs if your home is rendered uninhabitable for a period by fire, vandalism or another form of insured damage.

If you have possessions with a high value, it may be necessary to take out a separate policy or extension to cover them. These may include jewellery, antiques or financial documents (share certificates or bonds), where the value exceeds standard policy limits. As always, it's important to read and understand all the terms of a household insurance policy. You may also be required to

☑ SURVIVAL TIP

It's important to make sure that your contents are insured for their full value or claims can be reduced by the proportion your property is under-insured. For example, if your contents are worth €50,000 but you have insured them for €40,000 (i.e. 20 per cent under-insured), a claim will be reduced by 20 per cent.

show that you've done your best to minimise certain kinds of damage, e.g. by securing your possessions and home while you're absent; some policies replace stolen articles only when there's evidence of forced entry.

Many household policies cover only items kept in your home and may not include garages, exterior storage areas or other off-site property unless specifically mentioned. (You can buy insurance for mobile phones from phone companies.)

It isn't unusual to purchase a separate bicycle policy (*Fahrradversicherung*) or to add such cover to your regular household insurance, particularly if you use your bicycle for day-to-day transport or have a particularly expensive model. This insurance covers the theft of your bicycle under most circumstances excluded by a regular household policy, although you must lock your bicycle when you aren't using it and store it in a locked area or bicycle shed when at home. Should it be stolen while in use, the theft must occur between the hours of 6am and 10pm for cover to be effective.

If you have a non-family member (e.g. an au pair) living with you, you should check whether their possessions would be covered in a fire or other disaster. Non-related household members may need their own insurance cover for belongings or your policy may require you to notify the insurer when you have a long-term houseguest.

THIRD PARTY & LEGAL INSURANCE

It's customary in Germany to have *Privathaftpflichtversicherung* (third party liability insurance). To take an everyday example, if your soap slips out of your hand while you're taking a shower and flies out of the window and your neighbour slips on it and breaks his neck, he (or his widow) will sue you for €1 million (at least). With third party liability insurance, you can shower in blissful security (but watch that soap!). If you're renting accommodation, your landlord may insist on seeing proof that you have this cover so that he's adequately protected.

Third party liability insurance covers all members of your family and includes damage done or caused by your children and pets (for example, if your dog or child bites someone). However, where damage is due to severe negligence on your part, benefits may be reduced or even denied. Many policies specifically exclude cover for claims resulting from certain dangerous sports or hobbies (sky-diving, power-boating or mountaineering, for example) or if you regularly keep explosive or inflammable material in or near your home.

Legal insurance (*Rechtsschutzversicherung*) pays for consultations with a lawyer, and associated costs if you require legal assistance or are sued. You can even obtain insurance for a particular type of legal assistance, e.g. for your employment, for traffic accidents or for your apartment or house lease. Legal insurance doesn't cover legal fees for most non-adversarial situations, however, such as inheritance planning, patenting inventions or starting your own business. As always, you need to read a policy carefully to ensure that you understand the extent of its cover and how to file a claim.

Third party liability insurance usually costs around €75 per year, while legal insurance costs around €100 per year if purchased separately, but it's cheaper when combined with third party liability insurance.

HOLIDAY & TRAVEL INSURANCE

Holiday and travel insurance is available from a variety of sources, including insurance companies, banks and travel agencies, and can be purchased at airports and railway stations in Germany. Before taking out travel insurance, you should carefully consider the level of cover you require and compare policies. Most policies cover you for loss of deposit or holiday cancellation; missed flights; departure delay at both the start and end of a holiday; delayed and lost baggage and belongings; medical expenses and accidents (including evacuation home if necessary); loss or theft of money; personal liability (e.g. €1 million); legal expenses; holiday curtailment; and a tour operator going bust.

Travel policies may also cover medical evacuation or repatriation of family members who fall ill or who are injured while on holiday. German state health insurance covers you for medical emergencies throughout Europe, but when travelling further afield you need additional insurance.

If you travel abroad frequently you may find it more economical to have a permanent annual travel policy with worldwide cover that includes health insurance, than to purchase a travel insurance policy for each trip abroad. Annual policies are available from insurance companies that specialise in travel insurance, and some expatriate organisations offer attractively priced policies to members.

Germans are renowned travellers and favour package holidays booked through local travel agents. As a result, a number of consumer protections are written into German law regarding full or partial refunds for holidays spoiled by overbooking, incomplete facilities, inflated advertising claims, etc., and you can often obtain a refund (in cash, possibly including compensation for the fact that you've wasted a holiday period) for such situations simply by asserting your rights. For travel plans that go awry for other reasons, specific forms of travel insurance are available, including the following:

◆ **Travel cancellation insurance** (*Reiserücktrittsversicherung*) refunds your holiday fees in full or in part if you need to cancel or cut short your trip due to serious illness or the death of a family member; offered by most travel agents;

◆ **Baggage insurance** (*Reisegepäckversicherung*) covers damage to or loss of your bags while you're on holiday, which should be covered by a travel policy;

◆ **A 'Majorca policy'** (Mallorca-Police) brings the cover on a foreign hire car up to German levels and is particularly recommended for travel in southern European countries (not just Majorca!), where minimum mandatory car insurance is considered wholly inadequate by Germans. Before taking out such a policy, however, you should check your existing car insurance policy, as some German insurers include this cover in their standard policies.

☑ SURVIVAL TIP

It's advisable to always use a credit card when paying for travel-related expenses, particularly when paying for anything via the internet, as it affords extra protection.

Schloss Quedlinburg, Saxony-Anhalt

14.
FINANCE

O ne of the surprising things about the Germans, to some foreigners, is that they don't usually pay bills with credit cards, although this is changing. Many prefer to pay in cash (three-quarters of payments are still made in cash) or with local debit cards called *EC Karten*, and it isn't uncommon to find shops, restaurants and even some small hotels that don't accept cards! However, most such establishments will happily point you to the nearest cash machine! Compared with many other developed countries, particularly the UK and the US, Germany isn't a credit-oriented economy. Nevertheless, don't be fooled into thinking that this means the Germans are old-fashioned in their attitude towards money and avoid borrowing. The country has a highly efficient and dynamic banking system, which is one of the most advanced in the world.

When you arrive in Germany to take up residence or employment, ensure that you have sufficient cash, travellers' cheques, luncheon vouchers, gold sovereigns and diamonds to last at least until your first pay day, which may be some time after your arrival. During this period you'll also find an international credit card useful.

COST OF LIVING

No doubt you would like to know how far your euros will stretch and how much money (if any) you'll have left after paying your bills. First the good news: Germany has long had one of the highest standards of living in Europe, with above average wages (particularly in technical and engineering disciplines), relatively low inflation (under 2 per cent), and a strong and stable economy.

Food costs around 25 per cent more than in the US, but is similar overall to most other northern European countries, although if you're from southern Europe your food bill will almost certainly be higher than in your homeland. Shopping around for 'luxury' items such as hi-fi equipment, electronic goods, computers and photographic equipment at discount centres and online (see **Chapter 17**) can result in considerable savings.

In the Mercer 2016 Cost of Living Survey (www.mercer.com/costofliving) of 209 cities worldwide, the most expensive cities included Hong Kong (1), Zurich (3), Singapore (4), Tokyo (5), Shanghai (7), Geneva (8), Beijing (10), Berne (13), London (17), Copenhagen (24), Paris (44), Milan (50), Vienna (54), Rome (58) and Moscow (67), while German cities included Munich (77), Frankfurt (88) and Dusseldorf (107).

The fundamental flaw with most cost of living surveys is that they convert local prices into $US, which means that ranking changes are as much (or more) the result of currency fluctuations than price inflation. Therefore in the last few years, the Eurozone, Australia, Switzerland and Japan, with their harder currencies, have become more expensive in dollar terms, while the UK (e.g. London) and the US have become cheaper.

It's also possible to compare the cost of living between various cities, using websites such as Expatistan (www.expatistan.com/cost-of-living/country/germany). There are a number of websites that give you an idea of day to day costs in Germany (e.g. www.numbeo.com/cost-of-living/country_result.jsp?country=Germany and www.study-in.de/en/plan-your-stay/money-and-costs/cost-of-living_28220.php), although you should be wary of cost of living comparisons, as they're often wildly inaccurate and usually include irrelevant items that distort the results.

It's difficult to estimate an average cost of living, as it depends very much on where you live and your lifestyle. There are also large differences in prices (and above all rents) between the major cities and rural areas, and also between western (high) and eastern Germany (low). If you live in Munich, drive a Porsche and dine in expensive restaurants, your cost of living will be much higher than if you live in a rural area, drive a VW Polo and eat mostly at home. You can live relatively inexpensively by buying local produce (whenever possible) and avoiding expensive imported goods.

However, even in the most expensive cities, the cost of living needn't be astronomical. If you shop wisely, compare prices and services before buying, and don't live too extravagantly, you may be pleasantly surprised at how little you can live on.

GERMAN CURRENCY

The euro (€ – Euro in both singular and plural) has been the official currency of Germany since the mark's final bow on 1st July 2002. It's divided into 100 cents with coins minted in denominations of 1, 2, 5, 10, 20 and 50 cents and 1 and 2 euros. (Although they remain legal tender, some countries have dropped the 1 and 2 cent coins, with prices rounded up or down to the nearest 5 cents when payment is made in cash.) All euro coins have the same face, with a map of the European Union (EU) and the stars of the European flag. The obverse is different for each member country (designs on German coins include the Brandenburg Gate, an oak-leaf garland and an eagle – the state symbol), although all euro coins can be used in all eurozone countries – in theory, as minute differences in weight can cause problems with cash machines, e.g. at motorway tolls.

Euro banknotes are printed in denominations of 5, 10, 20, 50, 100, 200 and 500 euros. The design of the notes was subject to considerable debate and contention, and the winning designs depict 'symbolic' representations of Europe's architectural heritage. None of the images on any of the notes is supposed to be an actual building, bridge or arch, although there have been numerous claims in the press and elsewhere that the structures shown are actually landmarks in certain countries, including Germany.

When dealing with the euro, beware of counterfeit banknotes (especially €500 notes!). Genuine banknotes contain a number of anti-counterfeit devices, including watermarks, a metallic reflection strip and special inks and printing techniques, which change the colours you see depending on the angle from which you view the notes.

IMPORTING & EXPORTING MONEY

There are no exchange controls in Germany and no restrictions on the import or export of funds. A resident is permitted to open a bank account in any country and to export or import unlimited funds, although you're obliged to report to the Bundesbank any movements of cash into or out of the country exceeding €10,000.

When transferring or sending money to (or from) Germany you should be aware of the alternatives and shop around for the best deal. One of the safest and quickest methods of transferring money is to make a direct transfer or a telex or electronic transfer (e.g. via the SWIFT system in Europe) between banks. A SWIFT telex transfer should be completed in a few hours, funds being available within 24 hours. The cost of transfers varies considerably, not only in commission and exchange rates, but also in transfer charges.

Always check charges and exchange rates in advance and agree them with your bank (you may be able to negotiate a lower charge or a better exchange rate). Shop around a number of banks and compare fees. Some foreign banks levy a flat fee for electronic transfers, irrespective of the amount. When you have money transferred to a bank in Germany make sure that you give the IBAN number in full (you'll find it on your bank statement), otherwise money can be 'lost' while being transferred to or from a German bank account and it can take weeks to locate it.

If you're transferring a large sum of money in a foreign currency to Germany, e.g. to buy a house, it may be cheaper to use a specialist foreign exchange (FX) currency dealer to make the transfer. Dealers such as Moneycorp (www.moneycorp.com) and Currencies Direct (www.currenciesdirect.com) buy euros on your behalf and arrange the transfer. They claim to save you money by buying currency at the best rate and not charging for transfers, but you must open an account with them to use their services (which delays the process). You should also compare their rates with your bank, as in some cases your bank may be cheaper or will match rates. The charge for an international payment in euros anywhere in the EU should be the same as if it were a domestic payment in the country in which it's made.

> ### ☑ SURVIVAL TIP
> If at all possible avoid obtaining foreign currency at an aiport and always pay for card transactions in local currency (e.g. euros), wherever you are.

Most banks in major cities have foreign exchange windows and there are banks or exchange bureaux with extended opening hours at airports, major railway stations and in major cities. Here you can buy or sell foreign currencies, buy and cash travellers' cheques, and obtain cash with a credit or debit card. There are many private exchange bureaux in major cities and resorts with longer business hours than banks, particularly at weekends. They're easier to deal with than banks and, if you're changing a lot of money, you can usually negotiate a better exchange rate, but you usually get a better deal at a bank.

The exchange rate (*Wechselkurs*) against the euro for most major international currencies is listed in banks and daily newspapers. Exchange rates are usually better when obtaining cash with a credit or debit card, as you're given the wholesale rate, although there's a fee for cash advances and ATM transactions in foreign currencies.

BANKS

There are three broad categories of bank in Germany: private commercial banks (*Privatbanken*), public savings banks (*Sparkassen* and *Landesbanken*) and credit co-operatives or credit unions (*Genossenschaftsbanken*). The differences between the three types of bank relate principally to their legal forms and business structures, rather than the services they offer, and most banking institutions offer a full range of banking, investment and insurance services. Many banks also provide advice regarding property rental and purchase and personal financial planning, and it isn't unusual to find banks selling travel packages or tickets to local concerts and other events.

Private commercial banks include the so-called big four German banks: Deutsche Bank, Commerzbank (which acquired Dresdner Bank in 2009), Hypovereinsbank and Postbank, often described as 'universal banks'. The private banking sector also includes around 160 regional banks (e.g. Berliner Bank, Südwestbank, National-Bank) and branches of around 100 foreign banks (including Barclays and Citibank).

Public savings banks include the nine federal State banks (*Landesbanken*), ten Federal building and loan associations (*Landesbausparkassen*), and 450 or so local *Sparkassen* that are independently operated by town, district and municipal authorities. The *Landesbanken* and *Landesbausparkassen* (LBS) don't do business directly with the public, but operate through the *Sparkassen*. When you buy a home, for example, you can go to your *Sparkasse* and have them arrange it for you with the LBS.

Co-operative credit associations, once limited to members of specific trades or professions, long ago evolved into full service banks, mostly operating under the names of Volksbank or Raiffeisenbank.

Choosing among the hundreds of banks available is no simple matter. One important factor to take into account is that some businesses have a preferential arrangement with a particular bank, which may result in lower bank charges for employees. Comparisons between banks can be found on www.banken. de and www.dooyoo.de/banken.

Opening Hours

Normal bank opening hours are from 8 or 9am until 4pm, although banks are sometimes open as late as 6pm, with no closure over the lunch period in major cities and large towns. The main offices of many banks tend to keep similar hours to the local shops and may even open on Saturdays, at least for some counter services. Most banks in Germany have automatic teller machines (ATMs) and statement machines available 24 hours a day in a secure area, so that customers can withdraw cash, make deposits and check statements at their convenience.

The banking industry in Germany is one of the most dynamic sectors of the economy. Twenty-four hour telephone banking has

been available for many years, and even the smallest banks offer online (internet) banking.

Opening an Account

One of the first things you should do on arrival in Germany is open a bank account. Simply go to the bank of your choice and tell them you're living or working in Germany and wish to open an account. You're normally asked to provide standard identification and it may be useful to be able to offer a letter of reference from your bank in your home country or from a German employer, although this isn't usually necessary. If you prefer to open an internet-based account, you must generally complete a form on the bank's website, after which you receive an account information pack by post; although once you've opened an account you can perform most transactions online.

The 'default' method of paying bills in Germany is by direct bank transfer (see below), and cheques are more or less obsolete.

However, in order to be able to make a direct bank transfer you must have a giro account (*Girokonto*), which can be opened at any bank, including Postbank (see page 91).

After opening an account don't forget to give the details (account number and bank identification number – *Bankleitzahl* or *BLZ*) to your employer if you wish to be paid, as your salary usually goes directly into your bank account. Some companies have a preferential arrangement with a particular bank, which may result in lower bank charges for their employees. Your monthly salary statement is sent to your home address or given to you at work.

You can usually make arrangements with your bank to send statements to you monthly. However, some banks have discontinued this service, as an increasing number of customers use the internet to check their accounts. There is, of course, a charge for the traditional statement service. However, most banks provide a machine in their lobby or alongside an ATM that permits you to print statements free of charge.

Your statement is often the only notification you receive from the bank about the charges they've deducted, therefore you should check it carefully. At the end of the year it includes the annual totals required by the tax authorities and other reports. If you lose your copy of a statement you must ask your bank for a duplicate, for which you're charged a fee. If you use a bank's online banking services, be sure to print the statements you need periodically, and don't forget to make a copy of files if you download your banking information.

When writing figures in Germany (or anywhere in continental Europe), you should cross the down stroke of the number 7 in order to avoid confusion with the number 1, which is often written with a leading upstroke and resembles a seven to many non-Europeans (and Britons). Americans should note that Germans (like other Europeans) write the date with the day first followed by the month and year. For example, 01.09.2017 is 1st September 2017 and not 9th January 2017. The conventional US form of writing the date, e.g. 9/1/17 (1 September 2011), with the month first and slashes between the digits, must never be used in Germany.

Bank Transfers

The usual and most common method of making payments within Germany is a bank transfer. There are essentially two kinds of bank transfer, depending on whether you're instructing the bank to transfer money from your account to another account (*Überweisungsauftrag*) or are authorising the bank to allow a third party (e.g. a utility company) to take the money from your account (*Lastschriftverfahren*) – see below.

If you have an internet bank account you can usually set up, change and cancel single or regular payments online. Make sure that you keep copies of all transactions you authorise, plus the associated contracts or bills containing the bank account details and amounts. Your bank is responsible for correcting any errors made when transferring funds to or from your account, but corrections can be made much more quickly if you can produce documentation to back up your claim.

Überweisungsauftrag

An *Überweisungsauftrag* consists of a three-part form. You enter your name and account number and the identification number of your bank, and the name of the person or company you want to pay and their bank account and bank identification number. (This information must be printed on all bills and invoices sent to you for payment.) There's a space where you can enter the reason for the payment

(*Verwendungszweck*), which will be printed on your bank statement, and another for the amount you want to transfer. This can be done via online banking, which requires a transaction number (TAN), or at a bank service terminal. If it's done in person at the bank you complete the form by hand, sign it and keep one copy (the *Beleg für Auftraggeber*), giving the other two copies to your bank. Payment is generally made within one or two business days of the bank's receipt of the payment order.

Often when you receive a bill in the post it includes an *Überweisungsauftrag* form with the company's bank details and the amount already completed. You simply insert your bank details and sign the form before giving or sending it to your bank (don't send it back to the company!).

Dauerauftrag

To arrange a regular debit from your account (*Dauerauftrag*), contact your bank with the relevant payment information or arrange it yourself via online banking, including the bank account number of the person or company you want to pay, the amount and date(s) of payment.

An *Überweisungsauftrag* form doesn't include the date – either the date you submit the form to the bank or the date you want payment to be made – and payment is normally made within two business days of the bank's receipt of the payment order. If you want the transfer to be made on a specific date, you must request this (in which case the transfer is called a *Terminüberweisung*). You may wish to mark the date on your copy for reference. It's also wise to keep your copies of *Überweisungsaufträge* you've submitted to the bank in the same place as your bank statements, so you can check that payments have been made.

Lastschriftverfahren

Instead of directing your bank to pay a creditor, a *Lastschrift* is an authorisation permitting a creditor to debit a specified sum from your account, usually on a specific date (*Lastschriftverfahren* is the term for this process). While either an *Überweisungsauftrag* or a *Lastschrift* can be used to make a single payment, *Lastschriften* are often used to settle recurring expenses, such as rent, utility charges, car insurance premiums, magazine subscriptions and other regular payments made monthly, quarterly or annually (see **Dauerauftrag** box opposite). To set up a *Lastschrift* you must complete a form with your bank details and signature and send it to the receiver. Landlords, internet and telephone service providers and other companies usually require this type of payment.

Savings Accounts

You can open a savings account (*Sparkonto*) with commercial, co-operative and savings banks. Your employer may also offer a form of tax protected savings account at your own or another local bank. Most financial institutions offer a variety of savings and deposit accounts, with varying interest rates and minimum deposits, depending on the type of account and bank. In most cases the first €801 (€1,602 for a married couple) in interest is exempt from tax (the amount is called the *Sparerfreibetrag*), and there are additional tax advantages for savings accounts established to buy a home (*Bausparvertrag*). With deposit accounts (term deposits) you must be prepared to tie up your money for at least a month. The longer the term, the higher the interest earned.

You receive a pass book (*Sparbuch*) for a savings account, where all deposits and withdrawals are recorded. If you take part in an employer-sponsored savings plan, you need to take your pass book to the bank every few months to have the balance updated.

Cash & Debit Cards

German banks issue customers with a bankcard that enables you to obtain cash, balances, deposits and statements from an ATM. The bankcard also functions as a debit card and can be used to make purchases (e.g. petrol, clothing and groceries) from outlets displaying the relevant service sign (in the case of the Postbank card, for example, the sign to look for is Maestro). You're also issued with a PIN (number) which you should change to something you can easily remember (but not your birth date!) and should avoid writing it down anywhere. You can be held responsible for loss, improper use or forgery regarding bankcards.

Most Germans prefer to pay bills in cash and the use of credit/debit cards and contactless payment via a card or phone have met a lot of resistance. Only some two-thirds of Germans even have a credit card!

If you're banking with the Postbank (see page 91) or one of the associated Cash Group

of banks (which includes the Commerzbank, Deutsche Bank, Dresdner Bank and the Hypo Vereinsbank), cash withdrawals are free at these banks, although a withdrawal from an ATM of another bank will cost at least €5. There's a daily limit of €1,000 for Postbank Giro account withdrawals from any source.

> ☑ **SURVIVAL TIP**
> If you lose your bankcard, you must notify your bank as soon as possible.

MORTGAGES

Mortgages (home loans) are available from all major German banks, but the lending criteria may be quite different from what you're used to, particularly if you're from the UK or the US. Banks and other mortgage institutions base their loans on the value they assign to a property (*Beleihungswert*) rather than to its actual purchase price, and usually lend only 60 per cent of this value as a principal mortgage, although you may be able to negotiate a higher *Beleihungswert*. If necessary, a homebuyer must secure a second mortgage (at less favourable terms) for the remaining amount. The average German homebuyer takes out a 75-80 per cent mortgage repayable over 30 years.

It isn't uncommon for German employers (particularly family-owned companies in the *Mittelstand*) to lend to employees making home purchases, or even to co-sign or otherwise support a second mortgage through the employer's bank.

Mortgage loans in Germany can be at either a fixed or a variable interest rate, and most lenders require that all mortgages be repaid before the normal retirement age. Add to this between 4 and 10 per cent of the purchase price in fees, taxes and transfer costs, and it's easy to see why most people in Germany prefer to rent their homes.

If you take out a mortgage, the lender may require you to purchase term life insurance (*Risikolebensversicherung*) to secure the unpaid balance of the loan in the event of your premature death.

INCOME TAX

Income tax (*Einkommensteuer*) is the German government's main source of revenue, providing around 40 per cent of its income, followed by value added tax (VAT), which brings in some 22 per cent. It's often contended that German income tax rates are high compared with the rest of Europe, but this was never entirely true. The top rate is 45 per cent (for those who earn over €254,446 – poor them!) and the basic rate is 14 per cent.

As in many other countries, tax on employees' earnings (*Lohnsteuer* – literally 'salary tax') is deducted at source by their employers, i.e. pay as you earn (PAYE). The system used in Germany is extremely efficient and the amounts deducted usually cover your tax obligation almost to the cent, at least for those with no income other than from their regular employment. If you have no other source of income and no further credits or other adjustments to make for income tax purposes, you don't even need to file an income tax return (see below).

The information below applies only to personal income tax and not to companies. Note that unmarried couples aren't treated (for tax purposes) in the same way as married couples, the latter enjoying certain tax advantages.

Liability

Your liability for German taxes depends on where you're domiciled, which is usually the

citizens on income earned abroad, and requires a tax return to be filed, even if most or all of your income is exempt from taxation. US citizens can obtain information on tax filing requirements from an American embassy or consulate or via the internet (www.irs.ustreas.gov).

If you're in doubt about your tax liability in your home country, contact your country's nearest embassy or consulate in Germany.

Tax Card

Shortly after you register at your local Stadtverwaltung (see **Registration** on page 61), you receive a tax card (*Lohnsteuerkarte*) based on the information you provided on registration. You should check the information printed on the card, which includes your name, address, date of birth, church tax category (see page 61), and the number of children for whom you're claiming child credit or allowances. The tax card also shows your taxpayer identification number, which you should quote on all correspondence with the tax authorities, and your assigned tax class (*Steuerklasse* – abbreviated to *StKl*), which determines how much your employer should deduct from your pay for income tax.

If you're single, you'll probably be assigned to StKl I. (Single for tax purposes includes the divorced and widowed, and married people who are legally separated.) StKl II is for single people drawing certain types of assistance that entitles them to income tax reductions. Married people are assigned to one of three tax classes, according to whether their spouse is employed or not: StKl III is for a married person considered to be the primary breadwinner for the family. If a husband and wife are both employed full-time, both spouses will normally be assigned to StKl IV. StKl V is reserved for married people who

country you regard as your permanent home and where you live for most of the year. A foreigner working in Germany who has taken up residence there is considered to have his tax domicile in Germany. A person can be resident in more than one country at a time, but can be domiciled in only one country. Generally, people living in one country and working in another (known as 'border hoppers' – *Grenzenspringer*) pay taxes in the country where they live.

German residents are taxed on their worldwide income, subject to certain treaty exceptions, while non-residents are taxed only on income arising in Germany. Most countries exempt their citizens from paying income tax if they're living outside their home country for a certain period. Germany has an extensive network of double-taxation treaties in order to ensure that income that has already been taxed in one treaty country isn't taxed again in another.

⚠ Caution

There are ruinous fines and possible imprisonment for those caught evading tax, which is a criminal and not a civil offence in Germany.

Americans should be aware that the US is the only country that taxes its non-resident need or wish to have extra taxes deducted from their pay each month to make up for the fact that their husband or wife is already assigned to StKl III.

You should give your tax card to your employer as soon as you receive it, as it serves as the basis upon which taxes are deducted from your pay. At the end of the year your employer will provide you with an electronic statement (showing your income for the year and the social security payments and taxes deducted and paid on your behalf) for your tax declaration.

If your circumstances change – e.g. you divorce or have a child – you should contact your local tax office immediately to have any corrections made, both on your tax card and in your file.

Tax Number

If you're freelance or own your own business you need a tax number (*Steuernummer*) instead of a tax card. In order to obtain a tax number you must register your freelance status or company ownership at the tax office (*Finanzamt*). After around four weeks you'll receive your number in the post. It's against the law for any employer or contractor to pay you if you haven't got a *Steuernummer*. If you're self-employed or freelance you must file a tax declaration each year and report all income if

the total exceeds the base threshold (see **Tax Calculation** below); you then receive a bill from the *Finanzamt*. Your future tax payments are based on your previous year's earnings and may be paid in instalments.

Taxable Income

You must report your income in relation to the following categories:

1. farming and forestry;
2. trade or business;
3. independent services (i.e. self-employment);
4. employment;
5. capital investment;
6. rents and leases;
7. other income, including annuities, maintenance payments (alimony) and similar legally mandated payments between spouses or partners.

The good news is that if you receive payments that aren't defined in law as coming under one of the seven categories, they're tax-free! One of these is lottery winnings, which aren't subject to income tax in Germany. (Americans, however, are expected to pay income tax to their own government if they win the German lotto while resident in Germany!)

As mentioned above, your employer is responsible for reporting and paying the appropriate income tax on your employment income. Income from employment includes not only your salary, but also such things as overseas and cost of living allowances, profit sharing plans and bonuses, storage and relocation allowances, language lessons provided for a spouse, personal company car, payments in kind (such as free accommodation or meals), home leave or holidays (paid by your employer), and children's education expenses.

Your employer is required to value employee benefits and services and include them on your pay slip each month when calculating the taxes to be deducted from your salary, and include the amounts reported for the year on your tax card.

Allowances

The tax payments your employer makes for you take into account certain standard allowances against income, the most important of which are listed below (most allowances are indexed annually). Social security contributions are automatically deducted from your taxable income.

♦ the cost of getting to and from work if you don't have a fixed workplace or are temporarily sent to an external location by your employer, based on a flat rate per kilometre and a daily allowance, depending on how many hours or days you must remain there;

♦ a deduction for general employee expenses (*Arbeitnehmerpauschalbetrag*) of €1,000. You can deduct more (up to certain limits) if you have receipts to justify the sum.

♦ most insurance premiums, including life insurance, private health insurance, long-term care insurance, accident insurance, legal insurance and most forms of liability insurance (that insure the person, not possessions);

♦ contributions (*Spenden*) to charitable, religious or scientific research organisations, generally up to 5 per cent, but in a few instances up to 20 per cent of your income;

♦ costs incurred for 'extraordinary burdens' (*aussergewöhnliche Belastungen*) such as caring for a handicapped family member, hiring household help and private vocational training for a child;

♦ training, or continuing education in order to change or enhance your career (there are conditions and a maximum limit);

♦ two-thirds of childcare costs (up to a specified limit per child);

♦ the first €801 of income from interest on investments or savings (€1,602 for a married couple filing jointly);

♦ membership in a labour union;

♦ health care costs not covered by insurance;

♦ renovation costs for property let to tenants (not property that you live in yourself);

♦ payments to family in your home country (*Unterhalt*) who are in conflict countries/poverty;

♦ costs of a tax advisor or membership in a taxpayer's association (*Lohnsteuerhilfverein*).

There are many other allowances, which usually change annually. Any that aren't allowed for by your employer can be claimed on your annual tax return (see below).

Tax Calculation

The tax year in Germany is the same as the calendar year, from 1st January to 31st

December. Families and married couples are usually taxed as a single entity; however, married couples can elect to file separate returns if they wish to claim individual tax credits and allowances.

Children under the age of 18 are included on their parents' (or a parent's) tax return. Children over the age of 18 can be included on their parents' tax return if they're enrolled in school or a vocational training programme. Earnings for the school year from part-time jobs or training schemes must be declared on the family's tax return, although they aren't usually subject to income tax.

The tax payable is calculated according to your taxable income minus allowances. Income up to the base threshold (*Grundfreibetrag*) isn't taxed (or, officially, is taxed at 0 per cent!). In 2016 this level was €8,652. Above the threshold, income is taxed progressively at between 14 and 45 per cent, but on a sliding scale rather than in 'steps' as in most other countries, which means that you must wade through reams of income tax tables (*Einkommensteuer Tabellen*) to find out how much tax you owe. Alternatively, you can put your faith in the ever popular income tax calculators (*Steuerrechner*) found on the internet, e.g. www.icalculator.info/germany.html and www.parmentier.de/steuer/incometax.htm.

In 2017 the tax burden for single taxpayers (for a couple filing jointly the rates are doubled) was as shown in the table below:

Income Tax Rates

Taxable Income	Tax Rate
Up to €8,820	0%
€8,821 to €54,058	14%
€54,059 to €256,304	42%
Above €256,304	45%

Married taxpayers (but not unmarried partners) filing jointly pay taxes based on so-called 'splitting tables' (*Splitting-Tabelle*), whereby their combined income is taxed at the rate that applies to half the total; for example, if a couple earns €100,000 combined, they'll pay tax on the total but at the rate that applies to an income of €50,000.

Credits

Once you've calculated your tax due, you can claim a tax credit (*Kinderfreibetrag*) up to a maximum of €7,356 (2017) per child. Divorced parents with joint-custody arrangements are generally entitled to half a credit each per child, provided the child lives in Germany. It's possible to claim a credit for a child living outside Germany if you're legally obliged to support the child, e.g. under a divorce or separation agreement, or some other form of child support decree.

For more information, see www.kindergeld.org/kinderfreibetrag.html.

Surcharges

Once you've deducted any credits due, you must add surcharges! Those who declare themselves affiliated to certain religions must pay a church tax (*Kirchensteuer* – see page 61), which is levied at 8 per cent in Bavaria and Baden-Württemberg or 9 per cent (everywhere else) of the amount of income tax due.

There's also a solidarity surcharge (*Solidaritaetszuschlag*), imposed in 1995 to help finance the reunification of the former East and West German states, which is levied at 5.5 per cent of the income tax due; although the government claims to intend to reduce it further (it was originally 7.5 per cent of tax), there's currently no sign of this happening.

Tax Return

Some time in January your employer provides you with a printed electronic tax statement, with the sections related to earnings, allowances, credits and payments completed for the previous year. Usually, you also receive a set of tax forms and instructions from the local tax authorities (*Finanzamt*), but if you don't you can obtain copies from your town hall or the *Finanzamt* itself. Some post offices and banks also keep copies of the most common tax forms. There are also countless online tax calculation programs and other programs available on the internet that guide you as you complete the form online; then you simply print it out, sign it and send it in to the *Finanzamt*.

Employees who've had income tax deducted from their wages and who've no other source of income aren't required to file a return. Most employees can normally dredge up a few extra allowances, however, and generally wish to claim at least a small tax refund – in which case you must file a return. Self-employed people, business owners and other non-employees must file a tax return if their income from all sources exceeds the base threshold (€8,652 in 2016).

Unless your tax affairs are simple, it's prudent to employ a tax adviser (*Steuerberater*) to complete your tax return and ensure that you're correctly assessed, as the German tax system is somewhat complicated (especially if you don't have a good command of the language), and there are usually changes to allowances or allowable deductions each year. If you're self-employed or in business, finding a good adviser can mean the difference between success and failure – and his fee is tax-deductible! If you aren't self-employed, a cheap alternative to a tax adviser is the *Lohnsteuerhilfeverein*, a sort of club for tax advice. You pay a fee of around €100-150 per couple per year and receive unlimited tax advice and a completed tax return.

If you decide to do it yourself, many books, websites, magazines and computer programs are available to help you understand and save taxes, prepare your tax return and calculate your final tax bill. You must, of course, understand German well (and possibly have a good business or legal dictionary handy) to complete your tax return.

A general income tax form (*Hauptvordruck*) includes basic personal information such as your taxpayer identification number, name, address, occupation, spouse's name and your occupation. Most of this information will already be printed on the form if you received it by post from the *Finanzamt*. The tax authorities need your bank account number and the bank identification number (BLZ) for the account which you wish to use to pay your taxes or to receive a refund. If you haven't received an identification number by the time you file your form, leave that space blank and the tax office will assign you a number and send it to you with your bill or statement.

German tax returns, not surprisingly, are complicated and contain specialist (i.e. obscure) terminology. You must declare your income on the appropriate form(s) and also

Income Tax Forms

Form ID	Use
AUS	report foreign source income and tax paid abroad
AV	report retirement savings plans
Eigenheimzulage	claim tax benefits from the purchase or improvement of a residence
FW	claim certain benefits related to home ownership
GSE	report income and expenses from businesses you own or from self-employment
K	claim child credits (yes, these are separate forms!)
Kinder	identify the children for whom you're claiming credits
KSO	report income from other investments (interest or dividends, annuities, mutual funds or any other income not otherwise reported)
N	report employment income and marketing costs (*Werbekosten*)
U	report maintenance payments (alimony) or other support payments between separated or divorced partners
V	report income and expenses from the rental and lease of property
VL	report capital investments (this form is usually provided by the nvestment institution)

document your rights to the various allowances and credits. The form (*Anlage*) you require depends on the types of income you have to declare and includes those shown in the table above.

Forms don't help you calculate the amount of tax you must pay, but you can buy books and computer programs that include the appropriate tax tables along with instructions on estimating your final bill. You must include your tax statement with the return, so make sure to make a copy of your tax statement, as well as a copy of your return and any additional documents included.

Tax returns should be filed on or before 31st May of the year following the tax year for those required to file, e.g. self-employed, freelancers or those declaring additional income apart from their regular employment; for example, your return for the year 2017 should be filed by 31st May 2018. The tax office is authorised to grant extensions and normally does so on request up to the end of the year following the tax year, which is the absolute deadline for filing, i.e. 31st December 2018 for the 2017 tax return. If your return is prepared by a tax adviser the deadline is automatically extended to 31st December. If you haven't filed a return by this time you lose any claim you may have to a tax refund.

To request an extension, you normally need only include a letter with your return stating the reason you couldn't file by 31st May. Acceptable reasons include work, travel or family commitments. However, the tax inspector can impose a penalty of up to 10 per cent of the taxes due, so it's wise to file your return on time if there's any possibility that you'll owe additional tax. (Needless to say, the tax authorities won't pay you interest if you're late claiming a refund!) If you haven't filed your return by 31st May it's usually wise to have a tax adviser file it for you (the tax adviser's fee is deductible on your next tax return). Voluntary tax filers have between two and four years to send in their declaration.

Tax Bills

Within a few weeks of filing your tax return the tax office will send you a tax assessment (*Steuerbescheid*). If a refund is due, they'll advise you of the amount, which will be transferred automatically to the bank account listed on your return. If you owe money you'll be informed of the amount that will be debited from your account.

If you feel that your taxes haven't been correctly calculated you have one month after receipt of the tax assessment to make a formal protest (*Einspruch*). To make a protest, you must have a specific complaint about the calculation, and be able to show where and by how much the calculation is in error! The protest must be submitted in writing, and you should either follow an established model or have a tax adviser prepare the letter for you in order to ensure that you follow the correct procedure.

VALUE ADDED TAX

Value added tax (VAT) is called either *Mehrwertsteuer* (MwSt) or *Umsatzsteuer* (USt) in Germany (and is usually the difference between a fair price and too expensive!). The two terms are more or less interchangeable, although the legally correct term in Germany is *Umsatzsteuer*. Literally, it's a use tax rather

than a sales tax, as it's levied on all goods and services used in Germany, irrespective of where they were purchased. If you buy goods by mail-order from outside the EU, you may be charged VAT by the post office when they're delivered, although on small purchases (under around €50 declared value) they often don't bother to collect the tax.

Most prices in Germany are quoted inclusive of tax (*einschliesslich Mehrwertsteuer/ Umsatzsteuer*), although they're sometimes quoted exclusive of tax (*ohne Mehrwertsteuer/ Umsatzsteuer*). Germany has two rates of VAT: the standard rate of 19 per cent, which applies to most goods and services, and a reduced rate of 7 per cent that applies to certain food products and 'necessary' social services. There are also zero rated and exempt goods and services or those that are taxed in some other way, e.g. certain forms of life insurance that are actually investments.

There's no threshold for registering for VAT; if you're engaged in any 'economic activity' to earn a living rather than just as a sideline you're required to register with the local tax office (*Finanzamt*) and charge your clients VAT, even if you're barely making ends meet. This obviously adds to the bureaucracy of setting up as a self-employed person in Germany. However, 'small' businesses (*Kleinunternehmen*) can choose to opt out

Inheritance & Gift Tax Allowances		
Category	Relationship	Tax-Free Allowance
1	Spouse/civil partner	500,000
	Children, stepchildren, grandchildren/great-grandchildren of deceased children	400,000
	Grandchildren/great-grandchildren of living children	200,000
	Parents and grandparents	100,000
2	Siblings, nephews/nieces. Step-parents, relatives by marriage, divorced spouse	20,000
3	All other individuals, including legal entities	20,000

of charging VAT (invoices should be marked as 'VAT exempt'), although you then cannot reclaim the VAT paid to suppliers. A small business for VAT purposes is one that had a turnover of less than €17,500 in the previous year (VAT is included in this figure) and which expects its turnover to be no more than €50,000 (including VAT) in the current year. Once a small business has decided to become VAT exempt it's required to remain so for five years.

Some professions are exempt from VAT, such as doctors, physiotherapists and insurance brokers. All other businesses must include VAT at the appropriate rate on all their invoices, bills and receipts. VAT payments (or refunds) are normally paid monthly but in some cases quarterly.

CAPITAL GAINS TAX

Capital gains from the sale of non-business assets (e.g. a second home) are generally exempt from tax unless they're considered to be speculative. In the case of property, a sale is considered to be speculative if it takes place within ten years of purchase. Gains from the sale of a substantial share (i.e. more than 10 per cent) in a company are also taxable. Capital gains tax rates are the same as those for personal income.

If you think that you may be liable for capital gains tax, you should obtain advice from an accountant or tax advisor.

INHERITANCE & GIFT TAX

As in most other developed countries, dying doesn't free you (or rather your beneficiaries) entirely from the clutches of the taxman. Germany imposes both inheritance tax (*Erbschaftssteuer*) and gift tax (*Schenkungssteuer*) on its inhabitants, although it's the inheritor or the recipient of the gift (the beneficiary) who's responsible for filing a return and paying taxes, rather than the deceased's estate or the donor.

Inheritance tax (called estate tax or death duty in some countries) is levied on the transfer of property from the deceased to his heirs. The amount of tax due depends on the value of the property inherited and the relationship between the deceased and the beneficiary. Beneficiaries are grouped into three tax categories

(*Steuerklasse*) according to their relationship to the donor. Category I includes the spouse and children; category II parents, siblings and other blood relatives; and category III more distant relatives or unrelated beneficiaries. The tax-free allowances are shown in the table opposite. (Gift tax is levied in much the same way on property that's granted or donated to another person before the owner's death.)

There are strict rules and regulations regarding how property (both land and buildings) is valued, based on rental values and the use of the property at the date of the death or gift. Buildings that produce rental income are considered particularly valuable assets at tax time. The tax rates shown below apply to the amount of a gift or inheritance after the tax-free allowance has been deducted.

If you inherit property in Germany from abroad, you should consult a notary (*Notar*) or lawyer who's familiar with international tax law and treaties, or contact the *Finanzamt* directly before claiming your inheritance. Under tax treaties, the German *Finanzamt* usually recognises taxes already paid on an estate overseas, but it's important to know what documents you'll require to verify this when repatriating an inheritance from abroad.

It's possible to purchase life insurance to cover the inheritance tax your heirs will have to pay.

WILLS

It's an unfortunate fact of life that you're unable to take your hard-earned assets with you when you take your final bow (or come back and reclaim them in a later life). All adults should make a will (*Testament*), irrespective of how large or small their assets. The disposal of your estate depends on your country of domicile and, particularly if you own property (land or buildings), may also depend on where the property is located.

Under German law you can indicate your final wishes regarding the distribution of property and assets by drawing up a will. There are several kinds of will in Germany, but as with all official documents there are strict forms and rules to follow when writing them. It's therefore wise to consult a lawyer or notary (*Notar*) to ensure that you leave your final instructions in a legally valid form.

If you choose a notarial will (*notarielles Testament*), you can tell the notary how you wish to distribute your property and he'll draw up the legal documents for your signature. It's also possible to write your last wishes yourself

Inheritance & Gift Tax Rates

Taxable Value of Bequest	Tax Payable		
	Category I	Category II	Category III
Up to €75,000	7%	15%	30%
€75,001 to €300,000	11%	20%	30%
€300,001 to €600,000	15%	25%	30%
€600,001 to €6,000,000	19%	30%	30%
€6,000,001 to €13,000,000	23%	35%	50%
€13,000,001 to €26,000,000	27%	40%	50%
Over €26,000,000	30%	43%	50%

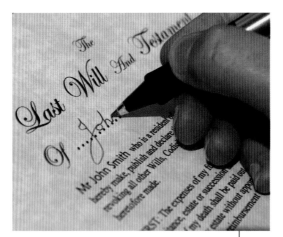

elsewhere. If you own property abroad, most legal experts advise you to have a separate will that's valid in the country where the property is situated.

German law doesn't allow you to leave your property to anyone or anything you choose, and you aren't permitted to disinherit entirely certain relatives, namely your direct descendants (children, grandchildren), your parents (if you have no children) and your surviving spouse. These privileged family members can claim their share of up to half the value of your estate if they discover that you've left them out of your will. They have up to three years after your death to assert their rights and can even recover any gifts made in the ten years before your death. It's important to consider this requirement when drawing up your will, so as to avoid leaving your heirs squabbling over what's left when you're gone – unless that's your intention! Under German law, your heirs will inherit not only your property, but also any debts. However, if you die leaving more debts than assets, your heirs can choose to reject the bequest altogether, thereby avoiding all tax and debt issues.

and give them (sealed or not) to a notary, who will register the existence of your will and hold it until you pass on. The notary's fee is based on the value of your estate, irrespective of whether he actually writes up the document or just registers the existence of your sealed last testament.

You can also prepare a holographic will (*eigenhändiges Testament*) – simply one written in longhand – provided you follow the form and regulations carefully. A holographic will is a cheap way of making a will without using a notary or lawyer. The only catch is that someone has to know where it is after you've gone! If you decide to write a holographic will, it's important that you hand-write the entire text of the will and sign the document legibly at the end, indicating the exact date and place (i.e. town) of signature. No witnesses are required; in fact, this type of will shouldn't be witnessed or it will complicate matters.

It's possible to have two or more wills – one covering your property in Germany and others for property owned abroad – although it's important to ensure that they don't contradict each other, or none of them may be valid! It may be wise to have a German will that simply refers to another will in your home country or

It's possible for married couples to prepare a joint will, of which there are several variations, each with its own legal requirements and restrictions. A *Berliner Testament*, for example, must be hand-written by one of the spouses and signed by both in order to be valid.

If you don't have a will (i.e. die intestate), your estate will be divided among your heirs according to German inheritance law. Simply put, this means that your closest category of living family members will receive your property (and debts) to share among themselves. The exact division depends on your marital status, the degree of relationship to surviving family members and any property-sharing agreements or conventions that apply between you and your spouse (often based on the property laws on the date and at the place you were married).

Keep a copy of your will(s) in a safe place, and another copy with your lawyer or the executor of your estate. Don't leave them in a bank safe deposit box, which in the event of your death is sealed for a period under German law. You should keep information regarding bank accounts and insurance policies with your will – but don't forget to tell someone where they are!

German inheritance law is a complicated subject, and it's important to obtain professional legal advice when writing or altering your will.

Carnival, Freiburg

15.
LEISURE

*T*he seventh most-visited country in the world, Germany attracts over 30 million international visitors annually. The country offers a huge variety of entertainment, sports and pastimes, and is blessed with an abundance of natural beauty – many tourists come to Germany to participate in outdoor sports, e.g. skiing and hiking, for which the country is famous. It's also noted for its wealth of historic cities and towns and is particularly famous for its 'high' culture – theatre, concerts and opera – which rates among the best in Europe.

Wherever you are in Germany, you can reach most other regions on a day trip thanks to the country's excellent transport infrastructure – except at the end of school terms, when everybody seems to want to go on holiday and trains are over-crowded, airports over-run and the famously fast *Autobahns* become gigantic car parks.

Leisure information is available from the German National Tourist Board (GNTB) and local tourist and information offices, many of which have a ticket agency, and a wealth of city and regional entertainment papers. Other information sources include local newspapers and radio programmes, and posters on those curious announcement pillars known as *Litfasssaülen*. Tourist information can also be obtained from a plethora of travel books and websites including www.germany-tourism.de, www.about-germany.org and www.lonelyplanet.com/germany, and most cities also have their own websites, e.g. www.berlin.de/en and www.muenchen.de/en.

TOURIST OFFICES

Most German cities have a tourist office or, at the very least, an information office (often located at the town hall), many of which also provide a hotel and event ticket booking service. They're usually open during normal business hours from Mondays to Saturdays and also on Sundays in major cities and areas where tourism is a major industry. Local tourist and information offices are listed in guidebooks.

The German National Tourist Board/GNTB (Deutsche Zentrale für Tourismus, www.germany.travel/en/index.html) has offices in many countries including Australia, Austria, Belgium, Brazil, Canada, China, the Czech Republic, Denmark, Finland, France, Hong Kong, Hungary, India, Israel, Italy, Japan, the Netherlands, Norway, Poland, Russia, Slovenia, Spain, Sweden, Switzerland, United Arab Emirates, the UK and the USA.

HOTELS

German hotels are generally spotless and efficient, and the standard of accommodation is invariably excellent, although the service may lack the friendliness one often finds in other countries. You can expect to find every type of accommodation in Germany, including cosy rooms in private homes (look for '*Zimmer frei*' or '*Fremdenzimmer*' signs in windows), holiday rooms on farms and simple guesthouses (*Gästehaus* or *Pension*, the latter in Bavaria) up to five-star luxury hotels. A *Gasthof* is a unique German institution roughly equivalent to a traditional English inn (a bar/restaurant with rooms). Generally, the smaller the place, the friendlier the service – guesthouses are often particularly cosy (*gemütlich*) and homely places to stay.

Room rates usually include continental breakfast (basically coffee and rolls), while in some larger establishments a buffet-style cooked breakfast is offered for an extra charge. Hotels with restaurants usually offer half board (breakfast and dinner) or full board (breakfast, lunch, dinner) at favourable rates. A Hotel Garni provides breakfast and drinks.

The cheapest accommodation in Germany is provided by the Ibis Hotels chain (www.ibis.com), which offers rooms from €30 per night in fairly central locations.

Rates usually vary from €40 to €50 per night for a single room (€50 to €70 for a double) in budget accommodation to over €350 per night at a top class hotel. The price charged for a room often has less to do with its quality or decor than with the local competition. In some popular cities such as Frankfurt and Munich, even small guesthouses charge five-star rates during trade fairs and it's common for them to raise their prices steadily as the better hotels fill up.

If you arrive in a city during a festival or international trade fair, you're likely to find yourself in poor quality, expensive accommodation on the outskirts of town, unless you've booked well in advance. This is especially true of Munich during Oktoberfest (mid-September until the first week of October), when it's necessary to book a hotel up to a year in advance. Hotels outside the major cities are generally more affordable.

Those interested in history or architecture may wish to stay at one of the many castles that have been converted into hotels, although you should be prepared to pay handsomely for the privilege. For information, see www.schlosshotels.co.at/en/hotels/neighbouring-countries/germany.html.

Germany is a member of Motorbike Hotels International (www.motor-bike-hotels.com), the European network of hotels offering special services for bikers. Hotels are located in popular motorcycling areas and offer free maps plus safe parking areas, bike washing and maintenance facilities, boot polishing equipment, and heated drying rooms for wet gear. First-time guests receive a 'biker's pass' that offers each tenth night free.

Local tourist offices provide a wealth of information about accommodation in their region and are happy to assist travellers in finding rooms and board. They also provide information for people with particular needs, such as those with children or pets, the disabled and those on particular diets. They may also provide a list of bed and breakfast establishments (B&Bs) and rooms to let in private homes. Tourist offices that provide a room-finding service (*Zimmervermittlung*) may make bookings free of charge or charge a small booking fee.

Most tourist guides contain a wealth of information about accommodation, and there are a number of specialised hotel publications in English and German, including the *Michelin Red Hotel and Restaurant Guide Germany* and *Hotels Deutschland*, published annually by the Hotel Verband Deutschland (www.hotellerie.de). You can also find German hotels via websites such as www.booking.com, www.hotels.com and www.trivago.com.

Hotel Lux 11, Berlin

HOSTELS

If you're travelling on a tight budget, the best way to stretch your financial resources is by staying at youth hostels (*Jugendherbergen*). Germany has one of the most extensive networks of hostels in the world, with over 500 throughout the country (there are even around 40 castles and stately homes that have been transformed into modern youth hostels). The vast majority are operated by the German Youth Hostel Association (Deutsches Jugendherbergswerk, www. jugendherberge.de/en), indicated by a 'DJH' sign. The DJH publishes an annual *Handbuch der Jugendherbergen in Deutschland* listing all its hostels with descriptions, facilities, photographs, travel instructions and rates. Although most hostels are open throughout the year, some are closed in winter and a number even close every other weekend.

Youth Hostels are open to everyone with no age limit: school classes, individuals and families, sports clubs or youth groups. However, you need to be a member of the Youth Hostel Association to stay in a hostel, which for those who live in Germany costs €22.50 per year for families and those aged over 27, and €7 per year for juniors (aged up to 26). DJH membership is the key to hostels and budget accommodation in hostels across the globe, and is valid in over 4,000 youth hostels in over 80 countries.

Guests are normally accommodated in dormitories, although single, double and family rooms may be available for an extra cost (bookings advisable or essential during peak periods). Almost all the rooms have washing facilities and many have their own shower and toilet. Around 150 Hostels are accessible to wheelchairs. Breakfast and bed linen are included in the price.

Hostel rates fall into four categories, depending on the services and facilities provided, with category 1 being basic and category 4 'first class' (some 60 per cent of hostels). Junior rates of from €15 to €31 per night for accommodation, breakfast and bed linen usually apply to guests aged under 27 and families with children. Those aged 27 and over usually pay a surcharge of around €4 per night. Children up to two years of age are free and children up to the age of five receive a 50 per cent discount on the total charge (or only on meals in some cases). Older children may also be eligible for reduced rates. A warm meal costs between €5 and €8 (less for a packed lunch) and inexpensive half- and full-board is usually offered.

Priority is given to those aged under 27, and those aged 27 or older are supposed to be accepted only when a hostel isn't fully booked by 6pm, unless they have a booking. In Bavaria, those aged over 26 aren't admitted to youth hostels unless accompanied by 'children' under 26. Bookings are held only until 6pm, unless the warden is informed that you'll be arriving late (10pm is usually the latest check-in time).

All hostels have a curfew, when the front door is locked, which may be as early as 10pm in rural areas, although it can be midnight or even 2am in major cities. The checkout time is usually 9am. The length of a stay at a youth hostel is limited to a maximum of three days, although this is usually enforced only when new arrivals would otherwise be prevented from getting a bed. However, some hostel wardens strictly enforce all rules, including some they make up as they go along!

Establishments run by the Friends of Nature Association (NaturFreunde Deutschlands e.V. (www.naturfreunde.de) are similar to youth hostels, although targeted more at older people. There are around 400, mostly in the countryside close to towns, providing accommodation in single and double rooms and/or small dormitories.

SELF-CATERING ACCOMMODATION

Self-catering accommodation (*Ferienwohnungen*) and furnished apartments (*Ferienappartements*) are available for short-term lease throughout Germany and can be rented through agencies or directly from owners. While they all look good in brochures and online, the quality varies hugely, and a high rental charge is no guarantee of quality. Most are spotlessly clean, but they're furnished and equipped to variable standards; some don't even supply toilet paper and if you don't bring your own bed linen and towels you may be charged an additional fee for laundry services. If you plan to arrive on a Sunday, bear in mind that the shops will be closed, so bring any necessities with you.

Generally, you're required to do your own daily cleaning, unless an apartment is part of a hotel complex where chambermaids are provided. In any case, you're usually charged a cleaning fee at the time of your departure.

Apartments are normally leased on a weekly basis from Saturday to Saturday, and you're required to vacate the premises before noon on the last day or face an army of cleaning ladies ready to remove you with the garbage.

The best way to find self-catering accommodation is via the internet from a wealth of websites including www.interchalet. co.uk, www.novasol.co.uk/holiday-cottages/ germany.html, www.tuivillas.com and www. vacation-apartments.com/europe/germany. You can also send an email to the tourist office of the town where you wish to stay, who will usually send you a list of available properties and prices, sometimes with a map of the town showing the apartments' locations.

Prices vary considerably with the season, quality, size and location, e.g. proximity to amenities such as ski-lifts or tourist attractions. The rental agreement is likely to require a deposit (payable in advance) and should specify any additional costs. In some areas there's a 'spa tax' (*Kurtaxe*) of a few euros per day, which is designed to help maintain the local spas and isn't included in room rates.

CARAVANNING & CAMPING

Germany has over 2,000 campsites, many in popular hiking and climbing areas, and camping anywhere else is frowned upon, although tolerated provided you have the permission of the landowner. Camping on public land is illegal, but you're permitted to spend one night in a caravan or mobile home in any public parking space.

Campsites are graded from 'good' to 'excellent' depending on their facilities, which range from basic washing and toilet facilities and perhaps a shop, to a wide range of amenities, including electricity connection, showers, sauna, washing machines, supermarket, lock-up storage for valuables and various sports facilities, which may include a swimming pool (outdoor and/or indoor) and tennis courts. Sites may also have facilities for golf or crazy golf, volleyball, cycling, table tennis, canoeing, fishing and boating. Large campsites usually also have a restaurant and a bar.

Prices are based on the facilities and location, and range from around €3 to €12 per person per night, plus around €4 to €8 per tent, with extra fees for cars and caravans. Most campsites are packed between June and September, and you should arrive by early afternoon if you haven't made a booking. Some camping areas are open only during the summer season, while others remain open year round.

A free list of caravan and camping grounds can be obtained from the German National Tourist Board, while comprehensive guides are published by the German Camping Club (DCC, www.camping-club.de) and the ADAC motoring organisation (*ADAC Reiseführer Camping*, https://campingfuehrer.adac.de/home/index.php). Useful camping websites include www.camping-in-deutschland.de and www.camping.info.

Caravans and mobile homes can be hired from companies throughout Germany including www.drm.eu and www.motorhomerepublic.com.

FESTIVALS

Every German town, no matter how large or small, has an annual festival. Most people are familiar with Munich's *Oktoberfest* and some may even have heard of the *Cannstätter Wiesen* or the *Bad Dürkheim Weinfest*. There are many hundreds more, which although smaller, possess that light-hearted German 'carousel-and-candy-floss' atmosphere. The larger festivals are invariably to celebrate the local beer and/or wine,

where you must usually pay a deposit on a beer mug at beer festivals or buy (or bring) your own glass at wine festivals – the organisers have learnt from long experience that many glasses don't survive the evening or are taken home as souvenirs. The number one rule on these occasions is never to drink and drive but to use public transport; the local police may be ill-humoured at having to work while everybody else is having fun and may apply the alcohol laws even more rigorously than usual.

There's also the carnival season (known as the 'fifth season'). *Karneval* or *Fasching* (pronounced 'fashing') is a Catholic festival usually beginning on Epiphany (*Dreikönigstag*, 6th January) – although it varies from region to region – culminating on the day before Ash Wednesday, i.e. Shrove Tuesday (*Faschingsdienstag*). *Karneval* is most popular in the Rhineland, and the party really gets going on the *Weiberfastnacht* (ladies' carnival) – the Thursday before Ash Wednesday – when women take control and run around cutting off men's ties. From Saturday to Tuesday, parades take place in many towns, the most important of which are on Rose Monday (*Rosenmontag*), which attracts hundreds of thousands of people. Things can get quite out of hand with revellers dressing up (political satire is an especially popular theme), drinking and trying to catch prizes thrown from floats (comparable to Mardi Gras in New Orleans, USA).

The largest festivities take place in Cologne, Dusseldorf, Mainz and Wiesbaden. Don't assume, however, that this is just fun and games – it's taken very seriously, particularly in the above towns. Once you get into the spirit of it you may wish to join a *Fasching* club, where you'll discover that what looks like lots of fun to the visitor is actually considerable hard work and quite expensive. In fact it's so costly that only millionaires can afford to accept the title of *Fasching* prince in the major locations. In Cologne it's estimated that the prince must spend around €60,000 just for the confectionery thrown from the parade's floats – a stiff bill for just 'three crazy days'.

There's a growing taste for medieval festivals in Germany, which are held in many parts of the country, particularly in the Angelbachtal and at Münzenberg Castle (near Butzbach) in spring and summer. An increasing number of people are drawn to this rather bizarre activity, which requires participants to make their own clothes, weapons and armour. Some of the groups involved, such as the Society for Creative Anachronism (www.sca.org and www.drachenwald.sca.org) take their hobby so seriously that they hardly talk about anything else. Medieval festivals offer arts and crafts exhibits, jousting knights, jesters, wandering minstrels, an outdoor theatre, and plenty of hearty food and drink. The castles are usually on hilltops, so be prepared for plenty of climbing.

THEME PARKS

Germany boasts a number of theme parks, including the top-rated Phantasialand (www.phantasialand.de) in Brühl, near Cologne, which has around 30 rides and seven shows, including some with animals. Free admission is provided for anyone visiting the park on his or her birthday (proof in the form of a passport or ID card is required). Movie Park (http://movieparkgermany.de), Bottrop (north of Essen) is a must for all fans of Spongebob Squarepants (a popular Nickelodeon cartoon character). Holiday Park (http://holidaypark.de) at Hassloch, between Mannheim and Karlsruhe, offers magic shows, a cypress garden and a waterski display; while the Europa Park (www.europapark.de) in the Black Forest (Rust, near Freiburg) is set in an old castle park with a French quarter, an Italian section, a Russian corner and a Dutch village. For information about Germany's leading theme parks, see www.germany.travel/en/specials/family-attractions/theme-parks/theme-parks.html.

You should plan to spend at least a day at any of the above theme parks. Parks provide plenty of parking, and coach trips are also offered by tour companies throughout Germany, usually on Saturdays or Sundays.

Deutsches Museum, Munich

MUSEUMS

The diversity and range of museums in Germany is unequalled in any other European country, where it's said that every town with over 10,000 inhabitants has at least two museums (Berlin alone has over 100!). While most relate to the history of the local area (*Heimatmuseum*) others are world-renowned, such as the Deutsches Museum in Munich (www.deutschesmuseum.de), the world's largest museum of science and technology welcoming around 1.5 million visitors a year; the Pergamon Museum in Berlin (www.smb.museum/en/museums-institutions/pergamonmuseum/home.html), which houses remains and reconstructions of ancient monumental architecture, such as the Altar of Zeus from Pergamon and Ishtar Gate; and the Gutenberg Museum in Mainz (www.gutenberg-museum.de), one of the oldest museums of printing in the world. Details of all Berlin's museums can be found at www.smb.museum/home.html and information about museums throughout Germany at www.worldartantiques.com/germanymuseums.htm.

State museums aren't always where you may expect to find them; for example, the Hessian state museum (www.hlmd.de) isn't in either Frankfurt (Hessen's largest city) or Wiesbaden (the capital of Hessen), but in Darmstadt, which was the capital until 1918.

One of Germany's most remarkable museums is the Technik Museum in Sinsheim (http://sinsheim.technik-museum.de), where you can hire some of the vehicles on display and take them for a 'spin' – from a 1930s racing car to a Second World War tank – although the hire charges and insurance aren't exactly cheap. For those of a bloodthirsty disposition, exhibits at the Middle Ages Criminal Museum (Mittelalterliches Kriminalmuseum, www.kriminalmuseum.eu) in Rothenburg o.d.T., open from April to October, include chastity belts, neck violins, human cages, a witch's chair and even the dreaded Iron Maiden.

There's also a humorous side to some German museums; anybody who thinks the Germans have no sense of humour need only visit the Karl Valentin Museum in Munich, where a bowl of water is labelled 'a splendid snow sculpture, until brought inside'. Other unusual museums around Germany include the Bee Museum (Knüllwald, www.lebendiges-bienenmuseum.de/livbeemu.htm), the Chair Museum (Rabenau, www.deutsches-stuhlbaumuseum.de), the Chocolate Museum (Cologne, www.schokoladenmuseum.de/en), and the Toy Soldiers and Tin Figures Museum (Kulmbach, https://plassenburg.byseum.de/de/die-museen/deutsches-zinnfigurenmuseum).

Note that many museums close on Mondays (in eastern states they may close on two days a week) and on public holidays.

Germany also has many interesting open-air museums and attractions, including the slate mines (*Schieferbergwerk Besuchergrube*) in Bundenbach/Hunsrück and the silver mines (*Reiche Zeche*) in Freiberg. If you're interested in architecture, and 17th-century half-timbered buildings in particular, head for New Anspach (near Frankfurt) to see the open-air museum (*Freilicht Museum*) at Hessen Park.

Admission charges vary considerably from around €2 to €10, while some museums offer free admission, particularly those run by a local authority or university. In most major cities public transport tickets also provide admission to museums.

GARDENS, PARKS & ZOOS

Many of Germany's botanical and zoological gardens are world famous, such as the

Schloss Bellevue, Berlin

Hellabrunn Zoo (www.hellabrunn.de/en) in Munich and Frankfurt's Palmengarten (www.palmengarten.de). Almost every major German city has a zoo, which may be called a *Vivarium, Tierpark* or *Tiergarten*. There are also around 30 Wildlife parks (*Wildpark*) in Germany, which are nature preserves with regional animal habitats only, such as deer, wild boar, bears and falcons. They usually offer animal petting and feeding areas, birds of prey shows and huge playgrounds, and are very popular with children.

In addition to general botanical gardens (*botanischer Garten*) there are so-called 'teaching trails' (*Lehrpfade*) in some locations, designed to educate visitors about the local flora and agriculture. These are usually free unless the services of a guide are required. Garden lovers may also be interested in the German Federal Garden Show (www.bundesgartenschau.de), held in a different city each year. A list of botanical gardens and zoos can be obtained from the GNTB, and information is provided in most guidebooks. (see also www.gardenvisit.com/gardens/in/germany and www.thegardeningwebsite.co.uk/gardens-to-visit-in-germany-c6989.html).

Many regions have areas designated as national parks or nature reserves, indicated by a triangular white sign with a green border reading '*Naturschutzgebiet*'. There are no admission fees but the strictly enforced rules include no camping, no fires, no picking flowers, no disturbing the animals and no dogs running free, while in some reserves visitors are restricted to marked paths.

German zoos and animal parks (all 863 of them!) are listed on www.zoo-infos.de/index-en.html and national parks on the Federal Agency for Nature Conservation's website (Bundesamt für Naturschutz, www.bfn.de/0308_nlp+M52087573ab0.html).

CINEMAS

Cinema flourishes in Germany, which has a long tradition of film-making, although the majority of films shown nowadays are American imports (dubbed into German). There are numerous cinemas (*Kinos*) in German cities, mostly with four to six screens (although some have 16 or more), and most towns have at least one. Most cinemas show films only in German, although in most large cities there's at least one 'art-house' or 'alternative' cinema (*Kommunales Kino* or *Programmkino*) showing original-language versions, indicated by '*OF*' (*Originalfassung*) or '*OV*' (*Originalversion*). A foreign film with German subtitles is indicated by '*OmU*' (*Original mit Untertiteln*) after the title. In some cities there may be a cinema showing only English-language films.

There are strict age restrictions for many films, which are shown by the word *ab* (from) followed by a number and *J.* (short for *Jahren*, meaning 'years'), as follows:

Films suitable for all are classified *o. ALTB.* (*ohne Altersbegrenzung*). It isn't unusual for cashiers or ticket collectors to ask to see some form of identification if you look younger than the age limit, and anyone who cannot prove his age is refused admission. Tickets can be quite expensive, e.g. for a Saturday night showing of a first release, although discounts of up to 50 per cent are generally offered one day a week (*Kinotag*) and the average ticket price is only around €8.

Most cinemas accept telephone and internet bookings, and you can often buy tickets at box offices in advance. In most cities you can obtain programmes by calling a local hotline (numbers can be obtained from tourist offices) or checking entertainment websites. Some cities, e.g. Berlin and Munich, stage annual international film festivals, during which participating cinemas are open 24 hours a day. For information about cinemas in Germany, see http://cinematreasures.org/theaters/germany.

Film Classifications

Rating	Restriction
o. ALTB.	unrestricted
ab 6 J.	6 years and over
ab 12 J.	12 and over
ab 16 J.	16 and over
ab 18 J.	18 and over

THEATRE, OPERA & BALLET

High-quality theatre, opera and ballet performances are staged in all major cities, many by resident companies, which receive generous government subsidies (including over 400 theatre companies). This doesn't, however, mean that tickets are cheaper than in other European countries – indeed, the opposite may be true. In many cities it's possible to buy a subscription, which includes a seat at each production during a season. Tickets for popular theatre, opera and ballet performances at the most famous venues are in high demand and must be ordered well in advance. If you're planning to attend the annual Wagner festival in Bayreuth (www.bayreuther-festspiele.de) or the Passion Play held every ten years in Oberammergau (www.passionsspiele-oberammergau.de/en), you must literally book years in advance.

Political and satirical *Kabarett* entertainment, featuring monologues and short sketches, is common in larger cities, particularly Berlin (where the musical *Cabaret* was set). Top British musicals, such as those of Andrew Lloyd-Webber, are performed (usually in German) in some cities and are extremely popular, so much so that an entire tourist industry has sprung up around them. Tour companies offer overnight or weekend package deals that include transport, hotel accommodation and tickets to shows. These all-inclusive deals usually represent good value, often costing little more than the price of a couple of tickets alone if you buy them from the box office.

Theatre performances are generally in German except for occasional international workshops, tours by American or British companies, or community theatres such as the English Theatre in Frankfurt (www.english-theatre.de). The Morale, Welfare and Recreation (MWR) division of the US armed forces sponsors English-language performances at its bases in Heidelberg, Kaiserslautern, Mannheim and Wiesbaden, which are open to the public. The Amerika Haus (www.amerikahaus.de) centres in Munich, Nuremberg and Cologne also stage English performances.

CONCERTS

Germany has a long tradition of classical music and opera and is the birthplace of many of the world's greatest composers. Every major city has a symphony orchestra and operatic company, many performing at the highest level. Classical concerts, music festivals and solo performances are regularly held throughout the country. Germany boasts not only some of the world's best concert houses, but three of its finest orchestras: the Berlin Philharmonic Orchestra (*Berliner Philharmoniker*), the Bavarian Radio Symphony Orchestra (*Symphonieorchester des Bayerischen Rundfunks*), based in Munich, and the Leipzig Gewandhaus Orchestra (*Gewandhausorchester Leipzig*). Although all three perform almost nightly during the season, it doesn't mean that obtaining a ticket is easy as most concerts are sold out well in advance. If you wish to attend a concert, you should book as far in advance as possible.

Free concerts are often staged at the various Amerika Haus centres (see above), where Americans touring Europe 'stop off'. There are also many free classical and choral performances in parks and churches, some sponsored by local tourist boards. Look out for notices in local newspapers and magazines, and for posters in cities. Upcoming concerts are also listed on various ticket websites such as http://concertful.com/concerts/Germany and www.ticketmaster.de/?language=en-us.

Many German cities (including Berlin, Essen, Frankfurt, Hamburg and Munich) are venues on the world tours of major popular artists and bands, some of which stage concerts in all five cities, while others take in only one or two. Tickets are available from record shops, local information offices and ticket agencies. In spring and summer huge outdoor rock concerts are staged in the major cities, attracting tens of thousands of fans. The price of tickets for pop music concerts is generally high, and in the case of superstars and top bands, astronomical. Don't, however, neglect the wealth of homegrown talent; Germany has a thriving club scene where everything from blues and jazz to folk and rock can be enjoyed nightly.

SOCIAL CLUBS

Club life has a special place in German culture, and most Germans belong to a number of clubs or associations, including sports clubs. There are many social clubs and expatriate organisations in Germany catering for both foreigners and Germans, including Ambassador clubs, American Women's and Men's Clubs, Anglo-French clubs, Business Clubs, International Men's and Women's clubs, Kiwani Clubs, Lion and Lioness Clubs and Rotary Clubs.

> ### ☑ SURVIVAL TIP
>
> If you want to integrate into your local community or German society in general, one of the best ways is to join a German club. Ask at the local town hall or library for information.

Expatriates from many countries run clubs in major cities, a list of which can usually be obtained from embassies and consulates. Many local clubs organise activities and pastimes such as chess, bridge, art, music, sports activities and sports trips, theatre, cinema and visits to local attractions. Joining a local club is one of the easiest ways to meet people and make friends (and, if you join a German club, improve your German!).

DISCOS & NIGHTLIFE

The availability, variety and quality of nightlife in Germany varies considerably with the town or region. In some small towns, you may be fortunate to find a bar with live music or a discotheque, while in major cities such as

Berlin, Hamburg and Munich, you'll be spoilt for choice and can party round the clock (and then some). The major cities offer a wide choice of entertainment, including jazz clubs, cabarets, discos, sex shows, music clubs, trendy bars, nightclubs and music halls. The liveliest places are the music clubs, which are infinitely variable and ever-changing with a wide choice of music from jazz to rock, funk to folk. The most popular clubs are listed in newspapers and entertainment magazines. For those with less tolerant eardrums, establishments such as a *Tanz-Club*, *Tanz-Café* or *Jazz-Club* may be more suitable.

Berlin and Hamburg are famous for providing opportunities for new groups and acts (it wasn't only the Beatles who made their name here). One place worthy of special mention is the Tiger Palast Club in Frankfurt (www.tigerpalast.de), a successful combination of nightclub, circus and variety show.

Discos are very much part of youth culture in Germany, where the usual fare includes pounding techno music (Germany is its spiritual home) played at deafening volume. Many discos are selective about who they admit (unless business is slow), especially those with a fashionable reputation such as the P1 in Munich, where you must be either 'famous'

> Irish-style pubs offering Guinness and other Irish beers are common throughout Germany, where they have almost a cult following and often offer live music. Darts can be played at many British and Irish pubs in Germany.

or conform to a rigid (often outrageous) dress code to get past the doorman (or be strikingly beautiful).

Discos generally don't admit those aged under 18 after midnight, and may ask them to leave (even if accompanied by adults) after that time. Places that cater only to teenagers aren't allowed to serve alcohol (although beer isn't reckoned to be an alcoholic drink in Bavaria!). Youth discos open as early as 7pm and generally close at midnight, while those targeted at adults often don't get going until 11pm and close between 3am and 5am. The admission fee to discos (and other nightclubs) is usually from €5 to €15, although it can be as much as €20, which may include a 'free' drink or two, or there may be a minimum drink purchase. Some clubs offer free entry, but drinks are very expensive. German discos are listed at www. discolist.de.

Germany is one of the world's more tolerant countries as far as LGBT is concerned, and most cities have thriving gay scenes. For listings of gay men's clubs, consult *Gab Magazin*, a monthly magazine and website (www.inqueery. de/gab), while both gay and lesbian establishments can be found via Travel Gay Europe (www.travelgayeurope.com/ destination/gay-german y). Local guides to gay establishments are distributed in popular cafés and bars in

trendy districts, and are usually identifiable by their pink colour.

CASINOS & GAMBLING

There are around 50 casinos in Germany, and most states have at least one licensed casino, many of which are situated in spa towns. The casino (*Spielbank*) and spa combination is

Baden-Baden Casino

a centuries-old tradition in Germany, where resorts such as Baden-Baden (established 1810), Bad Ems (1710), Bad Homburg (1841) and Wiesbaden have achieved huge popularity, although casino clientele is much changed from the elite crowd that used to frequent Baden-Baden and Wiesbaden in the 19th century.

Nowadays you can expect to find punters in casual dress, and even wearing T-shirts and shorts during the afternoon. However, most casinos insist on formal attire in the evening, or at the very least a collar and tie for men and a dress for women. All the usual temptations to part with your money are on offer, including roulette, blackjack, poker and craps, plus an endless array of slot machines. Most casinos

have a high maximum stake and, if Lady Luck is with you, 'breaking the bank' is still a (remote) possibility – though, of course, you're far more likely to lose your shirt. There's a nominal entrance fee of around €5 and you must show your passport or identity card.

Perhaps surprisingly, most gambling outside casinos is illegal. Among the few exceptions are the state and national lotteries, and slot machines limited to a small maximum pay-out. Sadly, the latter seem to be among the most addictive form of gambling in the world, and no matter what initiatives are taken by the authorities (short of outlawing them) they're responsible for an increasingly large number of compulsive gamblers. State lotteries donate around half their profits to charities or community programmes (e.g. *Aktion Mensch*, which funds programmes for mentally and physically disabled people), and pay out the other half in winnings.

The only other legal way to gamble in Germany is on horse racing, where bets are accepted at courses and through the (government-controlled) national lottery outlets. Horseracing includes both trotting (the most popular form) and flat racing – most medium and large cities having at least one racetrack.

BARS & PUBS

There's at least one bar (*Bierlokal*) or inn (*Gasthof*) in every town and most villages in Germany, although they can be rather seedy establishments. If you're looking for a place with a bit of class, you should seek out a *Gaststätte* (called a *Kneipe* in some regions), which may open as early as 10am and close well after midnight – they must usually close by

2am, although *Kneipen* in Berlin are required to close for only one hour in every 24 hours for cleaning (and most are best avoided)! While some are purely drinking establishments, others offer a variety of fairly basic, traditional dishes.

Southern Germany has a wealth of traditional beer halls known variously as a *Brauereikeller*, *Brauerei* or *Bierkeller*, where food is often served to the accompaniment of a brass band (and possibly dancing if you can still stand). In many Bavarian beer gardens you're permitted to bring your own food and you're usually required to pay a deposit on your glass.

As you'll quickly learn, drinking toasts is extremely popular in Germany, especially in beer halls and at festivals, where the band encourages them by playing the Prosit song every three minutes (a sneaky trick to make you consume more beer – it isn't compulsory to toast!). Toasting requires proper etiquette, which Germans are only too happy to teach you. The basic technique is as follows:

◆ When you get your drink, you must clink glasses with everyone within reach, while looking each individual in the eye, and say *Prost*, or *zum Wohl*; do so whenever a new person comes to the table and gets a drink or simply whenever you feel like it. If you cannot reach someone, make eye contact and nod before drinking.

◆ Be sure not to 'cross glasses' with others, which is considered bad luck.

◆ In some regions, you should bang the beer mat with your glass once before drinking.

◆ Never toast with water or a non-alcoholic drink!

The main draught beer served in a bar or pub varies with the region, but will generally be of one of the following varieties: *Pils* (Pilsen style, particularly in the north), *Weizenbier* (wheat beer, mostly in Bavaria), *Helles* (lager, only in Bavaria), *Berliner Weissbier* or *Kölsch* (Cologne style). Most bars have only one kind of beer on draught but a variety of bottled beers. In Bavaria, there are some beers that are served only at certain times of the year, such as at around Christmas. One such beer is *Starkbier* (strong beer), which has an alcohol content of as much as 18 per cent, and, needless to say, should be drunk slowly. If you're a real beer fan, you may wish to visit the Brewery Museum in Cologne, the Oktoberfest Museum in Munich or, better still, a real brewery (most offer tours and tastings).

Bars also serve a variety of other drinks, including soft drinks, wine, spirits, champagne or German sparkling wine (*Sekt*) and the usual range of cocktails, although the prices of the latter can be astronomical. The wine list varies with the bar and the region, local wines usually predominating. In wine-growing areas (but rarely elsewhere) there are wine bars (*Weinstuben*) and cellars (*Weinkeller*).

In Frankfurt you can hop aboard the Apple Wine Express, a vintage tram that winds through the city streets on weekends and public holidays. Apple wine (cider) is a Frankfurt tradition and the celebrated drink is produced only in a limited number of centuries-old, family-run establishments. Apple wine (called *Ebbelwei* in the local dialect), served in a blue-and-grey pottery jug called a *Bembel*, is made from a mixture of apples, water, sugar and yeast, and the cloudy, alcohol-rich result can make your head hurt for days if you drink too much. Apple wine pubs (*Apfelweinwirtschaft*) can be found throughout the old district of Sachsenhausen in Frankfurt, where customers sit outdoors at long wooden tables and toast each other with their apple wine glasses (known as a *Schobbeglas*). Those in the know order cheese in vinaigrette as an accompaniment or the local speciality, *schweinshaxe* (pork knuckle).

German bartenders rarely demand payment after each drink, but note each drink on your beer mat, with the possible exception of popular tourist haunts and Irish and other 'foreign' pubs. Most bars close on one day a week (*Ruhetag*), which is noted on a sign on the door. Most German bars are now smoke free, unless they have some sort of smoking ban loophole, such as a separate 'smoking' room.

You'll usually find at least one local newspaper and perhaps also a regional one in bars for customers to read. Card playing is permitted (although not if it involves gambling!) as well as chess and draughts/checkers (boards are provided in many places). A popular card game is *Skat*, a three-player, 32-card game, which is an institution in Germany where *Skat* clubs abound.

In most establishments there's a table reserved for regular customers called the *Stammtisch* – the locals may be upset if an outsider (i.e. anyone but a local regular customer) dares to sit there, which particularly applies in Bavaria.

CAFÉS

Cafés (*Café*) don't usually serve many alcoholic drinks, with the possible exception of sparkling wine and two or three types of beer. Instead, they offer a good selection of coffee (including iced versions) and tea. An establishment offering a wide range of fine cakes and pastries may be called a *Cafékonditorei*, while one specialising in ice cream, an *Eiscafé*. Usually you must go to the counter to choose your cake or pastry, which will then be served with the rest of your order. Snacks are available and usually include salads, homemade soups and simple toasted sandwiches, although you shouldn't expect much beyond this.

Cafés are an institution throughout Germany. They aren't simply a place to grab a cup of coffee or a bite to eat, but are meeting places, shelters, sun lounges, somewhere to make friends, talk, write, do business, study, read a newspaper or just watch the world go by. Germans spend a lot of time in cafés, perhaps nursing a single drink, and nobody will usually rush you to finish, unless it's the height of the tourist season and people are waiting for tables. Some are elegant places, visited as a Sunday outing, while others have a pianist or other entertainment, and most (like bars) provide free newspapers and possibly also a few magazines. Cafés generally close on one day a week.

RESTAURANTS

The only field in which complete multicultural integration has been achieved in Germany is in its restaurants. No matter what cuisine you fancy, whether it's Chinese, Greek, Indian, Italian, Japanese, Spanish, Thai, Turkish, Yugoslavian or Vietnamese, you should be able to find it somewhere in the major cities. The quality varies widely, from Michelin-starred *haute cuisine* to fast food at its direst. Prices are comparable with those in other central European countries and service is generally good (and seldom provided by Germans!).

Germany isn't noted for its food, although it isn't exactly a gastronomic wasteland, and, with the proliferation of ethnic restaurants, it has become increasingly difficult to find places offering traditional German cuisine. They do exist, however, and are well worth seeking out. Sausage (*Wurst*) is the most popular (virtually the national) dish in Germany, where it's allegedly possible to eat a different variety every day for more than four years! There are sausages made from beef, pork, veal or a combination of these, in a plethora of recipes. *Wurst* is usually accompanied by *Sauerkraut* (fermented cabbage cooked with apple, sometimes – in the cheaper varieties – with wine added to speed up the fermentation process), hot or cold potato salad, or dumplings. Game (particularly venison and wild boar) is popular throughout Germany, particularly in the autumn.

Germany also boasts a number of regional specialities, and there are many books on German regional cuisines. In Bavaria a popular dish is leg of pork stuffed with red pepper, assorted minced meats and breadcrumbs; Berlin has its *Berliner Leber* (veal liver cooked with apples and onions); a Bremen speciality is chicken casserole simmered in cream, cognac and white wine; Frankfurt has its *Rippchen mit*

Schweinehaxe (pork knuckle)

Kraut (thick, salted pork chops, boiled in water, cooked with juniper berries and served with sauerkraut); Mecklenburg offers breast of duck with carrots and apples (flavoured with butter, pepper, sugar and marjoram); a Hamburg speciality is *Aalsuppe* (eel soup, with plums and vegetables); Saarland is noted for its rabbit cooked in red wine and garlic; Swabia for sliced veal with cream sauce, served with noodles flavoured with juniper berries; and Thuringia is famous for its sauerkraut rice and sausage slices with onions, apple wine and paprika. *Guten appetit!*

Germany isn't exactly a Shangri-la for vegetarians, but meat-free alternatives can be found. Among the best bets are Chinese (a *Buddhaplatter* is simply vegetables and rice) and Indian restaurants (where many rice dishes are served without meat, and vegetable curry is a favourite). Salad bars can be found at caféterias in department stores and also at fancy hotels offering over-priced Sunday brunches. In fact, there's usually at least one meat-free dish on the menu at any German restaurant, although the quality is variable and most options are heavy on potatoes. True vegetarian restaurants are few and far between, although they do exist, particularly in the major cities (www.happycow.net/europe/germany). If you eat fish, you can get fish salads and sandwiches at the Nordsee fast food chain, but fresh fish isn't a regular item on the average German menu.

Restaurants are required to display their menu and price list outside the main entrance so that you can see what's on offer and the price (which includes tax and service) before entering. You can buy a filling meal for around €10 at ethnic restaurants or by choosing the set menu of the day (see below), but for a good meal with wine you should be prepared to pay at least €20 per head (or much more in a top restaurant).

Don't expect to be shown to a seat; you must find your own. In a busy restaurant in Bavaria it's common for strangers to share tables, and you shouldn't be surprised if someone asks to join you at your table. Many restaurants allow dogs and it's common for customers to bring their dogs with them.

A menu is called a *Karte* or *Speisekarte*, while in German a *Menü* (or *Tagesmenü*) is a set meal. Wine lists (*Weinkarten*) range from a few local house wines to the best French vintages at astronomical prices, although most good restaurants offer a selection of reasonably-priced wines from around the world. Water isn't provided unless you ask for it, and generally only sparkling mineral water is available (and charged to your bill). Bread is included only if it's stated on the menu; if you

request it as an extra it will also be added to your bill.

Note also the following regarding restaurants in Germany:

- ◆ Don't be surprised if you're presented with the bill (*Rechnung*) halfway through the meal, as this is common practice when staff are changing shifts, when the waiter must balance his account.

- ◆ Tipping (*Trinkgeld*) isn't a big thing in Germany, and you don't need to feel uncomfortable if you haven't got any change or have just a few small coins – you just simply round up the bill to the nearest euro or so. Tips aren't a waiter's wages, but are considered a 'thank you' for a job well done (see **Tipping** on page 282).

- ◆ Many restaurants have a separate room that's provided free of charge for social functions, provided the participants book (you cannot just turn up with a party) and order plenty of drinks or food.

- ◆ Most restaurants close for one day a week (*Ruhetag*), which is shown on a sign by the door.

The best restaurant guides for Germany include the *Michelin Red Hotel and Restaurant Guide: Germany* and the *Schlemmer Atlas*, both published annually. Alternatively there's a wealth of information available online for free.

Heidelberg, Baden-Württemberg

Toni Kroos

16.

SPORTS

*W*ith the introduction of gymnastics into schools during the Napoleonic wars in the 19th century – as as a means of pre-military training and the development of a physical culture (*Körperkultur*) – Germany was largely responsible for sport's role in modern society. In modern times few régimes have attempted to exploit sport as a means of gaining international prestige as much as those of the Nazis and communist East Germany (although Hitler's 'Aryan' 1936 Berlin Olympic Games famously came unstuck when black American sprinter James 'Jesse' Owens won four gold medals).

Although not as successful as the East Germany of pre-unification days, which was a (drug-fuelled) superpower in world sports, the united Germany remains a force to be reckoned with. The most widely practised sports include football, tennis, gymnastics and shooting, while athletics, handball, table-tennis, horse riding, skiing and swimming are also popular. Hiking, cycling, hockey (grass and ice), basketball, squash, motor sports, watersports and aerial sports also have many dedicated fans.

Responsibility for sport is shared between the federal authorities, the states and the municipalities, the last being responsible for providing sports facilities. Most towns have a public municipal sports and leisure centre with a host of facilities, including a fitness centre. Facilities are excellent in the western states, although not so good in the eastern states, where sport was formerly an elitist pursuit. Participation in and watching some sports is expensive, but costs can be reduced through the purchase of season tickets and by joining a club.

The Germans are sports-crazy, as both participants and spectators, and their enthusiasm is second to none (a number of TV stations are devoted solely to sports). Almost every sport is organised and performed somewhere in Germany, where there are over 90,000 sports clubs (*Sportvereine*) affiliated to the German Olympic Sports confederation (Deutschen Olympischen Sportbund/DOSB), which has 16 regional federations, some 60 national federations and numerous associated sports groups. Around one-third of all Germans (over 27 million) are members of a sporting club, while a further 10 million enjoy sports activities outside formal clubs. Unlike those in many other countries, such as the UK and the US, German schools and universities don't compete against each other in inter-school/college sports competitions, and the main nurseries for professional sports in Germany are amateur club competitions.

The DOSB sponsors physical fitness programmes such as the long-running *Trim dich* (literally 'trim yourself') campaign and 'sport for everybody' (*Sport für Jedermann*), which has encouraged millions of Germans to abandon their TVs and take up active sports. Jogging paths and work-out areas abound throughout the country to assist in these aims, and the DOSB awards bronze, silver and gold 'badges, known as *Deutsche Sportabzeichen*, to qualifying amateur sportsmen and women (around 1 million annually).

Various publications that promote sports events and list local sports venues are available from tourist offices, and most states and cities publish comprehensive booklets listing local sports organisations, facilities and classes. The addresses of national and state sports associations in Germany can be obtained from the DOSB (www.dosb.de/en), which also publishes a sports yearbook (*Jahrbuch des Sports*). There are also dozens of sports' magazines in Germany.

AERIAL SPORTS

Germany has many areas that are ideal for aerial sports such as gliding, hang-gliding, paragliding and hot-air ballooning. The Alps are a favourite spot due to the updraughts and the low density of air traffic (apart from all the gliders, hang-gliders and balloons!). Hang-gliding (*Drachenfliegen*) is especially popular in Germany, which has many schools, as is paragliding (*Gleitschirmfliegen*), which entails jumping off steep mountain slopes dangling from a parachute. Participants must have the proper equipment and complete an approved course of instruction, after which (if they survive) they receive a proficiency certificate and are permitted to go solo.

Ballooning has a small but dedicated band of followers. Balloon ownership is generally limited to the wealthy, but a balloon trip can be had for around €200. There is, however, no guarantee of distance or duration, and trips are dependent on wind conditions and the skill of your pilot (for information, see www.ballonfahrten.de). Light aircraft (including microlights) and gliders (sailplanes) can be hired with or without an instructor from most small airfields in

Germany, where there are also many gliding clubs.

Free-fall parachuting (sky-diving) flights can be made from most private airfields, costing around €200 per jump, including equipment and a certificate. For further information, visit www.tandemfun.de.

Further information about aerial sports is available from the German Aero Club (Deutsche Aero Club, www.daec.de).

CYCLING

Cycling is popular in Germany, not only as a means of transport and as a serious sport, but also as a relaxing pastime for the whole family. The country has over 170 long-distance cycling tracks totalling more than 40,000km (25,000mi), forestry tracks (*Forstwege*), city cycling trails and tourist routes. Scenic bike route maps and suggested itineraries for bike trips can be obtained from the Allgemeiner

Deutscher Fahrrad-Club (see below), while cycling maps (*Radwanderführer*) are published by Kompass.

Cycle racing has a huge following and races are organised at every level, including mountain bike races. Germany has a good record in international racing, particularly track racing, although the world's premier cycle race, the Tour de France, has been won only once by a German (Jan Ullrich in 1997).

Cyclists must use cycle lanes where provided, and mustn't cycle in bus lanes or on footpaths. As required by law, German motorists generally give cyclists a wide berth when overtaking, but cycling in some major cities is still dangerous. If you cycle in cities, you should have flashing lights and wear reflective clothing, protective headgear, a smog mask and a St Christopher medallion.

Bikes must be roadworthy and be fitted with a horn or bell, front and rear lights and an anti-theft device such as a steel cable lock (the only police-approved bike lock), although they still aren't thief-proof. If your bicycle is stolen you should report it to the local police – but don't expect them to find it! Some insurance companies cover bicycle theft.

You can hire a bike from railway stations participating in the 'Call-A-Bike' scheme operated by Deutsche Bahn. For other bike hire companies, look on the internet under *Fahrradverleih*.

There are a number of cycling organisations in Germany, including the Allgemeiner Deutscher Fahrrad-Club (www.adfc.de), which publishes a free brochure in English, *Discovering Germany by Bicycle*, and the Bund Deutscher Radfahrer (www.rad-net.de).

FISHING

Fishing is very popular in Germany, which has an abundance of well-stocked waters. However, there are no free fishing waters (apart from the sea), as all inland water belongs to the state, private individuals or fishing clubs, and you must buy a licence and, if applicable, pay the owner of a stream, river, pond or lake a fee. A daily permit (*Tageskarte*) can be purchased for between around €5 and €20 for most waters, although some of the most famous and productive locations can cost as much as €60 per day. No permit is required for deep-sea fishing, which is popular in the North Sea and the Baltic off Germany's northern coast, where boats can be hired from many ports.

German residents must complete months of instruction on fish habitat, biology, regulations and general knowledge, and pass a test costing around €30 before they can become licensed anglers – an excellent example of Germany's obsession with bureaucracy (see https://fishinggermany.jimdo.com/taking-my-german-fishing-license)! You receive a certification card (*Fischereischein*) costing €10 to €30 per year. Non-residents aren't required to take a test, but must have an appropriate fishing 'qualification' to obtain (from local tourist offices) a temporary licence to fish in Germany. Each state has different prices and different rules, e.g. an annual licence in Bavaria costs around €8.

Germany's main sport fish are trout (rainbow, brown, brook), grayling and carp. Fishing for brown trout and grayling is popular in mountain streams in the south, where Bavaria offers the best opportunities for fly fishing. The trout season usually runs from 1st May to the end of October, although in some waters the dates vary from year to year. There are strict regulations regarding the season, minimum size of catch and the number of fish that can be caught. For more information contact the Federation of German Sport Anglers (Verband der Deutscher Sportfischer, www.vdsf.de). The Landesfischereiverband Bayern (www.lfvbayern.de) publishes a fishing guide for Bavaria entitled *Angelführer Bayern*.

FOOTBALL

Football or soccer (*Fussball*) is Germany's unofficial national sport, with literally thousands of amateur football clubs, and it's one of the most successful nations in the world at both club and international level. Germany has won the World Cup four times, in 1954, 1974, 1990 and 2014 (only Brazil has won it more often), and was the runner-up in 1966, 1982, 1986 and 2002; it has also won the European Championship three times, in 1972, 1980 and 1996 (and was runner-up in 1976, 1992 and 2008). Germany hosted the World Cup in 1974 and 2006.

Although Germany has a large number of foreign players in its domestic league, they also produce a lot of home-grown talent and most of the national team plays for German clubs. Those that play abroad play mostly in the UK and Spain – which has affected the performance of top club teams in European competition, although German football clubs have a long and distinguished record here. Though not quite as rabid as Italian or Spanish fans, German fans can become rowdy, although it's generally safe to take your family to a football match.

The federal football league (*Bundesliga*) is Germany's premier competition, comprising 18 teams, among which the top dogs in recent years have included Bayern Munich, Borussia Dortmund, Bayer Leverkusen, FC Schalke, 1899 Hoffenheim, Hamburg SV, Werder Bremen and VfB Stuttgart. Bayern Munich (who play at the Allianz Arena in Munich) is Germany's richest and most successful club side – it seems that most other *Bundesliga* teams are simply feeder

clubs for Bayern, who snap up most of Germany's talent. (Almost every village or town has an amateur football club and there are local leagues throughout Germany.) For more information or details about forthcoming professional games, see the *Bundesliga* website (http://bundesliga.de).

The football season runs from September to Christmas and mid-February to June (there's a mid-winter break), with most matches played on Saturday afternoons (although games are also played on Fridays and Sundays) and attended by an average of around 25,000 spectators. German cup (DFB) matches are usually played during the week, as are European competition matches. Tickets can usually be purchased at grounds on the day of matches or from ticket offices, and cost from around €15 for standing places (*Stehplätze*) and from €20 for seats, while tickets for top matches and internationals cost at least €70. Ticket prices in Germany are lower than in many other European countries, particularly the UK, in large part because most clubs are actually owned by the fans.

For more information about football, see the Deutscher Fussball-Bund website (www.dfb.de).

GOLF

Although traditionally an élitist sport in Germany, golf has enjoyed increasing popularity in the last twenty years, boosted by the success of Bernhard Langer, who was in the top ranks of world golf in the '80s and '90s, and Martin Kaymer, who won the PGA championship in 2010 and the US Open in 2014 and was ranked world No 1 in 2011. The country now boasts over 500 clubs with some 300,000 members; numbers have increased considerably in the last few decades.

Martin Kaymer

However, most are private clubs, some with long waiting lists for membership, and there are few public golf courses in Germany. Club information is available on the internet (www.vcg.de, www.golfeurope.com/euro_clubs/germany-golf-courses.htm and www.1golf.eu/en/golf-courses/germany).

Most clubs admit non-members with a handicap card for a fee of between €50 to €75 for 18 holes during the week and €60 to €90 at weekends and public holidays. For famous golf clubs in the Munich area, one of the most popular cities for golf and tournaments, you can pay well over €75 during the week and more than €100 at weekends, although if you're playing with a member the fee is reduced. Annual club membership costs from €2,000 to over €10,000 for a top club.

Two major men's golf tournaments are held in Germany annually and are part of the European Tour: the BMW International Open (in Munich) and the Mercedes-Benz Championship (in Pulheim, near Cologne). The Unicredit Ladies German Open (held at Gut Häusern near Munich) is part of the Ladies European tour. For more information contact the German Golf Federation (www.golf.de).

HEALTH CLUBS

There are gymnasiums and health and fitness clubs in most towns in Germany, where 'working out' has become increasingly popular, and many companies provide health and leisure centres or pay for corporate membership of private clubs for senior staff. In addition, most public sports centres have tonnes of expensive bone-jarring, muscle-wrenching apparatus. To join a club, you must usually pay an initial fee, which ranges from €100 to €400 depending on the cachet of the club and the type of membership chosen, and then a monthly fee of €50 to €200. Usually, the higher the initial sum paid, the lower your monthly fee. You can reduce the fee by opting to use the facilities during off-peak times only, for example during the mornings or before 5pm.

In addition to gymnasiums, most clubs offer aerobics and keep-fit classes, a sauna and/or Jacuzzi and a swimming pool, and some also have tennis, squash and badminton courts (for which an additional fee is payable, depending on your membership). Other facilities may include a beauty salon (offering massage and aromatherapy) or a spa area and child care. Clubs allow you to buy a daily card (from around €20 to €40) or take a 'sniff' (*Schnupper*) day to assess whether you want to join. Clubs usually provide free personal training programmes for members.

Many top-class hotels have health clubs and swimming pools that may be open to the public, although access to facilities may be restricted to certain times.

HIKING

Germans are keen hikers. Although the main hiking season is from May to September, hiking isn't just a summer sport and most winter sports resorts keep trails open for walkers throughout the winter. Germany is a great hiking (*Wandern*) country with over 100,000km (62,000mi) of marked hiking and mountain-walking tracks administered by regional hiking clubs (*Wandervereine*) and mountaineering groups. It has a national network of paths with routes of various degrees of difficulty, although most are moderate or easy. Hikes

take in romantic forests, beautiful landscapes and tranquil lakes, and most pass through picturesque villages where there's usually somewhere you can stay overnight.

Germany has some of the most beautiful hiking country in Europe, but the terrain isn't usually as rugged as in some other countries, such as Austria, France, Spain or Switzerland. The most popular hiking areas are Bavaria and the *Schwarzwald* (Black Forest), stretching from the resort town of Baden-Baden to the Swiss border. Other popular hiking areas include the Erzgebirge, the Thuringian Forest, the Harz Mountains, the Sauerland, the Rhön, the Fichtelgebirge and the Swabian Mountains. Those who feel up to it may wish to try the challenging 60km (37mi) 'Allgäu high-level' route between Oberstdorf and the Oberjoch in the Alps, staying overnight in forest huts. Slightly less ambitious are the organised 'social' hikes (*Volksmarsch*), usually up to 42km (26mi), which attract huge numbers of participants, who usually receive a certificate, badge or medal for completing a hike.

> Free hiking maps are available from tourist offices, although the best hiking maps (*Wanderkarten*) are the *Wanderführer* series published by Kompass.

Those who are keen on Alpine walking should contact the German Alpine Association (Deutsche Alpenverein, www.alpenverein.de), which maintains around 15,000km (over 9,000mi) of Alpine paths and some 50 mountain huts. It runs courses in mountaineering and offers touring suggestions for both summer and winter routes, while a number of mountaineering schools run courses ranging from basic techniques for beginners to advanced mountaineering. Mountain walking shouldn't be confused with hiking, as it's generally done at much higher altitudes and in more difficult terrain. It's dangerous for the untrained and should be approached with much the same degree of caution and preparation as mountaineering.

For more information, contact the Federation of German Mountain and Hiking Clubs (Verband Deutscher Gebirgs- und Wandervereine, www.wanderverband.de), the German People's Sports Federation (Deutscher Volkssportverband, www.dvv-wandern.de) or the Federation of German Ski and Mountain Guides (Verband Deutscher Berg und Skiführer, www.bergfuehrer-verband.de).

RACKET SPORTS

Tennis is the second most popular participation sport in Germany (after football), and the German Tennis Association (Deutsche Tennis Bund) has over 1.5 million members and the largest club network of any country, with some 10,000 tennis clubs, over 40,000 outdoor courts and around 4,000 indoor courts. Tennis flourished in Germany in the '80s and '90s thanks to the success of stars such as Boris Becker, Steffi Graf and Michael Stich (all Grand Slam winners) and more recently Angelique Kerber, who was world number 1 in 2017 (and a former Australian and US Open winner), although the best the men could do was world number 20 (Alexander Zverev).

Alexander Zverev

Many towns have public courts, although they aren't as common as in many other countries, where you can book a court by the hour. Most courts are clay or Astroturf (artificial grass), while hard (asphalt) and grass courts are rare. When playing

on an indoor court you must wear shoes with non-marking soles – if you don't have any, they can usually be purchased or hired. Court fees vary from €15 to €30 per hour, depending on the season, day of the week and the time of day (they're usually cheaper before 5pm on weekdays); indoor courts are more expensive than outdoor courts, but the latter are more difficult to book on sunny days. Local courts and clubs are listed in the Yellow Pages under *Tenniscenter* and *Sportanlagen*.

Germany stages a number of annual professional tournaments as part of the ATP World Tour, among them the German Open in Hamburg (July), the BMW Tennis Open in Munich (April/May) and the Mercedes Cup in Stuttgart (July). Top German and foreign tennis players compete in the Federal Tennis League. For more information, contact the German Tennis Federation (Deutscher Tennis Bund, www.dtb-tennis.de).

Squash and badminton are popular in Germany, although the country has yet to make an international impact in either sport. Squash courts cost between €10 and €20 for 30 minutes, while badminton courts cost between €10 and €20 per person, per hour, courts generally being cheaper before 5pm.

SKIING

Millions of Germans ski regularly, although the majority head to neighbouring countries. Germany doesn't have many large ski centres and most are small, long-established resorts with 'traditional' lift systems. Where there are a number of nearby ski centres, sometimes including centres in Austria, you may be able to buy a pass covering all of them (although they're rarely linked by ski-lifts). German resorts are noted for their traditional architecture and the country doesn't go in for the purpose-built (i.e. concrete) resorts that are common in France. Most resorts offer good *après-ski* and many have excellent facilities for other winter sports.

The skiing season runs from the middle of December to the end of March, although at higher altitudes, such as the Zugspitze Glacier near Garmisch (up to 2,830m/8,490ft), you can often ski from November until the middle of May.

The Alps of southern Bavaria are Germany's main winter sports region, where Garmisch-Partenkirchen (720-2,966m/2,362-9,730ft) and Oberstdorf (700-2,224m/2,296-7,296ft) are the top resorts, both regular venues on the World Cup downhill circuit. Other Alpine resorts, suitable mainly for beginners and moderate skiers, include Bayrischzell, Berchtesgaden, Mittenwald and Schliersee. As an alternative to the Alps, you can ski in the Allgäu, Black Forest (*Schwarzwald*), Erzgebirge, Fichtelgebirge, Harz, Rhön, Sauerland (a cross-country paradise), Swabian Mountains and the Thuringian Forest, although many resorts have just a few downhill (*Alpin*) runs or offer only cross-country (*Langlauf*) skiing. Among the most popular resorts outside the Alps are the Black Forest resorts of Furtwangen, Schonach, Todtmoos and Todtnau. The upper Harz (Hochharz) is also noted for its excellent cross-country skiing and ski hikes.

Lift passes are fairly pricey, costing between around €15 and €42 for an adult for a day (€11-€23.50 for a child). The most expensive area is Garmisch-Partenkirchen, where the ski pass covers 38 lifts and provides access to 55km (34mi) of ski terrain, including the world famous ski runs of Kandahar and Olympia (both of which have snow-making equipment). Here a one-day weekday ticket cost €42 in 2016 (€23.50 for a child) and €234 for a 6-day pass (€117 for a child). See www.onthesnow.co.uk/europe/skipass.html for other ski pass prices.

Family passes (two adults and two children) are available in most resorts and off-season or 'white week' (*weisse Woche*) rates are offered by most winter resorts for cross-country and downhill holidays, which include bed and breakfast or half board plus ski lessons. Equipment (skis, poles and boots) can be hired for between €20 and €50 per day for adults and between €10 and €25 for children. Booking all-inclusive

package deals online with accommodation, ski passes and equipment can save you money.

The ADAC motoring organisation provides a recorded 'snow conditions' telephone service for most regions or you can check online, e.g. www.snow-forecast.com/countries/germany/resorts/A-A. For further information about skiing in Germany, contact the German Skiing Federation (Deutscher Skiverband, www.ski-online.de).

SWIMMING

Swimming is popular in Germany, where an estimated two-thirds of the population swim regularly. There are outdoor pools (*Freibad*) and indoor pools (*Hallenbad*) in most German towns and resorts, many open year-round. Swimming caps may be required at some pools and are usually sold at reception. There are a number of large indoor swimming centres and aquatic and water parks in Germany, where the facilities may include hot-water pools, sulphur baths, thermal whirlpools, connecting indoor and outdoor pools, wave machines, huge water slides, solariums and saunas (many mixed sex). The entrance fee is relatively high, e.g. €15 to €25, usually for a limited period, although they make a pleasant change from an ordinary pool. Spas throughout Germany have thermal or mineral-water indoor pools, where day visitors can swim or relax in the water.

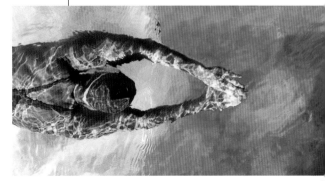

Germans are keen on nude bathing and many pools have days or times restricted to nude bathers; nudity is also permitted on certain beaches, shown by a sign reading 'FKK' (Freiekörperkultur). There are indoor sea-water pools in coastal areas and many lakes have swimming areas that are off-limits to other water sports enthusiasts. Swimming in rivers, particularly the larger ones, isn't recommended and in some cases is prohibited ('Baden verboten'), due to shipping, pollution or dangerous currents.

Most swimming pools and clubs organise swimming lessons for all levels (beginner to fish) and run life saving courses. Children can join a swimming team at a local pool that competes against other teams (competitions are organised by Schwimmvereine). For information contact your local swimming club or visit www.dsv.de. You can find a list of public swimming pools in your local area under Freizeit-, Hallen- und Freibäder in the journal section of the Yellow Pages or via the web.

> For further information, contact the German Swimming Association (Deutscher Schwimm-Verband, www.dsv.de).

WATERSPORTS

All watersports, including sailing, motor boating, windsurfing, waterskiing, rowing, canoeing and sub-aquatic sports are popular in Germany, which has a good record in world and Olympic competition, particularly in rowing and sailing. Boats and equipment can be hired on most lakes and at coastal resorts, where instruction is available for most disciplines. A licence is required for a boat with an output of over 3.6kW (around 5hp).

Windsurfing is particularly popular on Bavarian lakes, and rowing and canoeing is possible on most lakes and rivers. River surfing has also become a popular sport in Munich on the Eisbach and Flosslände, which have 'standing waves' (rather like the Severn bore); in fact, Munich is one of the few places in the world to stage an annual river surfing competition, the Munich Surf Open. Wetsuits are recommended for windsurfing, waterskiing and sub-aquatic sports, even during the summer.

The North Sea and Baltic coasts are a Mecca for sailors, as are the Bodensee (Lake Constance), Chiemsee, Müritz, Schweriner See and Starberger See (all lakes). The most popular rivers are the Danube, Elbe, Main, Neckar, Oder, Rhine, Saale and Weser. There are some 200 sailing schools on the North Sea and Baltic coasts, where Kiel and Rostock are the main sailing centres.

For further information about watersports in Germany, contact the appropriate organisation below:

- **Canoeing:** Deutsche Kanu-Verband (www.kanu.de);
- **Motor boating:** Deutscher Motoryachtverband (www.dmyv.de);
- **Rowing:** Deutscher Ruderverband (www.rudern.de);
- **Sailing:** Deutscher Seglerverband (www.dsv.org);
- **Waterskiing & Wakeboarding:** Deutscher Wasserski- und Wakeboard-Verband (www.wasserski-online.de);
- **Windsurfing:** DWSV (www.dwsv.net).

My Ziel shopping centre, Frankfurt-am-Main

17.
SHOPPING

*A*lthough not one of the world's great shopping countries, Germany offers a wide choice of shopping, ranging from exclusive specialist shops and world-renowned department stores to traditional farmers' and Christmas markets. As with so many aspects of German life, commerce is subject to a plethora of rules, regulations and legal constraints, which influence when, where and how you can shop. On the other hand, the abundance of regulations also affords considerable protection to consumers and high quality products, albeit rather expensive compared with some other countries. However, Germans are expert bargain hunters, particularly in the south of the country, where the Swabians claim to be Europe's penny-pinching champions.

Much retail regulation stems from German labour laws designed to protect shop employees from exploitation. Shop opening hours are strictly controlled and staff can only be required to perform the job they were hired to do – and even then, often apparently against their will. Even Germans joke about the surly customer service you can encounter in much of Germany.

Most shops accept exchanges or offer refunds on production of your receipt. As part of Germany's environmental legislation, shops are required by law to take back or keep the packaging from the goods they sell, so you should check that that goods are in order (as far as possible) before leaving a shop. Some shops have recycling bins in their car parks or near entrances for cartons and other packing material. If you have goods delivered to your home you can ask the delivery person to take the packing material away with them.

OPENING HOURS

Until recently, shopping hours (*Öffnungszeiten*) were strictly controlled under federal labour law, which meant that everything was

All prices advertised or quoted to individuals in Germany include value added tax and are the total price you pay.

closed by 8pm, Mondays to Fridays, and all day on Sundays and public holidays. The 'liberalisation' of shopping hours that began in the '90s led to opening hours being decided at the state level, and therefore they now vary from state to state. Most states allow shop-owners to open on four to six Sundays/public holidays a year (usually during the Christmas season), and on weeknights and Saturdays they may remain open later than 8pm, e.g. 10pm. Bakeries can open for a few hours on Sunday mornings to sell fresh bread and rolls. The exception is Bavaria, where the state government, shop owners and even the customers seem to prefer the status quo, so opening hours are more restricted. Smaller shops, particularly those in towns and villages, often close for an hour or so at lunchtime to allow employees to have their main meal of the day.

The only retail outlets that are exempt from normal shopping hours are those at airports, railway stations and petrol stations. Frankfurt airport has an extensive underground shopping area, which includes a grocery store that's open all day on Sunday and until late in the evening during the rest of the week. Petrol stations, particularly those on or near motorways, often operate a convenience shop, where you can find most 'essentials' (albeit at inflated prices).

PRICES & BARGAIN SHOPPING

There's minimal bargaining over prices in most shops, although some may offer discounts to members of a local sports club or other social or civic association. Prices aren't controlled but retailers cannot easily change prices, once posted, and most smaller stores adhere to the manufacturer's recommended retail price. A shopkeeper may reduce prices on a single line of products in order to sell off remaining stock, but such price reductions are limited to a small proportion of the total goods available, and generally apply only where the product was a one-time purchase that won't be re-ordered.

Major sales normally occur twice per year: at the end of the winter season (*Winterschlussverkauf*) and at the end of the summer season (*Sommerschlussverkauf*). The dates used to be set by regional authorities, but now shops are allowed to decide their own. In general the *Winterschlussverkauf* starts at the end of January and the *Sommerschlussverkauf* at the end of July. Price cuts during these sale periods are generous and it's an excellent time to stock up on seasonal merchandise, e.g. skiing and winter clothes in the end-of-winter sales, and swimming and holiday wear at the end of the summer. Goods purchased at a discount during end-of-season sales generally aren't returnable, therefore you need to shop carefully.

Due to the high overall level of prices there's an active market in Germany for second-hand goods, especially furniture (including complete kitchens) and appliances. Second-hand clothing and appliance stores can be found in most towns with over 5,000 inhabitants, and are listed in local phone books, on the internet and in local newspapers (some devoted solely to second-hand goods).

Shopping on the German versions of Amazon (www.amazon.de) and Ebay (www.ebay.de) is a good way to save money, while outlet malls are another option for savvy shoppers (see www.outlet-malls.eu/Germany)

Many towns run an annual flea market (Flohmarkt or Trödelmarkt) where locals can set up a stall (for a small fee, payable to the town) to sell off used household and other items (they're a good source of toys, children's clothing and kitchen equipment).

SHOPPING CENTRES & MARKETS

Germany has a variety of indoor shopping centres, located mostly in the larger towns and cities, and there's a wide range of shops and services in the underground passageways of most major railway stations, e.g. Frankfurt and Munich. The Germans haven't gone in for building vast indoor shopping malls on the outskirts of cities and towns, as are common in Britain and the USA, although there are small clusters of large stores (usually hypermarkets and discount stores) in industrial and commercial estates on the periphery of many towns. These developments have a down-to-earth practical air, but offer free parking, which is rare in towns.

> Other outdoor markets include flea markets (*Flohmarkt* or *Trödelmärkt*) and wine, crafts and other festivals organised by local authorities. Keep an eye out for posters around town announcing these events or ask at the local town hall or tourist office.

Most German towns have a pedestrianised shopping street (*Fussgängerzone*), except for early morning deliveries. In most cases, it's in the centre of town and well served by public transport. Parking in the centre of most cities and towns is expensive and difficult, particularly on Saturdays and during sale periods and the Christmas shopping season.

Most towns and all cities have regular open-air markets throughout the year. Most popular is the farmers' (Bauernmarkt) or food market, which is usually a weekly event (in Freiburg, for example, there's an open-air market six days a week in the Münsterplatz). Open-air markets aren't to be missed, particularly for regional and seasonal specialities such as white asparagus (*Spargel*) – available only in the spring – and the various types of wild mushroom (*Pilz*), an autumn speciality. Other treats you'll find in open-air markets include locally produced honey (*Honig*), cheeses (*Käse*), sausages (*Wurst*) and hams (*Schinken*), along with a wide variety of fresh fruit and vegetables. Market vendors set up at around 6 or 7am and usually cease trading in the early afternoon.

In the run-up to Christmas, many towns stage vast Christmas markets (*Adventmärkte* or *Christkindlmärkte*) offering local craft items, traditional Christmas ornaments and plenty of *Lebkuchen* (a form of gingerbread), *Stollen* (iced fruit loaf), *Spekulatius* or *Spekulatus* (an almond-flavoured biscuit) and other Christmas goodies – including *Glühwein* (mulled wine) to keep your Christmas shopping spirits up! The best include Nuremburg, Dresden, Cologne, Dusseldorf, Berlin, Rothenburg ob der Tauber, Stuttgart, Erfurt, Konstanz and Freiburg.

DEPARTMENT & CHAIN STORES

Germany has no shortage of excellent department stores, both indigenous and foreign, but after a long period of stability this sector has become the scene of mergers and takeovers in recent years. After the dust had settled Germany was left with just two major department store chains, Kaufhof (www.galeria-kaufhof.de) and Karstadt (www.karstadt.de). These are both high-quality chains, but Germany's flagship store is KaDeWe in Berlin (www.kadewe.de/en), continental Europe's largest department store, perhaps best known for its remarkable food department where shoppers can sample exotic delicacies at the many gourmet counters and wash them down with champagne and fine wines. In most large cities there are foreign chain stores such as H&M and C&A, while east Berlin even boasts a Galeries Lafayette in its KuDamm shopping district.

Department stores offer a dizzying variety of high-quality merchandise, with all famous brands represented as well as a range of good-value own-brand items. Practically all department stores accept major credit cards, which isn't always the case with other shops. At some stores you can apply for a loyalty card, which provides a discount and/or bonus points on all purchases.

The department store chains of Karstadt and Kaufhof have excellent food markets, typically on the ground floor or at basement level. Here you can usually find fresh, good-quality, pre-packaged foods, which is helpful if your German is basic and you're looking for something recognisable to cook for dinner.

Chain stores are popular throughout Germany, including US-style speciality chains such as Toys 'R' Us. There's at least one large hardware and DIY chain (*Baumarkt*) store, e.g. OBI, Bauhaus, Toom or Praktiker, on the edge of most towns, and there are also a number of discount electronics chains (e.g. Conrad, Media Markt and Saturn Hansa) where you can buy TVs, appliances and stereo equipment at competitive prices. The easiest way to compare prices is online – see **Internet & Mail-Order Shopping** on page 260.

SUPERMARKETS & HYPERMARKETS

Most towns in Germany have one or more supermarkets offering a full range of food and drinks and some small household items. Among the major chains are Tengelmann, Edeka, Rewe (which also owns Penny Markt) and Real (which is owned by Metro). There are many smaller international supermarkets, particularly Italian, Greek, Turkish and Asian, which can be good for unusual vegetables and specialist foods. In Munich, the classy Dallmayr

gourmet food shop rules the roost, with its upscale assortment of delicacies and coffees.

Metro is a huge discount retailer club (similar to Sam's Club or Costco in the US). You need to be a member to shop there, and all items are sold at wholesale prices and in bulk for small business owners. The large discount chains include Aldi, Lidl, Netto, Penny Markt and Plus, where some good bargains can be found, although the selection is limited and shops can become very crowded, especially when weekly special offers come out – so you may have to wait a long time at the checkout.

Supermarkets sell primarily food. Germany also has a wide range of hypermarkets – shops with over $2,500m^2$ ($27,000ft^2$) of floor space, selling electronic goods, household appliances, books, clothing and hardware, as well as food – usually found on the outskirts of major towns and cities. The main hypermarket chains are E-center, Globus, Kaufland, Real and V-Markt. Although some of the brand names may be unfamiliar, most products are similar to those found in supermarkets in other European countries and can meet most of your daily requirements.

Supermarkets in Germany don't provide free carrier bags or pack your purchases at the checkout. You can usually buy plastic carrier bags for €0.10 to €0.30, but it's more economical (and ecological) to bring your own bags. At most supermarkets, a €1 coin (or similar size token) is required to unlock a trolley from a rack, which is returned when you replace the trolley.

Some supermarkets offer online shopping but it isn't as popular as it is in the UK and USA. See websites for information.

Service in some supermarkets and hypermarkets can be particularly brusque. Don't expect cashiers to wish you Guten Tag or even to smile, and don't be surprised to find full pallets of merchandise left in the middle of an aisle blocking access to shelves in some discount stores, where staff are at a premium. If you buy anything from the produce section, you're sometimes expected to weigh and label it yourself; don't make the mistake of arriving at the checkout without weighing your fruit or vegetables (a cardinal sin!).

FOOD

Although you'll find it easier to shop in supermarkets than in small shops if your German is poor, don't overlook the smaller specialist food shops, which include butchers, bakers and greengrocers (although fishmongers are few and far between, except in coastal areas). Germany boasts a fine range of *Wurst* (which translates as 'sausage' but also includes cured and smoked meats, salamis and processed meats) and cheeses. You may also be surprised at the variety of bread, rolls and buns on offer in even the smallest grocery shop. The Germans make bread (*Brot*) from almost every form of grain – maize, wheat, rye, barley, spelt, etc. – typical German bread being heavy textured and thinly sliced. Foreign products, such as the more idiosyncratic British and American foods, although Stilton cheese and peanut butter can be found in some shops.

The quality of fruit and vegetables varies and is categorised from I (the highest quality) to III (the lowest), shown on labels. Some supermarket chains pride themselves on the quality (category I) and freshness of their produce, while others stock only category II and III produce, the indifferent quality being matched only by the unattractive displays and low, low prices! Many fruit and vegetables are treated with fungicides and must be thoroughly washed before eating.

Bio (BEE-oh) refers to organic goods in Germany, where Bio markets can be found in most towns.

Shops in rural areas often buy fruit and vegetables from local farmers, which is generally fresher and of better quality than that available in towns and cities and may also be cheaper. It helps to find out when your local shops receive deliveries and time your shopping trips accordingly. In general, Mondays are the worst days if you're looking for fresh produce or baked goods, and Saturday mornings are also to be avoided if possible, as this is the busiest time in most shops.

Eggs aren't generally washed or polished, giving them a more 'rustic' appearance than you may be used to; however, the fact that an egg doesn't shine doesn't mean that it's any less wholesome. As in many countries there are four kinds of eggs available: free-range (marked *Freilandhaltung*), organic (*Ökolog Erzeugung*), barn laid or cage free (*Bodenhaltung*) and battery cage (*Käfighaltung*). Milk is sold in three varieties: full-cream milk (*Vollmilch*), low fat/skimmed .5 or 1.5 per cent (*Fettarme Milch*), and heat-treated (*H Milch*). H Milch (UHT) doesn't need refrigeration until it's opened, as it has been sterilised. It may come as quite a shock that most kinds of milk aren't refrigerated in German supermarkets.

If you plan to do any baking, note that the quality of flour is indicated by the 'type number' on the packaging: the less refined, the higher the number, e.g. cake flour carries the number 405, while wholemeal flour is in the 1600 range. Freshly ground coffee can be purchased at most supermarkets (you can even grind it yourself).

ALCOHOL

Drinking alcohol is a popular pastime in Germany, despite strictly enforced drink-driving laws and growing concerns over alcoholism. Beer is the number one tipple, although its consumption is falling – in 2014 the average German consumed 114 litres compared with a record 171 litres in 1992. However, a possible shortage of beer, as was threatened a few years ago, can still bring the country to the brink of collective nervous breakdown.

Spirits are drunk in moderation, the most popular being Schnapps, which is also deemed to be the major cause of alcoholism!

Beer

Almost a third of the world's breweries – some 1,300 at the last count – are in Germany (half in Bavaria), producing around 5,000 brands of beer. Beer is brewed everywhere and styles differ considerably from area to area. Some of Germany's best brews are associated with monasteries, most notably the Kloster Weltenburg on the Danube, famous for its strong, chocolate-dark ales. *Roggenbier*, also from Bavaria, is brewed by the Princes of Thurn and Taxis in the medieval city of Regensburg, using rye instead of barley; malted and effervescent, it's almost a meal in itself. Another

Bavarian beer enjoying growing success in world markets is *Weizenbier* (wheat beer), also known as *Weissbier* (white beer), which is brewed using wheat, yeast and barley malts. Tangy, fruity and full-bodied, it's best drunk slightly chilled.

From eastern Germany there's *Schwarzbier* (black beer), brewed using burnt barley malt, with a stout-like consistency and a toasted flavour. The speciality of Cologne is *Kölsch*, a light, dry pale brew with virtually no effervescence, typically served in small fluted glasses. Some people find that it lacks flavour compared with the nutty beers of southern Germany, but it's easier to drink and seems to bloat less.

Alt (old) beers are popular around Dusseldorf. The term doesn't mean that the beer has been 'aged' but that it's brewed according to traditional, top-fermenting methods. Alt beers are dark and can taste hops-bitter or malt-sweet, depending on the recipe. *Bock* beers, in contrast, which are particularly associated with Munich, are bottom-fermented and quite strong. They can be dark or light. *Pilsner* (or Pils) beer is the most widely brewed in Germany and has become famous in other parts of the world. Strictly speaking, the term describes a brewing method first practised in the Bohemian town of Pilsen in 1842. The main ingredients of a Pilsner beer are pale malt, soft water, bottom-fermenting yeast and aromatic hops. Most Pils is a pale golden colour, although you'll occasionally come across a darker version brewed with dark malt.

German beer has a well deserved reputation for quality and flavour, which is due, at least in part, to the *Reinheitsgebot* (purity law) promulgated by the Duke of Bavaria in 1516. Brewing throughout Germany is still regulated by this decree, whereby beer made and marketed anywhere in the country may

German Wine Grades

Description	Meaning
Kabinett	fine, usually light wines, made from fully ripened grapes. The lightest of the Prädikat wines, they're excellent with food or on their own.
Spätlese	wines of superior quality made from grapes harvested after the normal harvest. Spätlese wines are more intense in flavour and concentration, but not necessarily sweet. They're good with richer, more flavourful foods or on their own.
Auslese	wines made from selected, very ripe grapes. They're intense in bouquet and taste, and usually, but not always, sweet.
Beerenauslese	wines made from selected overripe berries. These are rich, sweet dessert wines, which can also be enjoyed by themselves.
Eiswein	wines of Beerenauslese intensity, made from grapes harvested and pressed while frozen (hence the name 'ice wine'). The flavour is unique, with a remarkable concentration of fruity acidity and sweetness.
Trockenbeerenauslese	wines made from grapes which are overripe and dried almost to raisins. TBAs are rich, sweet, luscious, honey-like wines.

contain only grain malt, hops, yeast, water and, in some cases, sugar. Only natural ingredients are allowed, with preservatives and other additives strictly forbidden. The Germans successfully used the purity law to bar the import of most foreign-made beers until they were taken to the European Court of Justice by other EU members for unfairly restricting trade. A 1987 decision by the court forced Germany to accept foreign beers that didn't meet the purity criteria, although they haven't made much of a dent in the market, as Germans aren't generally willing to buy them.

Further information about German beer can be found on the brewing industry's website (www.bier.de).

Wine

The reputation of German wine has suffered in recent decades, although any visitor soon discovers that Germany offers much more than the saccharine Liebfraumilch, so popular in the UK during the '70s and '80s. The German wine trade is reverting to older traditions and making better quality wine of all types. Aided by a string of good vintages, German wines are re-establishing themselves, although inevitably (for climatic reasons) they lack the variety and range of French or Italian wines.

Germany has 13 official wine-producing regions, all of which are located along rivers or around lakes: Ahr, Baden, Franken, Hessische Bergstr., Mittelrhein, Mosel-Saar-Ruwer, Nahe, Pfalz, Rheingau, Rheinhessen, Saale-Unstrut, Saxony and Württemberg. These regions are loosely grouped into areas, of which the principal two are the Rhine (whose wine is sold in brown bottles) and Moselle (green bottles). Until recently, Germany had only been known

Wine drinking has grown in popularity over the last few decades, over 24 litres now being consumed per person per annum; this is calculated per head of population, so the average adult drinks considerably more than this.

for its white wines, but now with increased planting of red grapes (around 30 per cent), that's starting to change. Germany is now the third-largest producer of Pinot Noir. A tiny amount of rosé wine is produced in the Ahr valley, but all of it is drunk locally.

German wine is, by law, divided into two main categories, the lower of which is *Tafelwein* (table wine). Better quality wine is labelled *Qualitätswein*, which is roughly equivalent to the French Appellation Contrôlée and should signify a wine that's at least drinkable. *Qualitätswein* is further divided into *Qualitätswein eines bestimmten Anbaugebietes* (usually abbreviated to *Qualitätswein b.A.* or just QbA) and the best quality, *Qualitätswein mit Prädikat* (QmP), which literally means 'quality wine with distinction'. QmP wines, which are made entirely with natural ingredients, include the finest Germany has to offer. However, it should be noted that a wine made from riper grapes isn't necessarily of better quality, simply one that's likely to be sweeter and/or stronger.

QmP wines have six grades or 'attributes' corresponding to the ripeness (sugar content) of the grapes they were made from. These are, in ascending order of ripeness (but not necessarily sweetness), shown in the table on the previous page.

When buying, look for '*Erzeugerabfüllung*' or the new, more strictly defined '*Gutsabfüllung*' on the label, which indicate a wine bottled by the producer or estate. Wines without these words are likely to be blended from several producers. The grape type should also be indicated on the label; if it isn't, the wine is likely to be a blend of inferior grape juices and of poor quality. The classic German grape variety is Riesling, but some others can also be good, such as Ruländer (Pinot Gris) and the new varieties of Kerner and Scheurebe.

Legally, however, a wine needs to contain only 85 per cent of the declared grape variety.

Alcohol levels tend to be low in German wines. Dry *Auslesen* generally have the highest alcohol levels, up to 15 per cent in some cases, while *Kabinetts* and even TBAs can come in at under 8 per cent. If a wine's sweetness isn't indicated on the label, it's likely to be slightly to extremely sweet, in rough proportion with the ripeness level. If you want a dry wine, look for one labelled *trocken* (dry) or *halbtrocken* (semi-dry). Wines up to *Auslese* level may be produced in a dry style.

Most wines of the QbA and *Kabinett* grades are ready to drink when marketed and are at their best when young; they should be kept for no more than five years. *Spätlese* may also be consumed young, but the wine is likely to be enjoyable up to ten years after bottling. The 'higher grades' (*Auslese* and above) are usually longer-lived, generally reaching their peak when seven to ten years old, and with good storage can remain at their best for much longer. Wines from the Rheingau often take longer to reach their potential, while other Rhine wines – from Rheinhessen, Pfalz and Nahe – tend to mature faster. The wines of the Mosel-Saar-Ruwer are the most delicate, and the lesser grades from this region should be drunk sooner rather than later. It's also wise to sample stored wines from time to time so that they don't go past their best without you noticing.

A good source of information about German wine is the German Wine Institute (Deutsches Weininstitut, www.deutscheweine.de/ www.germanwines.de), which has branches in the UK (www.winesofgermany.co.uk) and the US (www.germanwineusa.com). Both provide a range of useful information on their websites, including a German wine and food pairing guide. Wine buffs may also wish to visit the comprehensive German winegrowers' website (www.germanwine.de).

Many people arrange to have drinks delivered to their homes rather than struggle with heavy crates. Deliveries are often made by the local brewery representative or the neighbourhood drinks market (Getränkemarkt) or supermarket.

Schnaps

In German, the word *Schnaps* (US spelling is Schnapps) refers to all kinds of spirits, including vodka, whisky and the like, although English speakers associate the word with typical German spirits. *Schnaps* is served mainly as an aperitif or a digestive, although it's also sometimes drunk with a glass of beer – what Americans and Britons would call a chaser. Either way, it's normally served neat, at room temperature, in a one-shot glass called a *Kleine-kleine* ('small small'). Many regional

brands exist, although they all look and taste much the same. Most are fruit-based – not to be confused with American Sweet Schnapps (e.g. peach schnapps) – and have a real kick.

Popular varieties include apple (*Apfelschnaps*), pear (*Birnenschnaps*), apple and pear together (Obstler), plum (*Pflaumenschnaps* or, in Bavaria, Zwetschgengeist) and wheat (*Kornschnaps*). Others contain a high proportion of roots and herbs (*Kräuterschnaps, Kräuterlikör*) arnica, angelica, bloodwort, etc., and all have a high alcohol content (from 25 to 60 per cent) and should be consumed with caution. The extravagant health claims sometimes made for schnapps – that it cures everything from indigestion to infertility – should be taken with a large pinch of Salz!

Other Drinks

Supermarkets sell beer, soft drinks and mineral water by the crate, which usually represents excellent value. Due to the (many) ecological and recycling laws, you must pay a deposit (*Pfand*) on both the bottles and the crate, which is refunded when you return the empties to the store. Most supermarkets have a bottle return station where you return your bottles and receive a credit slip to redeem at the checkout. Some shops are equipped with machines that do this automatically; you simply place the bottles on a turntable, press a button and the machine issues a receipt.

CLOTHES

In general Germans aren't known as flashy dressers and people of all ages, male and female, dress roughly as people do in the UK and North America, although perhaps a little more conservatively. One major factor in this is, of course, the climate. The winter months in most parts of Germany are cold and damp, and winter clothing, including warm gloves, hats, boots and waterproofs, is essential. Lightweight clothes are suitable for the summer, which rarely becomes uncomfortably hot.

Germans, it must be said, can be intolerant when it comes to unusual clothing. In some parts of the country, if you wear an unconventional outfit, such as a kilt or sari, you're likely to become an object of curiosity or even derision. Therefore, if you don't wish to stand out from the crowd you should observe how your German friends and neighbours dress and copy their 'style' (it isn't, however, mandatory to wear *Lederhosen*). In some rural areas Germans are still expected to wear their 'Sunday best' on Sundays, while in the cities attitudes are far more relaxed. For everyday wear, jeans and T-shirts are as popular in Germany as anywhere else and are acceptable for most leisure activities. At more expensive restaurants, men are usually expected to wear smart casual (and possibly a tie in the evening), while fashion-conscious women wear stylish outfits to restaurants (and to the theatre), particularly in the larger cities.

Although conservative, the dress code for business is less rigid than it once was, and is similar to North America and most northern European countries, with top management dressing more conservatively than those lower down the food chain. For men, a well-made jacket (preferably dark) with contrasting trousers is acceptable, but a muted business suit is the best choice in most situations and a tasteful tie is essential. For women, conservatively tailored suits and dresses are appropriate, and tight or revealing clothing should be avoided.

Clothing sold in Germany is generally of good quality, but tends to be expensive. All styles can be found in the major cities, but continental sizes may differ from those in other countries such as the UK and the US (see tables in Appendix B). Britons and Americans may have difficulty finding shoes that fit, as German feet tend to be wider and shorter.

Department and chain stores in German cities and larger towns offer an extensive range of clothing and sportswear (see **Department & Chain Stores** on page 249), particularly fashion chains such as C&A, Hennes & Mauritz (H&M) and Peek & Cloppenburg (P&C). P&C stocks good quality brands at reasonable prices, and is the place to go for stylish but conservative apparel. H&M is a Swedish chain found throughout Germany, which targets the young and trendy on a budget, while C&A appeals to budget customers with more conservative preferences. Winter sportswear is a best buy in Germany, where locally made garments are world class. Leatherwear is also a speciality, although the styling may not appeal.

NEWSPAPERS, MAGAZINES & BOOKS

Newsagents and bookshops are plentiful throughout Germany and most supermarkets, hypermarkets and department stores also sell a selection of books and magazines. There are no truly national newspapers in Germany other than the *Bild Zeitung* (generally known as *Das Bild*), a low-brow tabloid. The leading serious newspapers are the *Frankfurter Allgemeine Zeitung*, generally referred to as the FAZ, and *Die Welt* ('The World' – along with its sister publication, *Die Welt am Sonntag*), both conservative; their counterparts on the centre-left, are the *Süddeutsche Zeitung* (SZ) and the *Frankfurter Rundschau* (FR). These are available in 'national' editions throughout the country, although the FR includes a local news section in its Frankfurt edition; the same applies to the Munich edition of the SZ.

There are also numerous excellent regional newspapers, including the *Berliner Zeitung*, *Münchner Merkur*, *Stuttgarter Zeitung* and *Westfälische Nachrichten*. The newspapers with national scope tend to have fewer advertisements and fewer photographs, while regional newspapers (not surprisingly) provide more local information, including advertisements, cinema and theatre listings, and news of civic events. Regional or local newspapers are generally much easier to read than the FAZ, particularly if you're learning German. Many city and town newspapers distribute a free weekly edition to local homes, containing selected articles and local shop and classified advertising.

Most German newspapers have websites, which can be found at www.onlinenewspapers.com/germany.htm; for English-language publications and news websites in Germany, see www.world-newspapers.com/germany.html.

For decades, the major weekly news magazines in Germany have been *Der Spiegel* and *Stern*. *Der Spiegel* is known for hard news and thorough analysis of issues and events, while *Stern* is a larger format magazine with more pictures and a softer news content that includes celebrity interviews and features. In recent years, *Focus* (est. 1993) has emerged as a competitor to its more established rivals, modelled on the American-style news weeklies (*Newsweek* and *Time*), *Focus* combines hard news with more photographs, graphs and graphics than *Der Spiegel*.

Many newspaper kiosks, even in small cities, sell major European English-language newspapers and magazines, including the *International Herald Tribune*, the *Wall Street Journal*, the *Financial Times Deutschland* and the London *Times*, as well as *Time* and *Newsweek* magazines. Many are printed in Germany, with the content sent electronically from the home country to German printers. There are international news kiosks in city centres and at major railway stations and airports offering a much wider range of foreign newspapers and magazines. Expect to pay a premium for English-language publications, particularly those available on the day of publication. In smaller towns, the issues on sale may be anything from a day to a week old, depending on the publication.

If you prefer to subscribe to your favourite publications, most now have onlne versions. You can, of course, subscibe to the printed version, but it can be prohibitively expensive when postal charges are added and it can take days (weeks?) before you receive them. Some publications offer special international editions that are available from newsstands in Germany.

German publication subscriptions work somewhat differently from those in other countries. The subscription price for most magazines is slightly higher than the news-stand price. Most subscriptions are for a year and are automatically renewed unless written notice is given at least three months before the expiry date.

Bookshops

Most bookshops in Germany, even those in fairly small towns, usually offer at least a small selection of English-language books. In major cities, large bookshops, such as Hugendube (www.hugendubel.de) and Thalia (www.thalia.de), have well stocked English-language sections, and most bookshops selling technical or computer books stock a range of English-language titles. Prices for imports, as always, tend to be high, but competition from foreign mail-order and internet booksellers has reduced prices a little.

The leading internet bookseller is Amazon, which has German (www.amazon.de), British (www.amazon.co.uk) and American (www.amazon.com) websites, among others. The German branch of Amazon sells both German and English-language books, at prices considerably below those charged by most shops. Delivery within Germany is free from the German branch with Amazon Prime and books should arrive within a day or two at most.

Anyone who loves books should visit the Frankfurt Book Fair (*Buchmesse*, www.buchmesse.de) at least once, which is the world's premier publishing industry fair, held annually in early October. On Saturday and Sunday the fair is open to the public for a fee of around €15 per day, although at other times you need some form of 'professional' credentials to gain access, such as a business card with a title suggesting that you work in publishing, printing or book retailing.

FURNITURE & FURNISHINGS

Germans take great pride in their homes and furniture. The lounge or living room usually contains a large cupboard or sideboard called a *Wohnschrank*, made of solid wood and very heavy, which is used to store dishes and dinner services for entertaining, wine glasses, table linen, etc. It also frequently serves as a home for the TV, DVD player and music centre. Even if you arrive in Germany with your own furniture, you may eventually decide to indulge in a *Wohnschrank*.

Wohnschränke and other items of furniture are available in a wide variety of styles, quality and price ranges. German tastes range from traditional, massive wood-and-upholstered pieces to high-tech glass and stainless steel, often in bold colours and avant-garde designs. Prices in design shops tend to be high, but the quality is usually excellent and designs unusual. In many large cities you can find a branch of the upmarket chain Roche Bobois, as well as several local furniture stores. If you're looking for serviceable furniture at more reasonable prices, there's a range of do-it-yourself and discount furniture retailers.

IKEA, the Swedish furniture manufacturer, has outlets throughout Germany where you can buy stylish, modern Scandinavian furniture at reasonable prices for home assembly. IKEA stores (www.ikea.com/de) have free crèches and a restaurant. There are also a number of German furniture chains – such as Segmüller, Höffner and XXXLutz – and individual retailers who offer discount prices on a wide range of furniture and household goods.

If you're in the market for custom-made furniture, the town to visit is Kelkheim in southeast Germany (Taunus), known as the *Möbelstadt* (furniture town), where

craftsmen have been employed for centuries creating fine furniture. Local manufacturers sponsor an annual furniture exhibition (*Möbelausstellung*) in the autumn, where they proudly display their wares.

Most large items of furniture must be ordered as shops don't keep them in stock, and some, such as upholstered chairs, are made to order even at discount stores. Delivery takes from 4 to 12 weeks in most cases, unless you're buying a display item, in which case the shop will usually deliver within a week. Shops normally require a deposit when you order, with the balance paid on delivery by cheque or in cash (if you plan to pay by credit card you must usually pay the full amount in advance).

Carpets and curtains can be purchased at specialist shops, general furniture shops and department stores. Note, however, that many apartments and houses have external metal blinds, and the fashion is to have net curtains only inside. There are many carpet stores, some of which seem to have a permanent sale.

If you're bringing a bed from the UK or North America, you must bring bed linen (*Bettwäsche*) with you, as standard German bed linen (e.g. pillow cases, duvet covers and fitted sheets) is unlikely to fit; alternaively if you don't bring a bed don't bother to bring sheets and blankets also, as they won't fit German mattresses. The Germans use duvets and huge (very comfortable) pillows typically measuring 80cm x 80cm (31in x 31in). Bed linen sets contain duvet covers and pillowcases but you must buy a fitted sheet (*Spanntuch*) to cover the mattress. Most fitted sheets cover mattresses ranging from 90 x 180cm (36in x 72in) to 100 x 200cm (39in x 78in), but check before buying. Double beds typically have two separate (single) mattresses with separate duvets (with no top sheet), and double duvets are difficult to find; if you prefer sleeping 'together' bring your own with you.

Kitchens

One of the first surprises to hit many newcomers to Germany is the discovery that many rented apartments and houses don't include kitchen appliances or even cupboards and a sink unit. It's sometimes possible to purchase the kitchen from the outgoing tenant, thus saving considerable time, money and effort.

Most furniture shops and nearly all DIY stores offer kitchens and kitchen appliances in a wide range of styles and colours; you may be able to install the units yourself, but a licensed plumber and electrician are required by law to connect appliances. IKEA offers attractive, good quality products at keen prices. The good news is that cupboards, cabinets and appliances come in standard sizes, and can be taken with you if you move to another apartment or house. If you don't fancy doing the installation yourself, most furniture and kitchen stores will do it for you (it may even be included in the price).

HOUSEHOLD GOODS

Germany boasts a number of world famous manufacturers of high-quality household electrical appliances, including AEG, Bosch, Braun, Miele and Siemens. German products tend to be a bit more expensive than most of their competitors, but German consumers

☑ **SURVIVAL TIP**

Before buying any appliances check the efficiency rating (e.g. A, B), which is shown on all new appliances, to see how expensive an appliance will be to run; it's usually worth buying a slightly more expensive model as it will save you money in the long run. It's also worth checking the decidel (db) rating to see how loud it is (particularly for dishwashers).

expect reliable and well designed products, and the appliances you buy in Germany will last a long (long) time and have low running costs.

Americans, who cannot understand how Germans function with such 'tiny' refrigerators, will be pleased to hear that American-style refrigerators (with ice and cold water dispensers in the door) are becoming popular in Europe and can be purchased locally. However, they aren't among the most economical when it comes to running costs, and running water pipes to the refrigerator isn't an easy or cheap task (although you can now buy models that don't require plumbing). You may also have trouble fitting them into a standard German kitchen.

LAUNDRY & DRY CLEANING

All towns and shopping centres have dry cleaners (*chemische Reinigung*), most of which also do minor clothes repairs, alterations and dyeing. However, 'express cleaning' may mean a few days rather than hours, even where dry cleaning is done on the premises. You usually pay in advance and charges are quite high, particularly for leather garments. Note that unless you purchase special insurance for your clothes, the dry cleaner's liability for damage is limited to 15 times the cost of the cleaning.

There are few self-service launderettes in Germany, other than in cities and large towns. Most German families have their own washing machines. Those who live in an apartment block usually have access to communal drying rooms, but the preferred method of drying clothes in Germany is to hang them in the fresh air outdoors, either on a clothes line or using a folding drying rack on a balcony or terrace.

Ironing services (*Bügelservice*) are available in many areas. Look for signs in windows or announcements on shop notice boards, as this is a popular way for housewives to earn extra money in small towns.

HOME SHOPPING

Mail-order shopping has long been popular in Germany and, given the stringent regulations and efficient postal system, it's a safe and convenient way to buy many items. Catalogue shopping is dominated by two vast companies: Neckermann (www.neckermann.de) and Otto-Versand (www.otto.de), both long established and well respected. Both also offer online shopping. You'll see advertisements for these companies in many popular magazines and are likely to receive promotional leaflets in your letterbox. They have established a reputation for their own brands, particularly for household appliances and electronic equipment, and are noted for providing quality products at considerably lower prices than those in shops, with iron-clad guarantees and warranties.

Neckermann and Otto-Versand also have stores in most German cities and maintain agencies in smaller cities and towns where customers can consult catalogues and place orders. Smaller items are often delivered within 24 hours and even larger appliances and furniture are usually delivered quicker than by local stores, e.g. in a matter of days rather than weeks. Both companies provide a 24-hour

ordering service, seven days a week, via the internet.

Among the most popular internet sites are the ubiquitous Amazon (www.amazon. de) and Ebay (www.ebay.de), which are as popular in Germany as elsewhere. Other popular ecommerce sites include Idealo (www. idealo.de, general), Zalando (www.zalando. de, fashion), Bobprix (www.bonprix.de, fashion, home), Shopping 24 (www.shopping24.de, various), Tchibo (www.tchibo.de, fashion, home), Conrad (www.conrad.de, electronics) and Weltbild (www.weltbild.de, books, music, etc.).

SHOPPING ABROAD

Shopping abroad can be a pleasant day out and can also save you money. Germany's neighbours include Austria, Belgium, the Czech Republic, Denmark, France (popular for food and wine), Luxembourg, the Netherlands, Poland and Switzerland. Don't forget your passports or identity cards, car papers, dog's vaccination papers and foreign currency where relevant. When visiting countries that are signatories to the Schengen agreement there are no border controls, and you won't need to change currency if you're shopping in eurozone countries. Most shops in border towns in non-eurozone countries gladly accept euros (because they offer a poor exchange rate!), but it may pay you to use a credit card when shopping in non-euro countries, when you usually receive a better exchange rate. You're also offered some security if goods are found to be faulty.

When buying goods abroad, ensure that you're dealing with a bona fide company and that the goods will work in Germany; and when buying expensive goods abroad, always have them insured for their full value.

Although there are no restrictions, there are 'indicative levels' for certain items, above which goods may be classified as commercial quantities and therefore liable for import duty (if not prohibited altogether). Those aged 17 or over may import the following amounts of alcohol and tobacco into Germany, usually without question:

♦ 10 litres of spirits (over 22° proof);

♦ 20 litres of fortified wine (under 22° proof);

♦ 90 litres of wine (or 120 x 0.75 litre bottles or ten cases), of which a maximum of 60 litres may be sparkling wine;

♦ 110 litres of beer;

♦ 800 cigarettes, 400 cigarillos, 200 cigars and 1kg of smoking tobacco.

There's no limit on perfume or toilet water. If you exceed the above amounts, you may need to convince the customs authorities that you aren't planning to sell the goods.

 Caution

There are fines for anyone who sells duty-paid alcohol and tobacco, which is classed as smuggling.

Duty & VAT

When buying goods overseas, take into account whether you'll be liable for duty and VAT (*Mehrwertsteuer* – see page 211). There's no duty or tax on goods purchased within the EU or on goods worth below around €50 purchased in most other countries, depending on the shipping method. If you make purchases from a mail order catalogue company or internet vendor outside the EU, you may receive a separate bill for VAT and/or customs duty, depending on the declared value of your shipment and the method of shipping. Parcels shipped from outside Europe by express mail services are more likely to be charged VAT, irrespective of their declared value, due to the customs clearing methods used by shippers. Where charges are due, the postman will collect them when he delivers the parcel or leave a notice in your letterbox instructing you to collect the parcel and pay the charges due at the local post office.

Duty-free Allowances

Duty-free shopping is available when travelling to and from non-EU countries (such as Switzerland). For each journey outside the EU, travellers aged 17 or over are entitled to import duty free:

- ♦ four litres of still table wine;
- ♦ 16 litres of beer;
- ♦ one litre of alcohol over 22° volume or 38.8 per cent proof (e.g. spirits) OR two litres not over 22° volume (e.g. fortified or sparkling wines);
- ♦ 200 cigarettes OR 100 cigarillos OR 50 cigars OR 250g of tobacco;
- ♦ 60cc/ml (50gr or 2fl oz) of perfume;
- ♦ 250cc/ml (8fl oz) of toilet water;
- ♦ other goods (including gifts, souvenirs, beer and cider) to the value of €300.

Duty-free allowances apply on both outward and return journeys, even if both are made on the same day, so that the combined total (i.e. double the above limits) can be imported into Germany. Duty-free sales are 'vendor-controlled', meaning that vendors are responsible for ensuring that the amount of duty-free goods sold to individuals doesn't exceed their entitlement. Duty-free goods purchased on board ships and ferries are noted on boarding cards, which must be presented with each purchase.

RECEIPTS

When shopping in Germany ensure that you receive a receipt (*Quittung*) and retain it until you've reached home. This isn't just in case you need to return or exchange goods, which may be impossible without the receipt, but also to verify that you've paid if an automatic alarm sounds as you're leaving a shop or any other questions arise. When you buy a large object that cannot easily be wrapped, a sticker should be attached to it as evidence of purchase.

It's wise to keep receipts and records of all major purchases made while resident in Germany, particularly if your stay is for a short period only. This may save you both time and money when you leave Germany and are required to declare your belongings in your new country of residence, and may also be useful for tax reasons.

CONSUMER PROTECTION

Germans are usually well versed in consumer laws and regulations and in the event of a dispute with a merchant it's often only necessary is quote the relevant law or regulation to receive satisfaction. On the other hand, if the law establishes a limit on the merchant's liability or responsibility you're unlikely to sway him with any form of logic.

If you have a complaint against a retailer or manufacturer that you're unable to resolve with them, your first stop should be the local consumer association advice bureau (*Verbraucherzentrale*) to determine your legal position and rights. *Verbraucherzentrale* are found throughout Germany and, while privately owned and operated, are funded by the federal government and the states. For a list of your local *Verbraucherzentrale* see www.verbraucher.de or contact the umbrella organisation (Verbraucherzentrale Bundesverband e.V., www.vzbv.de).

Stiftung Warentest is a respected, independent and non-profit-making foundation that compares and tests products and services (rather like *Which?* and the Consumers' Association in the UK, and *Consumer Reports* in the US). Some 1,700 products (from grapefruit juice to hi-fi equipment) are tested each year, as well as services related to investments, health, tourism and transport. Companies whose products receive good or very good ratings often indicate this in their advertising.

Stiftung Warentest publishes two monthly magazines: *Test* for all types of consumer products, and *Finanztest* for financial products, such as insurance, property and banking services. You can take out a subscription to either magazine for €59.90 per year (12 issues), or you can sign up for a trial subscription for three issues for just €7.50 (www.test.de). You can also pay a flat rate of €7 per month for unlimited online access.

Reichstag, Berlin

18.
ODDS & ENDS

*T*his chapter contains miscellaneous information that's of general interest to anyone living or working in Germany, from citizenship to tipping and toilets.

CITIZENSHIP

There are three ways of becoming a citizen of Germany: you can be born in Germany to a German mother or father, you can be naturalised (*Einbürgerung*) or you can exercise the so-called 'right of return' available to 'Germans' living in eastern Europe. Germans take the issue of citizenship and nationality very seriously, and for years Germany's citizenship laws were strictly based on the principle of *jus sanguinis* ('rights of blood' or nationality by inheritance rather than place of birth). Until 1975, a child born in Germany had to have a German father in order to claim German nationality, and a German woman married to a foreigner couldn't transfer her nationality to her children. This changed in 1975, when the law was revised to permit either parent to transfer German nationality to their offspring, although the father's nationality is always registered automatically. If you want your child (born in Germany) to have its mother's nationality, you must make a formal request to the local authority.

In 2000, the citizenship law was amended again to allow children born to foreign couples in Germany to become German citizens, provided one of the parents had been temporarily resident in Germany (i.e. with a *befristete Aufenthaltserlaubnis* – see **Residence Permits** on page 52) for at least eight years, or had held a 'permanent' residence permit (*unbefristete Aufenthaltserlaubnis* or *Niederlassungserlaubnis*) for at least three years, on the day a child is born. It's also possible under certain circumstances for a child to have dual nationality (i.e. German and the nationality of his parents or one parent), but only until the age of 23, by which time he must choose one or the other.

To obtain German citizenship by naturalisation you must have resided legally in Germany for eight years (which can be reduced to seven years if you take a German-language integration course). You must be able to prove that you haven't been convicted of a serious crime and can support yourself and your family without resort to public assistance (though naturalisation won't limit your eligibility for future assistance). Applicants for German citizenship must also demonstrate their proficiency in the German language and declare their allegiance to the constitution (*Grundgesetz*). The language test is very much practical rather than literary. There's also a citizenship test (introduced in 2008), which comprises 33 questions (the pass rate is 17 correct) in B1 level German about the country's laws, history and people. There's a fee of €25 (€18 if your application is refused).

On taking German citizenship, you're expected to give up your previous citizenship.

Most Germans don't believe that a person can properly honour an allegiance to two nations (and Germans who move abroad and take on a new citizenship are expected to give up their German nationality, unless they can demonstrate close personal or property ties in Germany). There are a few exceptions to the ban on dual nationality, which include recognised political refugees, elderly individuals who would suffer 'unreasonable hardship' (such as the loss of their foreign pension rights), and cases where the second country imposes high fees or other unreasonably harsh conditions on anyone renouncing their citizenship.

CLIMATE

Overall, Germany's climate is moderate, with warm summers and cool winters. Now and then Germany experiences a particularly hot spell in summer or a vicious cold snap in winter, but these phenomena are usually short-lived. In winter, it can seem as if the country is almost upside down, temperatures in the north averaging several degrees higher than those in the south (which is more mountainous). Summers are damp and warm, and while many Germans like to spend their summer holidays on the beaches in the north of the country, the weather there is hardly as balmy as on the Côte d'Azur or in Majorca – both favoured spots among Germans. It's unusual to find air-conditioning anywhere in Germany, and for the most part it isn't needed.

The Alps are a major influence on the climate in the southern region, where winters are long and cold and snowfall is frequent. In Bavaria, annual rainfall can be as high as 200cm (79in), while in the rest of the country, annual rainfall of 60 to 80cm (24 to 31in) is normal, summer being the wettest season, while ice and freezing rain are more frequent hazards in winter than heavy snow.

Germany isn't normally subject to catastrophic weather conditions such as tornadoes or cyclones. However, in spring there's a danger of flooding, even in some of the minor river valleys, if heavy rains combine with melting snow from the mountains. In the north, storms sweeping across the Arctic Circle, referred to somewhat euphemistically as 'Icelandic lows', bring strong winds and gales to the coastal regions. These are moderated by the warm Gulf Stream, however, and winter temperatures along the North Sea coast average a degree or two above freezing. Centres of high pressure to the east of Germany can bring periods of cold, bright weather in winter.

When a low pressure system crosses the central part of the country, conditions are ripe for the *Föhn*, a warm dry wind from the south. Due to the changes in atmospheric pressure that create the *Föhn*, don't be surprised if you

Average Temperature High/Low °C (°F)				
Location	Spring	Summer	Autumn	Winter
Berlin	13/4 (55/39)	23/14 (73/57)	13/6 (55/43)	3/-3 (37/27)
Frankfurt	16/6 (61/43)	24/14 (75/57)	14/7 (57/45)	4/-1 (39/30)
Hamburg	13/3 (55/37)	22/13 (72/55)	13/6 (55/43)	3/-2 (39/28)
Leipzig	14/4 (57/39)	24/13 (75/55)	14/6 (57/43)	3/-3 (37/27)
Munich	14/3 (57/37)	23/13 (73/55)	13/4 (55/39)	2/-5 (36/23)

come down with a headache when the wind is from the south!

Average day-time maximum/minimum temperatures in Celsius and Fahrenheit (in brackets) for selected cities are shown in the table opposite. (A quick way to make a rough conversion from Centigrade to Fahrenheit is to multiply by two and add 30.)

The German weather forecast is available via TV and radio and in daily newspapers, and also includes the pollen count (*Pollenbericht*) from March to July and the *Biowetterbericht*, which reports what ailments you're likely to face due to the weather! You can also get a German weather forecast online, e.g. from the Deutscher Wetterdienst (www.dwd.de – German only) or the World Meteorological Organization (www.worldweather.org/016/m016.htm), via a computer or mobile phone.

CRIME

Compared with some developed countries, Germany has a low crime rate, which has been steadily decreasing since 2005; theft remains by far the most common of all reported crime, followed by fraud and vandalism. Violent and sexual crimes have also fallen, but fraud, bribery and corruption (so-called white collar crime) have increased significantly and become a preoccupation of the authorities. The murder rate is very low (under 1 person per 100,000 population) and around the same as the UK.

Germany is at the crossroads of Europe, not only for trade but also for organised crime, Berlin often serving as its centre of operations. Drugs are a major concern for law enforcement officials and the country is both a market for illegal narcotics and a transit point for the distribution of marijuana, heroin and cocaine to Scandinavia and the UK. Other activities associated with organised crime include car theft (particularly luxury models), counterfeiting, arms smuggling, prostitution and gambling. German tabloid newspapers and TV documentaries feature periodic *exposés* of white slavery rings, which are said to lure women to Germany with promises of office work or au pair positions, while selling them into prostitution. While such stories are sometimes sensationalised for the viewing audience, it pays to be aware that offers of easy employment, free from the usual immigration formalities, are unlikely to be legitimate.

During the '70s and early '80s, Germany developed something of a reputation as a centre for terrorist activity, mostly connected with radical left-wing groups such as the Baader Meinhof Gang and Red Army Faction (*Rote Armee Faktion*), which carried out attacks on government and business targets. By 1992, the left-wing groups had sworn off violence in pursuit of their goals, but a right-wing fringe had taken their place in the headlines with equally violent attacks on refugees and asylum seekers. Key operatives in the September 11th attacks in New York are believed to have originated from a Moslem extremist cell in Hamburg, and there have been at least two foiled bomb threats in Germany since then. In recent years there has been a number of terrorist attacks, which many people attribute to the huge increase in Muslim refugees, although in general refugees are responsible for very little crime (apart from fare-dodging on public transport).

While racist violence is still a problem in Germany, there's no reason for undue anxiety or paranoia about 'ordinary' crime. Basic common sense and being 'street wise' will ensure that you avoid most sources of trouble. Muggings and armed robbery are rare in most of Germany, where you can safely walk almost anywhere, day or night. Larger cities, especially Berlin, have their seedy areas, which you should avoid (particularly after dark) – ask a policeman, taxi driver or other local person which districts to avoid.

In cities, most apartments are equipped with sturdy locks and spy-holes, as well as a telephone entry system so that you can identify visitors before admitting them. In contrast, in rural areas there are still villages and small towns where people don't lock their homes and cars, although these are fast disappearing.

A physical map of Germany is shown inside the front cover and a political map showing the 16 states is inside the back cover.

GEOGRAPHY

Germany is the third-largest country in western Europe (after France and Spain), covering an area of almost 357,000km^2 (140,000mi^2) and stretching 840km (520mi) from north to south and 620km (385mi) east to west. It has borders with nine countries: Poland and the Czech Republic to the east; Switzerland and Austria to the south; France, Luxembourg, Belgium and the Netherlands to the west; and Denmark to the north. Its land boundaries total 3,621km (2,250mi), while the coastline (which is entirely in the north, bordering the North and Baltic Seas) extends for 2,389km (1,484mi).

Germany's geography has played a major role in much of its history, and has contributed greatly to the standing of the country within Europe. Located in the centre of the continent and sharing borders with so many other countries, Germany has long been a link between eastern and western Europe. The nation state of Germany has existed only since 1871, when Bismarck created the German Empire following the defeat of France. Prior to that, 'Germany' consisted of numerous small kingdoms, duchies, principalities and city states, some of which are reflected in the names and borders of the 16 modern states (*Länder*) that make up the country. Although Germany is one of the few modern European states without overseas territories, parts of many of its neighbouring states have been German at one time or another.

Geographically, Germany consists of three principal regions. The south is mountainous, including the Bavarian Alps and the foothills of the Swiss Alpine mountain range. The Central German Uplands in the centre consist of forested black mountains and intermediate plateaux that are part of the same formation as the Massif Central in France and continue east into Poland. The north of the country is part of the North European Lowlands, made up of marshes and mud flats extending to the coast and into Denmark. The country generally 'slopes' from south to north, starting with the Zugspitze, the highest point in the Bavarian Alps (2,962m/9,718ft), and dropping to sea level along the two sea coasts in the north. Germany is criss-crossed by many rivers, including the massive and spectacular Rhine, which forms part of its border with France.

GOVERNMENT

As its official name (Federal Republic of Germany) indicates, Germany is a federal republic. The current form of government was established in 1949, after it became clear to the occupying forces of West Germany (the Americans, British and French) that the Soviet Union wasn't going to reach an agreement with them on the future of Germany. Administrative structures had already been re-established by the occupying forces at state level (the *Länder*), so these were charged with selecting delegates to a council which would become the German Parliament. The Parliamentary Council drafted a constitution, called the 'basic law' (*Grundgesetz*), which was then approved by the states. The first national elections to the Parliament were held in August 1949.

Ten states comprised the former West Germany: Bavaria, Baden-Württemberg, Hesse, Lower Saxony, North-Rhine Westphalia, Rhineland-Palatinate, Saarland, Schleswig-Holstein, and the cities of Hamburg and

Bremen. West Berlin was accorded non-voting status as an 11th state, as it has always been considered the 'real' capital city of Germany, although Bonn was established as the 'temporary' capital and seat of government. Upon reunification in 1990, the five eastern states were added: Brandenburg, Mecklenburg-Western Pomerania, Saxony, Saxony-Anhalt and Thuringia, with Berlin (east and west) becoming a state in its own right.

> The *Bundestag* makes and changes federal laws, makes constitutional amendments, debates government policy, approves the federal budget and ratifies treaties dealing with Germany's external interests. It's the *Bundestag* that elects the prime minister, called the chancellor (*Kanzler*).

Most governmental authority is vested in the states, each of which has its own constitution, parliament, judiciary, cabinet of ministers and even a Minister-President (although not many citizens know who he is!). With reunification, the German government could finally realise the long-held dream of re-establishing Berlin as its capital city. The transfer of the seat of government from Bonn to Berlin got under way in 1999.

Parliament

The German legislature is a parliamentary system, consisting of two houses called the *Bundesrat* and the *Bundestag* (there's no word in German for both legislative bodies together). The *Bundesrat* is the upper house of parliament, made up of delegates selected by the state governments to represent the interests of the states. Each state has between three and six representatives in the *Bundesrat*, depending on its population. The *Bundesrat* has the right of veto over legislation passed by the lower house (*Bundestag*), and they must approve certain types of legislation affecting the states.

Members of the *Bundestag* are elected by voters using a two-vote system combining proportional representation for political parties with the direct election of candidates within districts. Each voter has two votes in a parliamentary election. One is cast for individual candidates running within the legislative district, the winner gaining a seat in the *Bundestag*. The second vote is cast for a political party and all its state representatives (*Landesliste*), and the total number of seats each party receives in the *Bundestag* is determined by the result of this second vote.

In theory, there are two seats for each voting district in Germany, making a total of around 630 (the number varies as additional seats may be added to reflect the actual balance).

Chancellor Angela Merkel

Chancellor & President

The chancellor (currently Angela Merkel) is the head of government and responsible for setting the policy guidelines within which the federal ministers run their departments. The government is accountable to the *Bundestag* for its actions but (yet another demonstration of the German devotion to order and stability) the

Bundestag can only unseat the chancellor in a vote of no-confidence if they've elected a new chancellor at the same time by an absolute majority. The *Bundestag* cannot unseat individual ministers.

There's also a federal president (currently Frank-Water Steinmeier), who's the official head of state of Germany, charged with responsibility for appointing and dismissing federal ministers, judges, civil servants and officers of the armed forces. The post, however, is largely ceremonial, although recent presidents have wielded considerable influence over public opinion.

Political Parties

Five political parties are represented in the *Bundestag*: the Christian Democratic Party (CDU), founded in 1945 by Konrad Adenauer; the Social Democratic Party (SPD), which has its roots in the working class movements of the late 19th century; the Christian Social Union (CSU); the Alliance 90/Greens (usually referred to simply as the Green Party); and the Left Party.

The CSU is primarily a Bavarian party and reflects the strong Catholic influence on the Bavarian state government. At the national level, the CSU is aligned with the larger CDU, which has broad support in the business and agriculture sectors. Five of the seven post-war chancellors have been Christian Democrats.

Alliance 90 was predominantly an East German environmental party, which allied with the western Greens in 1993. The Greens were an important partner in the coalition that strongly supported SPD Chancellor Gerhard Schröder. Although the Greens aren't part of any coalition, their popularity has increased dramatically in recent years, winning 63 seats in the 2013 election (with Alliance 90).

The Left (*die Linke*), previously known as PDS/WASG, has its roots in the former state

The CDU is the party of Helmut Kohl, post-war Germany's longest-serving chancellor and once seen as the father of reunification. The current chancellor, Angela Merkel, also belongs to the CDU and is the first woman to hold the office.

party of the German Democratic Republic, and represents mostly east German voters, although its appeal is expanding in the west. The Free Democratic Party (FDP) is a right-wing 'liberal' party, which tends to represent the interests of independent professionals and the owners and managers of small and medium-size businesses; in the 2013 election, the FDP failed to reach the 5 per cent threshold and didn't gain any seats in the *Bundestag*. There are a number of smaller parties active in the states, although none has been able to amass the 5 per cent required for representation in the *Bundestag*.

German law permits the free establishment of political parties, but requires parties to conform to democratic principles in their structure and to publicly account for the sources of their funding. Before it can nominate candidates, a new party must have a written constitution and a platform. Any party that seeks to impair or abolish the free democratic order or to endanger the existence of the Federal Republic of Germany can be banned. So far, the federal courts have banned two national parties, both in the '50s, one a far right-wing group and the other the Communist Party of Germany.

States

The federal government derives its authority from the states, rather than the other way around. The states are responsible for their own legislation, government and the administration of justice, whereas the federal government is responsible for matters of national importance, such as defence and foreign policy.

Elections

German citizens are eligible to vote at the age of 18 provided they've lived in Germany for at least the three months before the election date. Those living abroad can vote by absentee ballot for ten years after leaving Germany. Citizens of the EU resident in Germany may only participate in local elections and vote and stand for election as representatives to the European Parliament. The next federal election is due in September 2017, after this book went to press (the next elections to the European Parliament are due in 2019.)

Elections are based on a system of proportional representation.

LEGAL SYSTEM

The German legal system is based on the civil codes enacted by the *Bundestag* (see above). The national constitution is called the 'basic law' (*Grundgesetz*), and spells out in minute detail the division of power between the individual states (*Länder*) and the national federation. At times it seems that there are laws and regulations for literally everything, and many Germans jokingly explain the

German Constitutional Court

legal system with the phrase 'anything not expressly permitted is prohibited' (as opposed to the French system, where 'anything not expressly prohibited is permitted'). However, the Germans seem to find security and stability (*Ordnung*) in having laws or regulations to cover almost every conceivable situation.

Judges and prosecutors are appointed by the state and enjoy a status similar to that of a career civil servant. At federal level, judges are chosen by panels composed of the relevant federal ministry, the appropriate state ministries and deputies from the *Bundestag*. The court system is decentralised and within each state there's a variety of specialised administrative, criminal and civil courts.

In a German court it's a judge (or a panel of judges) who asks the questions and tries to determine the facts of the case. The prosecutor or defence counsel is permitted to ask questions or cross-examine defendants or witnesses, but this is rarely done (courtroom practice is considerably less dramatic than in the US). The judge determines the facts of the matter and then rules according to the law that applies. There are strict laws limiting publicity, both before and during a trial, therefore it's rare to see or read details about an ongoing case on TV or in the newspapers.

An unfavourable decision can be appealed in a superior court, but only on points of law, not on the facts of the case. There are five federal courts that handle appeals in their respective areas of jurisdiction: the Federal Court of Justice (civil and criminal cases) in Karlsruhe; the Federal Administrative Court in Berlin; the Federal Financial Court in Munich; the Federal Labour Court in Kassel; and the Federal Social Court, also in Kassel. The Federal Constitutional Court deals solely with matters involving basic law, federal/state disputes and legislation on appeal from lower courts or the states. This 'supreme' court also rules on the constitutionality of political parties and on charges against the federal president. A decision in a superior court overrules a lower court's decision, but only for the facts and circumstances of that particular case, as German law doesn't recognise the notion of precedence, where a decision in one case is used as a model for future cases (as in the UK).

In Germany, a person is presumed innocent until proven guilty under the law and has the right to legal counsel. The judge will appoint a defence lawyer in cases where the accused is unable to pay for one, particularly in complicated cases or where a defendant is believed to be unable to defend himself. An accused person can only be imprisoned pending trial (i.e. on remand) where there's strong evidence that he committed a crime and a judge issues a written arrest warrant.

MARRIAGE & DIVORCE

As in many other developed countries, marriage in Germany is becoming less popular. Many unmarried couples prefer not to get married and the average age at which people marry for the first time is increasing; it's currently around 30 for women and over 33 for men. The majority of weddings in western Germany are celebrated in church, but only a small percentage of those in the east. In

this means obtaining a form from the local *Einwohnermeldeamt* (to establish their own residence and marital status), and providing an official extract from their parents' *Familienbuch*, which provides the necessary family history details.

Many registrars also require a medical certificate, which primarily involves blood tests to screen for congenital and other diseases. Foreigners planning to marry in Germany must provide a certified copy of their birth certificate, showing their parents' names and their marital status at the date of birth. If the prospective bride or groom is widowed or divorced, he or she must provide the appropriate certificates or decrees to verify this. All documents must be translated into German by a certified translator. Foreigners must also provide a so-called 'Certificate of No Impediment' from their home country. This is issued by the national authorities of the foreigner's home country and states that under the law of that country there's no reason why the person cannot get married.

A number of countries (including the US) don't issue such certificates, in which case you must apply to the President of the Higher Regional Court (*Oberlandesgericht*) for an exemption. The local registrar can draw up a request for this so that you don't need to go to court. If you want the titles of any qualifications (e.g. an MA or a PhD) to be included in the wedding documents or announcements, you may be asked to provide the relevant certificates.

All paperwork must be submitted to the registrar around four to six weeks before a wedding is planned. Germany no longer requires 'publication of the banns' – the practice of posting notice of an impending marriage on the *Rathaus* notice board for a week or two in case anyone wants to oppose your marriage. Foreign nationals may also be

Germany the civil wedding ceremony at the registrar's office (*Standesamt*) is the most important one. A church wedding, which is optional, can take place only after the civil ceremony. Most friends and family members will, however, expect a big party to celebrate the wedding, irrespective of where the formalities take place.

Same sex registered life partnerships (*Eingetragene Lebenspartnerschaft*) has been legal in Germany since 2001 and in June 2017 the *Bundestag* passed a bill allowing same sex marriage.

The local registrar will tell you what documents to provide, but in all cases you'll need identification (national identification card or passport), documentation establishing your residence and marital status, and the names of your parents and their marital status at the time of your birth. For most Germans, required to notify their embassy or consulate of their impending marriage.

Marriage in Germany is legally similar to any other contract or legal obligation, so both partners must be of legal age (i.e. 18). It's possible for someone to marry at 16 with the permission of their parents, but only if the other partner is of legal age.

> In order to get married in Germany you must apply at the registrar's office in the town where one of the partners is resident. If neither partner is resident in Germany you can contact the central registrar office in Berlin (www.berlin.de/standesamt1), which can grant permission for any office in Germany to perform a wedding for non-residents.

Most couples take the traditional route and use the husband's last name as both their married names, but a married woman can keep her own name if she wishes. Either the husband or wife or both can use a double-name (*Doppelname*), by adding the wife's maiden name to that of the husband. On the birth of their first child, however, a couple must choose a single family name (*Familienname*), which will be the surname for that child and other children born within their marriage.

Unless they opt for a marital contract (*Ehevertrag*), a couple is covered by a form of communal property arrangement (*Zugewinngemeinschaft*), under which they automatically have joint ownership of all assets attained since their marriage. In the event of divorce, the household property (and any debts) acquired during the marriage are split evenly between the partners. However, it's possible to maintain complete separation of each partner's assets and debts by entering into a marital contract, either before or during the marriage, which must be drawn up by a notary or lawyer.

Marriage of a non-German citizen to a German citizen doesn't confer any preferential rights on the foreigner when it comes to taking German citizenship (see page 265).

Divorce

Any married couple resident in Germany can be divorced under German law, which has largely abandoned the traditional need for one spouse to accuse the other of some wrongdoing. The first step in getting divorced is generally that of establishing a separation (Trennung) between the partners, which involves not only the segregation of financial affairs but also the physical separation of the household. (It isn't always necessary for one of the partners to move out, and it's possible to establish a separation with both spouses still living under the same roof.)

Unless there are extraordinary circumstances a couple won't be eligible for divorce until after at least a year's formal separation. If both parties agree to the divorce at that time, a court reviews the division of property and rules regarding any child support claims, after which the divorce becomes final. Where one of the partners isn't willing to go through with the divorce, the court will intervene to

determine the state of the marriage and rule whether or not to finalise a divorce.

After three years' separation, a divorce will be granted automatically unless there are grave extenuating circumstances (such as serious illness or mental problems of one of the partners).

MILITARY SERVICE

Since 1994, German troops have been permitted to participate in various military operations under UN auspices with the approval of the *Bundestag*. Defence spending – over €36 billion per year or around 10 per cent of the federal budget – is a sensitive political issue given Germany's recent history. Germany is a member of the North Atlantic Treaty Organisation (NATO) whose members pledged (in 2014) to spend 2 per cent of their GDP on defence by the year 2024; currently only five of the 28-member alliance meet this target (of which the UK is one). Germany currently spends around 1.2 per cent of GDP on defence.

Germany's armed forces (*Bundeswehr*) consist of around 200,000 military personnel. Between 1956 and 2011 male citizens were subject to conscription between the ages of 18 and 23, but this was suspended in 2011. Military service is generally considered excellent preparation for the working world, and many young men display their service records proudly on their CVs when seeking their first job. Women weren't subject to the draft, although there are around 13,000 serving in various roles in the military.

Soldiers in the German military can join a soldiers' union, although they aren't permitted to strike. They even have a parliamentary ombudsman (*Wehrbeauftragter des Deutschen Bundestages*) to whom they can take their complaints without having to go through other channels.

PETS

If you plan to take a pet (*Haustier*) to Germany, it's important to check the latest regulations. Make sure that you have the correct papers, not only for Germany, but for all the countries you'll pass through to reach Germany if not flying direct. Careful consideration must be given before exporting a pet from a country with strict quarantine regulations. If you must return, even after just a few days in Germany, your pet may need to go into quarantine, which, apart from being expensive, is distressing for both pets and owners.

Importing Pets

Since 2000, qualifying pets, e.g. cats and dogs, arriving from certain countries can enter Germany without any restrictions under the Pet Travel Scheme (PETS). Under the scheme pets must be microchipped (they have a chip inserted under the skin in their neck) and vaccinated against rabies, undergo a blood test and be issued with a 'health certificate' ('passport'). Note that the PETS certificate isn't issued until six months *after* the above have been carried out! Pets must also be checked for ticks and tapeworms 24 to 48 hours before embarkation on a plane or ship. With a passport, which must be kept up to date abroad, an animal can return to the UK without needing to be quarantined.

The scheme is restricted to animals imported from rabies-free countries and countries where rabies is under control; this includes all EU countries plus Andorra, Australia, Iceland, Liechtenstein, Monaco, Norway, San Marino, Switzerland and the Vatican, as well as Canada, the USA and many others. The quarantine requirement still applies to pets coming from most parts of Africa, Asia and South America. Member countries and conditions change, therefore it's important to check well in advance of travel. For the latest regulations, contact the Department of the Environment, Food and Rural Affairs, DEFRA, PETS helpline UK (0870-241 1710, www.defra.gov.uk/wildlife-pets/pets/travel/pets/index.htm).

A PETS passport costs pet owners around £200 (for a microchip, rabies vaccination and blood test), plus £60 per year for annual booster vaccinations and around £20 for a border check. Shop around and compare fees from a number of veterinary surgeons and don't leave arrangements too late.

There's no quarantine for pets arriving in Germany but they need a health certificate (bilingual, German-English) issued by an approved veterinary surgeon. Dogs and cats need a rabies vaccination not less than 20 days or more than 11 months prior to the date of issue of the health certificate. Animals aged under 12 weeks are exempt but must have a health certificate and a certificate stating that no cases of rabies have occurred for at least six months in the local area. Animals may be examined at the port of entry by a veterinary officer.

If you're transporting a pet by ship or ferry, you should notify the shipping company. Some companies insist that pets are left in vehicles (if applicable), while others allow pets to be kept in cabins. If your pet is of a nervous disposition or unused to travelling, it's best to tranquillise it on a long sea crossing. Pets can also be transported by air, but a number of conditions apply so contact a pet travel agent for details.

Dogs & Cats

If you own a dog that belongs to a breed that could be deemed a fighting dog (*Kampfhund*), e.g. bull terriers, pit-bull terriers, Staffordshire bull terriers, American Staffordshire bull terriers or crossbreeds, it's unlikely that you'll be permitted to bring it to Germany. The states also have varying regulations on the subject. German diplomatic missions can provide detailed information if you think these restrictions may affect you.

German consulates can provide a list of the veterinary authorities in each state (also listed on www.tierarzt-onlinesuche.de/verzeichnis), who can usually provide bilingual forms for your vet to use for vaccination and health certification.

Dogs must be licensed in Germany, which involves having a rabies certificate. The cost of a dog licence varies from town to town, e.g. between €80 and €150 per year for one pet (and up to double for a second or third pet dog). Owners must also have personal liability insurance for their dogs.

Dogs are considered a potential nuisance in Germany, with their tendency to make noise and foul pavements. Owners are expected to train their dogs, keep them on a lead in public areas and (most importantly) clean up any mess they make. A well-trained dog, however, is usually welcomed everywhere, and it shouldn't surprise you to find a dog quietly dozing under a table in a café or restaurant while its owner is enjoying a meal or a beer. Shops which don't permit dogs usually post a polite message asking your dog to wait for you outside (evidently most German dogs can read), and they sometimes provide bowls of water and rings on the wall for you to tie up your pooch to in case it's tempted to disobey.

Cats needn't be licensed in Germany, although if they roam free it's wise to keep up to date with the recommended vaccinations, particularly for rabies. An outdoor cat should also have a collar and identification tag so that the local animal shelter (*Tierheim*) can contact you if it's lost.

Other Pets

You can take up to five dogs, cats, rabbits or hares into Germany. (A female cat or dog with a litter of kittens or puppies under the age of three months counts as a single animal.) You must have a certificate for each animal showing that it was vaccinated against rabies within the last 12 months and at least 30 days before your arrival in Germany. The certificate must be issued by a licensed veterinary surgeon or state veterinary agency and indicate the address of the issuer clearly as part of the seal

or stamp. Reptiles, aquarium fish, hamsters and guinea pigs aren't subject to import restrictions.

Up to four parrots or parakeets can be imported into Germany, provided they have a health certificate issued no more than ten days before their arrival. All other birds require an import permit from the highest veterinary authority of the state (*Land*) where you enter Germany. Birds from countries with outbreaks of avian flu are prohibited.

You should contact the German state veterinary authority if you're planning to import an animal not mentioned above.

POLICE

Police (*Polizei*) forces in Germany are organised and maintained by each state and include several specialist services. The *Schutzpolizei* are responsible for general law and order, traffic control, patrolling of streets, and much of the on-site investigation of crimes and accidents. The *Kriminalpolizei* get involved in serious crimes and 'remote' investigations into murders, robberies, organised crime and terrorism. The *Bereitschaftspolizei* is a national unit formed from state ranks that's controlled jointly by the states and the federal government. It provides security in the event of natural disasters or catastrophic

accidents and also assists with crowd control at demonstrations, sporting events and other large gatherings, major traffic control measures and other large-scale police operations.

The police in Germany wear green uniforms and drive green and white police cars, which range from small Opels to Porsches, marked prominently with the word *Polizei*. It isn't unusual for a police car to sport a powerful loudspeaker system, which is used to tell you exactly where and how to pull over and stop when you've been driving too fast or have committed some other offence. If you start to turn the wrong way into a one-way street you may hear what sounds like a voice from on high barking out a command in German to 'Halt!' It's rather unnerving the first time it happens, but it can save you from a nasty accident. All German police are armed (so be polite to them).

In general, Germans have a lot of respect for their police, as they represent the law and help maintain order, which is so important in German society. Your dealings with any member of the police force will usually be formal, precise and strictly according to the rules and regulations, as prescribed by law. German police don't have a particularly 'warm and friendly' image, but they also aren't normally considered brutal, prone to abusing their powers or corrupt.

POPULATION

The population of Germany is around 83 million, with an average population density of around 230 inhabitants (*Einwohner*) per km^2 (600 per mi^2), one of the highest in Europe. However, population density varies enormously according to the region. The highest average density is in the industrial belt of North Rhine-Westphalia (529 per km^2) and the lowest is in Mecklenburg-Western Pomerania (73 per km^2) in the east. The 12 largest cities in Germany account for around 15 per cent of the population, with Munich the country's most densely populated city with over 4,300 inhabitants per km^2. The largest city in Germany is Berlin, with over some 3.5 million *Einwohner* and a density of just over 3,860 per km^2. The next largest cities are Hamburg (1.8 million), Munich (1.4 million), Cologne (1.06 million) and Frankfurt (730,000). In the east the largest cities are Leipzig and Dresden, both with populations of around 525,000.

The government of Germany considers itself under a moral obligation to accept and welcome Jewish immigrants from Eastern Europe.

Since reunification, many easterners (known as *Ossis*) have relocated to the west in search of jobs and the rumoured good life, with only limited movement to the east by westerners (*Wessis*). Most of the growth in population in the last few decades is attributed to the influx of foreigners, particularly refugees in recent years. Deaths have exceeded births in Germany since 1972. The average life expectancy in Germany in 2015 was 83.4 for women and 78.7 for men (and increasing). Meanwhile the birth rate is declining. Over two-thirds of households in Germany comprise just one or two people and the number of households with three or more is falling fast.

There are around 8.2 million foreigners officially living in Germany or roughly 10 per cent of the population. In the '60s and '70s the Federal Republic recruited large numbers of foreign workers, mostly from Mediterranean countries, who were euphemistically called 'guest workers' (*Gastarbeiter*), in response to labour shortages. Many guest workers stayed at the end of their contracts and there were over 2 million foreigners employed in western Germany in the '90s, the largest national groups being from Turkey, the former Yugoslavian states, Italy and Greece. The now defunct German Democratic Republic recruited a number of Vietnamese workers, several thousand of whom now live and work in what was formerly East Germany.

According to official figures, half the foreigners in Germany have lived there for over 20 years, while a third have lived in the country for longer than 30 years (not counting recent refugee arrivals). Until recently, it was extremely difficult even for long-time residents of Germany to obtain German nationality (see page 265).

Negative attitudes towards foreigners in Germany attract disproportionate press cover abroad, but immigrants' experiences vary widely and most are positive. In general, foreigners from the EU are accepted throughout Germany, although a small segment of the population still harbours xenophobic (or racist) attitudes towards certain immigrant groups.

Germany can justly pride itself on having some of the most liberal and open policies on political asylum in Europe. When the former Yugoslavia disintegrated, for example, Germany took in far more refugees and asylum seekers than most of its neighbours, despite already having enormous financial commitments with the reunification of the two German states.

RELIGION

Some 60 per cent of the German population is Christian, split fairly evenly between the Roman Catholic and Protestant faiths. The remaining 40 per cent includes some 4 million Moslems, 100,000 Jews and around a third of the population who claim to have no religion at all, at least as far as church tax registration is concerned (see page 61).

Cologne Cathedral

The northern part of Germany is primarily Protestant, while the southern states (particularly Baden-Württemberg and Bavaria) are predominantly Catholic. Bavaria, in particular, takes its Catholicism seriously in both political and educational matters, and the southern states observe additional public holidays thanks to the influence of the Catholic Church (see page 41).

The Jewish community in Germany tends to be Orthodox, with little remaining of the Conservative or Reform branches of the religion commonplace before the war. Berlin, Frankfurt and Munich have the largest Jewish communities, plus smaller communities in at least 80 other towns.

While there's no official state religion, recognised churches receive funding from the state in exchange for operating a variety of public services, such as hospitals, nursing homes, day care centres and workshops for the disabled. Because of the relatively recent arrival of Islam in Germany, the state hasn't got around to officially recognising the Moslem faith, and mosques are only now beginning to receive public funds, although Moslems are exempt from church tax.

Freedom of religion and a ban on discrimination based on religious observance are incorporated into the German constitution and rigorously enforced. Religion is taught as a subject in state schools, where children normally attend Christianity-focused religious education classes, although parents can choose to have children take an ethics course instead.

SOCIAL CUSTOMS

All countries have their social customs and Germany is no exception. As a foreigner, you'll probably be excused if you accidentally insult your host (although you may not be invited again!), but it's better to know what constitutes acceptable and unacceptable behaviour in advance. Bear in mind that there's a variation from region to region, and by and large, small towns and conservative states in the south adhere more closely to tradition than cosmopolitan cities elsewhere.

♦ When you're introduced to a German, you should address him or her as Mr (*Herr*) or Mrs (*Frau*) followed by his or her family name, and shake hands without gloves (unless it's 20 degrees below freezing). When saying goodbye, it's customary to shake hands again. Note that *Frau* is used nowadays for most women over the age of 18, whether or not they're married.

♦ When you're introduced to someone, always use the formal form of address (*Sie*). Don't use the familiar form (*du/ihr*) or call people by their first names until invited to do so. If you're on formal terms with someone, there's quite a bit of ceremony attached to the decision to change to the familiar form of address (*duzen*, as opposed to *siezen*), often involving going out for a drink (and sometimes three or four!) to celebrate.

♦ Especially in small towns and conservative cities, it's customary to say good day (*guten Tag*) or good morning (*guten Morgen*) – in Bavaria, God greets you (*grüss Gott*) – on entering a small shop, a doctor's waiting room, or arriving at your place of work, and to say goodbye (see below) on leaving. However, if you do this in a more progressive city, such as Hamburg, you may get some strange looks (or you'll simply be 'dismissed' as a southern peasant).

♦ The Germans are well known for their 'wish' greetings among friends or close associates. Rather than saying simply good-bye (*auf Wiedersehen* – literally 'until seeing again'), it's considered more sociable to wish someone a good evening, a good weekend, even a good meal! At lunchtime in many workplaces people say *Mahlzeit* to each other; this literally means 'mealtime' but is code for 'have a good lunch'. On leaving work in the evening, the usual expression is *Feierabend* (literally, 'quitting time' or 'evening off'), and on Fridays people wish one another a *schönes Wochenende* (literally 'beautiful weekend'). If someone is leaving on holiday, you should wish them *schönen Urlaub* or (if you know they're off on a trip) *gute Reise*. Other options are *viel Spass* ('have fun') and *kommen Sie gut Heim/nach Hause* ('have a safe trip home'). The all-purpose response *gleichfalls* ('same to you') is usually the appropriate response.

♦ When you're dining with another person, whether he's a family member or a stranger, you shouldn't begin to eat until you've wished him *guten Appetit*.

♦ Don't arrive late for an invitation and don't overstay your welcome. The Germans are extremely punctual and will invite you for exactly the time they expect you to arrive. If the invitation states a finishing time, you're expected to make your move for the door at the appropriate hour.

♦ If you're invited to someone's home, it's usual to take along a small present of flowers, a plant or chocolates. If you take flowers, there must be an odd number (in some places), and you should unwrap them before handing them to the hostess. Flowers can be tricky, as there are specific meanings attached to certain kinds of flowers, and these may differ considerably from what you're used to. To Germans, who take these things seriously, carnations mean bad luck, chrysanthemums are for cemeteries and roses signify love. For newcomers, a potted plant or a box of chocolates could be a safer bet.

♦ It's a good idea to close inside doors behind you when visiting someone's home. In many German households, inside doors are kept closed when rooms aren't in use, including toilets and bathrooms. You should also get into the habit of turning off lights as you leave a room.

♦ Always identify yourself before asking to speak to someone on the telephone, and don't call people at meal times or after 9pm unless you're sure they're night people (or foreigners). Incidentally, goodbye on the

telephone is *auf Wiederhören* ('until hearing again').

♦ If you're planning a party, you should notify your neighbours so that they don't call the police and complain about the noise. Some people will advise you always to invite your neighbours, and in some areas there's an unofficial policy of not calling the police the first time someone throws a noisy party, provided the neighbours have been invited. If you're the one who calls to complain you could find yourself the neighbourhood pariah – at least for a few weeks afterwards.

♦ It's considered bad luck to wish someone a happy birthday (or happy anniversary of any kind) or give them a present before the actual date. Stay up late and wait until just after midnight or catch them the next day.

♦ If you live in an apartment with a communal laundry room or clothes line (outdoors or indoors), check whether each apartment has a scheduled day and time for using them or whether there's a roster. There's

Time Difference						
BERLIN	**LONDON**	**JO'BURG**	**SYDNEY**	**AUCKLAND**	**L. ANGELES**	**NEW YORK**
noon	11am	1pm	10pm	Midnight	3am	6am

certainly no quicker way to alienate your neighbours than to use communal facilities out of turn. If you hang your laundry out to dry on your balcony or anywhere that's visible to the public, check whether there are any local by-laws against drying clothes on Sundays or public holidays, which are most common in small towns in the south of Germany.

TIME DIFFERENCE

Like most of the continent of Europe, Germany is on Central European Time (CET), which is Greenwich Mean Time (GMT) plus one hour in winter and two hours in summer. The Germans change from winter to summer time and vice versa at the same time as the rest of central Europe, i.e. at 2am on the last Sundays in March and October. Time changes are announced in local newspapers and on radio and TV so that you don't forget.

The time in selected major cities when it's noon (in winter) in Germany is shown in the table above.

Times (e.g. in timetables) are usually written using the 24-hour clock, when 10am is written as 1000 *Uhr* and 10pm as 2200 *Uhr*. Midday is 12 *Uhr* and midnight is 24 *Uhr* or *Null Uhr*. The 24-hour clock is also often used in speech; for example, 7pm may be referred to as *neunzehn Uhr* (1900) rather than *sieben Uhr abends*. Be careful if people say they'll meet you at *halb acht*, because in German this is 7.30, not 8.30, and they won't be happy if you turn up an hour late! Similarly *Viertel acht* ('quarter eight') is 7.15 (a quarter of the way to 8 o'clock), unless

clearly stated as 'quarter to' (*Viertel vor*) or 'quarter past' (*Viertel nach*) the hour.

TIPPING

Most restaurants and hotels include a 12.5 to 20 per cent service charge in their prices, so leaving a tip (*Trinkgeld*) is optional. Normally, if you want to show your appreciation for the service, you round up the price you're quoted to the next whole euro, permitting staff to keep the change. Rounding up to the nearest 5 or 10 euros is a way of indicating that you found the service exceptionally good, and of course is always appreciated. If you're out with a group of people, each person (or couple) is normally expected to settle his own portion of the bill. Obviously if each member of a large party rounds up his portion of the bill, the waiter will have been suitably rewarded for his efforts.

Although tipping is optional in most other situations, it's traditional to leave a couple of euros for the maid when you check out of a hotel room. Taxi drivers normally receive around 10 per cent of the fare, a tour guide a few euros at the end of a tour, and at the hairdresser you should leave a couple of extra

euros for the shampoo girls (often trainees or apprentices). Porters, toilet attendants and cloakroom personnel often advertise their charges, therefore an additional tip isn't necessary.

TOILETS

Public toilets (*Toiletten*) in Germany can be in short supply. When you're in a town and need one, your best bets are large department stores, cafés and restaurants, or the foyers of large hotels. On the motorway, rest areas (*Raststätten*) with public toilets are clearly marked (*Toiletten*), although cleanliness varies. A bathroom is a *Badezimmer*, although this term is never used for a toilet. Public toilets are usually labelled *Herren/Männer* (gentlemen/men) and *Damen/Frauen* (ladies/women) or simply *H* and *D*.

Pay toilets are normal in Germany, particularly in railway stations and some department stores, although urinals (*Pissoir*) are sometimes free. The fee ranges from 10 to 50 cents, usually paid by means of a coin-operated lock, so be sure you have some change with you. Some toilets have a sign indicating the charges for various 'services' such as using a urinal or WC and washing your hands with hot water, while others have an attendant who you should usually 'tip' on your way out.

The traditional German-style toilet may come as a bit of a surprise to unsuspecting newcomers. For some reason, the main part of the toilet bowl is rather shallow, forming a sort of platform. When you flush, the water flow from the tank (often concealed in the wall) pushes anything on this platform to the front of the bowl, where it's carried away down the disposal pipe. Some claim that this unique design caters to the German obsession with monitoring their health!

Oktoberfest, Munich

19.
THE GERMANS

Who are the Germans? What are they really like? Let us take a candid (and unashamedly prejudiced) look at the German people, tongue firmly in cheek, and hope they forgive our flippancy or that they don't read this bit (which is why it's hidden away at the back of the book).

The typical German is a Green, a businessman, proud, bureaucratic, subservient, militaristic, punctual, competitive, a unionist, chauvinistic, private, a sun worshipper, angst-ridden, unsympathetic, organised, perfect, superior, honest, industrious, hygienic, a workaholic, taciturn, healthy, tidy, frugal, selfish, well educated, insecure, rigid, arrogant, affluent, conservative, authoritarian, formal, malleable, responsible, self-critical, a pacifist, stoical, materialistic, ambitious, intolerant, reliable, a beer lover, conscientious, obstinate, efficient, enterprising, unloved, obedient, liberal, stolid, orderly, insensitive, xenophobic, meticulous, inventive, prejudiced, conventional, intelligent, virtuous, egotistical, dependable, law-abiding, a good footballer and infuriatingly Teutonic.

You may have noticed that the above list contains 'a few' contradictions, which is hardly surprising, as there's no such thing as a typical German. Modern Germany is a patchwork of former feudal states with enclaves and cities reflecting the tribalism and eccentricities of the country's former dukedoms and principalities. Germans are first and foremost inhabitants of a particular city (Berliners, Dresdeners, Frankfurters, Hamburgers, Müncheners, etc.) followed by Bavarians, Frisians, Hessians, Prussians, Saxons, Swabians or whatever. They're Europeans third and Germans a distant fourth – and only then among foreigners and because it says so on their passports. However, while it's true that not all Germans are stereotypes – some are almost indistinguishable from 'normal' people – we refuse to allow a few eccentrics to spoil our arguments...

There has long been a north-south divide; the more conservative northerners dismiss the less inhibited southerners as lazy and soft, while the southerners reciprocate with taunts of 'dour' and 'dull'. There's a less tangible divide between the parochial Saxons in the east and the cosmopolitan Rhinelanders in the west, although this has been sharpened by the reunification of the inhabitants of the former West Germany (*Wessis*) and East Germany (*Ossis*). To the *Ossis*, West Germans are seen as arrogant and greedy colonisers, while East Germans are viewed by *Wessis* as lazy socialists, more than happy to live off state handouts.

Although not always the xenophobes they're painted, Germans don't exactly like foreigners (particular those living in their country), but respect most English-speakers as equals, including (some) Americans, Australians, Britons (all of whom are 'English' to Germans), Canadians, Irish and New Zealanders. They also have a grudging regard for Austrians, French, Dutch, Scandinavians and Swiss

(most of whom are more 'Germanic' than the Germans). They tolerate the people of other countries in the European Union (because they have to and they like to holiday in the sun), but are generally somewhat prejudiced against southern or eastern Europeans, not to mention non-Europeans.

Unlike many other countries with a large foreign population, Germany isn't an ethnic melting pot but a jumble of splinter groups living entirely separate lives with their own neighbourhoods, shops, restaurants, clubs and newspapers. The Germans' attitude to foreigners is typified by their name for foreign workers, 'guest workers' (*Gastarbeiter*), who were supposed to leave once they'd done the jobs they were invited to do. However, millions of foreigners, particularly Greeks, Italians, Spaniards, Turks and former Yugoslavians, failed to leave, and many 'guest' families are now into their third generation. Germany has an ageing population and a low birth rate, which makes immigration essential if the natives are to maintain their high standard of living and German industry remain supreme.

However, very few people immigrate in the true sense of the word, making a permanent home in Germany, changing their names to Fritz or Frieda and acquiring citizenship (which

isn't easy). Germany is also a magnet for the homeless and dispossessed, and has attracted huge numbers of refugees and asylum seekers in recent years, whom it initially welcomed with open arms but is now less enthusiastic towards.

Germans pride themselves on their lack of class-consciousness and apart from some with aristocratic names (surnames beginning with *von*) and a few who still live in castles, Germans generally consider themselves to be middle or working class. However, Germany is far from being a classless society and status is as important there as it is anywhere else, although it's invariably based on money (or how big your car is) rather than birthright. Germany generally has no 'old school tie' barriers to success (unlike the UK and France) and almost anyone, however humble his origins, can fight his way to the top of the heap – although ethnic barriers aren't so easy to overcome.

There's no truth in the rumour that laughter is forbidden (*Lachen ist verboten*) in Germany, although you may sometimes wonder whether there's a tax on humour. To Germans, humour is something to be taken very seriously – they don't even laugh when you tell them they have no sense of humour! Germans have no sense of sarcasm, although the misfortune of others is a source of much pleasure – called *Schadenfreude* – which is similar to what everyone else feels when the Germans lose at football (as someone aptly said, "Happiness is an agreeable sensation arising from contemplating the misery of another."). Of course, not all Germans lack a sense of humour, although foreigners are unlikely to understand their complex 'jokes', and locals who appreciate a good laugh have usually been corrupted by working too long with frivolous foreigners.

It's difficult to become close friends with Germans – even for other Germans – and Germans from other parts of Germany living in small towns and villages can remain 'outsiders' for decades. You may even be unaware that you have German neighbours, except when they complain. But once you've broken through the barrier, you normally have a loyal and lifelong friend and can call on them (and be called upon) unannounced (when Germans entertain a stranger, everything must be spotless and in perfect *Ordnung*).

> It's often said that in Germany everything that isn't illegal is forbidden (*verboten*), while everything else is compulsory.

In business, Germans can be even more formal. In older, conservative companies, colleagues who've worked together for years may still address each other as Herr Schmidt or Frau Müller, using the formal *Sie* form of address. In international companies, *du* is often used between colleagues, although it's safer to start with *Sie* until told otherwise. Germans aren't usually so strict with foreigners and, if you speak to them in English, you may find yourself on first name terms after a relatively short period. Like most people, they're less formal and more relaxed when entertaining guests in their own homes, although you may not receive an invitation right away (or ever).

Germans are law-abiding and follow most rules and regulations (except speed limits) to the letter. Anyone loitering in town at 3am is more likely to be waiting for a green light to cross the road than preparing to rob a bank. The Germans not only slavishly follow all rules and regulations but also delight in pointing out others' transgressions. In Germany there

are rules for everything – which, no matter how trivial, certainly aren't made to be broken. If you use an IN door to exit, or park a few centimetres over a line, it will invariably be brought to your attention by an upstanding German citizen.

On the surface, Germans appear to be reasonably healthy, but in reality they all suffer from something, even if it's 'only' stress brought on by worrying about their possible or latent health problems (and whether they'll ever have enough money to retire). Fortunately, Germany has a lot of spas, which are a cure for everything from *Kreislaufstörung* ('circulation disorder' or generally feeling under the weather) to the common cold. However, there's no cure for the national plague of anxiety (*Angst*), which permeates all facets of German society.

The Germans worry about every aspect of their lives, from their diet to their bank balance, their appearance to their sex lives, their careers to what their friends and neighbours *really* think

of them. But their *Angst* extends far beyond their own lives, and they worry incessantly about the environment, their country's image and place in the world, the national football team, mad cow disease and the melting of the glaciers that will bring about the end of the world… This constant worrying leads to another unique German complaint, *Weltschmerz* (literally 'world pain'), which roughly translates as weariness of life or sheer pessimism.

Germany isn't exactly noted for its food and there's no such thing as German cuisine. German food consists mostly of sausages (*Wurst*), pork, dumplings, potatoes, cabbage, sauerkraut, black bread and cake, washed

down with huge steins of beer. Not for Germans some prissy *nouvelle cuisine*; they want simple, hearty peasant food – and plenty of it. One thing Germans never worry about is starving. They're among the world's most committed carnivores, and vegetarians are thin on the ground. On the other hand, they're particular about what they eat and are careful to avoid anything remotely connected with a health scare.

The Germans also know a thing or two about drinking and are among the world's most prolific consumers of alcohol, particularly beer, although you'll rarely see a legless German – unless it's at a *Bierfest* (and even then it's unlikely). They produce a vast variety of beers, all of which are made to standards and with ingredients laid down in the 16th century (foreign beer is labelled to warn consumers that it's 'unclean'). In stark contrast to their excellent beer, much of Germany's wine is 'plonk' and leaves much to be desired (do people still drink Liebfraumilch?), although there are some notable exceptions.

Germany is renowned for its excellent motorway network, and the Germans are second only to Americans (and Australians) in their worship of all things automotive – provided they're made in Germany. They have a passionate and enduring love affair with their cars, which are more important than their homes, spouses and children (combined). In Germany you are what you drive: Mercedes are for doctors, politicians and captains of industry (and football managers); Porsches are for flashy media types, pop stars and football players; while BMWs and Audis are for middle managers, engineers and hairdressers. The peasants drive Fords, Opels and Volkswagens, although those who are really beyond the pale drive foreign cars.

However, even worse than a foreign car is a dirty car – anyone who doesn't pamper his car (usually a foreigner) doesn't deserve to own one! In Germany your car says more about you than what you wear, where you live or even how much money you have. When they aren't stuck in traffic jams, it's mandatory for Germans to drive everywhere at over 200kph. A German car must above all be reliable and, if one should ever break down, it's likely to be blamed on the *Gastarbeiter* who built it.

> Many German men still believe that a woman's place is in the church or home, cooking or taking care of the children – a position summed up by the three 'K' words *Kinder, Küche, Kirche*.

Sport is a source of great national pride or shame, depending on whether the Germans are thrashing everybody in sight – usually the case – or unluckily losing narrowly to opponents who cheated, bribed the referee or caught the Germans on a bad day (Germans are **never** beaten by superior opponents). Sports stars are icons and national heroes and fêted wherever they go, and are to be found on chat shows at all times of day and night expounding on a variety of topics, including (sometimes) sport.

The German attitude towards sex is open and up-front, and they delight in flaunting their bodies (and body hair) at every opportunity. German newspapers, magazines and television are obsessed with sex, and routinely carry out surveys of the nation's (and other nations') sexual habits, while late night TV is dominated by explicit sex scenes. Germans are unembarrassed about discussing sex with strangers and will relate the most intimate details of their love lives at the drop of their *Lederhosen*. Sex clubs, bars and shops abound in most towns, mixed nude bathing and saunas are commonplace, and Germans are enthusiastic naturists.

Germany isn't exactly a land of milk and honey for the dedicated career woman, who's considered something of an eccentric, and very few receive equal pay with their male colleagues or make it to the top of the heap. Although women theoretically have equal rights with men, in reality this often isn't the case, and they usually must be at least twice as qualified and three times as smart as men to compete on an equal footing. Until fairly recently, women didn't even have rights over their own bodies: abortion was legalised only in 1974 (and was punishable by death in the '30s). However, most women don't appear overly concerned about the status quo and many seem to enjoy their subservient role, provided they're treated as ladies.

The Germans' seemingly permanent prosperity and stability was jolted in the early '90s by the recession and reunification, which cost the Germans far more than they bargained for. On top of that, they're the largest financial contributors to the poorer EU countries, whose admittance to the EU they whole-heartedly supported (more customers for German goods!). They're encumbered by myriad petty

rules and regulations, and beset by red tape at every turn. Among the major concerns facing the nation are asylum seekers and refugees (and their integration), drug addiction and crime, intolerance and racism, the environment, the Euro and bailing out other EU countries, terrorism, burgeoning social security costs and housing shortages (not necessarily in that order).

To be fair, Germans do have a few good things going for them (but whatever you do, don't tell them – they're conceited enough as it is). They're excellent footballers, master brewers, and superb architects, engineers and designers, and their products are famous worldwide for their quality and reliability. They're generally slow to make changes, both individually and as a nation, but they're quick to embrace new technology, particularly when it will make them rich(er). Their society is a model of functionality and orderliness compared with most other countries, and they have a strong sense of community and social justice. Germany enjoys a high standard of living, low inflation, good industrial relations and a very impressive economy.

They have superb public services and excellent social security benefits; superb health services (which they constantly complain about) and hospitals (no waiting lists); efficient local government; exceptional working conditions and employee benefits; and a first-class transport system with magnificent motorways and amongst the world's fastest trains. They also have a rich cultural history and have produced many great artists, composers, poets, philosophers and writers, including such world-famous names as Bach, Beethoven, Brahms, Brecht, Duden, Dürer, Goethe, the Grimm brothers, Handel, Hegel, von Humbolt, Luther, Mann, Marx, Mendelssohn, Nietzsche, Schiller, Schubert, Schumann and Wagner, to name but a handful.

Today, Germany remains at the forefront of the arts, particularly classical music, and has some of the world's leading conductors, composers, musicians, orchestras, theatres, galleries and museums.

While doing battle with German bureaucracy is enough to discourage anybody, Germans are generally welcoming, and, provided you're willing to meet them halfway and learn their language, you'll invariably be warmly received. Contrary to popular belief, Germans aren't baby-eating ogres and, although they can be difficult to get to know, when you do get to know them you invariably make friends for life. The mark of a great nation is that it rarely breeds indifference in foreigners – admiration, envy, hostility or even blind hatred, but seldom indifference. By that standard, Germany is indisputably a great nation. Love it or hate it, it's a unique, vibrant, civilised, bold, sophisticated and challenging country. Germans enjoy one of the world's best lifestyles and an enviable quality of life, and although foreign residents may criticise some aspects of German life, most feel privileged to live in Germany and few seriously consider leaving.

Auf Deutschland! **Long live Germany!**

Neuschwanstein Castle, Bavaria

20.
MOVING HOUSE OR LEAVING GERMANY

*W*hen moving house or leaving Germany, there are numerous things to be considered and a 'million' people to inform. The checklists contained in this chapter are intended to make the task easier and may even help prevent an ulcer or nervous breakdown, provided of course you don't leave everything to the last minute.

MOVING HOUSE WITHIN GERMANY

When you're moving house within Germany, you should consider the following points:

♦ You must usually give your landlord at least three months' notice before vacating rented accommodation (refer to your contract). If you don't give your landlord sufficient notice or aren't leaving on one of the approved moving dates you must find someone to take over the property. Your resignation letter must be sent by registered post to reach your landlord by the third day of the month, otherwise the notice period will apply from the following month. Arrange a date with your landlord for the hand-over.

♦ You'll need to inform the following:

– your employer;

– your present council a week before moving house and your new council within a week of taking up residence (see **Registration** on page 61);

– your electricity, gas, telephone service, internet service, cable/satellite TV and water companies;

– your insurance companies (e.g. health, car, house contents and private liability); banks, post office, stockbroker and other financial institutions; credit card and hire purchase (credit) companies; lawyer; accountant and local businesses where you have accounts;

– your family doctor, dentist and other health practitioners – health records should be transferred to your new doctor and dentist, if applicable;

– your children's schools. If applicable, arrange for schooling in your new community. Try to give a term's notice and obtain a copy of any relevant school reports or records from your children's current schools.

– all regular correspondents, subscriptions, social and sports clubs, friends and relatives. Give or send them your new address and telephone number. This can be arranged over the internet or by using address cards available free from post offices. Arrange to have your post redirected by the post office (see **Change of Address** on page 91).

– your local consulate or embassy if you're registered with them.

♦ If you have a German driving licence or a German registered car, you must contact the driving licence office (*Führerscheinstelle*) of your local district administration office (*Landratsamt*) and the local motor vehicle branch (*Kfz-Zulassungsstelle*) in your new town;

- Return anything borrowed, e.g. library books.

- Register your dog with your new council.

- Arrange removals or transport for your furniture and belongings.

- Arrange for a cleaning company and/or decorating company for your apartment, if necessary.

- If applicable, ensure the return of the deposit from your landlord.

- Cancel newspaper and other regular deliveries.

- Give notice to your employer, if applicable.

- Ask yourself (again): 'Is it really worth all this trouble?'

LEAVING GERMANY

Before leaving Germany for an indefinite period, the following items should be considered in addition to those listed above:

- Check that your own and your family's passports are up to date.

- Check the entry requirements for your country of destination, e.g. regarding visas, permits and vaccinations, by contacting its embassy or consulate in Germany. An exit permit or visa isn't required to leave Germany.

- Your private company pension contributions may be repayable. Before your pension fund will repay your funds you must provide a statement from your council stating that you've de-registered and are leaving Germany.

- Arrange to sell anything you aren't taking with you, e.g. house, car and furniture. Find out the exact procedure for shipping your belongings to your country of destination .

- If you have a German registered car that you plan to take with you, you must import and re-register it in your new country of residence within a limited time.

> ☑ **SURVIVAL TIP**
>
> You may qualify for a rebate on your income tax (see page 204) and pension insurance. Your employer and council will assist you with these. Tax rebates are normally paid automatically.

- Contact Deutsche Telekom and other phone companies to cancel your contract, and pay the final bill (see **Chapter 7**).

- Pets may require vaccinations several months in advance of your move, or need to go into quarantine for a period on arrival in the new country.

- Arrange health, travel and other insurance (see **Chapter 13**).

- Depending on your destination, you may wish to arrange health and dental check-ups before leaving Germany. Obtain a copy of your health and dental records, and a statement from your health insurance company stating your present level of cover.

- Terminate any German loan, lease or hire purchase (credit) contracts, and pay all outstanding bills; allow plenty of time as some companies are slow to respond.

- Check whether you're entitled to a rebate on your road tax, car and other insurance. Obtain a letter from your German motor insurance company stating your no-claims bonus.

- Check whether you need an international driver's permit or a translation of your German or foreign driving licence for your country of destination.

- Give friends and business associates in Germany an email address where you can be contacted.

Gute Reise! **Have a good journey!**

Skyline, Frankfurt-am-Main

Mosel vineyards

APPENDICES

APPENDIX A: USEFUL WEBSITES

*T*he following list of websites (by subject) will be of interest to newcomers planning to live or work in Germany.

Culture

Every Culture (www.everyculture.com/Ge-It/Germany.html).
German Culture Council/Deutscher Kulturrat (www.kulturrat.de).
German Culture (http://germanculture.com.ua).
German Way (www.german-way.com/history-and-culture). German history and culture.
Goethe Institut (www.goethe.de/en). The official national cultural institute, which promotes the study of German abroad and encourages cultural exchange.
Live Science (www.livescience.com/44007-german-culture.html). German culture: facts, customs and traditions.
Museums in Germany (http://webmuseen.de).
Wikipedia (https://en.wikipedia.org/wiki/Culture_of_Germany). Wiki's German culture pages.

Education

Campus (www.campus.de). Information for foreigners planning to study in Germany.
Deutschebildungsserver (www.bildungsserver.de). Everything about German education.
German Academic Exchange Service/DAAD (www.daad.de).
Privatschulberatung (www.privatschulberatung.de). Information about private schools in Germany.
Humbolt Instutut (www.humboldt-institut.org/en). Offers German courses for foreigners.
Study in Germany (www.study-in.de/en/plan-your-studies/higher-education-system). Higher education system explained.
Studying in Germany (www.studying-in-germany.org). Comprehensive guide to tertiary education in germany.
Wikipedia (https://en.wikipedia.org/wiki/Culture_of_Germany). Wiki's German education pages.
Young Germany (www.young-germany.de/topic/study/the-german-school-system-explained). The German school system.

Government

Bund (www.service.bund.de/Content/EN/Home/homepage_node.html). The main German government website for public services in Germany (in English).

Federal Government/Die Bundesregierung (www.bundesregierung.de/Webs/Breg/EN/Homepage/_node.html). Federal government website in English.

Federal Insurance Agency/Deutsche Rentenversicherung (www.deutsche-rentenversicherung.de/Allgemein/en/Navigation/englisch_index_node.html).

Federal Statistics/Statistisches Bundesamt (www.destatis.de/EN/Homepage.html).

German Embassy in London (www.uk.diplo.de/Vertretung/unitedkingdom/en/Startseite.html).

German Embassy in Washington (www.germany.info).

German Federal Labour Office/Bundesagentur für Arbeit (www.arbeitsagentur.de).

German President/Bundespräsident (www.bundespraesident.de/EN/Home/home_node.html).

Living & Working

Accommodation (www.immobilienscout24.de; www.atHome.de, www.immowelt.de, www.immonet.de, www.wohnungsboerse.net and www.wohnung-jetzt.de). Accommodation for rent and sale.

American Chamber of Commerce (www.amcham.de).

Association of German Chambers of Industry & Commerce/Deutscher Industrie-und Handelskammertag (www.diht.de/en).

Berlin Mietspiegel (www.stadtentwicklung.berlin.de/wohnen/mietspiegel). Information on rents in Berlin.

British Chamber of Commerce in Germany (www.bccg.de).

Central Placements Agency/ZAV (www.arbeitsamt.de).

Doing Business (www.pwc.com/hu/hu/german_business_group/assets/doing_business_in_germany_guide_2017.pdf). Price Waterhouse guide to Germany.

German-British Chamber of Industry & Commerce (http://grossbritannien.ahk.de/en).

Institute for Foreign Relations/Institut für Auslandsbeziehungen (www.ifa.de).

Jobs (www.jobs.de; www.monster.de; www.job-world.de; www.stepstone.de). A selection of Germany's leading job websites.

Living in Germany (www.gov.uk/guidance/living-in-germany). British goverment advice.

Make it in Germany (www.make-it-in-germany.com/en). German government advice.

Media

Deutsche Welle (www.dw.com/en). Website of the German equivalent of the BBC World Service.

Der Spiegel (www.spiegel.de/international/germany). In English.

Frankfurter Allgemeine Zeitung (www.faz.net). The online version of one of Germany's most respected newspapers.

Frankfurter Rundschau (www.fr-online.de). The online version of Germany's principal left-leaning liberal newspaper, the equivalent of *The Guardian* in the UK.

Online Newspapers (www.onlinenewspapers.com/germany.htm). Links to most German newspapers.

Paperball (https://paperball.news). Search engine for the German press.
Süddeutsche Zeitung (www.sueddeutsche.de). The online version of Germany's top broadsheet newspaper.
Die Welt (www.welt.de/english-news). One of Germany's leading newspapers (the website is available in English, French and German).

Miscellaneous

Allgemeiner Deutscher Automobilclub (www.adac.de). Germany' premier automobile club.
Berlin (www.berlin.de/en). The official website of the German capital, containing copious information about all aspects of life in the city.
British Council (www.british council.de/en). The UK's international organisation for cultural and educational opportunities.
Deutschebibliothek (www.ddb.de). Website of the German National Library.
Focus Money (www.focus-money.de). Financial information.
Frankfurt-am-Main (www.frankfurt.de). Official website for Frankfurt (available in English).
Germany Info (www.germany.info). Comprehensive information about many aspects of Germany in English.
German Sports Federation/Deutscher Sportbund (www.dsb.de).
Munich (www.munich.de). Official website of the city of Munich.
Shopping24 (www.shopping24.de). Web shopping portal for everything from flights to flowers.
Sport (www.sport.de). Portal to comprehensive sports coverage but with the emphasis on football and Formula 1 motor racing.
Tickets & Concerts (www.eventim.de).
UK-German Connection (www.ukgermanconnection.org/home). Organisation dedicated to increasing contacts and understanding between young people in the UK and Germany.
Weihnachten Info (www.weihnachten-info.de). Information about Germany's Christmas markets.

Travel

Buses in Germany (www.goeuro.com/buses/germany).
Deutsche Bahn (www.db.de). German railway website.
Ebookers (www.ebookers.de). Last-minute travel and hotel bookings.
Flugplan (www.flugplan.de). Flight timetables to just about everywhere.
Germany Travel (www.germany.travel/en/index.html). German National Tourist Board website.
Eurowings (www.eurowings.com/de.html). Budget airline.
Lufthansa (www.lufthansa.de). Germany's national airline.
Skyscanner (www.skyscanner.net/flights-from/de/cheap-flights-from-germany.html). Cheap flights.
Trivago (www.trivago.co.uk/germany-655/hotel). One of the best hotel websites.

APPENDIX B: WEIGHTS & MEASURES

*T*he metric system of measurement in used in Germany. Those who are more familiar with the imperial system of measurement will find the tables below useful. Some comparisons shown are only approximate but close enough for most everyday uses. In addition to the variety of measurement systems used, clothes sizes often vary considerably with the manufacturer (as we all know only too well). Try all clothes on before buying, and don't be afraid to return something if it doesn't fit.

Women's Clothes										
Continental	34	36	38	40	42	44	46	48	50	52
UK	8	10	12	14	16	18	20	22	24	26
US	6	8	10	12	14	16	18	20	22	24

Pullovers												
	Women's						Men's					
Continental	40	42	44	46	48	50	44	46	48	50	52	54
UK	34	36	38	40	42	44	34	36	38	40	42	44
US	34	36	38	40	42	44	sm	med		lg	xl	

Men's Shirts										
Continental	36	37	38	39	40	41	42	43	44	46
UK/US	14	14	15	15	16	16	17	17	18	-

Men's Underwear						
Continental	5	6	7	8	9	10
UK		34	36	38	40	42	44
US		sm	med		lg	xl

NB: sm = small, med = medium, lg = large, xl = extra large

Children's Clothes						
Continental	92	104	116	128	140	152
UK	16/18	20/22	24/26	28/30	32/34	36/38
US	2	4	6	8	10	12

Children's Shoes	
Continental	18 19 20 21 22 23 24 25 26 27 28 29 30 31 32
UK/US	2 3 4 4 5 6 7 7 8 9 10 11 11 12 13
Continental	33 34 35 36 37 38
UK/US	1 2 2 3 4 5

Shoes (Women's & Men's)												
Continental	35	36	37	37	38	39	40	41	42	42	43	44 45
UK	2	3	3	4	4	5	6	7	7	8	9	9 10
US	4	5	5	6	6	7	8	9	9	10	10	11 11

Weight			
Imperial	**Metric**	**Metric**	**Imperial**
1oz	28.35g	1g	0.035oz
1lb*	454g	100g	3.5oz
1cwt	50.8kg	250g	9oz
1 ton	1,016kg	500g	18oz
2,205lb	1 tonne	1kg	2.2lb

Length			
British/US	**Metric**	**Metric**	**British/US**
1in	2.54cm	1cm	0.39in
1ft	30.48cm	1m	3ft 3.25in
1yd	91.44cm	1km	0.62mi
1mi	1.6km	8km	5mi

Area			
British/US	**Metric**	**Metric**	**British/US**
1 sq. in	0.45 sq. cm	1 sq. cm	0.15 sq. in
1 sq. ft	0.09 sq. m	1 sq. m	10.76 sq. ft
1 sq. yd	0.84 sq. m	1 sq. m	1.2 sq. yds
1 acre	0.4 hectares	1 hectare	2.47 acres
1 sq. mile	2.56 sq. km	1 sq. km	0.39 sq. mile

Capacity			
Imperial	**Metric**	**Metric**	**Imperial**
1 UK pint	0.57 litre	1 litre	1.75 UK pints
1 US pint	0.47 litre	1 litre	2.13 US pints
1 UK gallon	4.54 litres	1 litre	0.22 UK gallon
1 US gallon	3.78 litres	1 litre	0.26 US gallon
NB: An American 'cup' = around 250ml or 0.25 litre.			

Oven Temperature		
Gas	**Electric**	
	°F	**°C**
-	225–250	110–120
1	275	140
2	300	150
3	325	160
4	350	180
5	375	190
6	400	200
7	425	220
8	450	230
9	475	240

Air Pressure	
PSI	**Bar**
10	0.5
20	1.4
30	2
40	2.8

Power			
Kilowatts	Horsepower	Horsepower	Kilowatts
1	1.34	1	0.75

Temperature	
°Celsius	°Fahrenheit
0	32 (freezing point of water)
5	41
10	50
15	59
20	68
25	77
30	86
35	95
40	104
50	122

Temperature Conversion

Celsius to Fahrenheit: multiply by 9, divide by 5 and add 32. (For a quick and approximate conversion, double the Celsius temperature and add 30.)

Fahrenheit to Celsius: subtract 32, multiply by 5 and divide by 9. (For a quick and approximate conversion, subtract 30 from the Fahrenheit temperature and divide by 2.)

NB: The boiling point of water is 100°C / 212°F. Normal body temperature (if you're alive and well) is 37°C/98.6°F.

APPENDIX C: USEFUL WORDS & PHRASES

*T*he following lists provide words and phrases you may need during your first few days in Germany. They are, of course, no substitute for learning the language, which you should make one of your priorities. All verbs are provided in the polite German form, which is the correct form to use when addressing a stranger.

Asking for Help

Do you speak English?	*Sprechen Sie Deutsch?*
I don't speak German	*Ich spreche kein Deutsch*
Please speak slowly	*Bitte sprechen Sie langsam*
I don't understand	*Ich verstehe nicht*
I need ...	*Ich brauche ...*
I want ...	*Ich will ...*

Communications

Telephone & Internet

landline	*Festnetz*
mobile phone	*Handy (popular) or Mobiltelefon*
no answer	*kein Antwort*
engaged/busy	*besetzt*
internet	*Internet*
email	*E-mail, Mail*
broadband connection	*Breitband Verbindung*
internet café/wifi spot	*Internet Café/Wifi Spot*

Post

post office	*Postamt*
postcard/letter/parcel	*Postkarte/Brief/Paket*
stamps	*Briefmarke*
How much does it cost to send a letter to Europe/North America/Australia?	*Wie viel kostet es, einen Brief nach Europa/Nordamerika/ Australien zu senden?*

Media

newspaper/magazine	*Zeitung/Zeitschrift*
Do you sell English-language media?	*Verkaufen Sie Englisch-sprachige Median?*

Courtesy

yes	*ja*
no	*nein*
excuse me	*entschuldigen Sie*
sorry	*sorry* (popular)*, es tut mir leid*
I don't know	*Ich weiss es nicht*
I don't mind	*es ist mir egal*
please	*bitte*

Bitte has three meanings: please, you're welcome, and 'here you are' (when handing someone something).

thank you (very much)	*danke (schön/vielen dank)*
you're welcome	*bitte (schön) or gerne*

Days & Months

All days and months are capitalised in German.

Monday	*Montag*
Tuesday	*Dienstag*
Wednesday	*Mittwoch*
Thursday	*Donnerstag*
Friday	*Freitag*
Saturday	*Samstag*
Sunday	*Sonntag*
January	*Januar*
February	*Februar*
March	*März*
April	*April*
May	*Mai*
June	*Juni*
July	*Juli*
August	*August*
September	*September*
October	*Oktober*
November	*November*
December	*Dezember*

Driving

car insurance	*Autoversicherung*
driving licence	*Führerschein*
hire/rental car	*Mietauto*

How far is it to ...?	*Wie weit ist es zum/zur ...?*
Can I park here?	*Kann ich hier parken?*
unleaded petrol (gas)/diesel	*bleifrei Benzin/Diesel*
Fill the tank up, please	*Volltanken, bitte*
I need €20/30/40 of petrol (gas)	*Ich brauche für zwanzig/dreißig/vierzig Eu Benzin.*
air/water/oil	*Luft/Wasser/Öl*
car wash	*Autowaschanlage*
My car has broken down	*Mein Auto hat eine Panne*
I've run out of petrol (gas)	*Ich habe kein Benzin mehr*
The tyre is flat	*Ich habe einen platten Reifen*
I need a tow truck	*Ich brauche einen Abschleppwagen*

Emergency

Emergency	*Notfall*
Fire	*Feuer*
Help	*Hilfe*
Police	*Polizei*
Stop	*Halt*
Stop, thief	*Halt, Diebe*
Watch out	*Pass auf or Vorsicht*

Finding your Way

Where is ...?	*Wo ist ...?*
Where is the nearest ...?	*Wo ist der/die nächste ...?*
How do I get to ...?	*Wie komme ich auf ...?*
Can I walk there?	*Kann ich da zu Fuß hingehen?*
How far is ....?	*Wie weit ist ...?*
I'm lost	*Ich habe mich verirrt*
map	*Straßenkarte/Landkarte or Stadtplan*
left/right/straight ahead	*links/rechts/gerade aus*
opposite/next to/near	*gegenüber/gleich neben/nahe*
airport	*Flughafen*
bus/plane/taxi/train	*Bus/Flugzeug/Taxi/Zug*
bus stop	*Bus Haltestelle*
taxi rank	*Taxistand*
train/bus station	*Zug/Bus Bahnhof*
When does the ... arrive/leave?	*Wann kommt der ... Wann fährt der ...?*
one-way/return	*einfach/hin und zurück*
bank/embassy/consulate	*Bank/Botschaft/Konsulat*

Greetings

Hello	*Hallo*
Goodbye	*Auf Wiedersehen*
Good morning	*Guten Morgen*
Good afternoon	*Guten Tag*
Good Evening	*Guten Abend*
Good night	*Gute Nacht*

Health & Medical Emergencies

I feel ill (dizzy)	*Ich fühle mich krank/schlect (schwindelig)*
I need a doctor/ambulance	*Ich brauche ein Arzt/Krankenwagen*
doctor/nurse/dentist	*Arzt/Krankenschwester/Zahnarzt*
surgeon/specialist	*Chirurg/Spezialist*
hospital/healthcentre	*Krankenhaus/Poliklinik*
A&E (emergency room)	*Notaufnahme*
chemist's/optician's	*Apotheke/Optiker*
prescription	*Rezept*

In a Bar or Restaurant

Waiter (male/female)	*Herr Ober/Fräulein*
menu	*Speisekarte*
bill	*Rechnung*
well done/medium/rare (for meat)	*durch gebraten/medium/englisch*
vegetarian	*vegetarisch*
meat/fish	*Fleisch/Fisch*

Paying

How much is it?	*Wie viel ist es?*
The bill, please	*Die Rechnung, bitte*
Do you take credit cards?	*Akzeptieren Sie Kreditkarten?*

Socialising

Pleased to meet you	*Es freut mich Sie kennenzulernen*
My name is ...	*Mein Name ist ... or Ich heisse ...*
This is my husband/wife/son/ daughter/colleague/friend	*Das ist mein Mann/Frau/Sohn/ Tochter/Kollege*
How are you?	*Wie geht es Ihnen?*
Very well, thank you	*Sehr gut, danke*

Shopping

What time do you open/close?	*Wie sind Ihre Öffnungszeiten?*
Who's the last person (in the queue)?	*Wer ist der letze in die Reihe?*
I'm just looking (browsing)	*Ich möchte nur schauen*
I'm looking for ...	*Ich suche ...*
Can I try it on?	*Kann ich das anprobieren?*
I need size ...	*Ich brauche Größe ...*
bigger/smaller/longer/shorter	*grösser/kleiner/kürzer*
a bag, please	*eine Tasche/Tüte, bitte*
How much is this?	*Wie viel ist es?*

Numbers

1	*eins*
2	*zwei*
3	*drei*
4	*vier*
5	*fünf*
6	*sechs*
7	*sieben*
8	*acht*
9	*neun*
10	*zehn*
11	*elf*
12	*zwölf*
13	*dreizehn*
14	*vierzehn*
15	*fünfzehn*
16	*sechszehn*
17	*siebzehn*
18	*achtzehn*
19	*neunzehn*
10	*zwanzig*

INDEX

The Best of London: Capital of Cool

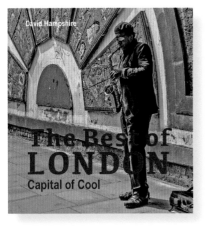

ISBN: 978-1-909282-92-6, 256 pages, £11.99
David Hampshire

There are great world cities, from classical capitals to modern metropolises, and then there's London – the yardstick by which other cities are measured. It has the most astonishing ability to reinvent itself, always staying one step ahead of the pack, a magnet for creatives – be they writers or artists, designers or thinkers – and a melting pot of cultures from around the globe. New York may be hip, Paris may be chic, but London is surely the Capital of Cool.

In creating this book we decided that the best way to illustrate London's cool credentials was to illustrate the very best that the city has to offer across a wide range of interests. Some names are instantly recognisable, from the British Museum to the Shard, while others may surprise – and all are among the very best that London offers – and, by definition, among the very best in the world. We trust that you'll enjoy exploring them and that you'll agree that London – at its best – is truly unbeatable.

London's Architectural Walks

ISBN: 978-1-909282-85-8, 128 pages, £9.99
Jim Watson

London's Architectural Walks is a unique guide to the most celebrated landmark buildings in one of the world's major cities. In thirteen easy walks it takes you on a fascinating journey through London's diverse architectural heritage with historical background and clear maps.

Some of the capital's most beautiful parks are visited, plus palaces, theatres, museums and some surprising oddities. With the author's line and watercolour illustrations of all the significant buildings this book is an essential companion for anyone interested in the architecture that has shaped this great city.

SKETCHBOOK SERIES

£10.95

ISBN: 978-1-907339-37-0
Jim Watson

A celebration of one of the world's great cities, London Sketchbook is packed with over 200 evocative watercolour illustrations of the author's favourite landmarks and sights. The illustrations are accompanied by historical footnotes, maps, walks, quirky facts and a gazetteer.

Also in this series:

Cornwall Sketchbook (ISBN: 9781909282780, £10.95)
Cotswold Sketchbook (ISBN: 9781907339108, £9.95)
Devon Sketchbook (ISBN: 9781909282704, £10.95)
Lake District Sketchbook (ISBN: 9781909282605, £10.95)
Yorkshire Sketchbook (ISBN: 9781909282773, £10.95)

London's Secrets: Peaceful Places

ISBN: 978-1-907339-45-5, 256 pages, hardback, £11.95

David Hampshire

London is one of the world's most exciting cities, but it's also one of the noisiest; a bustling, chaotic, frenetic, over-crowded, manic metropolis of over 8 million people, where it can be difficult to find somewhere to grab a little peace and quiet. Nevertheless, if you know where to look London has a wealth of peaceful places: places to relax, chill out, contemplate, meditate, sit, reflect, browse, read, chat, nap, walk, think, study or even work (if you must) – where the city's volume is muted or even switched off completely.

London for Foodies, Gourmets & Gluttons

ISBN: 978-1-909282-76-6, 288 pages, hardback, £11.95

David Hampshire & Graeme Chesters

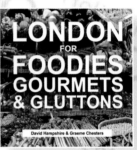

Much more than simply a directory of cafés, markets, restaurants and food shops, London for Foodies, Gourmets & Gluttons features many of the city's best artisan producers and purveyors, plus a wealth of classes where you can learn how to prepare and cook food like the experts, appreciate fine wines and brew coffee like a barista. And when you're too tired to cook or just want to treat yourself, we'll show you great places where you can enjoy everything from tea and cake to a tasty street snack; a pie and a pint to a glass of wine and tapas; and a quick working lunch to a full-blown gastronomic extravaganza.

London's Cafés, Coffee Shops & Tearooms

ISBN: 978-1-909282-80-3, 192 pages, £9.95

David Hampshire

This book is a celebration of London's flourishing independent cafés, coffee shops and tearooms – plus places serving afternoon tea and breakfast/brunch – all of which have enjoyed a renaissance in the last decade and done much to strengthen the city's position as one of the world's leading foodie destinations. With a copy of London's Cafés, Coffee Shops & Tearooms you'll never be lost for somewhere to enjoy a great cup of coffee or tea and some delicious food.

London's Best Shops & Markets

ISBN: 978-1-909282-81-0, 256 pages, hardback, £12.95

David Hampshire

The UK is a nation of diehard shoppers. Retail therapy is the country's favourite leisure activity – an all-consuming passion – and London is its beating heart. It's one of the world's most exciting shopping cities, packed with grand department stores, trend-setting boutiques, timeless traditional traders, edgy concept stores, absorbing antiques centres, eccentric novelty shops, exclusive purveyors of luxury goods, mouth-watering food emporiums, bustling markets and much more.

see www.londons-secrets.com

London's Best-Kept Secrets

ISBN: 978-1-909282-74-2, 320 pages, £10.95

David Hampshire

London Best-Kept Secrets brings together our favourite places – the 'greatest hits' – from our London's Secrets series of books. We take you off the beaten tourist path to seek out the more unusual ('hidden') places that often fail to register on the radar of both visitors and residents alike. Nimbly sidestepping the chaos and queues of London's tourist-clogged attractions, we visit its quirkier, lesser-known, but no less fascinating, side. *London Best-Kept Secrets* takes in some of the city's loveliest hidden gardens and parks, absorbing and poignant museums, great art and architecture, beautiful ancient buildings, magnificent Victorian cemeteries, historic pubs, fascinating markets and much more.

London's Hidden Corners, Lanes & Squares

ISBN: 978-1-909282-69-8, 192 pages, £9.95

Graeme Chesters

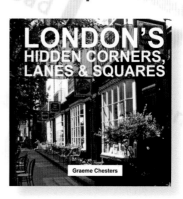

The inspiration for this book was the advice of writer and lexicographer Dr Samuel Johnson (1709-1784), who was something of an expert on London, to his friend and biographer James Boswell on the occasion of his trip to London in the 18th century, to 'survey its innumerable little lane and courts'. In the 21st century these are less numerous than in Dr Johnson's time, so we've expanded his brief to include alleys, squares and yards, along with a number of mews, roads, streets and gardens.

A Year in London: Two Things to Do Every Day of the Year

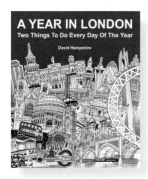

ISBN: 978-1-909282-68-1, 256 pages, £11.95

David Hampshire

London offers a wealth of things to do, from exuberant festivals and exciting sports events to a plethora of fascinating museums and stunning galleries, from luxury and oddball shops to first-class restaurants and historic pubs, beautiful parks and gardens to pulsating nightlife and clubs. Whatever your interests and tastes, you'll find an abundance of things to enjoy – with a copy of this book you'll never be at a loss for something to do in one of the world's greatest cities.

LONDON'S HIDDEN SECRETS

ISBN: 978-1-907339-40-0
£10.95, 320 pages
Graeme Chesters

A guide to London's hidden and lesser-known sights that aren't found in standard guidebooks. Step beyond the chaos, clichés and queues of London's tourist-clogged attractions to its quirkier side.

Discover its loveliest ancient buildings, secret gardens, strangest museums, most atmospheric pubs, cutting-edge art and design, and much more: some 140 destinations in all corners of the city.

LONDON'S HIDDEN SECRET'S VOL 2

ISBN: 978-1-907339-79-0
£10.95, 320 pages
Graeme Chesters & David Hampshire

Another volume of the city's largely undiscovered sights, many of which we were unable to include in the original book. In fact, the more research we did the more treasures we found, until eventually a second volume was inevitable.

Written by two experienced London writers, LHS 2 is for both those who already know the metropolis and newcomers wishing to learn more about its hidden and unusual charms.

LONDON'S SECRET PLACES

ISBN: 978-1-907339-92-9
£10.95, 320 pages
Graeme Chesters & David Hampshire

London is one of the world's leading tourist destinations with a wealth of world-class attractions. These are covered in numerous excellent tourist guides and online, and need no introduction here. Not so well known are London's numerous smaller attractions, most of which are neglected by the throngs who descend upon the tourist-clogged major sights. What London's Secret Places does is seek out the city's lesser-known, but no less worthy, 'hidden' attractions.

LONDON'S SECRET WALKS, 2nd edition

ISBN: 978-1-909282-93-3
£10.99, 320 pages
Graeme Chesters

London is a great city for walking – whether for pleasure, exercise or simply to get from A to B. Despite the city's extensive public transport system, walking is often the quickest and most enjoyable way to get around – at least in the centre – and it's also free and healthy!

Many attractions are off the beaten track, away from the major thoroughfares and public transport hubs. This favours walking as the best way to explore them, as does the fact that London is a visually interesting city with a wealth of stimulating sights in every 'nook and cranny'.

see www.londons-secrets.com